D1104014

A. R. E. SINCLAIR, formerly staff ecologist at the Serengeti Research Institute, is currently assistant professor at the Institute of Animal Resource Ecology, The University of British Columbia.

THE AFRICAN BUFFALO

WILDLIFE BEHAVIOR AND ECOLOGY
George B. Schaller, Editor

THE AFRICAN BUFFALO

A Study of Resource Limitation of Populations

A. R. E. Sinclair

THE UNIVERSITY OF CHICAGO PRESS
Chicago and London

A. R. E. Sinclair, formerly staff ecologist at the
Serengeti Research Institute, is currently assistant
professor at the Institute of Animal Resource
Ecology, The University of British Columbia.

The University of Chicago Press, Chicago 60637
The University of Chicago Press, Ltd., London

© 1977 by The University of Chicago
All rights reserved. Published 1977

Printed in the United States of America
81 80 79 78 77 9 8 7 6 5 4 3 2 1

Library of Congress Cataloging in Publication Data

Sinclair, Anthony Ronald Entrican.
    The African buffalo.

    (Wildlife behavior and ecology)
    Bibliography: p.
    Includes index.
    1. African buffalo.   2. Mammal populations—
Africa.   I.   Title.
QL737.U53S53   599'.7358   76-22955
ISBN 0-226-76030-8

Contents

CONTENTS   vii

Plates follow page 52

To all my family
They made it possible

Acknowledgments

I first went to the Serengeti in 1965 to study birds as an assistant to Professor Arthur Cain, and it was in the course of these ornithological studies that I became acquainted with mammals. By the time I returned in 1966, the Serengeti Research Institute had been set up by the initiative of John Owen, then director of the Tanzania National Parks. It was his farsightedness that brought ecological studies to the Serengeti in the early sixties. I would like to thank him for his support while I was there. The trustees of the Tanzania National Parks have set an example for the rest of the world in their conservation efforts. I would like to thank them for their continued support and encouragement of the research projects and for permitting me to work in the Serengeti.

This work is based upon six years' fieldwork, with a year in the middle spent at Oxford University. All the parks staff helped me at some stage, but I would like to thank particularly the park wardens, Myles Turner and Sandy Field, who did much of the flying for me in the early days and gave logistical support in many of my activities.

Much of the fieldwork would not have been possible without the help of the assistants, particularly S. Makacha, J. Moshi, B. Gwamaka, A. Laurie, A. Cassells, and T. Munthe. Without complaining, they spent many long days and nights with me observing animals and collecting material.

My study was part of an integrated program at the institute, and most of my colleagues aided me at one time or another. From the very start Hans Kruuk and George Schaller helped in many ways, and they provided valuable advice throughout. At the same time their own work was a valuable base upon which to build this study. These remarks also apply to the work of Richard Bell and Murray Watson, who organized the early censuses and provided me with valuable advice. Jeremy Grimsdell has been especially helpful by keeping me informed of the progress of his work in Uganda. Mike Norton-Griffiths and Colin Pennycuick provided constant help through both discussions and fieldwork. Most of the institute members volunteered to help in the annual aerial censuses. I would like to thank all of them here for the long and unpleasant hours they spent bumping their way across the Serengeti on my behalf. Harvey Croze, Peter Jarman, Bob Bradley, and John Bunning were among those whose experience I depended on for these censuses. The navigation was considerably helped when A. MacFarlane produced his map in 1968, and in 1971 George Jolly paid a special visit to advise on sampling procedures for various kinds of census.

Much of the autopsy work in the Serengeti was carried out by Alan Young and Bernd Schiemann. But I also received considerable help from veterinarians at other centers: C. Staak, D. Protz, and C. Groocock of the Arusha Veterinary Investigation Centre came to the Serengeti to help with autopsies; W. Plowright of the East African Veterinary Research Organisation carried out much of the serum analysis for rinderpest and other diseases. At the East African Agricultural and Forestry Research Organisation, botanical and chemical analyses of rumen, plant, and fecal samples were carried out by M. D. Gwynne, A. D. McKay, and J. Osborne. I would like to thank all of them for their help.

At Lake Manyara Park, Iain Douglas-Hamilton extended generous hospitality. I will not forget quickly the various incidents concerning elephants that I shared with him. At Arusha Park the late D. Vesey-Fitzgerald provided considerable help by arranging with his assistant, Frank, for the collection of grass samples on Mount Meru in 1968 and 1969. The many conversations I had with Vesey led me to appreciate the depth and breadth of his knowledge about African ecology.

I started radio-telemetry work on buffalo in 1971 with the help of Brian Bertram, and work on wildebeest later became possible after Jack Inglis had developed the system of aerial tracking of these animals in the year he spent at S.R.I. I would like to thank both of them for their consideration and patience.

At Oxford University Professor Tinbergen provided me with financial support and much valuable advice. It was directly through him that I was able to start the buffalo work. At various stages of analysis I was helped by a number of people, particularly Mike Cullen, Richard Dawkins, John Phillipson, and Professor George Varley.

I would like to thank them and also Professor John Pringle for providing space and facilities in the Zoology Department.

In Australia I had the advantage of working with the Commonwealth Scientific and Industrial Research Organization. I would like to thank the executive and other scientists for the help they gave me, particularly after the Darwin cyclone. During the fieldwork in the Northern Territory I was helped by Bob Collins and Don McPhie. My colleagues of the Wildlife Division helped in many ways, particularly Drs. H. J. Frith, Ken Myers, Alan Newsome, Mike Ridpath, Reg Barrett, Jon Dunsmore, and David Spratt. The efforts of librarians B. Staples and R. McJannett were invaluable.

Various earlier drafts of this book have been read by a number of people. Chapter 2 was read by A. Gentry; chapter 3, by L. Pennycuick; chapter 6, by P. J. Jarman, J. N. M. Smith, and in part by R. Mykytowycz; chapter 7, by M. Griffiths, K. Williams, and in part by R. M. F. S. Sadleir; chapter 8, by G. Caughley, I. Parer, and J. J. R. Grimsdell; and chapter 9, by J. Dunsmore and D. Spratt. Frank Knight drew figures 1, 3, 4, and 9, and David Shackleton drew figure 38. In addition to reading earlier drafts of some chapters, George Schaller read the whole manuscript. I would like to thank all of them and the two referees for their many helpful comments. Needless to say, the errors in this book are mine alone.

Blackwell Scientific Publications, Ltd., has kindly given permission to reproduce figures 20, 25, 28, 55, 70, and 80, and to redraw figures 22, 56, and 58.

This work was funded by the East African Wildlife Society, the Royal Society, the Science Research Council of Great Britain, the Caesar Kleberg Programme of Texas A & M University, and the African Wildlife Leadership Foundation, Washington, D.C. To these organizations I am extremely grateful.

Finally, I would like to thank Dr. Hugh Lamprey, who was director of the S.R.I. for much of the time I was there and who supervised my work. His patience, understanding, and constant support through many difficulties allowed me to complete this project. Since I started this work George Schaller has given me constant encouragement, particularly during the writing stage.

My wife Anne has been a part of this throughout, helping in the field by collecting skulls, carrying out autopsies, and radio tracking. She also typed all the drafts of this book. Without her I would not have been able to do the work.

This is a scientific study, dry and impersonal. But it is based on a fascinating six years with the African wildlife. The sights, sounds, and smells of Africa are left out; yet it is these that make the experience memorable, that stirred my emotions, and stimulated and maintained my interest.

THE AFRICAN BUFFALO

1 Introduction

In August 1965 scientists in the Serengeti National Park completed an aerial photographic census of the African or Cape buffalo (*Syncerus caffer*). Their count of 35,000 animals was surprising, since just four years earlier an aerial census had recorded only 15,000. Hunters who have known the area intimately for twenty or thirty years shook their heads in disbelief. How could there be 35,000 buffalo? they asked. I asked a different question: Why weren't there more?

Why, indeed, does a population have a certain number of individuals at a certain time and place—not more, not less? We now know that the wildebeest (*Connochaetes taurinus*), a grazing bovid like the buffalo, numbers close to one million animals in this area. But a closely related grazing species, the kongoni, or Coke's hartebeest (*Alcelaphus buselaphus*), numbers only about 9,000 in the same area. This study attempts to answer the question, What determines the size of a population? This question can be asked about any species' numbers, and its relevance to human population is obvious. At the time I started this study in October 1966 there was an impressive array of theories about this question and an equally impressive paucity of comprehensive data to support them. But much of wildlife management policy, and even human attitudes (e.g., Ardrey 1970), is colored by such theories. Clearly there is a need to understand how animal populations in general are determined, and perhaps mammal populations in particular.

The buffalo has acquired a quite unjustified reputation as one of the most dangerous animals in Africa. It is reputedly fierce and mean and is even supposed to show cunning by circling back on its tracks to ambush a hunter. Its whole reputation has developed from hunters' tales, particularly from the tales of hunters who have wounded animals and tried to follow them. Consequently, until recently what little was known of the behavior of the species concerned what ani-

3

mals did as the hunter pulled the trigger or immediately afterward. The behavior of frightened or mortally wounded animals is liable to be somewhat aberrant. Little was mentioned about herds of buffalo grazing like cattle over green fields, or about how timid they are, taking flight at the mere suspicion of human scent just like gazelle. Nevertheless, with the romance established hunters went out of their way to shoot the bulls for trophies. C. R. S. Pitman, a game warden in Uganda nearly half a century ago, describes a rather unusual hunt in which 150 African spearmen surrounded a buffalo herd, guided by observers in trees, while he and his guides waited inside the ring:

> The combatants in the ring, the spearmen closed in, guided by shouts from above, and contact with the herd was quickly established—off went the buffaloes with a drumming of hoofs. I was utterly bewildered, and very lonely, for whenever danger threatened, my followers disappeared with the agility of monkeys. Pandemonium reigned supreme; round and round the ever-decreasing circle pounded the frightened creatures; hither and thither I ran in the wake of my confident guides who, constantly on the lookout for the chance of a shot, invariably rushed headlong in the direction of the most noise.
>
> After nearly half an hour of this I was not only exhausted but thoroughly frightened, and wondered where it was going to end. Momentarily I expected the maddened herd to come charging along the path upon which I stood: escape would be impossible, for the great brutes could have swept through the bushes with ease. Opportunities for shooting did not arise and the ring of spearmen held their ground to such good effect and yelled so lustily that every few minutes there would be a thunderous roar in the vicinity of my precarious position, and I would catch a glimpse of huge, black bodies vanishing in a dense dust cloud. At last the buffaloes began to feel the strain of the chase, and the herd, passing closer to me than it had previously done, suddenly halted. The dust blew away, the animals stood their ground and offered me the long-awaited chance; the hindmost beast—not twenty paces distant—collapsed mortally stricken, only to be enveloped immediately in the swirling dust-cloud raised by the disappearing herd, which this time was not to be denied and carried its determined, panic-stricken rush through the surrounding foe. "All's well that ends well," and no harm had been done; but I admit that my feelings when the proceedings terminated were those of distinct relief.
>
> If any big-game hunter seeks a new thrill, where the odds are all against him, I recommend buffalo hunting as conducted by a large party of Marakwet spearmen! [Pitman 1943]

The buffalo prize became even more valuable as a result of a serious decline in numbers near the end of the nineteenth century, so that the animals were only occasionally encountered. This decline was the result of a catastrophic panzootic caused by the virus rinderpest. Before this occurred in 1889, the buffalo was one of the most numerous species in eastern Africa. Thus Lydekker (1908) quotes F. C. Selous, one of the more objective naturalists of the time, as saying of the buffalo:

> Till the end of 1889 and the beginning of 1890 it was however exceedingly common being found all over the country where there was good grass and water. It occurred on the coast opposite Lamu, on both banks of the Tana . . . , and near Mombasa. The real stronghold of the species was, however, the Masai country, where with perhaps the exception of Burchells zebra and hartebeasts, it was the most common of all the big game. From the southern slope of Kilimanjaro to Lake Baringo buffaloes were practically unmolested by the natives. . . . In the northern part of Masailand between Lakes Elementaita and Baringo they occurred in extraordinary numbers. . . . The banks of the Turkwel formed another stronghold; while on the Mau plateau they were also abundant and might be seen in dense black masses on the open grassy downs at all hours of the day. On the coast they were confined to the thick bush, and only came out to feed in the late evening.
>
> In 1890 rinderpest appeared amongst the native cattle and spread among the buffaloes so rapidly that by the end of April they were decimated and there are now (1900) few left.

Rinderpest is a disease of cattle. According to Branagan and Hammond (1965), it was introduced to Somalia from either Arabia or India during an Italian military expedition to Ethiopia in 1889. It spread rapidly, and by 1892 it had reached Malawi. These authors comment, "The rinderpest panzootic which swept Africa during the last decade of the nineteenth century was not only one of the major natural disasters of recorded history but was also an event of profound political and economic significance." It was also of profound ecological importance. The extent of the mortality in cattle is highlighted by the accounts of widespread starvation and death of the nomadic tribes that depend upon cattle for their livelihood. The effects upon the buffalo and some other bovids such as wildebeest were also severe, for several authors have corroborated Selous's account. For example, Hinde and Hinde (1901) write, "Ten years ago the buffalo was the commonest animal in East Africa but owing to rinderpest and pleuro-pneumonia, it is now reduced to some 3 or 4 herds." This is perhaps an overstatement; nevertheless, it seems that buffalo were more affected at that time than other wild bovids.

Ford (1971) describes some of the important ecological consequences of rinderpest in Sukumaland, the region bordering the Serengeti on the southwest. Buffalo were present in the region (and presumably in the Serengeti) before the rinderpest, for Stanley and Emin noticed abundant tracks of this species when they traveled through in 1889 (Ford 1971). The rinderpest caused considerable mortality among buffalo and cattle in the region, and this resulted in a reduction of the human population due to famine and emigration. Lack of cultivation by humans and lack of grazing allowed the bush to grow up, and this was colonized by tsetse flies as soon as the wild bovid population had recovered. The presence of these flies then prevented the human population from reentering the area with their cattle because of the trypanosomiasis disease transmitted by the flies. It was not until the 1930s that the spread of the tsetse fly was stopped with the help of modern bush-clearing methods. This allowed the subsequent expansion of the human population. In short, the effects of the rinderpest panzootic were still being felt some forty years later.

The buffalo population in East Africa recovered between 1900 and 1920, and by 1920 the species was becoming numerous in some areas (Roosevelt 1910; Percival 1924). In August 1913 the hunter S. E. White walked through what is now the northern part of the Serengeti National Park. Although he refers to seeing a few buffalo, clearly they were very scarce compared with present times (White 1915). However, other bovids were still relatively plentiful:

> In the bottom lands were compact black herds of wildebeest, grazing in close formation, like bison in a park, and around and between them small groups of topi and zebra—two or three, eight or a dozen —moving here and there, furnishing the life and grace to the picture of which the wildebeest were the dignity and the power. And every once in a while, at the edge of a thicket, my eye caught the bright sheen of impala, or in the middle distance the body stripes of gazelle, or close down in the grass the charming miniture steinbuck or oribi. [White 1915]

Similarly, when in July 1912 the game warden A. B. Percival (1928) camped on the Mara River near the present Kenya-Tanzania border, he noted that wildebeest were very concentrated in the area due to the prevailing drought, but he thought that their numbers had not dropped greatly because of it. Topi were also numerous then. Over the past decade wildebeest have moved into the northern Serengeti and Kenya during the dry season months of July to October (Pennycuick 1975), and their movements seem similar to those in 1912 and 1913: the gross pattern of their movements may not have changed substantially during this century even if their numbers have changed.

Rinderpest continued to affect the Serengeti buffalo and wildebeest until the 1960s. Buffalo remained relatively uncommon for most of this time. Moore (1938) remarks that in the 1930s she had to make a special journey to the northern Serengeti in order to see them, and she has confirmed their scarcity in the central and western areas at that time (A. Moore, personal communication).

An understanding of ecosystem processes or of population dynamics requires some sort of experimental perturbation. Unfortunately, in wildlife biology such experiments are either impossible or prohibitively expensive, and so our understanding of wildlife systems is necessarily incomplete relative to other areas of biology. However, there are occasions when the required perturbation is done for us—for example, through logging or agricultural practices or the construction of dams, fences, and other barriers. The introduction of the exotic disease rinderpest and its subsequent removal by inoculation campaigns in the areas surrounding the Serengeti provided a perturbation of the buffalo population. I have used this disturbance to analyze the dynamics of the population in order to distinguish between the various theories of population regulation. I have attempted this because Andrewartha (1961), Lack (1966), and Reddingius (1971) have all pointed out that there is little direct evidence for density-dependent regulation in animal populations—especially vertebrate populations. At the outset of this study I was aware only that the buffalo population was changing, and it was far from clear that rinderpest was implicated. But in the course of the work evidence accumulated on the causes of the various population processes. Large mammals are particularly suitable for studies on causes of mortality because carcasses are relatively easy to find and can be autopsied.

I have attempted to test empirically the various theories on population control. I identify three groups of hypotheses which emphasize different aspects of this problem: (1) Density-independent control, in which it is postulated either that regulation does not take place (Andrewartha and Birch 1954) or that it does so only occasionally and is masked by independent environmental factors (Ehrlich and Birch 1967; Ehrlich et al. 1972). (2) Regulation through extrinsic factors such as food shortage, disease, or predators, which are supposed to be negative feedback mechanisms governing the size of a population. The theory for this has been reviewed by a number of authors (e.g., Nicholson 1933; Solomon 1964; Clark et al. 1967; Wagner 1969; Varley and Gradwell 1970). Lack (1966) has suggested that food is a limiting resource, at least in birds, but Hairston et al. (1960) and Slobodkin et al. (1967) have argued that predation regulates the dominant members of the herbivore trophic level. One way to test these two theories is to find whether any resource is limiting for the dominant herbivores, whether that resource is food, and whether in the herbivore trophic level the major part of it is consumed. (3) Regulation through intrinsic factors: I have termed this the "self-regulation" hypothesis. It states that extrinsic factors do not regulate the population, but that intrinsic factors such as social behavior and genetic polymorphism result in increased mortality or reduced fertility. In this way the population is supposed to reach a level below that at which resources are limiting (Christian 1961; Christian et al. 1965; Krebs 1972; Krebs and Myers 1974).

Those who advocate regulation do so on the grounds that since populations remain within relatively narrow limits for long periods and do not become extinct, some density-dependent factor must be influencing their size. If this were not so then populations would drift to extinction. However, since all populations do eventually become extinct—as Reddingius (1971) puts it, the probability of extinction is unity—then the difference between the regulation and nonregulation schools becomes one of relative time of population survival: those populations experiencing regulation are supposed to survive longer than those without a governor. But how much longer becomes impossible to say. Furthermore, Reddingius (1971) has shown from a theoretical viewpoint that it is possible for populations to remain within well-defined limits for finite periods of time whether or not they are regulated. Although the theoretical basis of the original regulation hypothesis is now somewhat unsatisfactory, this does not mean that populations are not regulated. The issue can be resolved only by examining real populations. Thus Reddingius (1971, p. 197) says, "I think it can be inferred that in order to derive reliable conclusions about the being regulated of representative field populations we need both further results in theoretical statistics and more biological data. The quarrel between the 'regulationists' and their adversaries has been premature in the sense that none of the opposing parties possesses sufficient data to support their assertions."

The rationale behind the "intrinsic regulation" school of thought is that food-limited populations would damage their resources and thus eventually become extinct. This hypothesis can be tested by observing whether natality is density-dependent and whether food is in superabundance. If neither of these conditions holds in the long run then this hypothesis is unlikely to be true. Conversely, the "extrinsic regulation" hypothesis can be tested by observing whether a density-dependent mortality is caused by lack of some external resource or by disease or predators. The evidence normally used to detect intrinsic factors does not prove the "self-regulation" hypothesis. For example, endocrine imbalance can be caused by stress through lack of food as well as by aggression in social interactions. Regular fluctuations in the frequency of genotypes in a polymorphic population can be caused by differential mortality or reproduction in the genotypes as much through extrinsic factors as through social factors. In fact, the "self-regulation" hypothesis is difficult to prove because it is based upon the negative argument that extrinsic factors are not playing a part in regulation. It can, however, be disproved.

In this study I ask two basic questions: Is regulation taking place? and, if so, What are the causes of this regulation? By "regulation" I mean that if a population is experiencing a stable negative feedback process it is being regulated by "density-dependent factors." I have used Klomp's (1962) definition of density-dependent factors as those that either increase the percentage of mortality or reduce the reproductive rate as the population rises. I also recognize a distinction between the action of direct or automatic density-dependent factors such as the food supply and the delayed density-dependent action of factors such as predators (Varley and Gradwell 1970).

2 Taxonomy, Distribution, and Evolution

The African buffalo is a member of the family Bovidae, tribe Bovini, which also includes oxen and bison. In the past the species was distributed over most of Africa south of the Sahara. In South Africa it once occurred in some parts of the southwest arid zone and avoided only the Kalahari, Karroo, and Namib deserts. Selous (cited in Ansell 1972) mentioned that there was considerable desiccation in southwest Africa during the nineteenth century, and this may have been one reason the species disappeared from this area. Previously buffalo ranged from the Kalahari east through what is now Botswana to the Orange River in South Africa. Lydekker (1908) wrote that the French traveler Le Vaillant met with buffaloes on the Orange River in about 1783, but the missionary John Cambell did not mention seeing any during his travels in 1813.

Sidney (1965) reviews the information on present-day distribution up to 1960, and Ansell (1972) includes the more recent data (fig. 1). Buffalo have been exterminated from most areas in South Africa except the Addo and Kruger national parks. For the rest of Africa the distribution shows that the original range is becoming fragmented as human populations increase, particularly in the western African countries where the coastal lowland forest has been cleared extensively. In eastern Africa, buffalo are absent from the arid zone of Somalia, eastern Ethiopia, and northern Kenya. Similarly, much of central and southern Tanzania is thick dry scrub unsuitable for the species.

Buffalo are found in most of the major vegetation types shown by Moreau (1966), including the dense lowland forest of the Congo basin, montane forest in East Africa, moist and dry woodlands of central and southern Africa, and *Acacia* grasslands of the Sahel zone in West Africa and the plains of East Africa—in fact, wherever permanent water is found. They reach altitudes over 4,000 m on some

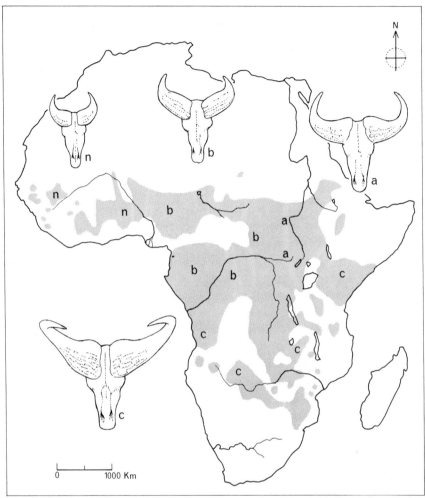

Fig. 1. The distribution of the African buffalo: c, *Syncerus caffer caffer*; a, *S.c. aequinoctialis*; b, *S.c. brachyceros*; n, *S.c. nanus*. Skulls are to scale.

mountains, where they experience frosts at night, but in West Africa they tolerate high ambient temperatures with high humidity. Stewart and Stewart (1963) state that in East Africa buffalo move into dry scrub in the wet season but they are not found in areas with a mean annual rainfall of less than 250 mm. In short, the species is much more catholic in its habitat choices than other bovids.

Syncerus

Although recent taxonomists (Ansell 1972; Grubb 1972) consider that there is only one species of buffalo in Africa, they have described a number of subspecies, and clearly there is considerable variation, particularly between West and East Africa. Of the four generally recognized subspecies illustrated in figure 1, *caffer* is the largest, standing 140–60 cm at the shoulder, with males weighing up to 700 kg, females to 500 kg. They are black and have relatively wide horns, reaching a span of 130 cm. The males are characterized by a heavy boss of horn on the top of the head. This race extends from South Africa and Angola, through central and East Africa, to the southern borders of Sudan and Ethiopia. The smallest race, *nanus*, is only half the size of *caffer* (105 cm at the shoulder) and is reddish brown. *Nanus* has only a slight thickening of the boss in males, or it may be absent altogether. This race is found in both dense lowland forest and savanna from the Ivory Coast westward.

Intermediate between these extreme races are *brachyceros* and *aequinoctialis*. The former extends from the Ivory Coast through Nigeria to Lake Chad and southeast through northern Cameroon, the Central African Republic, the Congo (Brazzaville), and northwest Zaire. This form grades into *aequinoctialis*, which can be found in the forests of eastern Zaire, to the west of lakes Tanganyika and Kivu, in the Albert National Park, and there are even some traces of this race in the Ruwenzori National Park, Uganda. Farther north it is found from Lake Chad east through southern Sudan and into Ethiopia, merging with *caffer* in the upper Nile region and along the southern borders of these countries. All races show variation in color, body size, and shape of horns, and they intergrade with each other. Thus there is no hard and fast distinction between races, and type names are mainly a matter of convenience. It may be better to consider *Syncerus caffer* as a polytypic species (Cain 1954) in a state of active radiation.

Other Species

Apart from *Syncerus*, the Bovini include the three genera *Bubalus*, *Bison*, and *Bos*. On morphological grounds, the closest relative of *Syncerus* is the Asian water buffalo *Bubalus bubalis*. Both have horn cores which tend to be triangular in cross section. The parietals form a wide zone on the roof of the cranium and are separated from the frontals. In *Bubalus* the horns emerge from the head more posteriorly than in *Syncerus*, there is no boss of horn in either sex, and the horns are long (100–10 cm in males, 110–30 cm in females) and crescent-shaped (fig. 3). In *Syncerus*, the vomer and palatinum remain separate, whereas in *Bubalus* they are fused. In the African buffalo the hair on the midline of the back is normally directed backward, the ears are large and heavily fringed with hair, and the skin contains many sweat glands; in the Asian buffalo the hair on the midline grows forward from rump to nape, the ears are small and not fringed, and the skin has few sweat glands and is relatively hairless. These skin differences are possibly adaptations to the more aquatic life this species leads. Similarly, *Bubalus* has wide hooves with joints which are very flexible for walking in mud (Cockrill 1967). It is short-legged (130 cm at the shoulder) and cannot run fast, but this may also be an aquatic adaptation, for these animals swim well and readily. I have watched them grazing on floating vegetation while swimming out of their depth and even submerging to reach underwater vegetation.

B. *bubalis* occurs in the wild as several subspecies over southern Asia. The largest race, *arnee*, occurs at present only in very small patches on the plains of the Ganges and Brahmaputra in Assam, the largest group being seven hundred animals in the Kaziranga Park. There are a few isolated groups elsewhere (Daniel and Grubh 1966). In former times they ranged from Mesopotamia to Indochina, and in the seventh century A.D. they were hunted in Persia (Epstein 1971). This race of buffalo was among the earliest domesticated animals; evidence of domestication has been found in India as early as 5,500 years ago (Epstein 1971). The domestic form extends from Italy and Egypt to China and northern Australia, where it is feral, and also occurs in South America. Two other races occur on islands: the tamarou (*B. b. mindorensis*), found only on Mindoro Island in the Philippines, is a small animal, 100–120 cm at the shoulder and weighing only 400 kg. It lives in forest and tall-grass jungle, but otherwise little is known of its ecology, and it is now very rare (Talbot and Talbot 1966). The other dwarf race, the anoa (*B. b. depressicornis*), is even smaller (60–100 cm at the shoulder) and occurs only on Sulawesi (Celebes). Still less is known about this animal. Epstein (1971) regards it as a separate species from *B. bubalis*.

In general the range of the water buffalo covers the humid tropics. The animal is well adapted to swamp country and eats sedges, grasses, and aquatic plants as well as some bushes and trees. It inhabits forests and swamps over much of its range, living in family groups of about 10 animals in small home ranges (McKay and Eisenberg 1974).

Both of the cattle and bison groups are distinguished from the buffaloes by horns which are round in cross section. In the genus *Bos*, the horns arise from the back of the skull and the frontals are long. Apart from the two domestic cattle species—the zebu (*B. indicus*) of Asia and *B. taurus* of Europe—there are four other wild species, namely, the yak (*B. grunniens*) of Tibet, the rare kouprey (*B. sauveli*) of Cambodia, the banteng (*B. banteng*) of Southeast Asia, and the gaur (*B gaurus*) of India and Southeast Asia. The yak was originally classified as a separate genus, *Poephagus*, but taxonomists (Simpson 1945; Ellerman and Morrison-Scott 1951) have now relegated this to a subgenus of *Bos*. Similarly the kouprey, banteng, and gaur have sometimes been assigned to the subgenus *Bibos*. These three are distinguished from the others by elongated neural spines on the thoracic vertebrae, which give them a dorsal ridge. They also have broad parietals, whereas domestic cattle and the yak have narrow parietals. The zebu has peculiar elongated bifid neural spines on the cervical and thoracic vertebrae (Epstein 1971), unlike any of the other species.

The yak lives in the high mountains (above 2,000 m) of central Asia. It is long-haired and adapted to cold climates. The only other species in the *Bos* group that originally lived in temperate regions is the extinct aurochs (*B. primigenius*), the wild form of *B. taurus*, which occurred in Europe. Otherwise the *Bos* group—including the zebu—is adapted to tropical climates. The range of the gaur extends from India through Burma and Malaya to Indochina but not Indonesia. The banteng ranges from Burma to Indochina and is present on the islands of Java and Borneo. It was originally present in Sumatra and only just enters north Malaya (Wharton 1968). Kouprey were known only in northern Cambodia and along the borders of Laos and Vietnam, and the population was thought to be only a few hundred (Wharton 1957; Pfeffer 1969). In view of the unsettled conditions in that area over the past decade, this species may well be close to extinction. Schaller (1967) states that the gaur is a forest animal which comes out onto the meadows only to eat and drink during the hot season after its forage in the forests has been burned and the stream beds dry up. Its habitats are largely undisturbed tracts of evergreen and moist deciduous forests, but it penetrates the dry deciduous forests at the periphery of its range. In the past it may well have inhabited the Gangetic plains or similar areas. It is both a grazer and a browser, preferring green grass when available, but in the dry season it consumes a variety of herbs and leaves mixed with coarse dry grass along stream beds. At this season Schaller (1967) found that rumens contained approximately 85% coarse dry grass, the rest being dicotyledonous material. Gaur live in small groups of 5 to 10 individuals, and large bulls become solitary. These males are black with white lower legs and have a dorsal ridge and dewlap.

Banteng live in dry woodland and glades and do a significant amount of browsing as well as grazing. The males are also black but have a less pronounced ridge and dewlap. They have white lower legs and also a white rump patch. The females are light brown, smaller than the males, and have small lyre-shaped horns. Like gaur, they live in small family groups and are extremely timid. Kouprey eat grasses and sedges along riverbanks and green regrowth after fires in the savanna areas, but they also eat young shoots from trees in the open deciduous woodland that predominates over their range (Wharton 1957). They prefer more open habitats than the gaur, which also occurs in Cambodia, but Wharton (1957) has seen mixed groups of kouprey and banteng. Male kouprey are large (700 kg) and black with white lower legs, and old animals may have gray sides. Their dewlap is so large that it drags through the grass. The nostrils are an unusual crescent shape. The horn tips have the outer layer conspicuously frayed back, so it looks like a tassel, a result of horning the ground during agonistic displays. Females are small and gray brown. In general this group of tropical species is not particularly associated with water, preferring the drier deciduous woodland and forest. Although these animals are grazers they also browse, particularly during the dry season. They live in small groups, and adult males become solitary.

Unlike cattle, bison are adapted to temperate regions only. There are two species, the wisent (*Bison bonasus*) in Europe and *B. bison* in North America, the only bovine to reach that continent. In this group the frontals are broad, and the large interparietals separate the small parietals, thus forming a broad but short skull. As with some of the *Bos* species, the neural spines of the thoracic vertebrae are elongated, producing a dorsal hump. The wisent was once common in the deciduous forests of Europe, but it is now reduced to a few hundred animals (about 370 in 1966), with some living free in the Bialowieze Forest of Poland (Krysiak 1967). Borowski and Kossak (1972) found that the diet of free-ranging wisent was composed of 61% grasses and sedges, 6% herbs, 27% shoots of trees, and 6% bark in summer. Experimental work by Gebczynska and Krasinska (1972) produced results similar to the field observations. These authors commented on the large numbers of plant species consumed by the wisent. Since in a mixed deciduous woodland the biomass of each plant species is small, the wisent has evolved catholic tastes in order to meet its relatively large food requirement. In winter when the ground is snow covered the content of browse in the diet—particularly bark—increases because this is the only forage that is accessible. The American bison, although it also inhabits forests, has in the past utilized the extensive grasslands of the Midwest, where it was presumably more of a grazer than a browser. Nevertheless, it does incorporate browse in its diet (Fuller 1961; Meagher 1973). This species occurs in larger herds of several hundred animals.

EVOLUTION

The phylogenetic origin of the Bovidae (fig. 2) presumably was a small generalized animal such as *Archaeomeryx* of the Eocene (Pilgrim 1947). This species was about the size of existing chevrotains, had no horns, and possessed upper incisors and four digits on front and back limbs. Whether it was a true ruminant is uncertain, for it lived 45 million years ago, between the appearance of pigs, 63 million years ago (Corbin and Uzzell 1970), and the first bovids, and so it may still have been at an intermediate stage in the evolution of the ruminant stomach. The first clear bovid appears to be *Eotragus*, living some 15–17 million years ago in the Miocene (Pilgrim 1947). This animal had short upright horns with circular cores. Gentry (1967) suggested that there followed a lateral compression of the horn cores in forms like *Protragocerus*, so that they became angular in cross section. An increase in size led to *Pachyportax* and *Parabos* in the Upper Miocene and Lower Pliocene about 5–6 million years ago.

At this point there appeared to be a radiation in the Bovini, for by 3 million years ago the main lines leading to *Bos* and *Bubalus* were already distinct: *Leptobos* in Europe and India during the Upper Pliocene (2–3 million years ago) had round horn cores, but there were some traces of the original angular keels. The *Bubalus* stock derived from *Proamphibos* (3–4 million years ago in the Pliocene) and the large *Hemibos* of Upper Pliocene India, both with anteriorly placed horns, triangular in cross section. Gentry (1967) notes that in fossil genera from both lines at this time—notably *Pro-*

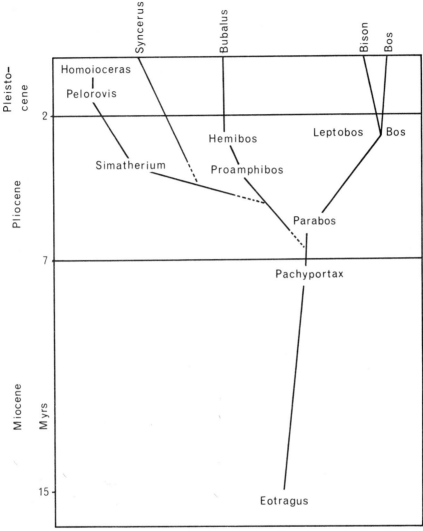

Fig. 2. Suggested phylogenetic relationships between *Syncerus* and other Bovini.

leptobos, Leptobos and *Proamphibos*, and *Hemibos*—males had horns but the females remained hornless. In all present-day Bovini the females have horns, except the diminutive water buffalo of Celebes, the anoa.

The phylogenetic origin of *Syncerus* in Africa, however, is far from clear. The earliest fossils, *Simatherium*, occur 4 million years ago in the Upper Pliocene. *Simatherium*, according to Gentry (1967), was about the size of a buffalo, but the slightly flattened horn cores arose from behind the orbits, farther back than in *Syncerus* but not so far back as in *Pelorovis*. It was older than *Hemibos* and *Leptobos* in Eurasia. Gentry considered *Simatherium* ancestral to the giant *Pelorovis* of the middle Pleistocene (fig. 3). *Pelorovis*, originally thought to be related to sheep, has been shown by Gentry (1967) to

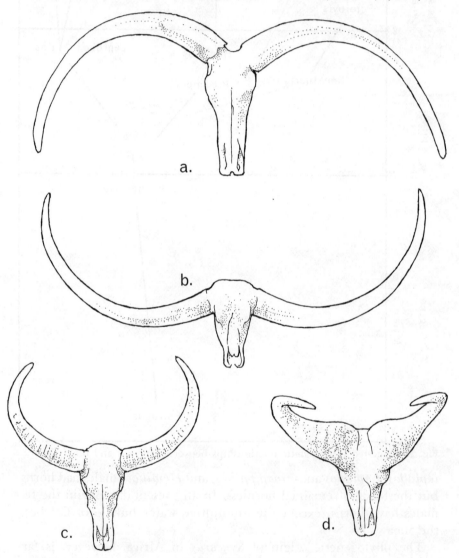

Fig. 3. The horns of the two fossil buffalo are very much larger than those of the present-day buffalo. a, *Pelorovis*; b, *Homoioceras*; c, *Bubalus*; d, *Syncerus*. Skulls are approximately to scale.

be a bovine phyletically nearest to *Syncerus* among present-day genera. *Pelorovis* and *Syncerus* both have narrow frontals and no contact between vomer and palate, and there are certain resemblances in their horn cores. However, there are obvious differences also. Not only do the horns arise from the back of the *Pelorovis* skull, but they are very large, forming a bow shape outward and downward. The length of a horn can reach 150 cm, compared with only 90 cm in *Syncerus*. The skull is long and was held pointing downward to balance the heavy weight of horn. The teeth are relatively simple compared with those of modern genera, and Gentry thinks the animal may have eaten soft aquatic vegetation. He further speculates, "The 1952 find of *Pelorovis* was of a herd, and it might be thought that these animals could have been plains-dwelling grazers like *Alcelaphus*. However this may be carrying the comparison too far, and it is awkward to accommodate with the primitive occlusal pattern of the molars. The only ecological possibility likely for a bovid which I would eliminate for *Pelorovis* would be eye-level browsing." Nevertheless, herd living is not inconsistent with aquatic grazing habits, as can be seen in *Syncerus* and particularly *Bubalus* today.

The differences in the skulls of *Pelorovis* and *Syncerus* make it very unlikely that the former was directly ancestral to the latter. In the late Pleistocene there appeared a large buffalo, *Homoioceras* (fig. 3), which existed until recent times, perhaps even until 12,000 years ago. Early man hunted it, and it appears in several rock drawings in North Africa (Zeuner 1963; Epstein 1971). This animal apparently died out as conditions became drier in Africa after the last ice age. Bate (1951) writes that "the African genera *Homoioceras* and *Syncerus* resemble each other in essential and primitive skull characters; they differ in minor skull characters and in the totally dissimilar shape of the horns." *Homoioceras* is much larger than the present-day buffalo. The horns originate from the skull more posteriorly than those of *Syncerus* but not so far back as those of *Pelorovis*, and there is also a suspicion of a basal thickening of the horn cores. In fact, the base of the horns resembles that of female *Syncerus*. Gentry (1967) mentions that the upper molars are no less advanced than those of *Bubalus* and are more advanced than those of *Syncerus*. The frontals are narrow, as in *Syncerus* and *Pelorovis* and unlike *Bubalus*. In skull characters *Homoioceras* is more like *Pelorovis* than is *Syncerus* in its larger size, long horn cores, absence of bosses, and a number of other characters (Gentry 1967). In fact, Gentry (personal com-

munication) has commented that apart from the type specimen
H. singae, all other *Homoioceras* types should be considered as one
species and called *Pelorovis antiguus*. *Homoioceras* was really the
last stage of the extinct *Pelorovis* lineage. *Syncerus* is related but has
an independent lineage. Gentry (personal communication) has also
noted that some fragments of molars found with *Pelorovis* probably
belong to this lineage leading to *Syncerus*. He writes, "Fossils which
I would accept as *Syncerus* are now known from the Shungura Formation, Omo, Ethiopia, back to at least 2½ million years." He mentions that fossil *Ugandax gautieri*, classified as a hippotragine by
Cooke and Coryndon (1970), may in fact be a bovine and seems a
likely ancestor for *Syncerus*. So he concludes that the two lines *Simatherium* to *Pelorovis* and *Ugandax* to *Syncerus* may have split from
each other not much later than both split from other bovines. There
still remains no distinct connection between the African and Asian
bovine stocks in the fossil record.

Both *Homoioceras* and *Pelorovis* had long metapodials, whereas
Syncerus has relatively short ones. It may be of interest to note that
rock-dwelling and montane bovids such as klipspringer (*Oreotragus
oreotragus*) and goats (*Capra*) also have short metapodials to facilitate
walking on steep slopes. It is therefore possible that *Syncerus* may
have evolved in mountainous regions and only recently expanded
into plains habitats. As Bate (1951) points out, the extreme plasticity
of the genus *Syncerus*, which ranges from the dwarf forest form to
the large plains form, suggests that it has not existed long. The fluctuations of climate over the past million years in Africa (Moreau
1966), resulting in the repeated advance and retreat of montane forests, would have encouraged the rapid radiation of a montane species.

The evolution of the water buffalo is better known. A species of
Bubalus from the Pliocene has been found in the Siwalik hills of
India, and related species in India can be traced up through the
Pleistocene (Epstein 1971). There was a *Bubalus* species in Europe
during the Great Interglacial, but this died out (Zeuner 1963). In
recent times the wild *B. bubalis* has been confined to India and
Southeast Asia.

Bubalus probably belongs to a group containing the large *Hemibos*
and *Proamphibos*. Gentry (1967) considers the latter phyletically related to the early Pliocene bovines *Parabos* and *Pachyportax*. Possibly it was from these forms, 5–6 million years ago, that *Leptobos*
diverged and led to the *Bos* group. Although *Leptobos* had round

horn cores, there were still traces of a flattened edge, the keel, characteristic of the *Bubalus* line. *Leptobos* lived in Europe and India before the ice ages and was a contemporary of the earliest forms of *Bos*. These were the long-horned *B. acutifrons* in Upper Pliocene India and *B. sivalensis* and *B. palaeosinensis* in China, which were, in fact, bison (Gentry 1967). So this period produced the divergence of *Bos* and *Bison. B. acutifrons* could have given rise to the Pleistocene wild cattle *B. primigenius*, which occurred in two subspecies—*namadicus* in India and *primgenius* in Europe. The latter, commonly called the aurochs, was absent or rare in Europe during the Lower Pleistocene, which might suggest an Indian origin for the species (Zeuner 1963). It became fairly frequent in the Great Interglacial but was not abundant until after the Ice Age had ended. Unlike *Bison*, it never reached North America. The two subspecies of *B. primigenius* are thought to be the wild ancestors of the modern domestic types *B. taurus* and *B. indicus*, which interbreed freely with no loss of fertility.

The aurochs lived until modern times in Europe, the last survivor dying in Poland in 1627. In central Europe males were black with a white stripe along the back and white curly hair between the horns. Toward southwest Europe the line on the back became yellow or red. Females were mostly brownish red. In the past fifty years breeding experiments in the zoos of Munich and Berlin have tried to "reconstitute" the aurochs by crossing breeds of cattle. These have been fairly successful (Zeuner 1963). Domestication of the aurochs occurred before 4,500 years ago, for by that time there were already several domestic breeds. The origin of the zebu (*B. indicus*) is more obscure, since it is known only in its domestic form, for which evidence dates back to 6,500 years ago. It has several features in common with *B. primigenius namadicus*, however, and the fact that the zebu has been physiologically adapted to tropical climates from the earliest times, unlike the aurochs, suggests domestication from a tropical race such as *namadicus* in India.

The genus *Bison* appeared in the Upper Pliocene of eastern Asia as a number of small species (Kowalski 1967). By the early Pleistocene they had reached Europe, and twice during the middle and late Pleistocene they crossed the land bridge over the Bering Strait to North America, where they extended to Florida and Mexico, though never to South America. During the Pleistocene ice ages of Europe the very large *B. priscus*, probably a grazer, ranged over the steppe.

It died out as conditions became warmer toward the end of the Pleistocene. The present-day wisent (*B. bonasus*) probably evolved from small forest forms such as *B. schoetensacki* of the early Pleistocene rather than from *priscus*, because the wisent extended its range into northern Europe only in late postglacial times and has never ranged beyond the deciduous forest (Kowalski 1967). Guthrie (1970) has reviewed the evolution of bison in North America. He has suggested that bison species radiated on this continent because they lacked competition from related bovine forms. The first invasion of *B. priscus* in the early mid-Pleistocene gave rise to *B. latifrons* in the south of the continent, and this may have evolved into *B. antiguus* in the late Pleistocene. At this time the northern half of the continent was covered with ice. When conditions became warmer in the late Pleistocene a second invasion of either *B. priscus* or *B. bison* moved south. At this time the earlier species became extinct, and today *B. bison* remains as the only species. Geist (1971) presents some alternative views for these later invasions.

Both Pilgrim (1947) and Thenius (1969) indicate that *Parabos* may have been the form giving rise to the African Bovini as well as to the *Bos* and *Bubalus* groups. This leads to the conclusion that there was a radiation at this period, presumably in Eurasia, and that the African buffaloes are as distant from the Asian buffaloes as they are from cattle and bison. As Gentry (1967) says, "If my opinion of a relationship of *Pelorovis* to *Syncerus* is accepted, then *Pelorovis* reinforces the views of those who have held that Asiatic and African buffaloes are not very closely related, and provides no basis for connecting *Syncerus* with the *Leptobos-Bos* group instead. There is no diminution of the phenetic distance between the African Bovini and those of Eurasia. It is not clear how far bovine evolution has consisted of a few long-independent lineages advancing gradually and often in parallel, or how far there have been repeated radiations of similar adaptive types at successive levels of overall advance."

So for the present these are the conclusions derived from the fossil evidence. There is, however, some other evidence obtained from a comparison of present-day genera. Mross and Doolittle (1967) compared the amino-acid sequences of the fibrinopeptides A and B of eighteen species of artiodactyls. They mention that studies of such sequences from a large variety of vertebrates have shown that these molecules have undergone an unusual degree of variation during vertebrate evolution. Consequently they are useful for studying evolution and taxonomy. In general they found that the mutational changes in the amino-acid sequences of fibrinopeptides were consistent with classical taxonomic schemes. Thus sheep were the closest to the bovines, followed by deer, camels, and finally pigs. Within the bovines they found that the two buffaloes were more similar to each other than they were to cattle and bison. This indicates that *Syncerus* diverged from *Bubalus* later than either diverged from the *Bos* stock. However, *Syncerus* differed from *Bubalus* by one amino acid on the B fibrinopeptide and had a deletion of four amino acids on the A fibrinopeptide. Such a deletion is not seen in any of the other species and indicates that *Syncerus* is further from *Bos* and *Bison* than is *Bubalus*. The latter, therefore, would be the older and more conservative buffalo type, with *Syncerus* being more specialized. *Bos* and *Bison* differ from each other by a total of only 3 amino acids, which agrees with the evidence from the fossil record for their more recent divergence. Therefore, if, as the fossil evidence shows, buffaloes diverged from the *Bos-Bison* stock sometime between 5 and 6 million years ago, the African buffaloes became distinct from the Asian stock more recently than this, but earlier than the late Pliocene (2½ million years ago). At present there is a gap in the African fossil record covering this period.

Further evidence comes from a comparison of the agonistic behavior of various Bovini, described later in chapter 6. The behavior of *Syncerus* is more like that of *Bubalus* than like that of cattle or bison. For example, males of the latter genera bellow aggressively in the rutting season, but neither of the buffaloes show this behavior. Similarly, bison and some *Bos* species have developed special morphological features such as the dorsal ridge to emphasize threat displays. Such specialization is absent in the buffaloes. It appears that the buffaloes, being less specialized, may be more akin to the original stock from which the other Bovini evolved. On this evidence, *Syncerus* would have diverged from *Bubalus* after the *Bos-Bison* stock had become separated. Nevertheless, the African buffalo has a number of special features—such as the heavy boss used in fighting and the elaborate submissive display—that suggest it evolved from *Bubalus* not too recently. In fact, *Syncerus* and *Bubalus* are more dissimilar to each other than are *Bos* and *Bison*, and so the divergence of the buffalo species probably occurred before *Bos* and *Bison* split from each other. Furthermore, *Bubalus* resembles the latter two in agonistic behavior more than does *Syncerus*, again implying that *Bubalus* is more like the original ancestors and *Syncerus* is more specialized. Therefore, since the phylogenetic evidence from the comparative behavior tends to agree in most essential details with that from the amino-acid sequences in the fibrinopeptides, I suggest the relationship between the genera shown schematically in figure 2.

3 Regions of Study

The main part of my study of population ecology was conducted in
the Serengeti National Park of Tanzania. The numerous interacting
grazing ungulates, the several predators associated with them, the
large size of the populations, and the scale of the area involved combined to produce a complex problem. Consequently, I also turned to
two other areas where a simpler ecological situation appeared to exist.
One area was the Lake Manyara Park about 60 km east of the Serengeti Plains, the other was in the montane region of Arusha Park at
Mount Meru in northern Tanzania, 100 km farther northeast of
Lake Manyara. The Arusha Park was the most suitable place for behavioral studies, although some observations were also made in the
other two areas. Scientific names for plants and animals and the authorities for them are listed in Appendix A.

THE SERENGETI

Locality and Topography

The extraordinary abundance and movements of large mammals in
the Serengeti ecosystem result in part from the area's peculiar combination of geology, vegetation, and climate. This ecosystem is taken
to be the area utilized by the migratory wildebeest population and
covers some 25,000 km² (within 34° to 37° E, 1° 15′ S to 3° 30′ S) of
open plains and wooded grasslands close to the southeastern edge of
Lake Victoria, including territory in both Tanzania and Kenya (fig.
4).

The eastern boundary is formed by the forested hills to the east of
the Loita Plains in Kenya. These hills run south into Tanzania, and
between them and the crater highlands (including Ngorongoro
Crater) lie the arid Salai Plains also used by the Serengeti wildebeest.
The southern and southwestern borders, running to Speke Gulf of
Lake Victoria, are formed by dry, rocky woodland and cultivation,

25

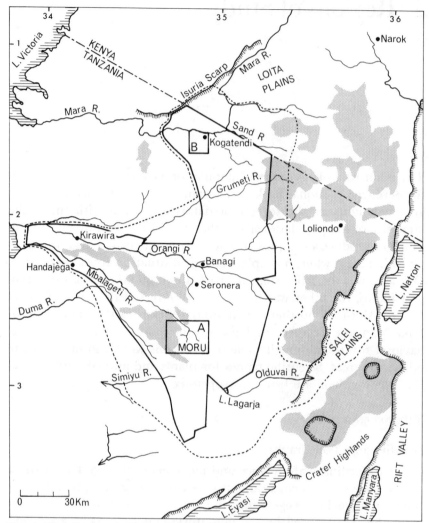

Fig. 4. The Serengeti National Park (*solid line*) and surrounding areas. The
dotted line describes the range of the migratory wildebeest population. The
areas A at Moru Kopjes and B on the Mara River indicate the two study areas.
Shaded areas indicate hills.

especially in the west. This part of the Serengeti forms a relatively
narrow extension that reaches almost to the lake. The northern
boundary of this extension and the western boundary of the park are
bordered by cultivation which continues onto the top of the Isuria
escarpment. This escarpment forms the northwestern boundary and
continues into Kenya. The northern boundary is rather indefinite
and runs along the southern edge of the Loita Plains. These plains

are rarely used by the Serengeti wildebeest when they are in the north during the dry season, for there is little water and no grass growth. However, the wooded regions of the Masai Mara Reserve of Kenya are included in the range of the Serengeti wildebeest.

The Serengeti slopes from a high point on the eastern plains (1780 m) to a low point at Lake Victoria (1230 m), with a more rapid change in altitude in the east so that the western extension is comparatively flat. Because of this, the northeast is dissected by many small tributaries draining into the main rivers—the Mara, Grumeti, and Orangi, which all run west to the lake. In the west there are fewer tributaries, and the main rivers—the lower Grumeti, Mbalageti, and Duma—meander westward, often with oxbows, and support a rich riverine forest.

The southeast of this ecosystem is composed of gently undulating treeless plains, with very few rivers. Those that flow for most of the year (and the two small lakes at the head of Olduvai Gorge) are alkaline because of a high concentration of sodium carbonate in the soil and consequently are not used by ungulates. These plains, covering some 10,000 km², are composed of volcanic ash derived from the crater highlands immediately to the east. One of these volcanoes, Kerimasi, deposited the ash during an eruption some 50,000 years ago (Pickering in Schaller 1972). The soil is friable and porous and does not hold rainwater for long.

From the crater highlands the plains extend west for 60 km and come to an end with a number of low hills, the southern and central ranges, the latter extending westward toward Lake Victoria as a sort of backbone to the western extension. These hills, although stony and sometimes precipitous, are no impediment to the moving herds and are often frequented by several ungulate species such as buffalo, impala, and giraffe. However, in the northeast of the ecosystem the Loita Hills and their southern extension, the Gol Mountains, are far less hospitable, for in the north they are covered with dense thicket and in the south they are extremely dry, so that few animals apart from some gazelle and the Masai cattle use the area. The Masai themselves occupy at low density most of the area to the east and north of the Serengeti National Park, including the Loliondo area and the eastern Serengeti Plains. Until 1959 they also resided at Moru Kopjes within the park. With the hills to the west of the plains comes an abrupt change to woodlands (plate 5), and this is associated with a change from the volcanic ash soil. Except for the two ranges of hills, the terrain is relatively flat over the west and central parts of the woodlands. Farther north gently sloping ridges and valleys form the area between the Grumeti and Mara rivers.

Climate

The annual distribution of rain in East Africa is dominated by the Intertropical Convergence Zone, a low-pressure area which follows the movements of the sun with a lag of about six weeks. The relatively dry northeast winds move south over East Africa in October and November and drop what little moisture they have as the "short rains." Again following the sun on its way north, the moist southeast winds bring the "long rains" from March to June, and these are often very heavy. In the Serengeti, numerous small watercourses start to flow, sometimes becoming raging torrents. The larger rivers in the flatter western parts overflow their banks and areas of low-lying ground on each side are flooded for weeks at a time, in some parts forming marshes that remain well into the dry season. Areas of impeded drainage become waterlogged, and one area in the far west, an old lake bed from times when Lake Victoria was at a higher level, is extensive enough to form a floodplain.

Since Norton-Griffiths, Herlocker, and Pennycuick (1975) describe the patterns of rainfall in the Serengeti area in some detail, I shall mention here only those aspects relevant to this study. A gradient of decreasing annual rainfall from the northwest to the southeast can be seen from the annual isohyets in figure 5. This gradient is the result of a number of local climatic influences. The crater highlands create a rain shadow on their western side so that the southeastern part of the plains receives as little as 500 mm of rain in the year and the short rains are abbreviated or nonexistent. This can be seen in the histogram of mean monthly rainfall over ten years at Olduvai Gorge (fig. 6). The effect of this rain shadow decreases farther west on the plains, as is seen, for example, on the Simiyu River, where the woodlands begin. But usually there is no appreciable rain until December, and rainfall lasts only until May. On the other hand, Lake Victoria causes increased precipitation over the western extension, and it is common in this area for the rain to come from the west as well as from the east. As a result, at Handajaga Hill (fig. 6) the short rains start earlier and are more consistent than on the plains, with heavy rain appearing in November and occasionally even in October; but there is still a pronounced dry season.

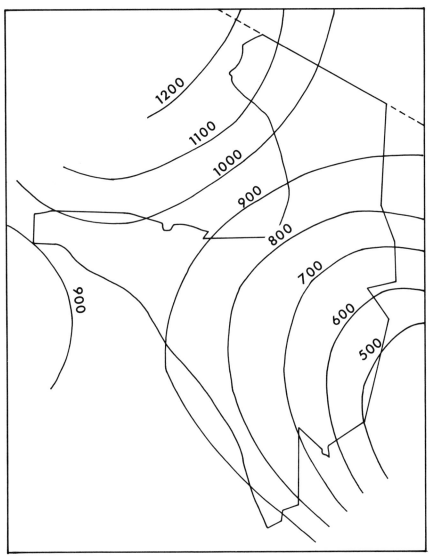

Fig. 5. Mean annual rainfall isohyets (mm) showing the decline from northwest to southeast. Redrawn from Norton-Griffiths, Herlocker, and Pennycuick (1975).

The northern part of the Serengeti Park is influenced not only by the lake basin rainfall but also by that from the Mau highlands farther north in Kenya, and by high-level northerly winds (Norton-Griffiths, Herlocker, and Penncuick 1975). The combined effect of

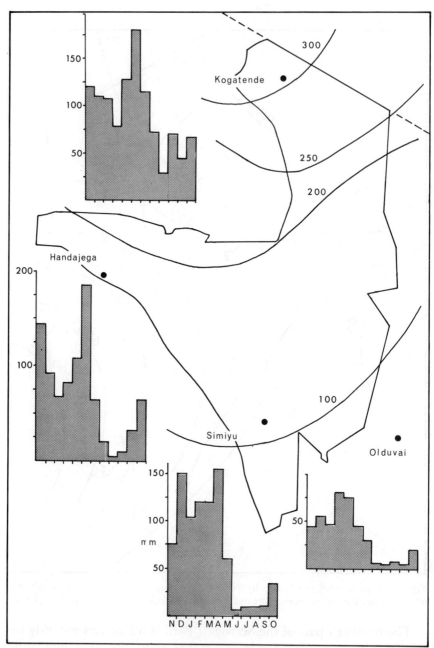

Fig. 6. Mean dry season isohyets (mm) showing the same gradient as in fig. 5. The histograms show the distribution of rainfall through the year at four stations. Isohyets adapted from Norton-Griffiths, Herlocker, and Pennycuick (1975).

these systems is to produce a high rainfall of over 1,000 mm in this area. Not only do the rains start early in November, but they often continue without a break until June. More important, there is also an appreciable amount of rain in the dry season. Consequently the rainfall gradient is also present in the dry season (fig. 6).

In the northwest the rain comes as locally distributed thunderstorms that have developed from the heat and smoke of grass fires (plate 7). But the far southeastern plains almost never receive rain during this season, and they become a dry, dusty, and desolate wilderness. The dry season lasts for four months covering July to October, but there is considerable variation in the start and end of this period. For purposes of analysis in this study these four months have been taken as the dry season. There is sometimes an intermediate dry period from January to March, between the two rains, but as often as not there is one continuous wet period from November to June with occasional breaks of a few weeks which may occur in any month. Hence, there is considerable temporal variability as well as spatial differences in the distribution of rain. However, it is rare indeed for there to be a complete failure of rains over the whole Serengeti ecosystem: even the drought of 1960–61, which seriously affected the areas to the east of the crater highlands around Lake Manyara and Arusha, did not have any noticeable effect in this region.

Rainfall has been highly variable from year to year (fig. 7), and there is little evidence of any trend over the past twenty years. The early sixties were wet years but in the mid-1960s a relatively dry period ensued. This in turn was followed by several wet years starting with 1971 (fig. 7), which may be part of the worldwide change that may have occurred since then (Kukla and Kukla 1974). Similarly, for the years 1963 to 1972 dry-season rainfall in the woodlands remained fairly constant until 1969, but thereafter there was a consistent increase. These later years, especially 1971 and 1972, were very wet, and rarely was there an occasion without abundant water and green grass in the dry season.

A number of other climatic factors are associated with the seasonality of rainfall. Mean daily temperature reaches a maximum in the dry season and a minimum in the long rains (fig. 8), and, conversely, relative humidity is at a minimum in the dry season. Winds also tend to be stronger and more consistent in this season. All these factors contribute toward making the dry season relatively unfavorable for the animals.

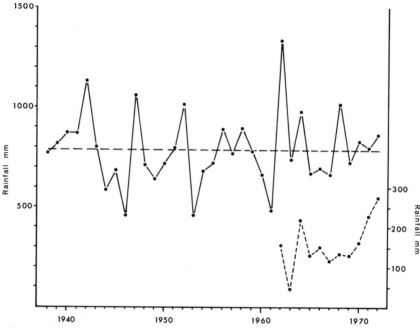

Fig. 7. Total annual rainfall (*solid line*) and rainfall during the dry season
(*dotted line*) at Banagi in the center of the park. The mean annual rainfall is
shown as a broken straight line and illustrates that there has been no long-term
change over the thirty-five years. Dry-season rainfall increased between 1969 and
1972.

Woodland Vegetation

Herlocker (1975) has described the woody vegetation of the Serengeti
National Park. Here I describe only the broad characteristics of the
woodlands, mentioning details relevant to buffalo. The distribution
of woodlands and open grasslands is shown in figure 9, together with
the main rivers containing year-round flowing water or pools. The
woodlands are dissected by numerous small watercourses a few meters
wide, which are usually dry. Between these watercourses the terrain
forms a gently sloping soil catena with light sandy soils at the top
grading down to fine black silt soils at the bottom, and this largely
determines the types of vegetation growing in an area. Of the trees,
thorny *Acacia* species tend to predominate. Particularly around the
periphery of the plains on the west and north sides, the umbrella-
shaped *Acacia tortilis* forms open, almost parklike stands, (plate 14)
and provides shade for ungulates. Farther into the woodlands a fine
mosaic of small stands of *Acacia hockii, A. senegal, A. clavigera, Commiphora trothae, Albizia harveyi,* and *Balanites aegyptiaca* is found

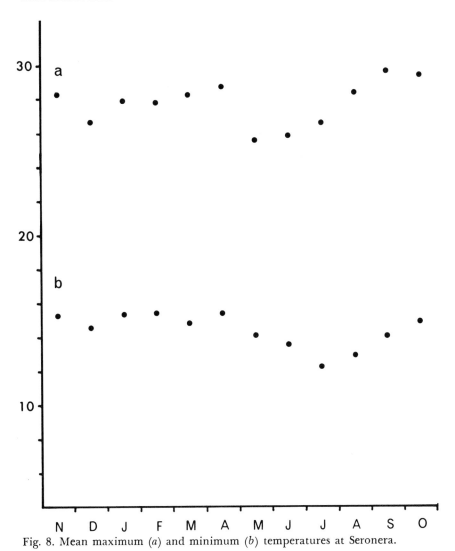

Fig. 8. Mean maximum (a) and minimum (b) temperatures at Seronera.

over most of the catena except in the drainage lines. The first two
species are short (rarely over 4 m), thin-stemmed trees providing
little shade. *A. clavigera* is a medium-sized tree (over 10 m) found
over the whole area, but it forms dense shady stands on poor, stony
soil at the foot of the central and southern ranges which are always
associated with swarms of bloodsucking tsetse flies (*Glossina* spp).

At the bottom of the catena, in areas of poor drainage, the black
silt soil becomes waterlogged in the rains but bakes hard in the dry
season. Two species, *Acacia seyal* on the very wet soils, and the

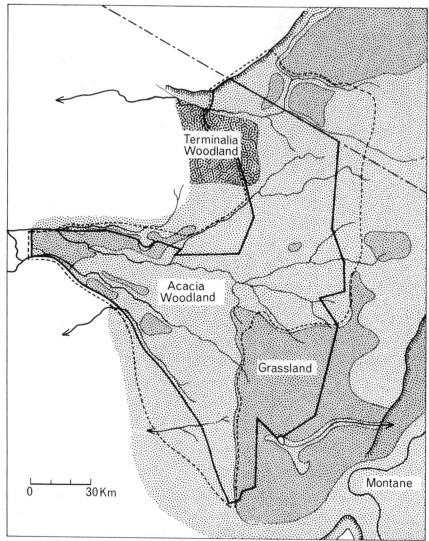

Fig. 9. Distribution of the major vegetation types in the Serengeti-Mara region.

whistling thorn, *A. drepanolobium*, on slightly less wet soils, form
almost pure stands, but being small they provide little shade for animals. However, in the far west on the extensive floodplain near Lake
Victoria, *A. seyal* provides the only shade available to buffalo. Along
some of the more permanent rivers in the south the tall *Acacia xanthophloea* forms a nearly closed canopy sometimes up to 50 m wide.
The small watercourses which flow only in the rains are characterized
by a thin line of bushes and herbs along the banks and even along

the bed itself. Apart from *A. brevispica*, a small thorny bush, commonly occurring species are *Grewia bicolor*, which is often browsed by giraffe (*Giraffa camelopardalis*), and *Ormocarpum trichocarpum* and *Capparis tomentosa*, both small bushes occasionally browsed by buffalo. This thicket is only a few meters wide, and although it provides shade and protection for solitary male buffalo, it is of little use for herds. However, along the larger rivers which either flow year round or at least contain permanent pools of water in the dry season a more extensive forest develops (plate 6), sometimes several hundred meters across and with large trees such as fig (*Ficus spp.*) and podo (*Podocarpus usambarensis*). This forest is found mostly in the north on the Mara River—especially in Kenya—and its tributaries, but patches also occur along the lower Grumeti, Mbalageti, and Duma rivers in the far west. It contains a rich understory of herbs, bushes, saplings, and lianas and so provides abundant food, shade, and protection for a number of herbivores. These include elephant (*Loxodonta africana*), rhinoceros (*Diceros bicornis*), bushbuck (*Tragelaphus scriptus*), and even large buffalo herds (plate 13).

In the north, on the Mara watershed and in the Loita Hills, the riverine forest extends up the catena as a thicket usually 5–6 m high and contains small trees such as *Croton dichogamus*, *Euclea divinorum*, and *Teclea nobilis*. From White's (1915) description it is evident that this thicket was fairly extensive seventy years ago in the northwest of the Serengeti Park. He describes how it took several days to push through eight miles of this thicket to reach the south bank of the Mara River. Nowadays there are only small pockets of such ridgetop bush in what is otherwise open grassland with scattered trees of *A. clavigera* (plate 7). The disappearance of this thicket has probably been caused by the extensive grass fires that every year kill the outside layer of bushes and prevent any regenerating rootstock from producing more than one year's growth before being burned back again. Each dry season the lining of orange-colored scorched bushes around every thicket is a common sight. The grass fires, lit by man, must have increased in the past half-century as human populations have increased their pressure on the northwestern and southwestern boundaries. These thickets are extensively used by elephant and buffalo and provide the main food supply for rhinoceros.

People living in the area start fires on the outskirts of the region either to attract animals to new growth for illegal hunting or, in the eastern sectors, to provide new grazing for the nomadic Masai cattle.

The strong easterly winds fan the fires, which spread across large areas of the woodlands (plate 10), sometimes lasting for several days. Hot fires late in the dry season burn off the new growth from young trees, and all the standing crop of grass and herbs. After such fires the ground is black and parched, with nothing for the ungulates to eat until a shower causes the roots of the perennial grasses to send up new shoots about 5 cm long, the "greenflush." These shoots soon dry and wither unless more rain falls, but for a short time they provide food for the wandering wildebeest, zebra (*Equus burchelli*), and Thomson's gazelle (*Gazella thomsoni*). Fires starting early in the dry season, when there is still a certain amount of green undergrowth, have less devastating effects upon the vegetation. Pockets of grass remain unburned, providing refuges for small animals, trees often escape unharmed, and after the first rain there develops a mosaic of different grass heights. The damp soils along rivers and on the spring-line prevent fires from encroaching into the riverine grasslands, and in some areas this is the only long grass remaining in the dry season.

Where the thickets have disappeared, open grasslands are found both in the adjoining Kenya Mara Park and in the northern Serengeti Park. However, a small area in the northwest Serengeti south of the Mara River (fig. 9) supports a different type of woodland containing broad-leaved trees, such as *Terminalia mollis* (plate 8) and *Combretum molle*, and scattered bushes of *Heeria mucronata* and the ubiquitous *Grewia bicolor*. *Acacia gerrardii* and extremely stunted *A. hockii* (only 1 m high) are two of the few *Acacias* growing in the area. The terrain is more markedly undulating than elsewhere, the soil is thin, and on the ridgetops there are areas of bare rock (plate 9).

The *Terminalia* woodlands occupy the top half of the ridges only. About halfway down there is an abrupt boundary with open, almost treeless grassland stretching down to the riverine forest in the valley bottom (plate 9). At this boundary of the woodland there is a seepage line where the water table meets the surface. It follows a contour and the seepage is only a few meters wide—rarely more than thirty—forming a band of green waterlogged ground which in wet years is maintained throughout the dry season (plate 9). Usually there is enough water to produce seepage streams running down through the open grassland every 100 m or so. Such lush green grass is a favorite area for buffalo, and mud wallows are frequently excavated in the wettest parts. Characteristic of this line are large termite mounds with their associated bushes of *Rhus natalensis*.

The central and southern ranges of hills have a thin stony soil and support a largely broad-leaved *Combretum* woodland with some bushes of *Pappea capensis* and *Harrisonia abyssinica*. The large outcrops of rocks, known as kopjes, are characteristic of the Serengeti woodlands and plains (plate 5). Those in the woodlands often support a dense vegetation. Fig trees are prominent and are favored by troops of baboons (*Papio anubis*) for their fruit. Apart from *Grewia*, there are other bushes such as *Cordia ovalis, Rhus natalensis,* and the thorny *Ziziphus mucronata* and *A. brevispica*. The whole provides a rich habitat for many mammals such as vervet monkeys (*Cercopithecus aethiops*) and hyrax (*Procavia, Heterohyrax*) as well as ungulate browsers such as klipspringer (*Oreotragus oreotragus*), which are especially adapted to running over rocks, and giraffe and eland (*Taurotragus oryx*). One important feature of these kopjes is that at the base of the large rocks seepage water often wells up, providing small areas of permanent green grass as well as drinking water in the dry season. Buffalo males use these areas, grazing the green growth and seeking shade and protection within the kopje vegetation. Such areas are also favorite resting places for predators.

Grassland Vegetation

The grasslands are of particular importance in the Serengeti because they support the major part of the ungulate biomass. The several grassland communities can be lumped into a few main types (fig. 9). Apart from the riverine grasslands, which are edaphic, and those on the plains, the rest are fire-induced derived grasslands. Over much of the wooded areas and the northwest section of the plains the grasses grow relatively long, to heights of approximately 100 cm. The two most common grasses are the red oats grass, *Themeda triandra,* and the coarse *Pennisetum mezianum*. Both can be found over most parts of the catena. A number of less abundant species are also widespread, including *Heteropogon contortus* and the palatable *Digitaria macroblephora*. The latter is so frequently grazed that it is difficult to find in a flowering state except where protected by *Acacia* bushes.

The composition of grass species changes according to the position on the catena, and this is particularly noticeable on the open grasslands of the western extension (Bell 1971). At the top a number of short, fragile grasses such as *D. macroblephora* and *Chloris pycno-thrix* are heavily grazed by wildebeest (*Connochaetes taurinus*) and Thomson's gazelle (*Gazella thomsoni*), but on the intermediate slopes the longer *Themeda* and *Sporobolus pyramidalis* predominate. At the bottom of the catena in impeded drainage areas of black silt soils *Pennisetum mezianum* is abundant and is often associated with whistling thorn (*Acacia drepanolobium*). However, other areas in the vicinity of the larger rivers which are frequently flooded support tall coarse grasses, such as *Panicum maximum*, which form thick clumps up to 2 m high. Within the riverine forest a similar tall grass, *P. infestum*, is found together with the broad-leaved grass *Setaria chevalieri*. Both are coarse grasses, but being in the deep shade of the forest they have some green leaves during the dry season, and these are grazed by the buffalo. Along the sandy riverbanks in the immediate vicinity of permanent water grows the highly nutritious creeping grass *Cynodon dactylon*, also heavily grazed by these animals.

The northern *Terminalia* woodland above the springline has a markedly different composition of grass species. A fine mosaic of different species is formed, each having almost pure stands covering about 100 m². Apart from *Themeda* the most abundant is *Loudetia kagerensis* (about 1 m high), but on the ridges *Hyparrhenia filipendula* grows to 2 m high, although on this stony ground the plants are widely spaced with low basal cover. *Eragrostis cilianensis* is also common, and in some areas so is *Setaria sphacelata*. Hence the tendency in other areas of the Serengeti toward short grasses at the top and long grasses at the bottom of the catena disappears in the *Hyparrhenia* grasslands. The southern and central ranges of hills support a similar grassland dominated by *Laudetia kagerensis*, but with less *Hyparrhenia*. Since the soil is thin and stony, the grasses are widely scattered with low basal cover and consequently the production and standing crop are relatively low.

The springline supports the grasses listed above and a number of sedges such as *Kyllinga alba*, *Cyperus obtusiflorus*, *C. teneriffae*, and *Mariscus mollipes*, all of which are heavily grazed. Below the springline, *Themeda*-dominant grasslands extend to the drainage line. In various parts of the Serengeti area these drainage lines are alkaline and support specially adapted grasses. In the drier parts *Sporobolus marginatus* and *S. spicatus* are abundant, but in the swamps there are stands of the coarse sedge *Cyperus laevigatus*. Chemical analysis of such grasses has shown that they do not contain abnormally high

amounts of alkaline salts, and *C. laevigatus* in the young stages contains the relatively high content of 8% crude protein; all these alkaline species are grazed by buffalo.

The northwest corner of the plains (fig. 9) is composed of long
Themeda grassland with small areas dominated by the aromatic
lemon grass, *Cymbopogon excavatus*, which in the mature stages is
avoided by most herbivores. Braun (1973) and Kreulen (1975) have
classified the rest of the plains into intermediate and short grasslands.
The intermediate grasslands in the southeast stand about 50 cm
when ungrazed and have a high basal cover. Such species as *Andropogon greenwayi, Sporobolus pellucidus,* and *Harpachne schimperi*
are common, with areas of herbs such as *Solanum incanum* and *Indigofera basiflora.* The short grasslands rarely have grasses over 15
cm in height and are heavily grazed by the migratory wildebeest and
Thomson's gazelle. They extend east to the foot of the crater highlands. In the dry season there is little standing crop of grass, no water,
no shade, and a constant desiccating wind over these plains: few
ungulates can support themselves there at this season.

The standing crop of grass at the end of the wet season is related
to the amount of rain that has fallen. This relationship, shown in
figure 10, was obtained from information collected during this study
and by Braun (1973) and applies to all the grassland types, although
individually each is slightly different. In the woodlands as much as
8,000 kg/hectare dry weight of grass has been produced over one wet
season (Braun 1973). During the dry season there is relatively little
growth and the standing crop declines through burning, grazing, and
decomposition.

Burning is an important factor in the long-grass areas (plate 10),
taking as much as 90% of the standing crop in some years. Between
1964 and 1972 burning removed an average of 62% during the dry
season. Also, if there is a dry period in February some parts of the
woodland may be burned twice in a year, as occurred in 1971 and
1972. Hence the standing crop is repeatedly removed and there is
little chance for litter to accumulate. Figure 11 shows the sequence
of burnings and growth on the outer edge of riverine grassland
which was available to buffalo in the northern part of the Serengeti.
Those fires in the intermediate dry spells of March were followed by
the long rains, and there was a rapid growth resulting in nearly 6,000
kg/hectare after only four months' growth, despite grazing by ungulates. The burnings in the long dry season were followed by little

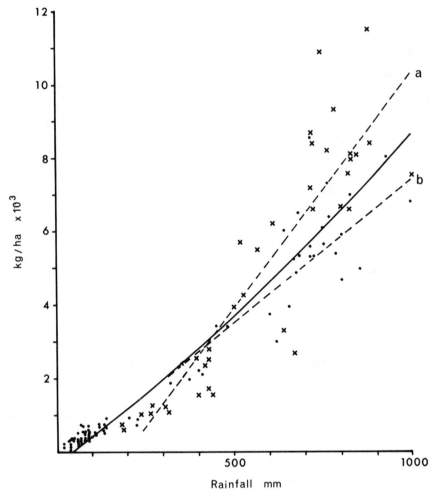

Fig. 10. The relationship between grass growth and rainfall in the period from the start of the wet season until the grass is cut. Information from the plains (Braun 1973) is shown as crosses, that from the woodlands as dots with their respective regression lines *a*, *b*. The solid curve was calculated from the combined data.

growth and intensive grazing pressure, so that there was little if any increase in standing crop for the rest of that season.

The standing crop of grass does not always represent food—particularly mature grass, which is composed of a considerable amount of stem, of very low nutritive value for ruminants. Usually the highest-quality food is the new growth resulting from recent rainfall. The rate of growth of new grass leaf is proportional to the amount of

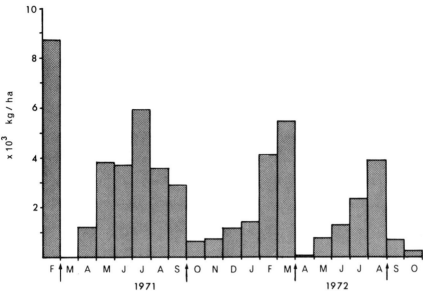

Fig. 11. Standing crop of grass at one site in riverine grassland in the northern Serengeti. Arrows indicate the approximate time of burning.

rain falling in the previous month (fig. 12), although there is some variation resulting from differences in soil dampness. Also, the rate of growth varies according to the position on the catena, with a higher rate of growth at the bottom than at the top.

One of the important food components for ruminants is the amount of protein, usually measured as the percentage of crude protein in oven-dried grass. Crude protein is highest in green leaves and lowest in stem and is inversely related to the amount of lignified fiber in these parts. The base of the leaf surrounding the stem—the leaf sheath—is intermediate in protein quality. Protein and soluble carbohydrates are transported to the grass roots, where they are stored when the grass dries and withers. The leaves then turn brown and are much lower in quality as food. Eventually during the dry season they disintegrate and fall off the stem to form litter which the ungulates cannot eat. Meanwhile the leaf sheath, normally closely wrapped around the stem, curls outward as it dries and becomes available to the grazers. Both the leaf sheath and the stem become more lignified in the dry season. After a grass fire the new growth of leaves from the base of the plant is very high in quality, having over 15% crude protein. As the grass grows this percentage declines, until

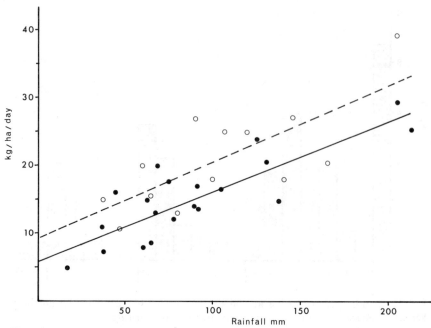

Fig. 12. The relationship between growth rate on a clipped plot and rain falling in the previous month. For any rainfall value, growth is always higher in riverine grassland (*open circles, broken regression line*) than in grassland halfway up the soil catena (*dots, solid line*).

in the mature flowering stage it is only 4% for the whole plant. In the dry season this falls still further to about 2.5% (fig. 13). The new growth at different times of year shows no change in the woodlands, remaining at approximately 15% crude protein; but in the intermediate grasslands Braun (1973) describes a decrease in protein content of the new growth toward the end of the rains.

Fauna

The immense numbers of wildebeest quite naturally play a dominant role among the grazers. There are five distinct populations of this species. Apart from the main migratory herd, which numbers some three-quarters of a million animals (table 1),* there are small populations of between five and ten thousand animals in the far western extension of the Serengeti Park, in the Loliondo area east of the park, on the Loita Plains in the north of the ecosystem and in Ngorongoro Crater itself. The migratory population overlaps the

*All tables will be found in Appendix D.

first three from time to time. In these studies all references are to the main migratory population, for it is by far the most important. These animals spend the wet season from November to May on the intermediate- and short-grass plains, and according to recent tracking results using radio transmitters, they move about the plains in a grazing rotation with a cycle of about four weeks.

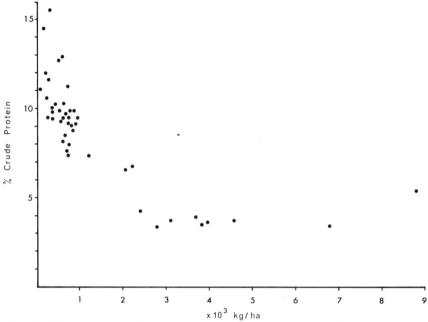

Fig. 13. The crude protein content is highest in new growth after burning and declines rapidly as the grass grows and matures.

When the plains dry up, they move northwest through the southern and central ranges in search of water and green grass in the western extension, where they concentrate along the permanent water supplies of the Mbalageti and Grumeti rivers. They use the western grasslands for June and July, until most of the edible grass has been consumed, and if there is no further rain they move to the north. Pennycuick (1975) has found that recently the population has moved off the plains earlier than it did a decade ago and spread more into the central woodlands as well as the west. In that time the population has tripled (Sinclair 1973a) and it appears that they now exhaust the food resources on the plains and in the west earlier. The movement to the north usually takes place in August and the population concentrates on the Mara River and its permanently flowing tributaries, both in Tanzania and Kenya. The farthest north they have been found is the edge of the Loita Plains, which at this season is an inhospitable dry area.

At the start of the rains in November the wildebeest move south as far as the new green growth allows, which is usually to the edge of the woodlands or onto the long-grass plains. They normally have to wait at least until December before they can move east to the short-grass plains where they drop their calves between January and March. If at any time the rains fail on the plains the wildebeest move west again. In general the wildebeest tend to move to the plains if enough rain has fallen there, but if not they will move to the nearest green area in the woodlands. Pennycuick (1975) has shown that the higher the rainfall on the plains the more the area is used, but the use of woodlands is inversely related to rainfall. This means that there are an increasing number of wildebeest overlapping with other grazing species in the woodlands as the dry season becomes more severe.

The zebra and the Thomson's gazelle form the other two large migrating populations utilizing the plains in the wet season. Zebra tend to move north earlier than wildebeest and continue into the Kenya Mara, although a separate group moves west and remains there for the dry season. They are often found in long dry *Themeda* and are less dependent upon the short greenflush that the wildebeest eat. Thomson's gazelle normally migrate west in the dry season and rarely move farther north than the central woodlands. Hence, by the end of the dry season the population is largely separate from the wildebeest and zebra. Although more tolerant of dry conditions, the gazelle avoid long-grass areas and tend to graze the short grass on catena tops in the western extension. The eland is the only other large herbivore exhibiting this migratory pattern. This small population divides into two parts, one moving west and the other north in the dry season, and although they eat some grass they usually rely on herbs and bushes at this time of year.

A number of grazing ungulate species remain in the woodlands year round. From information given in Hendrichs (1970) and Sinclair (1972, 1973a) and by M. Norton-Griffiths (personal communication) the approximate abundance and density of these are given in table 1. Buffalo contribute most toward the resident biomass of the woodlands, although impala (*Aepyceros melampus*) are numerically more abundant. Buffalo occupy the whole Serengeti woodlands and are sometimes found on the long-grass plains in the wet season. They move up to the highest and rockiest areas in the hills, and bachelor males climb up into kopjes. They rarely go out to the intermediate- and short-grass plains and are very sensitive to human interference, avoiding any areas with cultivation or continual poaching activity. The boundary of their distribution in the Serengeti is shown in figure 9. Densities are highest in the north between the Grumeti and Mara rivers and in the Masai Mara Reserve and lowest in the far south of the woodlands.

Impala are most common in the central woodlands. They prefer habitats where the vegetation is broken up into small mosaics (Lamprey 1963a) and can often be found on the edge of forest and thicket in the north. Although often found grazing, they also eat herbs and other browse (Azavedo and Agnew 1968). Topi (*Damaliscus korrigum*) form large herds of six or seven hundred animals on the long-grass plains in the western extension, but over the rest of the woodlands they are found in groups of about twenty animals. They tend to avoid hills, rocky areas, and dense vegetation. In the west, at the height of the dry season they can be found grazing the long riverine grasses that are also utilized by buffalo in that area (P. Duncan, personal communication; Bell 1970). Kongoni, or Coke's hartebeest (*Alcelaphus buselaphus*), somewhat similar in size and appearance to topi, are considerably less numerous. Although they overlap with topi in distribution over the southern, central, and northern woodlands, they are densest in the drier eastern part of the central woodland where topi are scarce. They are also found in the central and southern ranges of hills. Like topi, they are entirely grazers of the long-grass lands and hence a small number of both species are found on the long-grass areas of the Serengeti plains; there appears to be considerable overlap in the ecology of these two species.

Waterbuck (*Kobus defassa*) are relatively scarce in the region, being confined to the vicinity of the main rivers. But they graze the same riverine grasslands as the buffalo, and Field (1968b) has found little difference in the food species these two grazers prefer in the Ruwenzori Park, Uganda. Elephant also graze these grasslands in the dry season as well as browsing in the hill thickets and riverine forest. Small numbers of reedbuck (*Redunca redunca*) frequent swamps and reedbeds, but they emerge to graze riverine grassland also. The hippopotamus (*Hippopotamus amphibius*), on the other hand, tends to avoid the long riverine grasses and grazes the *Themeda* grasslands. This keeps the grass short, and as a result hippopotamus often change the composition of the grassland close to rivers. The small population of roan antelope (*Hippotragus equinus*) occurs mostly in the north on the *Hyparrhenia* grasslands. Oryx (*Oryx beisa*) are found only on the dry Salai Plains in the far east.

There are a number of browsers, but giraffe have the greatest effect on trees and bushes. In the fairly dense stands of *Acacia mellifera* trees along the western extension giraffe congregate in herds of more than a hundred. In these areas the browsing is sufficient to trim bushes and trees to conical shapes. Hill thickets in the northern Serengeti and Kenya Mara support the main population of black rhinoceros, although they are thinly scattered over the *Acacia* woodland. In the pig group, warthog (*Phacochoerus aethiopicus*) are ubiquitous daylight feeders over the woodlands and long-grass plains, where they both graze and root for tubers. Bushpig (*Potamochoerus porcus*) are said to occur, although little is known of them, and giant forest hog (*Hylochoerus meinertzhageni*) have been recorded once in thicket near the Mara River. Grant's gazelle (*Gazella granti*) spread over both woodlands and plains, and like oryx are among the few species able to exist on the plains in the dry season. Their food is mainly herbs.

Bushbuck, a medium-sized antelope, is found singly along all the main rivers wherever there are patches of thicket or forest. Greater kudu (*Tragelaphus strepsiceros*) are present in the dry rocky area to the south of the Serengeti. White's (1915) report that tracks of this species were found in the northern hillside thicket near the Mara River has never been confirmed, and probably the habitat has now altered unfavorably. One very small browser, the dikdik (*Madoqua kirki*) occurs commonly over all the woodlands wherever there are small thickets. The slightly larger steinbuck (*Raphicerus campestris*) is found in the drier *Acacia* woodlands and around the edge of the plains, while oribi (*Ourebia ourebi*) and gray duiker (*Sylvicapra grimmia*) occur more often in the wetter areas of the long *Hyparrhenia* grasslands. Klipspringer occur only in rocky areas of hilltops and on kopjes. Other denizens of the rocks are baboons, vervet monkeys, porcupines (*Hystrix cristata*), and the two species of hyrax.

Among the small mammal herbivores there are two species of hare (*Lepus*), one on the plains and one in the woodlands, which according to Hendrichs (1970) occur at a density of 20/km^2. Around the kopjes there are relatively large numbers of rodents, the most abundant being the daylight grass rat (*Arvicanthis*) and the spiny mouse (*Acomys*). After the very wet season of November 1967–July 1968

Arvicanthis showed a sudden population explosion and spread in large numbers throughout the *Acacia* woodlands and far out onto the long-grass plains. Numbers did not decline until the following November. Coincident with this eruption was an immigration of birds that preyed on the rodent, in particular the long-crested hawk eagle (*Lophoaetus occipitalis*), which numbered about fifty birds along the Seronera River where normally there were no more than two. The black-shouldered kite (*Elanus caeruleus*) and the black-headed heron (*Ardea melanocephala*) also appeared in numbers that have not been recorded before or since. How these species knew of the eruption remains a mystery. In normal *Themeda* grassland there are far fewer rodents; the biomass estimated from mark-recapture experiments during this study (Sinclair 1975) is about a quarter of what Hendrichs (1970) found in the kopjes. The short-grass plains support almost no rodents except the springhare (*Pedetes caffer*).

The invertebrate grazers of green grass are dominated by the Orthoptera, but their numbers vary considerably according to the stage of grass growth after a fire and according to the season. On greenflush after a fire there are only 0.02 kg/hectare dry weight of Orthoptera, but in long grass at the end of the rains this increases some sixtyfold to 1.20 kg/hectare. Consequently, during the rains Orthoptera eat as much grass as do the resident ungulates of the long grasslands, but in the dry season they eat only a negligible amount. Termites are the main herbivores removing litter and detritus, and it has been estimated (Sinclair 1975) that this could amount to over 15 kg/hectare dry weight.

The only carnivore of importance to adult buffalo is the lion (*Panthera leo*). Other large carnivores such as leopard (*P. pardus*), cheetah (*Acinonyx jubatus*), hyena (*Crocuta crocuta*), and wild dog (*Lycaon pictus*) are important predators on the migrating populations of ungulates. Kruuk (1972) and Schaller (1972) have discussed the ecology of these species in the Serengeti in some detail. There are also several smaller carnivores such as the jackals (*Canis mesomelas, C. aureus*), bat-eared fox (*Otocyon megalotis*), small cats (*Felis serval, F. libyca*) and mongooses which live on small mammals, birds, and invertebrates as well as carrion.

ARUSHA NATIONAL PARK

This area of northern Tanzania, covering approximately 100 km², includes the eastern slopes and the crater of Mount Meru in the western part, the Momella lakes in the center, and the Ngurdoto

Crater (plate 11) in the east. The vegetation is described in Vesey-Fitzgerald (1974). On the whole the area is montane, with the floor of Meru Crater lying at 2,600 m, the rim of Ngurdoto Crater being 1,800 m and its floor approximately 1,600 m. The lower slopes of Mount Meru and the Momella lakes reach 1,520 m. Annual rainfall in Meru Crater is very high, and measurements obtained by D. Vesey-Fitzgerald (personal communication) show that it can reach 2,300 mm; but this rainfall declines with altitude to 1,500 mm at 1,800 m and 1,100 mm at 1,500 m. Figure 14 shows the mean monthly rainfall distribution at 2,100 m on Mount Meru for 1967–9. As in the Serengeti, there are two main peaks in rainfall, but there is also an appreciable amount of precipitation in all months. Temperature also varies considerably over the year, and the variation increases with altitude. Temperatures may fall considerably at night, and in Meru Crater frosts may occur. There is a warm, wet period in November and a cold, wet season in April and May, followed by a relatively dry season which is initially cold but gradually warms up from June to October. There is never less than 60 mm rain per month at 2,100 m, a precipitation much greater than that in the Serengeti.

The vegetation on Mount Meru and Ngurdoto Crater is essentially montane forest. The tree line on Mount Meru occurs at about 2,400 m, and above this lies the heath zone. Eland are one of the few ungulates found at this altitude. The highest trees include *Podocarpus, Ilex,* and *Afrocrania,* and a little lower down juniper (*Juniperus procera*) grows on areas opened up by lava flows. However, a fire in the 1940s killed most of these trees, and the crater now contains only a strange, lifeless forest. Lower down there is a luxuriant montane forest with large canopy trees, lianas, and an often dense understory of small shade trees and bushes. An old landslide removed a segment of this forest and left an area of grassland stretching from the crater to below the lowest parts of the forest. Succession back to forest has been inhibited by grazing pressure. Within the forest there are open areas on the ridgetops, edaphic glades in the depressions, and semi-shaded clearings caused by tree falls. Vesey-Fitzgerald (1974) describes the latter on steep slopes above 2,000 m. When old *Juniperus* trees, some of which are over 60 m, fall, they bring down other trees round about and thus open up the canopy. This causes a draft pocket, and there is a tendency for other big trees in the vicinity to be blown down. With more light available, a greensward is established, which is maintained by grazing.

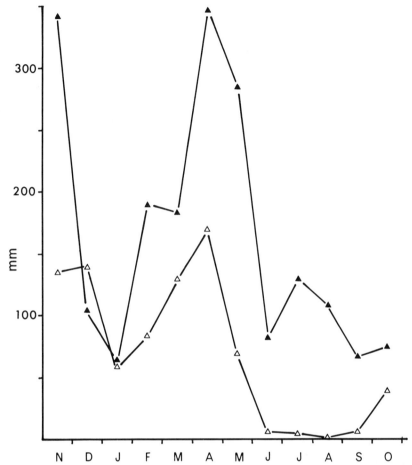

Fig. 14. Mean monthly rainfall for Lake Manyara Park (*open triangles*) and Mount Meru Park at 2,100 m altitude (Jekukumia station, *solid triangles*).

The forest at Ngurdoto contains relatively few glades on the outer rim, but there are many on the crater floor and there is open grassland around the swamp. In 1936 a fire spread onto the saddle between Meru and Ngurdoto, destroying part of the lower forest on Ngurdoto. This area is now covered by sagebrush, which in most parts is thin enough to allow grass to grow. The original edaphic glades are still present but are mostly covered with the semifloating grass *Leersia hexandra* and semiaquatic plants such as *Nymphaea*. The Momella lakes fill the depressions left in the old remains of the mountain when it erupted and fell away to the east.

On the lower slopes of Mount Meru, as in Ngurdoto Crater and around Momella, the main grasses are the creeping *Cynodon dactylon* and *Pennisetum clandestinum*, which form a thick mat of runners and stolons. On Mount Meru *P. clandestinum* takes over completely on the misty shoulders and in glades above 2,100 m. On the gloomy forest floor and along trails at this height the small grasses *Poa leptoclada* and *Eragrostis usambarensis* form a mixed sward with *Carex* sedges and creeping herbs such as *Alchemilla*. In some edaphic glades above 1,800 m there is a tall, coarse tussock grass, *Eleusine jaegeri*, which buffalo leave untouched. Over the rest of the area below this height a similar tussock grass, *Sporobolus greenwayi*, is abundant, but being very coarse it is also ungrazed. At the foot of Mount Meru there are a number of small marshes composed of *Cyperus laevigatus* and fringed with *Cynodon dactylon*. In Ngurdoto Crater the swamp which occupies about one-third of the area is covered with reeds (*Typha*), but around the shallower edges there is a zone of the broad-leaved swamp grass *Brachiaria brizantha*.

Buffalo are the only grazers abundant in the area. They can be found up to the tree line, especially old bulls. They graze the steep ridges and climb along the narrow ravines. They prefer the *Cynodon* and *Pennisetum* swards and rarely use the *Poa* grasses. Although there is rain all year round, the temperature becomes cold enough to prevent growth from July to September. At this season the animals move down to the marshes, where they graze *Cynodon dactylon* and *Cyperus laevigatus*, and at Ngurdoto they wade into the *Brachiaria* zone. Of the other ungulates a few waterbuck live near the Momella lakes but not on the mountain. Elephant are the dominant browsers on the woody vegetation, followed by giraffe, rhinoceros, and eland. In the forest, bushbuck and the small red forest duiker (*Cephalophus natalensis*) and suni antelope (*Nesotragus moschatus*) feed on the low carpet of herbs that proliferates in the cool damp shade. Warthog and bushpig frequent the forest glades, especially at Ngurdoto Crater. Buffalo have few predators, since there are no lions and few hyenas. Leopards, although not uncommon, attack only calves.

Lake Manyara National Park

This area lies to the southeast of the crater highlands at the foot of the rift-valley escarpment, which forms its western boundary (see fig. 4) by rising steeply to heights between 1,200 and 1,800 m. The park is a long, narrow strip formed from detritus and transported

soil and covers some 90 km² between the escarpment and Lake Manyara, which forms the eastern boundary. The area changes as the lake
level rises and falls. The altitude of the park is lower than that of the
Serengeti and Arusha parks (only 945 m), and consequently the temperature is somewhat higher. The rainfall is normally not high, the
average being 767 mm per year over the period 1958–68, and it falls
in the same two seasons (fig. 14) as in the Serengeti. However, a
number of permanently flowing springs above the escarpment flow
into the alluvial soils of the park, which retain considerable amounts
of groundwater. In the northern part this groundwater has allowed
the development of forest and swamp which would not otherwise be
possible in the existing climate. Greenway and Vesey-Fitzgerald
(1969) describe this groundwater forest as an edaphic climax type of
vegetation composed of several species of tall (30 m) evergreen, quick-
growing, and possibly rather short-lived trees. The characteristic tree
is *Trichelia roka*, which occurs throughout the forest and along river
fringes. Several *Ficus* species and *Tabernaemontana usambarensis* are
abundant, and lianas are frequent. The ground herbage is condi-
tioned by the amount of light reaching the forest floor and also by
elephant activity. Swamps formed from impeded drainage are en-
closed within the groundwater forest. Buffalo use the forest for shade
rather than food, but elephant, rhino, and baboons may be found
there frequently.

Most of the area south of the forest does not have so much groundwater, and in the semiarid environment the vegetation is unstable
(Greenway and Vesey-Fitzgerald 1969). The dominant tree is *Acacia
tortilis*, which reaches a height of 10 m. The trees are irregularly
grouped in clusters interspersed with open spaces, giving a parklike
appearance. They form even-age stands because of the relative rarity
of successful germination, and many of these stands are now old and
dying out, hastened by the debarking activities of elephants. Consequently, grassland dominated by *Cynodon plectostachyus* is replac-
ing the woodland. Until recently this grassland has been maintained
by fire, but since fires have now been stopped, changes may be expected.

The *C. plectostachyus* grassland is associated with the *Acacia* woodland. An ecotone between the woodlands and the alkaline soils of
the lake is characterized by *Sporobolus marginatus*. Below this on the
exposed lakeshore flats the small *Sporobolus spicatus* (50 cm height)
is dominant. It was extensive in the 1950s when the lake level was

low, but with the present high level the plant is restricted to a zone above high water. On slightly raised areas on the flats *S. consimilis* (*-robustus*) grows up to 2 m high in dense stands. In the more boggy and permanently waterlogged alkaline areas the sedge *Cyperus laevigatus* grows in pure stands 100 cm high. This forms a fringe along the lakeshore farther out than *Sporobolus spicatus*.

Douglas-Hamilton (1972) has studied the elephants and their effects on the woodland in this area. Buffalo were first counted by Watson and Turner (1965). Both of these species are at exceptionally high density in this area, possibly because of the good forage in the forest and on the alkaline grasslands. These grasslands are used extensively by buffalo. Of the other herbivores Schaller (1972) records impala as relatively abundant, about 700 animals, but giraffe, zebra, waterbuck, warthog, and bushbuck are all scarce—less than 100 animals each. Consequently buffalo, which number around 1,800, make up more than 90% of the potential biomass available to lions as prey. Perhaps not surprisingly, lions are also at a relatively high density and feed mainly on the buffalo, unlike the situation in the Serengeti where buffalo are not the most common prey. Since hyenas are uncommon, carcasses from lion kills remain intact, which helped when I investigated the effect of predation on buffalo at Manyara.

PLATES

Plate 1. African buffalo bachelor males

Plate 2. Wildebeest female and yearling

Plate 3. Wildebeest massing in a grazing front on the Serengeti Plains. March 1973.

Plate 4. Water buffalo male showing *flehmen* behavior

Plate 5. Moru Kopjes in the southern study area, where plains and woodlands merge at the hills. July 1972.

Plate 6. The Mara River flows throughout the year. Some patches of riverine forest and thicket grow along its banks. February 1971.

Plate 7. Scattered *Acacia clavigera* in the northern Serengeti. The unburned grass has been heavily grazed. In the distance the smoke from two fires has produced two cumulus clouds which later developed into thunderstorms producing localized rain. October 1972.

Plate 8. *Terminalia* woodland is found on the ridges in the northwest of the Serengeti Park. The grasses are *Hyparrhenia*, unburned but heavily grazed. September 1969.

Plate 9. The undulating terrain of the northern Serengeti. Exposed rocks can be seen on the ridges. The grass has been burned above and below the springline, which can be seen as a narrow strip contouring the hillside, with two seepage lines draining off it. August 1968.

Plate 10. Grass fires in the woodlands remove, on average, 62% of the standing grass crop in the dry season. September 1972.

Plate 11. Ngurdoto Crater. Buffalo graze the grasslands on the near side. The swamp occupies the center and far side of the crater.

Plate 12. Buffalo in tall riverine grass, the preferred dry season habitat

Plate 13. Buffalo in an opening in the forest, grazing riverine grass

Plate 14. Umbrella-shaped *Acacia tortilis* trees with Moru Kopjes in the distance

Plate 15. Young males wallow while the rest of the herd ruminates on dry ground

Plate 16. Male showing *flehmen* behavior. In the foreground a little egret searches for grasshoppers disturbed by the animals.

Plate 23. Subadult female with radio-transmitter

Plate 24. Tooth section from a seventeen-year-old male showing paired cementum lines.

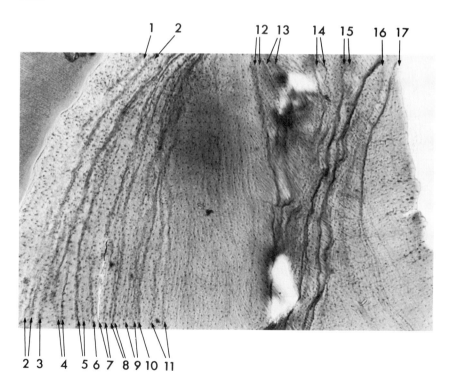

Plate 21. Hyenas chasing a two-year-old buffalo. They failed to pull it down.

Plate 22. Collared female used for plotting home range

Plate 19. Lion eating a bachelor male buffalo he has killed

Plate 20. Hyena scavenging on a buffalo carcass

Plate 17. Subadult males sparring

Plate 18. Herd animals resting in groups

Plate 25. Adult female with her newborn calf and her previous calf of eighteen months. One of her horns is deformed.

Plate 26. Closeup aerial photograph showing various ages and sexes

Male   2yr Male   2yr Female   Female   6mth Calf

Plate 27. A typical aerial photograph used for measuring fertility and recruitment

Plate 28. *From left to right*: young adult male, middle-aged male, and two-year-old juvenile male.

Plate 29. Very old solitary male. Note that both horns are broken.

Plate 30. Flooded *Cyperus laevigatus* swamp with dead *Acacia xanthophloea* trees killed when Lake Manyara water levels rose in the mid-1960s.

Plate 31. Temporary exclosure cages for measuring grass growth during the dry season. Northern Serengeti study area, September 1969.

Plate 32. Mount Meru. Foreground cage shows high standing crop of grass. Outside the cage the same *Pennisetum* grass is kept short by grazing. The other exclosures are for measuring growth rates. In the background tall *Eleusine jaegeri* is avoided by buffalo.

Plate 33. Females in poor condition at Lake Manyara. Late dry season, 1968.

Plate 34. Bachelor male in poor condition. Dry season. Note the dry but still heavily grazed grass.

Plate 35. This male was still alive when it was found in this position. He was in very poor condition. The grass, previously burned, had regrown as greenflush but was heavily grazed by wildebeest. Northern Serengeti, September 1969.

Plate 36. Wildebeest calves lost after trying to follow their mothers across Lake Lagarja. More than 3,000 died on this occasion. February 1973.

Plate 37. A park ranger inspects a pile of buffalo skulls that poachers have covered with foliage to hide them from vultures. The buffalo had been caught by snare lines set between the trees in the thicket behind. July 1972.

Plate 38. Mixed group of buffalo, zebra, and wildebeest grazing near water. Edge of Serengeti Plains, April 1973.

Plate 39. Buffalo and wildebeest grazing the same long *Themeda* grassland. Northern Seregenti, August 1972.

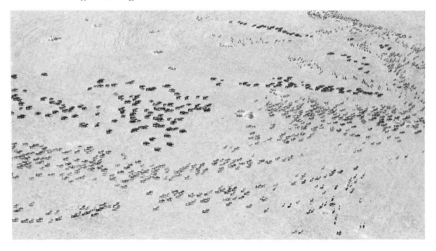

Plate 40. Wildebeest grazing riverine grass while waiting to cross the river

Plate 41. Die-off of Australian water buffalo in the dry season of 1972 after their food supplies were depleted. They died at the water's edge after becoming too weak to pull themselves out of the mud.

4 Resource Requirements

Of course any population study must first identify the types of resources the animals need: only after this can one attempt to quantify resources and needs. Since the morphology of the African buffalo varies, one might expect a related variability in ecological requirements. Consequently, any one population may have some degree of special adaptations and requirements. Thus each population under study should be described separately.

One might suggest that there are four basic needs of the animals—food, water, protection from climatic extremes, and protection from predators. In the Serengeti the first three needs are accentuated during the dry season, July to October, when resources are least abundant and the climate is most extreme. Apart from these four there may be a number of other special requirements such as protection from predation when calves are being born in the wet-season months of March to May. The vegetation types which provide for these needs may be described as habitats; they are one type of resource. Within the preferred habitats the buffalo eat some of the plant species but leave others. So in this chapter I shall describe the main vegetation types and plant species available to the animals and analyze which they prefer. I shall also discuss some of the reasons for these preferences.

HABITAT SELECTION

I encountered three particular problems in this investigation. First, as a result of the extreme clumping of the buffalo into compact herds, I had to cover large areas to obtain a reasonable amount of data. For this reason I undertook a complete aerial survey of two study areas; the more usual methods of placing transects across the vegetation strata would have resulted in too high a variance for significant results. The second problem arose in recording the number of animals within each vegetation type. Because juveniles follow their mothers,

53

they do not make an independent choice of habitat. Hence this "social facilitation" will confound the analysis of behavioral responses to different vegetation types, and individual animals cannot be taken as independent data points. So I considered only each herd or group of animals as one record on each sighting. Third, the "edge effect" phenomenon described by Lamprey (1963a), in which animals may be using one vegetation type for, say, feeding only if another type for, say, protection is close by, had to be taken into account. At the same time it was not always possible to delimit the boundaries of different types very accurately. Consequently vegetation maps of the two study areas were superimposed with a grid, and the number of cells of the grid containing each vegetation type was taken to be the approximate area of those types. The size of the cells, 0.25 km², was chosen so that not too many vegetation types occurred within each cell.

> Each study area was searched by aircraft at least once a month, and the positions of all buffalo herds, bachelor male groups, and wildebeest and elephant groups were plotted on vegetation maps (1: 50,000) with an accuracy to the nearest 300 m. For each survey, the positions of all groups were then analyzed to determine which vegetation types were in the same grid cells and which were not. The method therefore took into account the proximity of other vegetation types, and this was important when "edge effects" were operating.
>
> The statistical analysis involved an adaptation of Cole's (1949) coefficient of association. The cells on the vegetation map for each survey were scored for presence or absence of buffalo and of each vegetation type. These scores were then used in the formulas by the method described in Appendix B. Association, as defined by Cole, is the amount of co-occurrence in excess of that to be expected if two categories are independently distributed. The coefficient of association (C) ranges from $+1$ to -1, with zero representing random association. For this particular case the association was one-way, in that buffalo were associated with vegetation type and not the reverse. The advantage of this coefficient was that it gave a linear measure of magnitude of association and that a measure of significance could be obtained. In other words, it was possible to measure to what degree buffalo were selecting for or avoiding a vegetation type and also to compare the degree of selection between different types. Another advantage was that it allowed the use of small numbers of positive observations when there were large numbers of negative observations, which was usually the case.

The grid cell scores for each survey were summed for each month and for three-month periods representing the dry season, August–October, short rains, November–January, early long rains, February–April, and late long rains, May–July, and the coefficients were calculated. The mean monthly and quarterly coefficients over the period of study were also computed. The records of breeding herds and bachelor male groups were treated separately in the calculations, to detect whether social differences affected choice of habitat. With a view to measuring the overlap between buffalo and potentially competing species, the habitat choices of wildebeest groups in the northern area and elephant herds in both areas were also analyzed.

The two study areas were chosen because of their differences in density and distribution of animals; their location is shown in figure 4 (chap. 3). The southern Area A (660 km²) included the edge of the population's distribution on the Serengeti Plains and contained a relatively low density of 3.7 animals/km². The northern Area B (280 km²) was situated in the high-density (10.0 animals/km²) region on the south bank of the Mara River, where the mean rainfall was relatively high at 1,000 mm/yr, compared with 750 mm/yr in the south. One further difference between the areas was that large numbers of wildebeest were present throughout the dry season in the north, when they were absent in the south.

The Vegetation

For this study I distinguished twelve vegetation types which could be classified into three groups—riverine, nonriverine woodlands, and nonriverine grasslands. These types are described in detail in Appendix C, and some are illustrated by plates. Herlocker (1975) gives further botanical details. Riverine types included grassland, which predominated in the south but in the north occurred in small patches between stretches of forest (plates 6, 12, 13). In the north, forest and riverine grassland were lumped as "riverine vegetation." Also in this area there were narrow seepage lines that contoured the valley slopes (plate 9). In both areas there were gullies or watercourses with a thin strip of thicket along their banks providing cover for lone males. These gullies flowed only during the wet season.

Nonriverine woodlands in the south included several *Acacia* types. Typical "*Acacia* woodland" (plate 14) was characterized by *Acacia tortilis*, and I distinguished this from stands of the gall trees *A. seyal* and *A. drepanolobium*. "Hills" in this area were treated as a separate nonriverine woodland. In the northern area I distinguished only one type, characterized by a mixture of *Terminalia mollis* (plate 7) and *A. clavigera*, above the seepage line.

Nonriverine grasslands included the plains in the south and the "open grassland" below the seepage line in the north (plate 9). After dry-season grass fires a short greenflush occurred in both nonriverine grassland and woodland. This growth stage was distinguished from other vegetation types.

The degree to which these different vegetation types meet the needs of the buffalo is summarized in table 2. Initially I suggest that the animals' main needs are green grass and water, both of which are harder to find in the dry season. They also need protection from heat stress, which is most severe at this season, and protection from predators. Riverine grassland, particularly in the south, provides both food and water but offers neither protection from predators nor shade. The seepage line is a suitable feeding area for small male groups, but not for herds, which need larger areas. The forest appears to satisfy all needs, although the amount of food available is small. In the nonriverine woodlands shade is available in the dry season, but there is little protection from predators, particularly in long grass, and the food is poor. The open grasslands appear to fulfill none of the basic requirements. Greenflush, which may be found in all nonriverine types, is usually too short to provide food for herds.

Because of these differences between vegetation types, I shall examine which requirement is most important in the dry season by considering which vegetation type is selected most often. Hence I operationally defined the "optimum habitat" in the Serengeti study areas as that vegetation which is selected most often during the dry season. And "selection" is determined by the measurement of a significantly greater proportion of observations of animals in a vegetation type than would occur by a random distribution through all types available, using the association coefficient.

The Habitat Preferences of Buffalo Herds

Riverine vegetation types. The mean monthly association coefficients (fig. 15a) indicate that herds show a significant preference for the southern riverine grassland throughout the annual cycle, which was taken to begin with the first rains in November. This preference increased during the dry season. A similar result was found with the

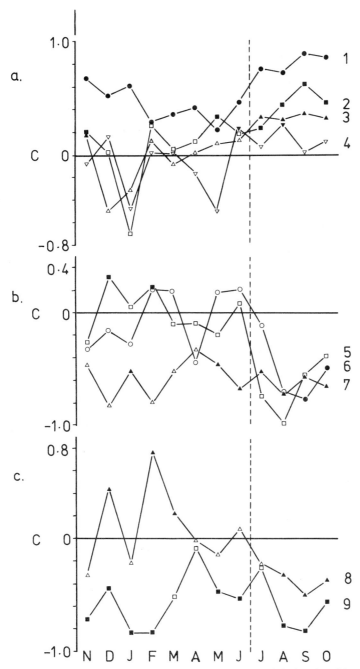

Fig. 15. Mean monthly coefficients of association for buffalo herds with various vegetation types: *1*, riverine grassland; *2*, riverine vegetation; *3*, forest; *4*, seepage lines; *5*, hills; *6*, *Acacia* woodland; *7*, *Terminalia* woodland; *8*, open grassland; *9*, plains.

riverine vegetation in the northern area except that there was a random distribution in the wet season, changing to a positive preference in the dry season. Although most of this was due to a preference for forest, there was also a small but significant association for the few patches of riverine grassland in this area. The herds showed no particular preference for the seepage line except perhaps during the early dry season. There was no preference for the wet-season watercourses at any time of year.

Nonriverine woodland. Herds showed a random association with both the *A. seyal* and *A. drepanolobium* types throughout the year (fig. 15*b*), and this was also the case for the *Acacia* woodland in general, except that at the height of the dry season they avoided it. They also avoided the hills at this season but developed a significant positive preference during the first rains. However, in the northern area the *Terminalia* woodland was significantly avoided throughout the year.

Nonriverine grasslands. The herds in the southern area avoided the plains for most of the year except during the long rains, when there was a random association and apparently no preference (fig. 15*c*). However, the mean monthly values from the whole period of study obscured the differences between the years 1967 and 1968. The association coefficients for individual months are shown for this vegetation type in figure 16*a*. During the dry season of 1967 the plains remained unburned and there was a large standing crop of dead dry grass, but in 1968 this area was completely burned early in the dry season and remained bare and parched for the rest of the season. Whereas the buffalo herds showed a random association with this area (positive but not significant at $p < 0.05$) in 1967, they distinctly avoided it throughout the 1968 dry period ($p < 0.001$). During the wet season the animals avoided the plains except during March and April of each year—the wettest months.

The open grasslands of the north were also avoided in the dry season, but were significantly preferred in the wet season (fig. 15*c*). This cycle can be seen repeating itself in the data for individual months, (fig. 16*b*), where positive association is found in the wet season and negative values occur in the dry months.

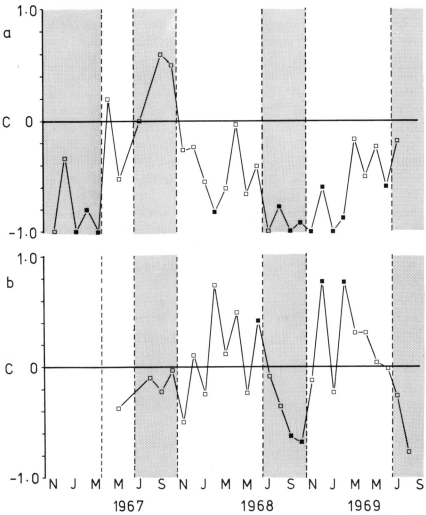

Fig. 16. Individual monthly coefficients of association for buffalo herds with *a*, plains, *b*, open grassland.

The optimum habitat. The highest positive association during the dry season was with riverine grassland in the southern area (C = 0.889, $p < 0.001$), and riverine vegetation in the northern area (C = 0.617, $p < 0.001$). The former habitat, as mentioned above, contains some green food and water but provides no protection against predators; in fact, the long, rank grass and reeds at the water's edge provide good hiding places for lions, and many kills were found in this area. These features of the grassland suggest that the needs for food and water were more important at this season than the need for protection from predators. Furthermore, there was no shade for the animals, and it was common to see them all lying out in the sun ruminating in the heat of the day. During the very dry months of September and October 1968, the animals remained in areas without shade for days and sometimes weeks at a time. Again this suggests that factors other than heat stress were determining their habitat; of course, heat stress might still have affected them.

In the northern area the preferred riverine vegetation was a combination of forest and riverine grassland. Although both of these were significantly preferred ($p < 0.001$), the former had an association coefficient of 0.323 while the latter averaged only 0.178 for the dry-season months. Perhaps this was not surprising, since forest provided most of the animals' more obvious needs, except that food remained fairly sparse. Riverine grassland provided more food.

From this analysis the "optimum habitats" for buffalo herds seem to be riverine grassland and riverine vegetation in the two areas under study. Also, it appeared that food and water rather than protection from predators and environmental extremes were the important factors determining the choice of habitat. During the wet-season months, although food was in abundance everywhere, buffalo continued to prefer riverine grassland above all habitats in the southern area. In the north, wet-season watercourses were preferred most in the first rains, from November to January, and open grassland was then preferred during the long rains from February to April. This reflected a gradual movement away from the main rivers as the area became wetter, and it could have two causes: the greater rainfall in north flooded the riverine grassland, forcing the animals out; second, open grasslands that had previously been burned regrew as a lush greensward which, at an intermediate stage of growth, was suitable for buffalo. At the start of the rains this grass was too short for the buffalo to eat, and so there was a delay before they moved onto these pastures. I will come back to this later.

The Habitat Preferences of Bachelor Males

Riverine types. Male groups were much smaller than herds, usually consisting of 3 or 4 animals and rarely including more than 50. Herds may comprise more than 1,000 animals. Only in the northern area were records of male groups sufficient for analysis.

Male groups, like the herds, showed a definite preference for riverine vegetation for most of the year (fig. 17a). The only period when
such a preference was not significant was during the long rains in

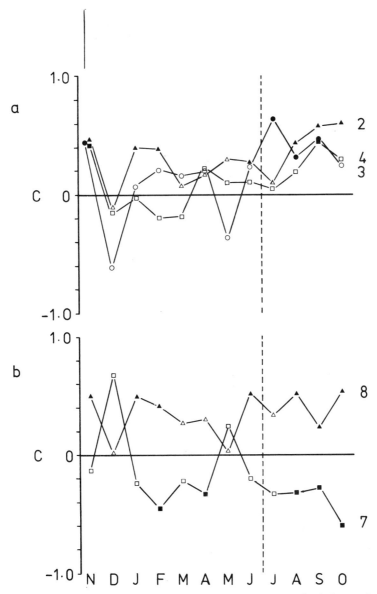

Fig. 17. Mean monthly coefficients of association for buffalo bachelor males with
various vegetation types: 2, riverine vegetation; 3, forest; 5, seepage lines; 7,
Terminalia woodland; 8, open grassland.

March to May. During the dry season these males showed their highest association with this type (C $= 0.560$, $p < 0.001$ as a mean value for the whole season) and, as with the herds, it was their "optimum habitat." The forest was also the most important part of this vegetation, with a significant preference in the dry season but random association in the wet months (fig. 17a). With riverine grassland there was a small but significant association (C $= 0.064$, $p < 0.001$) in the dry season but not in the wet season. The forest was therefore more important to these small groups of animals than to the large herds, perhaps because the small groups could feed on the scattered shade grasses in the forest more efficiently than the herds. At the same time the male groups had a greater need for protection from predators.

But the males also utilized other habitats not favored by the herds. One of these was the seepage line (fig. 17a), which was preferred during the dry season (C $= 0.353$, $p < 0.001$). These thin strips provided green food and also wallows for the small groups. A large herd would not find enough forage on these strips to spend much time grazing them.

Nonriverine woodland. The *Terminalia* woodland was avoided for the whole dry season and for some of the wet months as well (fig. 17b). For the rest of the year the bulls showed no particular preference, and in general they behaved much like the herds.

Nonriverine grassland. At all seasons males could be found grazing on the open grassland, but usually close to the forest (fig. 17b). They also used wallows in this grassland. Preference for areas with wallows was also noted by Field and Laws (1970) in Uganda. Since males but not females exhibited wallowing behavior, this may have contributed to the bachelor groups' higher utilization of open grassland. This grassland during the dry season was a combination of short greenflush after fires had burned through the area and unburned long dry grass with occasional blades of green grass. The males showed a preference for the long-grass areas but a random association with greenflush. The herds showed no preference for either area. Being in small groups, these males could search far and select the scattered green material, whereas the large, compact herds would be unable to find sufficient food.

The Habitat Preferences of Wildebeest and Elephant

Although wildebeest were present during the dry season only in the north, they were there in very large numbers, four or five times the density of the resident buffalo population. The "optimum habitat" of wildebeest at this season in the study area was the open grassland (fig. 18b), with the mean seasonal association reaching 0.158 ($p <$ 0.001). When this is compared with the figures for buffalo herds it can be seen that the two species do not overlap in their use of this habitat. Although buffalo males used open grassland, they represented less than 6% of the buffalo population and hence were of negligible importance. With riverine vegetation, wildebeest exhibited no particular preference (fig. 18a). However, when riverine grassland and forest were examined separately it was found that there was a small but significant preference (C $= 0.058, p < 0.001$) for the former and an increasing tendency to avoid forest (fig. 18c). Thus there was a certain amount of overlap in one part of the preferred habitat of buffalo, but none in the other part.

This overlap in the use of riverine grassland is caused by wildebeest moving to the rivers to drink or to cross in search of food. Usually they approach the rivers at places not surrounded by trees or thick vegetation which might conceal predators. These crossing-places are characterized by small patches of riverine grassland flanking the riverbanks. As the leading wildebeest hesitantly approach the crossing point, the herd builds up into a dense mass, and those at the back start to graze. Eventually one or two cross and the rest follow (plate 40), racing after each other in long lines, trampling the grass as they go, and often alarming drinking animals, who stampede away from the water, then approach again. In the course of all this some grass is eaten and much is trampled; and once the grass is broken down buffalo do not eat it. So the impact of wildebeest on the buffalo habitats can be substantial. I will discuss the measurements of their effect in chapter 10.

H. Croze (1974a) believes that there are northern and southern elephant populations in the Serengeti which rarely mix. Although elephants were present in both study areas, they tended to move out of the northern area during the height of the rains, March to April, and this coincided with the large aggregations of animals that formed in the center of the park at this time. Conversely, elephants from

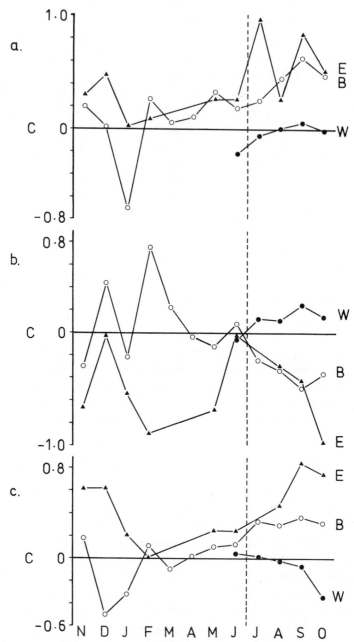

Fig. 18. The coefficients of association for buffalo herds (*B*), wildebeest (*W*), and elephant (*E*) with riverine vegetation (*a*), open grassland (*b*), and forest (*c*).

farther south outside the park moved into the southern area during April and May. Then they gradually dispersed back south as the dry season progressed, and their numbers reached their lowest point between December and February.

During the southern area dry season the elephants' highest association was with *Acacia* woodland (C = 0.626, $p < 0.01$), although they also preferred thickets along the wet-season watercourses. Riverine grassland was preferred toward the end of the long rains when the herb layer was at its tallest, but the association declined during the dry season. Several of the *Acacia* tree species produced a new flush of leaves during the dry season, and it was at this time that the elephants turned to breaking down and eating the foliage and woody material. At the same time the grass was very low in quality and often in quantity as well, after fires had burned the area. Not surprisingly, elephants avoided the plains at this time.

In the northern area the elephants' highest association was with riverine vegetation, mainly forest (fig. 18c). Consequently, although riverine grassland was preferred, forest appeared to be the "optimum habitat" in this area. The *Terminalia* woodlands were significantly avoided, as were the open grasslands. On this evidence alone overlap with buffalo during the dry season appears considerable, but the food consumed was very different, since elephant browsed while buffalo grazed. Jarman (1971) showed that in the Zambezi Valley the overlap in diet between elephant and buffalo decreased from 22.6% in the wet season to only 1.1% in the dry season. In the southern Serengeti, where *Acacia* woodland was the "optimum habitat" for elephant, there was little overlap with buffalo in either habitat or food choice.

To conclude this survey of habitat preference, buffalo require the riverine type of grasslands during the dry season, and if riverine forest occurs they make use of this also. In the northern parts of the Serengeti, but not in the south, wildebeest were potential competitors with the buffalo by grazing the riverine grassland part of the "optimum habitat" of buffalo, but they avoided the forest. Incidental observations indicated that a similar situation occurred with zebra. Although elephant preferred the forest at this time, they were eating different foods. Forest, therefore, appears to be the "ecological refuge" for buffalo if competition becomes severe in this area. The overlap zone is the riverine grassland patches which can be utilized by other grazing species. When competitors are completely absent and numbers of buffalo low, they may be able to extend into other habitats such as the open *Themeda* grasslands, as is demonstrated by the bachelor male groups.

A general feature of the habitat preferences of buffalo is the greater association with riverine vegetation when wildebeest move into the northern area. However, in the southern area there is a similar trend in magnitude of association although no other competitors were present, indicating that the move toward the riverine habitats is caused by factors other than competition.

The Effect of Environmental Factors on Habitat Preferences

So far I have pointed out that preferences for different vegetation types increase during the dry season and that this suggests that environmental factors are influencing the animals' behavior. Apart from rainfall, the degree of burning and the distribution of local rainstorms—reflected by the area of greenflush—could also have played a part in determining preferences. By correlating the association coefficients for each vegetation type with these three environmental factors, we can see some indication of their effects on the buffalo.

The effect of rainfall. The mean monthly rainfall calculated over the period 1967–69, when these observations were made, is given in table 3, and this was correlated with the monthly association coefficients. If there was a significant positive correlation between an association coefficient and the rainfall, it was possible that the rain was affecting the buffalo's choice of habitat. Table 4 gives the correlation between rainfall and habitat association for different vegetation types. Taking rainfall in the same month for which association coefficients were calculated, the only significant positive correlation was with association for hills. Since this occurred before grass could have grown high enough for food, it seems that the rain itself may have been important. However the association with hills remained high one month after rain had fallen, indicating that green food could also have been important. In the *Acacia* woodland there was no significant use by buffalo until one month after rain had fallen, and this use was higher still two months later. As with the hills, it suggests that the buffaloes' response was due to the growth of grass following the rain. But in the northern *Terminalia* woodland utilization remained low irrespective of the rainfall. With the nonriverine grasslands in both areas there was no significant correlation between rainfall and association, but there was a tendency for the correlation to increase two months after rain had fallen. With the plains data the mean monthly association calculations masked differences between years. Taking individual months, the correlation between rainfall and association with the plains two months later became more apparent ($p < 0.05$).

As expected, the movement into the riverine vegetation types was negatively correlated with rainfall. With both riverine grassland in the south and forest in the north, low rainfall in one month was correlated with a high association in the same month. This correlation was even more pronounced when the association one month later and even two months later is considered. Similarly low rainfall in one month could have caused greater association with the seepage lines in the following month. Again these relationships suggest that the progressive drying out of the other vegetation types made the buffalo retreat to the few remaining wet areas. This was unlikely to be the direct result of lack of water, for water was easily within reach of any of the avoided habitats during the dry season. More probably the observed preferences were a response to the change in the nature of the grass as it dried out and became unpalatable in the nonriverine vegetation types.

The effect of grass fires. When the association with plains was examined by individual months, the plains were avoided only when they had been burned. This was confirmed in the negative correlation between the association with plains and the area of burning ($r = 0.63$, $p < 0.05$). Similarly, the adjacent *Acacia* woodlands were avoided when they were burned ($r = -0.68$, N $= 12$, $p < 0.05$), as were the open grasslands in the north ($r = -0.71$, $p < 0.05$). And, as already mentioned, not until rain had fallen again and the grass had grown for one or two months did the buffalo move back to these areas.

The effect of greenflush. The distribution of local rainstorms as measured by the area of greenflush during the dry season had little effect on the degree of association with the different vegetation types except in the open grassland of the north. Here there was a negative correlation between the area of greenflush and buffalo association with the open grassland. This was the preferred habitat of wildebeest, and they concentrated on the greenflush rather than on the long, unburned part. Since this negative correlation with greenflush was not found for the south, where there were no wildebeest, it suggests that wildebeest were competitively displacing the buffalo. At the beginning of the wet period in November, rain fell first over the southern hills, thereby increasing the area of greenflush in this habitat. Consequently there was a positive correlation ($r = 0.58$, $N = 12$, $p < 0.05$) between the area of greenflush and the association with hills.

FOOD SELECTION

Since it appears that buffalo habitat preferences are affected by alterations in food, in this section I shall describe the types of plants on which buffalo feed and suggest some of the factors which might determine their food preferences. In recent years two approaches to this have developed. First, suggestions have been made that the various wild ruminant species in East Africa coexisted by eating different species of plants, thus making more efficient use of the grasslands than do domestic animals (Pereira 1961; Talbot 1966). This naturally led to study of the plant species being eaten (Talbot and Talbot 1962; Field 1968a, 1970), and it was implicit in this approach that interspecific competition was taking place.

However, at about the same time Vesey-Fitzgerald (1960) suggested that the various larger mammal herbivores were each altering the habitats so that another species could make use of them; far from competing, it appeared that each species was facilitating the existence of another. In the valley grasslands of the Lake Rukwa area of Tanzania, Vesey-Fitzgerald found that elephants ate or trampled the tall swamp grasses which grew up to 2 m high. They were followed by buffalo, who could then eat the regenerating shoots and who further trampled and grazed the area. Finally, topi moved in to graze the short grasses on the small patches which had been opened up. If the elephant and buffalo did not remain in these grasslands the small patches of short grass rapidly disappeared and the topi were not able to use the area. This situation led to investigations of which parts of the grass plant were being eaten (Gwynne and Bell 1968; Bell 1970, 1971).

In the Serengeti region there were indications that several grazing ruminants, in particular wildebeest, zebra, and Thomson's gazelle, were eating the same species of plant at different stages of growth (Bell 1969). Indeed McNaughton (1976) has demonstrated that when wildebeest grazed tall-grass communities it stimulated growth by forcing the grass to tiller and so produced a short, dense mat of green leaf suitable for Thomson's gazelle. Wildebeest were thus facilitating grass use by gazelle. Observations by Lamprey (1963a) suggested that buffalo were also eating grass species similar to those eaten by other ruminants, particularly since in the Serengeti wildebeest, waterbuck, and topi could all be found in riverine grasslands used by buffalo at the time of potential food shortage. Thus, although Field (1968a,b) suggested that buffalo were eating different grass species than other grazing ungulates, there also seemed to be a considerable overlap. Consequently, at the start of this study I decided to investigate whether buffalo were selecting both for particular species and for plant parts. Then I examined the selected food to find which attributes were most important to the animals.

Types of Food Eaten

A number of records have accumulated on the types of food eaten by buffalo in different areas of Africa. Even in the dense, wet lowland forests of the Congo the dwarf races eat mainly grasses along the riverbanks (Christy 1929), and in the more open regions of Nigeria Littlejohn (1938) mentioned that buffalo ate predominantly grass. In the former Albert Park, Congo, Bourliere and Verschuren (1960) found that the food was mainly grass, but that buffalo also ate herbs and shrubs; in the forest they consumed creeping grasses and some tree shoots. After fire they ate leaves of xerophytic bushes and stems of a riverine woody herb, *Pluchea ovalis*. In other high rainfall savanna areas such as Mount Meru, Tanzania, (2,000 mm rain/yr) grasses such as *Cynodon dactylon* and *Pennisetum clandestinum* as well as the sedge *Cyperus laevigatus* were important. In the Ruwenzori Park, Uganda (1,200 mm), Field (1968c) observed that grass was again predominant but that adults ate the prickly shrub *Capparis tomentosa*. Longhurst (in Bourliere and Verschuren 1960) found that leaves of this shrub were present in eight out of fifty-three stomachs. In the Serengeti area shrubs were relatively scarce, and few records of browsing were obtained—mainly incidental observations of browsing on *Grewia bicolor* and *Sesbania sesban* along rivers. Vesey-Fitzgerald (1969) observed that *Cyperus laevigatus* and the grass *Sporobolus spicatus*, both of which grow on the alkaline soils around Lake Manyara in Tanzania, were the most important species in the dry season, followed by *Cynodon dactylon*. In dry savanna such as Tarangire (680 mm), Lamprey (1963a) observed that 94% of plants seen eaten by buffalo were grasses, 1% were herbs, and 5% were shrubs. Leuthold (1972) in Tsavo, Kenya, recorded that the tall *Panicum maxi-*

mum was the dominant grass in the diet. In the *Combretum* wood-lands of the Zambezi Valley, where grass was very sparse, Jarman (1971) recorded that 55% of the food he saw eaten was trees and shrubs. In this area deciduous trees were browsed only when the leaves were green. Grasses became the principal constituent of the dry-season diet (74%), but evergreen trees and shrubs were also more prominent than in the wet season (22%). However, buffalo were at a very low density in this area. In the Kruger Park of South Africa, Pienaar (1969) observes that buffalo are grazers and lists as food a number of grass species common to eastern Africa as well. Small amounts of dicotyledonous plants are also eaten, the com-monest being *Grewia bicolor*, with *Heeria, Combretum*, and *Euclea* appearing among others. Still farther south in the Addo Elephant National Park of Cape Province, Graaff, Schulz, and Van der Walt (1973) have reported on the food eaten by buffalo that died during an extended dry period in dense semisucculent thorn scrub. Although all the animals ate grass, they were compelled to eat a number of succulent shrubs as well because grass—mainly shade species—was very scarce at this time.

These observations show that buffalo are largely grazers but are capable of eating a range of herbs and shrubs as well. Table 5 lists the commonest grass species eaten in seven areas of East Africa, with those growing in damp soils given first, those in dry areas last. *Cynodon dactylon*, a creeping riverine grass, is recorded most often, perhaps because it has a relatively high protein content (Plowes 1957). Of the many grass species available to buffalo throughout eastern Africa, very few appear to be important in their diet. Some, however, are the dominant species over much of the area (e.g., *Themeda triandra, Pennisetum, Hyparrhenia*), and their consump-tion by buffalo may merely reflect their abundance. There seems to be a general tendency for buffalo to eat plants associated with water in dry environments but to graze more widespread species in higher rainfall areas.

There are also a number of species which are avoided. Among these is lemon grass (*Cymbopogon excavatus*), avoided by most un-gulates, presumably because of its content of aromatic compounds. Coarse tussock grasses are also left untouched: *Aristida stenostachys* in Tsavo (Leuthold 1972), *Imperata cylindrica* in Uganda (Field 1968c), *Odyssea jaegeri* on the edge of Lake Manyara (Vesey-Fitzgerald 1969), and *Sporobolus greenwayi* and *Eleusine jaegeri* on Mount Meru are a few such species.

Grass Species Preferences

Investigations on whether animals specifically select for food items or merely take them in the proportions that are available have often met with the difficulty of measuring how much *is* available. Grass species can be measured merely by presence or absence, by numbers of plants, or by biomass. This last measure appears to be the most meaningful biologically, because it takes into account the size of the plant. However, to measure both the available biomass and that eaten by the animals is not usually feasible under natural conditions. Hence in this study I decided to set up experiments to test whether buffalo are capable of differentiating between a number of similar grass species that they are known to eat.

Two tame juvenile buffalo were used in the experiments. They were tested singly in a circular enclosure about 10 m in diameter by offering them bundles of a number of grass species laid out in a circle. The grass species commonly grew in mixed stands under natural conditions, and the animals were quite familiar with them. All were in the long green flowering stage. Approximately 1 kg of each species was cut per trial; this was divided into four bundles and each was then weighed. The grass of each bundle was cut into lengths suitable for eating and placed on the ground in such a way that it was not lying flat. The order of species in the circle was randomly determined for each trial before the animal was put in the pen. The buffalo was allowed to graze for approximately one hour. After each trial the bundles were reweighed, correcting for evaporation by calculation from control bundles. Samples of each species were oven dried to calculate the dry weights available to and eaten by the animal. During each trial the time the buffalo spent eating each species of grass was also measured. Since the experimental situation may have affected the animals' behavior in selecting species, a number of measurements were also made of the time they spent grazing two species of grass growing in small adjacent stands, when these were the only grasses available, to see whether similar results would be obtained.

Three sets of tests were carried out. Since *Cynodon plectostachyus* was commonly eaten in Manyara (Vesey-Fitzgerald 1969) and *The-*

meda triandra was often eaten in the Serengeti, these two were chosen for comparison in the first series of eight tests. In all tests more *Themeda* than *Cynodon* was eaten, and out of the total eaten 77% was *Themeda* (figure 19a). Because of the difficulty of replicating each test with similar quality grass, there was a certain variability in weights eaten. Because of this variability I used the Wilcoxon matched-pairs test (Siegel 1956): it appeared that *Themeda* was significantly preferred ($p < 0.01$) to *Cynodon plectostachyus*.

In the second series of tests one species, *Digitaria macroblephora*, which was known from incidental observations to be heavily grazed by buffalo, was compared with the preferred species in the previous test, *Themeda triandra*. These tests included *Sporobolus pyramidalis*, because it occurred frequently in the observations of Field (1968b), and *Pennisetum mezianum*, because it was abundant throughout the Serengeti long-grass lands. Twelve trials were conducted, with the four species presented simultaneously. The percentage of the totals eaten are shown in figure 19b. Clearly *Digitaria* was eaten most, accounting for 61.5% of the total weight consumed, *Themeda* and *Sporobolus* were almost equal, with 17.0% and 16.5% respectively, and *Pennisetum* accounted for only 5.5%. The Friedman two-way analysis of variance (Siegel 1956) was used to test the results. Assuming that no difference in weights eaten should be found if no preferences were shown, the results indicated that the animals were making a significant ($p < 0.001$) distinction between the grass species. *Digitaria* was preferred over all other species ($p < 0.01$), and that both *Themeda* and *Sporobolus* were preferred to *Pennisetum* ($p < 0.05$).

In the third set of trials *Digitaria* was replaced by *Eustachys paspaloides*, a common but apparently less-grazed species of grass. Although only three trials were completed before an unforeseen termination of the experiment (one morning lions killed one animal and injured the other), the results (fig. 19c) were sufficient to indicate that the animals were again selecting between these four species ($p < 0.05$). *Pennisetum* still accounted for a small proportion of the total weight eaten, but in the absence of *Digitaria* it now appeared that *Themeda* was eaten to a greater extent than *Sporobolus*.

These tests indicated that the buffalo were capable of selecting for or avoiding certain species of grass under the conditions of the experiment. However, since cut grass was not their normal food, it was possible that the distinction made between grass species in these trials

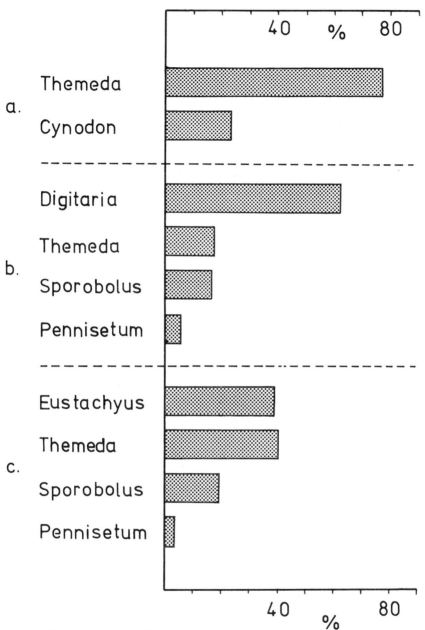

Fig. 19. The proportion of the total amount eaten in each experiment (*a–c*) where grass species were presented together in equal quantities to a tame buffalo.

was of less importance when the grass was growing normally. It was possible to test this with two species, *Themeda triandra* and *Penni-*

setum mezianum, since they are sometimes found in small homogeneous stands adjacent to each other. An animal was allowed to graze these stands while tethered by a rope, and the time eating the two species was recorded. Of nine trials carried out with a total of 149 grazing minutes, 76% was spent grazing *Themeda*, and in all trials buffalo spent more time eating this species. Since the previous experiments showed that the time spent grazing these species was related to the weight eaten, I concluded that more *Themeda* was eaten than *Pennisetum*. With the Wilcoxon test this result was significant to $p < 0.01$ and indicated that the previous experiments reflected a real ability of buffalo to select for different growing grass species.

Preferences for Plant Parts

To determine whether buffalo were selecting for certain parts of the plant, rumen samples were taken from dead animals at various times of the year. The proportions of the different plant parts found in the rumen were then compared, after corrections for differential breakdown, with their proportions in the available greensward.

> Rumen samples were preserved in 8% phenol or 10% formalin. The botanical analysis of samples collected between 1967 and 1969 was carried out by M. D. Gwynne at the East African Agricultural and Forestry Research Organisation, Nairobi; thereafter I did the analyses myself. The method followed that of Gwynne and Bell (1968). Stirred samples were washed first in 2% acetic acid to free particle aggregates bound by rumen fluids, then in water to remove the acid. Subsamples (40 g wet weight) were spread evenly in water on the bottom of aluminium trays, and a Perspex overlay inscribed with an 11×11 grid was placed on top so that the subsample was viewed in water through the Perspex with no air-water interface. The plant part immediately below each of the one hundred intersections was determined under the binocular microscope, and the results were recorded as a direct percentage. Gwynne and Bell (1968) found that the method produced closely similar results between different subsamples of the same sample (no proved significant difference), and that there was a close relationship between percentage frequency on a point-count basis and percentage dry weight.
>
> Dicotyledonous material was differentiated into leaf, stem, bark, seed, and fruit. In some rumen samples grass was classified as leaf (from the leaf tip to the ligule), sheath (from the ligule to the node below), stem (chiefly culm but including some rhizome), seed (all inflorescence components), and root. Grass was termed leaf sheath

only if it had been stripped free from the stem. In the present study all the dicotyledonous material fell into the categories leaf, stem, and seed, and the grass into leaf, sheath, and stem. In later samples grass was differentiated only into leaf + sheath, and stem.

The proportions of available grass components were measured by clipping quadrats of 0.25 m², drying the samples at 80° C, sorting them into two components of leaf + sheath, and stem, and then weighing them. A few grass species were sampled separately and sorted into leaf, leaf sheath, and stem.

The rate at which food passes through the rumen depends on its specific gravity, the lighter components floating to the surface of the rumen constituents and passing through to the omasum and abomasum. Therefore coarser particles of food remain longer than fine, fragile particles. Consequently there will be a greater proportion of coarse particles in the rumen samples than in the food as it enters the mouth. To measure this difference and correct for it, we used measurements of rate of passage of food in cattle (Campling, Freer, and Balch 1961). Components with high fiber stay in the rumen longer than grass leaves (both components have fiber contents similar to grasses eaten by buffalo). Using this information we divided the rumen contents of buffalo into the two components leaf + leaf sheath (1) and stem (s), and assumed the ratio of their residence times T_1/T_s to be $1/1.3$. The justification for extrapolating from cattle to buffalo comes from Glover and Duthie (1958), who showed that the process of digestion in different species of ruminants is very similar.

This ratio was used in the formula given in Sinclair and Gwynne (1972) to find the proportions of leaf + leaf sheath (I_1) in the diet at intake. Knowing the proportions of leaf + leaf sheath, and stem in the rumen to be R_1 and R_s respectively, then I_1 expressed as a percentage could be found by

$$I_1 = 100 / (1 + [\frac{1}{1.3} \cdot \frac{R_s}{R_1}]).$$

The correction factors in fact proved quite small. The largest correction occurred when stem made up 50% of the rumen contents. In this case it was 6% too high. When stem made up 20% of the rumen contents it was only 2% too high when compared with the proportion in the food as it was eaten.

The rumen samples were accumulated over a number of years. In figure 20 the earlier results of the rumen analysis are shown ac-

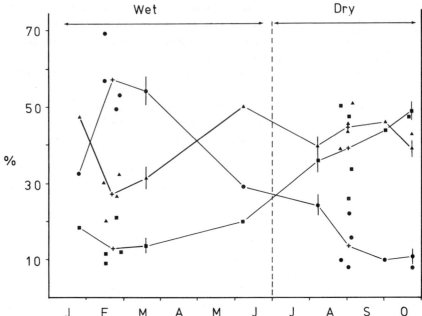

Fig. 20. Seasonal changes in the proportions of the main components of the buffalo's diet in the Serengeti: grass leaf (*circles*), leaf base (*triangles*) and grass stem
(*squares*). Redrawn from Sinclair and Gwynne (1972) with permission from
Blackwell Scientific Publications, Ltd.

cording to the month in which they were collected. Throughout the
year dicotyledonous material amounted to a very small proportion
of the diet, and in the dry season it was absent from most samples and
never reached more than 6%. Dicotyledons, therefore, must be considered unimportant as a food for buffalo in the Serengeti, where
buffalo eat grass almost exclusively. Of the grass parts eaten, the leaf
sheath showed the least variation as a food component in the different seasons. Grass leaf, however, declined from a maximum of
69% of the rumen sample in February to a minimum of 11% in
October at the end of the dry season, whereas the proportion of stem
in the rumen showed the opposite trend.

    In order to include the later samples and to compare them with
the available grass parts, the leaf and leaf sheath components are
combined and corrected so as to show the proportions present in the
food as it was taken from the greensward. The results are given in
figure 21, together with the proportion of the same component in the
grassland measured as a mean of a number of samples (between 10
and 20) collected every month during the years 1971 and 1972. In the

first few months after the rains began in November the new growth
of grass on the previously burned ground was almost all leaf, and the
animals seemed to eat this in the proportion that it was available.
After two or three months, depending on the rainfall, the grasses ma-
tured and produced flower heads. This took place over the relatively
short period of a few weeks, resulting in a large change in the ratio
of leaf + sheath to stem in the greensward. However, the buffalo
were still able to maintain a high proportion of leaf in their diet by
selecting for this component.

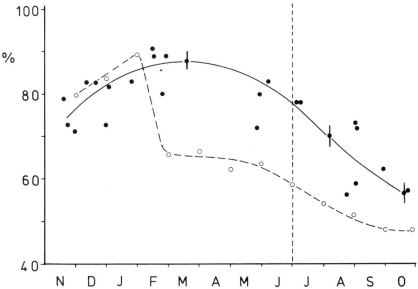

Fig. 21. The decline in the proportions of the combined leaf plus leaf base at
intake (*solid circles*) during the dry season. The proportion of the same component in the available sward is indicated by the open circles. The difference
between the two lines shows the degree of selection.

The ratio of leaf + sheath to stem in the available grass remained
more or less constant through the rest of the wet period until May.
Thereafter the proportion of leaf and sheath declined through the
dry season until it reached a minimum in October. There was a
similar decline of this component in the buffalo's diet, but it occurred at a faster rate. The difference between the proportion of
leaf and sheath in the diet and that in the greensward gradually became less, indicating that although food selection was still evident,
its effect was decreasing as conditions became harsher.

The proportion of leaf in the diet is correlated with the monthly rainfall below 100 mm per month (fig. 22). The proportions of leaf in the diet were similar during the month receiving 150 mm and that receiving 100 mm, suggesting that the amount of leaf eaten reached an asymptote. The decline in selection as the dry season progressed could have been due to the decreasing leaf-to-stem ratio. Stobbs (1973) has demonstrated that the greatest rate of intake in cattle occurred when the grass was of medium height with a high proportion of leaf, before the flowering stage. The lowest rate of intake occurred when the grass was mature and flowering, with a high proportion of stem. This indicates that the mature grass is more difficult for the animals to eat and offers less of the preferred food components.

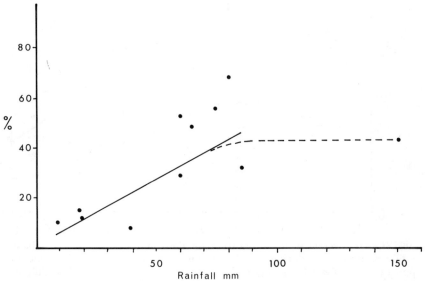

Fig. 22. The proportion of grass leaf in the rumen increases as the rainfall in the previous month increases to about 100 mm, but thereafter remains constant with further increases of rainfall. Redrawn from Sinclair and Gwynne (1972) with permission from Blackwell Scientific Publications, Ltd.

Young animals, with their smaller mouths, may be more able to select preferred food items. However, this is not borne out when the proportion of leaf in the rumen samples collected during October is plotted against age of animal (fig. 23), for there is no noticeable trend with age. A similar picture emerges from the sample collected in the early dry season. This further suggests that the coarseness of the grass

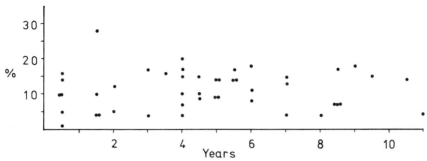

Fig. 23. The proportion of grass leaf in the rumen of animals of different ages collected from the same herd at the end of the dry season, October 1967. Proportion of leaf is not correlated with age.

during the dry season made it harder for animals to find the small amounts of grass leaf.

The Mechanism and Function of Food Selection

The dry weight leaf + sheath to stem ratio of the green, mature flowering species offered to the tame animals in experiment 2 was calculated as *Digitaria macroblephora* = 1.083 > *Themeda triandra* = 0.805 > *Sporobolus pyramidalis* = 0.695 > *Pennisetum mezianum* = 0.475, and this corresponds to the order of preference shown by the animals. Since leaf contains more protein and soluble carbohydrate than stem, the leaf/stem ratio reflects the content of these nutrients in the grass. It appears, therefore, that the nutrient content was the common factor ultimately determining the choice of both species and plant parts. Proximate factors could have been related to this by variables such as the tensile strength of the leaves: grass leaves with high protein and low fiber content break more readily than stem, so that the animals would find them easier to eat (M. D. Gwynne, personal communication). Other factors such as silica content (Field 1968a), essential oils (Oh, Jones, and Longhurst 1968), and phenolic compounds (Levin 1971) could be important, for they increase in conjunction with the crude fiber content as the plant matures.

Buffalo increase the proportion of protein and other nutrients in their diet by selecting for both species and parts of the plant. Obviously this behavior has the important function of raising the quality of food eaten above the average quality available. If other ungulates are selecting their food plants for the same reason, this is an evolutionary pressure tending to increase the overlap in their diets.

Overlap may be reduced by interspecific competition when resources are limiting. Such a process of trends in overlap is indicated in the results of Jarman (1971) in the Zambezi Valley: In the wet season, when resources were presumably not limiting the populations, the overlap in diet of buffalo with four other ungulate species combined —elephant, impala, rhinoceros, and greater kudu—was 75%, but in the dry season it was only 20%, and similar trends could be seen when buffalo were compared with each species separately.

To conclude, therefore, it appears that buffalo select for both plant parts and species in order to maximize their nutrient intake. This selection decreases during the dry season when the structure of the grass layer makes grazing difficult. Therefore this feeding selection would result in increasing rather than decreasing overlap between coexisting ungulate species. The decrease in overlap could result from a number of factors, one of which could be interspecific competition.

SUMMARY

1. Among the resources animals need are vegetation types in which they can find food and avoid climatic extremes and predators. Such vegetation types are called "habitats." In the dry season food is relatively scarce and climate more extreme. The vegetation utilized at this time is called the "optimum habitat."

2. During the dry season buffalo prefer riverine grasslands, but they also use forest if it is available. These are their "optimum habitats."

3. Wildebeest are potential competitors because they graze the riverine grassland in the dry season, but they avoid the forest. Elephant prefer the forest at this time but eat different food from the buffalo. Forest, therefore, is the "ecological refuge" for the buffalo if competition becomes severe. The zone in which they overlap with other grazers is the riverine grassland.

4. Changes in the buffalo's food supply determine their movements into and out of different habitats. As the grass dries out, becoming coarse and less nutritious in the nonriverine habitats, the buffalo move down the catena to the riverine habitats. The process is accelerated by fires. Conversely, rain causes the animals to move back, but only after sufficient growth has taken place.

5. Buffalo eat grass including very small amounts of herbs or shrubs. Experiments with tame animals showed that they were capable of selecting for particular species of grass.

6. Analysis of rumen contents and the available greensward shows that buffalo select for grass leaf. The degree of selection is greatest toward the end of the rains and declines through the dry season. This reflects an increasing difficulty in finding the preferred component and a consequent acceptance of less-preferred food.

7. The selected grass species and plant parts are high in both protein and carbohydrates. Hence feeding preferences appear to function to maximize nutrient intake.

8. Feeding selection would result in increasing rather than decreasing overlap between coexisting ungulate species. Decrease in overlap could result from interspecific competition.

5 Feeding Behavior and Environmental Physiology

So far I have shown that the quality of food available to the animals, measured in terms of the proportion of leaf in the food, declines during the dry season relative to the previous wet season. Added to this is the decrease in available drinking water as the temporary streams and waterholes dry up and climatic variables, such as temperature and solar radiation, become more severe. Although African buffalo graze mainly at night, they graze during daylight hours as well. They spend a similar length of time in rumination—the process whereby the semidigested grass in the rumen is regurgitated in small quantities (the bolus) and chewed down to smaller particles. In all, some 85% of the twenty-four hours is taken up with grazing and ruminating. In this chapter, I consider whether the animals can compensate for the potential resource restrictions during the dry season and alleviate the climatic stresses by altering their feeding behavior. In short, Can buffalo adjust their behavior so that they can obtain enough food without exposing themselves to severe climatic stresses?

CYCLES OF ACTIVITY

With the help of assistants, I followed a number of individual males for 96 consecutive hours in the wet season, and later for two periods of 72 and 36 in the dry season. Other isolated periods covering the day or night were recorded during both seasons. The animals were watched from a vehicle with which they had become familiar. Observers recorded in 6-hour shifts, noting the behavior at intervals of 5 min. This time interval was chosen on the basis of error measurements by Harker, Taylor, and Rollinson (1954). They made observations of cattle grazing at 1 min intervals and compared these with observations at longer intervals. Taking grazing times measured from observations at 1 min intervals as being essentially correct, they found that times measured from observations at 6 min intervals had an error of only 3.7%. Thermohydrograph records obtained in the same general area as the behavioral observations provided a continuous record of the surrounding environment.

Of the various behavior elements recorded, only grazing, ruminating, drinking, and wallowing are considered here. When ruminating, an animal either stood still or rested on its brisket. In the latter position the head was slightly raised, and this could be distinguished from the resting position, in which the chin was close to the ground. Resting occurred infrequently, only a few minutes at a time, as is typical of large bovids (Balch 1955). Occasionally an animal rolled onto its side while resting, but again only for a short time. Night observations were made during moonlit periods. Although this may have altered the nocturnal activity of the animals, it was a constant factor in the comparison of feeding activity between wet and dry seasons. In fact, Wilson (1961) found that moonlight does not alter the nocturnal activity of cattle, although wildebeest seem to show a difference in activities between dark and moonlit nights (D. Kreulen, personal communication).

The proportion of each half-hour period of the day an animal spent grazing was calculated as a mean over four consecutive days recorded during the wet season. Similar calculations were made on the same individual male as a mean over four days in the dry season, and these are shown in figure 24a, b. In both seasons there was considerable variability in the length of grazing bouts during the night, with the result that the mean values over four-day periods shown in the histograms indicate that grazing can take place at any time during the night hours.

In daylight hours there was a regular period of grazing in the early morning between 0600 h and 1000 h. In the wet season there was very little grazing during the middle of the day from 1100 h to 1600 h. However, in the dry season there were two noticeable changes. An increase in the amount of grazing relative to the wet season occurred during the hottest hours, 1400–1600 h. This was followed by a long period of ruminating in the early evening, and a similar period occurred at dawn, neither of these being very obvious during the wet season.

Because of the variability in day-to-day feeding activity I used an autocorrelation technique for further analysis (Delius 1969). I correlated the proportion of grazing in each half-hour period with that in the next half hour (lag 1), then the half hour later (lag 2), and so on for successive lags until the number of observations became too small.

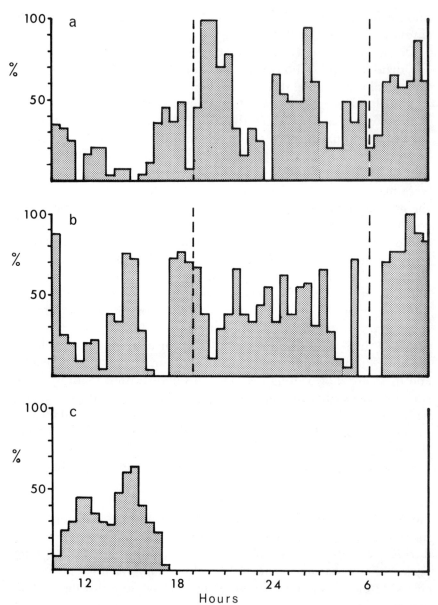

Fig. 24. The proportion of each half hour spent grazing by bachelor males during the wet season (*a*), and the dry season (*b*). The proportion spent in wallows is shown in (*c*).

The correlation functions were then plotted as a time-series correlogram. The technique is useful for detecting cycles where they are not readily apparent in the crude data. For example, the activity in one half-hour period will be strongly correlated with that in the same period 24 h later, if there is a 24-h rhythm, and this would show up at lags of 24 h and 48 h. The autocorrelation coefficient at zero lag is of course unity. Since the correlograms are symmetrical for positive and negative lags, the figures presented here show positive lags only. Where one behavior is cross-correlated with another event, the correlogram is not symmetrical (Delius 1969).

Figure 25 shows the autocorrelation functions for grazing activity plotted against the lag, for both wet and dry seasons. In the wet season the only obvious cycle had a 24-h period: in other words, graz-

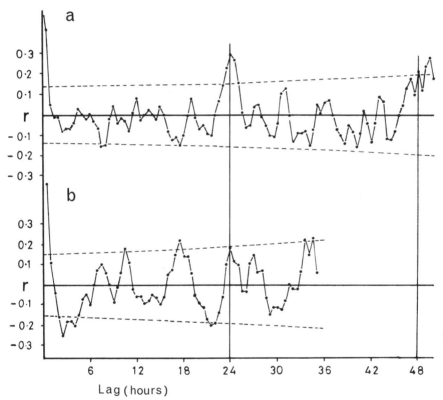

Fig. 25. Autocorrelation functions for grazing time per half hour plotted against time lag in the wet season (a) and dry season (b). Reproduced from Sinclair (1974d) with permission of Blackwell Scientific Publications, Ltd.

ing tends to take place at the same time each day, but the relationship between successive bouts of grazing within the 24-h period appears to be random. In the dry season, on the other hand, not only does the circadian rhythm show up, but one can see other cycles with periods of 8 h. The statistical analysis of these correlograms requires some previous prediction of the cycle period. Obviously one may predict a circadian rhythm, so that the result is significant if the correlation function exceeds the 95% confidence limits—as it does at both seasons—with a lag of 24 h. Since I had no obvious reason to expect an 8-h cycle to develop in the dry season, the fact that correlation functions exceeded the 95% confidence limits at a lag of 8 h could have arisen by chance. As an indication of the validity of this dry-season cycle, the order of the original 30-min periods of activity data were randomly shuffled and autocorrelated again. After this process no cycles of any sort could be seen. It appeared from this that the cycle in the original data was real.

The autocorrelation of the proportion of 30 min periods spent ruminating (fig. 26) showed a more obvious 24-h cycle in the wet season than that of the grazing, and in the dry season this was also super-

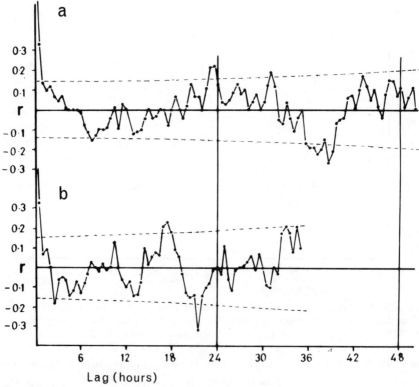

Fig. 26. Autocorrelation functions for ruminating time per half hour plotted against time lag in the wet season (*a*) and dry season (*b*).

imposed with a shorter cycle of 8-h period. When grazing was cross-correlated with ruminating (fig. 27), the expected inverse relation-ship was found: that is, when animals grazed at a particular time of day in the wet season, ruminating occurred 12 h later. In the dry season grazing was positively correlated with ruminating 2 h later and 9 h later, but the circadian rhythm was less noticeable. To sum-marize, these analyses indicate, first, that feeding behavior was or-ganized into somewhat regular bouts within the day in the dry sea-son, but much less so in the wet season. Secondly, there was a much stronger correlation between grazing and ruminating activity in the dry season.

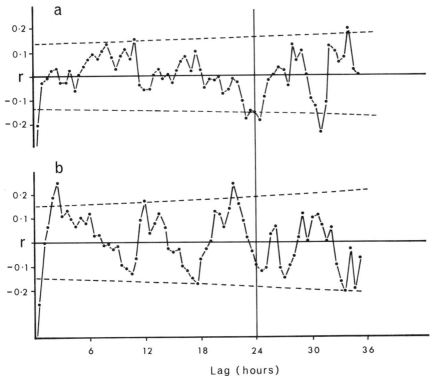

Fig. 27. Cross-correlation functions of grazing with ruminating plotted against time lag in the wet season (a) and dry season (b).

Cycles could also be seen in the feeding behavior of breeding herds, although the difficulties of observation precluded measuring differences between seasons. With the help of a radio transmitter attached by a collar to an adult female, a herd of 250 animals was followed throughout a 24-h period. The proportion of the herd grazing was recorded every 5 min, and the results are shown in figure 28. As with the bachelor males there were two main periods of

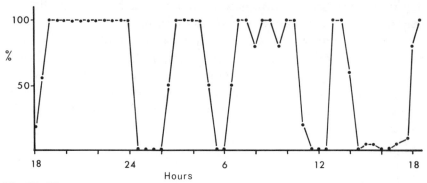

Fig. 28. The proportion of a herd (250 animals) grazing over a 24-h period. Note that the whole herd changes rapidly from grazing to nongrazing and vice versa. Reproduced from Sinclair (1974*d*) with permission of Blackwell Scientific Publications, Ltd.

grazing—in the early morning and during the first hours of the night —and there was also a resting period in the heat of the day. I recorded grazing activity of herds during daylight hours at Ngurdoto Crater near Mount Meru on a number of days. The midday grazing period was present during dry periods but almost absent in wetter seasons, much like the pattern of the bachelor males.

TOTAL ACTIVITY TIMES

So far I have discussed only when feeding occurs. Does the total amount of grazing and ruminating per 24 h differ between seasons? Figure 29 shows that grazing increased in the early dry season but later declined slightly, and the differences between seasons were not significant (Mann-Whitney test, $p = 0.2$; Siegel 1956). But there may have been an increase in ruminating time during the dry season, increasing the ratio of ruminating to grazing. This would indicate that more ruminating was required for the same amount of grazing, probably because of the increased fiber content of the food in the dry season.

    Arnold (1964) stated that grazing time in sheep increased as the amount of food decreased, but this reached a limit and then declined. Moreover, the rate of food intake declined as grazing time increased. Stobbs (1973) has shown that the rate of food intake in cattle de-

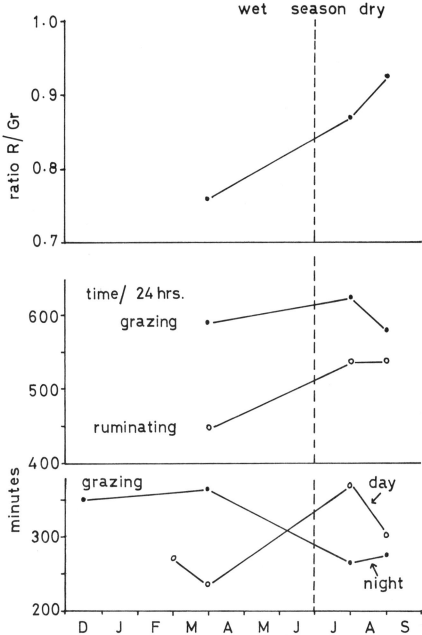

Fig. 29. The ratio of total ruminating time per day to total grazing time, and the changes of these two activities with season. Total ruminating time appears to increase in the dry season, and more grazing occurs by day than by night at this season.

clined to a minimum in the dry season as the grass became coarser with a higher proportion of stem. Other observations show that total grazing time of tropical cattle increased under these conditions (Joblin 1960; Harker, Taylor, and Rollinson 1954; Smith 1959), and in conjunction with this ruminating time also increased (Hancock 1954). Therefore with poor-quality forage the animals spend more time grazing and more time ruminating for a smaller amount of food than they would with good-quality forage.

When grazing times are divided into daylight and night hours (fig. 29), a significant increase in daylight grazing can be seen during the dry season ($p = 0.002$, Mann-Whitney test). This increase was due to the addition of a grazing bout during the heat of the day (fig. 24). It seems likely, therefore, that the poor-quality food resulted in a decrease in rate of food intake: this in turn caused a need for longer total grazing and ruminating times, and to organize this a more rigid alternation of these two phases was produced. Consequently such a feeding cycle necessitated the extra grazing period in the middle of the day. In the mild wet season the buffalo could spend as long as five hours without grazing during the midday period, presumably because of good quality food.

THE RATE OF RUMINATION

As the adult ruminant grows older the size of cusps and number of ridges on the teeth decline, and in very old animals the molars become quite smooth and are occasionally broken. Inevitably the grinding efficiency of the teeth declines with age, and old animals probably cannot obtain as many nutrients as young animals from the same amount of food, especially from low protein–high fiber grass, if they chew at the same rate. However, I thought it possible that old animals might compensate for their poor teeth by either chewing more or chewing faster on each bolus of food that is regurgitated.

Animals of all ages were timed by stopwatch with respect to the number of chews per bolus and the length of time per bolus; and from this I calculated the rate of mastication (chews per minute). Observations were made at Lake Manyara, Ngurdoto, and the Serengeti, and no differences could be found between the three areas; nor were there differences between the two sexes at the same age. The measurements are shown plotted against approximate age in figure 30. If the old animals were compensating for their poor teeth they should have chewed longer or faster on each bolus than the middle-

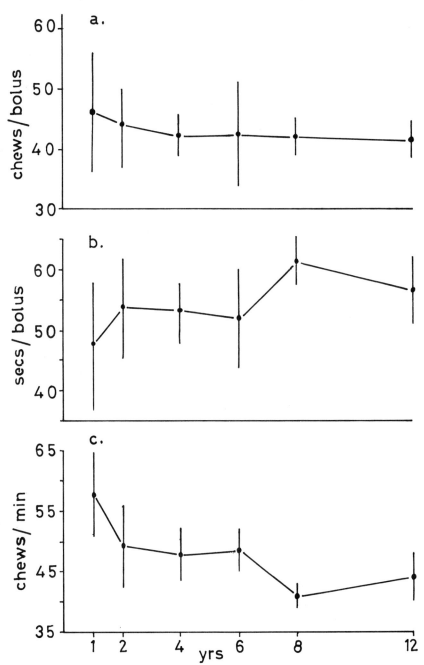

Fig. 30. The efficiency of chewing the food bolus during rumination does not alter with age in adults, as is shown in *a*, number of chews per bolus, and *b*, length of time needed to chew the bolus. These give rise to *c*, the rate at which the bolus is chewed.

aged animals, but no significant differences were found between these two age groups. Over all ages the trend was the reverse of what I expected, with young animals chewing faster. It is probable that the rate of chewing is a mechanical feature related to the size of the jaw, and once the jaw is full grown the rate remains constant. So this evidence suggests that the old animals were unable to compensate for the poor grinding efficiency of their teeth by increasing the amount or rate of chewing, and hence they obtained fewer nutrients than younger animals.

DRINKING AND WALLOWING

Bachelor males usually returned to the river to drink at dusk and just after nightfall, and 50% of the recorded instances occurred between 1800 h and 2100 h. They also drank during the first part of the morning, between 0630 h and 1000 h, but this was less frequent. Drinking always occurred during periods of grazing. Usually the buffalo grazed as they made their way slowly to the river, and once there took only 5 or 10 min to drink. Afterward they resumed their grazing but moved some four or five hundred meters away from the river. During the dry season the animals also drank occasionally at midday. Weir and Davison (1965), recording during the dry season in Rhodesia, found that buffalo herds usually drank in the period 1630 h–2000 h, with a smaller peak of drinking between 0830 h and 1030 h, behavior similar to that of Serengeti males. With these males the intervals between drinking were either 12–13 h or 23–25 h in the wet season. Although there appeared to be a greater variability in drinking intervals in the dry season (6–28 h), the mean interval was the same in the two seasons—16.5 h.

Taylor (1968) found from experimental animals in a constant environment of 22° C that the minimum water requirements were 10.37 kg/100 kg$^{0.75}$/day. Wilson (1961) found that under tropical conditions cattle required twice as much water during the dry season as during the rains.

Males in the Serengeti wallowed mainly during the wet season, because most wallows dried out at the end of the rains. But I have seen some animals during the dry season wallowing in the shallow waters of the Sand River and Mara River in the north. One particular animal at Kogatende returned to the same sandbank in the river each day, to lie half submerged in the flowing water for several hours. The times of day when wallowing occurred in the wet season are shown in figure 24*c*. These are derived from the mean proportion of each half-hour interval spent wallowing, from records of a number of animals over a period of seven days. They did not wallow before 1000 h and were rarely found doing so after 1600 h. There appeared to be two main periods for wallowing, with a break usually caused by a short bout of grazing. Buffalo rarely spent more than 3 h in a wallow on any one occasion. In the first bout of wallowing during the mornings, periods of only 20 or 30 min were common, but the second bout during the hottest time of day was usually longer, lasting about 2 h. Most wallows were not fit for drinking, often consisting of thick mud highly contaminated with urine. They were only large enough to contain one or two animals at a time. The males quite clearly knew the location of these wallows, for I have seen animals break off grazing and walk straight to a particular wallow half a kilometer away. Within their small home range these males might visit three or four wallows. Males in the breeding herds also wallowed when possible (plate 15), but females and young almost never did so, even when, as at Lake Manyara, there was ample opportunity. In fact, on some occasions when the herds settled down by the lake to ruminate, the dominant males in the herd moved off to the water while all the females and young lay along the lakeshore.

THE EFFECTS OF TEMPERATURE ON FEEDING

In order to measure daily fluctuations in surface body temperature, one of the male buffalo being observed for measurements of activity was immobilized and a thermistor inserted in the subcutaneous layers of the neck. The thermistor was connected to a radio transmitter constructed and operated by H. Baldwin and W. Holz. The radio transmitted in pulses whose rate increased as the thermistor became hotter. The receiver was connected to a recorder with a continuously moving chart on which was traced the pulse rate. Temperature was calculated using measurements from the initial calibration of the instrument.

Although the transmitters were rather too easily broken by these animals, records from three separate days were obtained during December 1967 when conditions were wet (figure 31). These show that subdermal body temperature rose above 40° C at its highest point and fell as low as 35.2° C during the night, thus producing a range of 5° C in the 24 h period. The highest body temperatures coincided with the normal afternoon break in grazing, which suggests that the

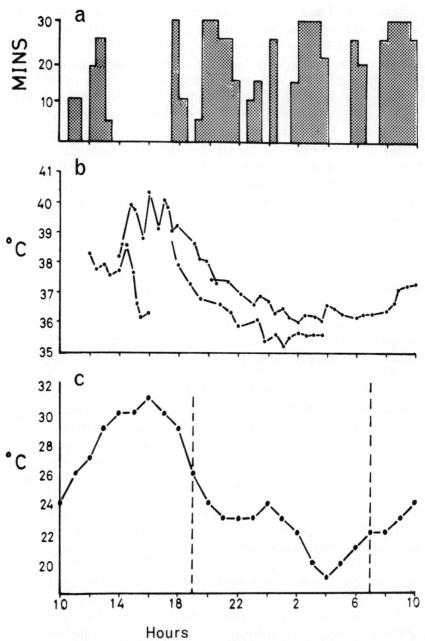

Fig. 31. a, Typical grazing activity of a bachelor male, showing the rest period in the afternoon: b, the subcutaneous body temperature is highest during the rest period. This occurs when the ambient temperature is also at its peak (c). a is from Sinclair (1974d) with permission of Blackwell Scientific Publications, Ltd.

timing of grazing is at least partly determined by heat stress on the animal. Body temperature was closely correlated with the ambient shade temperature. When the animal grazes in daylight hours it is for the most part exposed to solar radiation, and this imposes a heat load on the animal beyond that caused by air temperature. Bligh and Harthoorn (1965), using similar radiotelemetric methods, also found these fluctuations in deep body temperature of buffalo.

Taylor (1970*a, b*), in a series of experiments on East African ungulates, has added considerably to the understanding of strategies of temperature regulation of these animals. He exposed a number of species, including buffalo, wildebeest, and cattle, to a constant moderate temperature regime of 22° C and to a regime of 12 h at 40° C, alternating with 12 h at 22° C simulating conditions when animals are exposed to intense solar radiation. Also, comparisons were made between those that had free access to water and those with restricted access. Evaporative water loss from buffalo increased from 1.8 l per 100 kg body weight per day to 4.1 l when the moderate temperature regime changed to the hot regime. When water intake was restricted, evaporative water loss with both regimes was reduced by about 15%. With free access to water, the increase in evaporative water loss to dissipate the extra heat load under the hot regime amounted to approximately 2% of the body weight per day. However, when water intake was restricted the buffalo continued to evaporate water to dissipate heat and were unable to reduce this to any extent. In other words, buffalo are not able to tolerate water restriction for very long when temperatures become severe. Wildebeest are able to reduce evaporation under these conditions slightly better than buffalo, and zebu cattle do better still.

Body temperatures in the hot regimes fluctuated from 37.4° to 39.3° C when there was free access to water but increased to 40° C when water was restricted. Taylor (1970*a*) calculated that this increase in body temperature helped reduce the evaporative water loss by some 0.3 liters/100 kg/day. This range of body temperature was similar to that observed in the Serengeti animals. Taylor points out that heat storage, by allowing the body temperature to rise slowly through the day, is an effective means of saving water, but only for large animals, such as buffalo, with a small surface area and low metabolism in relation to body mass.

To investigate these physiological strategies further, Taylor (1970*b*) observed dehydrated animals in air temperatures as high as

50° C. Ungulates adopt two types of physiological responses to heat stress—panting and sweating. Buffalo and cattle sweat and wildebeest pant (Robertshaw and Taylor 1969). Taylor (1970b) found that rectal temperatures of buffalo, whether dehydrated or not, rose to about 40.5° C when the animals were exposed to air temperatures of 45° C (fig. 32a). Hence 40° C appears to be the maximum body temperature

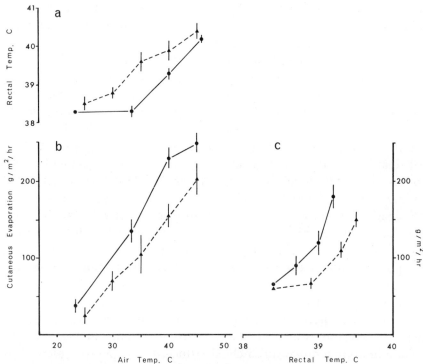

Fig. 32. The relationship between air temperature, rectal temperature, and sweating in hydrated (*solid line*) and dehydrated (*dotted line*) experimental buffalo. Redrawn from Taylor (1970b).

the species can tolerate under normal conditions. For air temperatures lower than 45° C, rectal temperatures were higher in dehydrated animals than in hydrated animals. Similarly, the dehydrated animals had lower rates of cutaneous evaporation (fig. 32b), and the onset of evaporative cooling began at higher body temperatures during dehydration (fig. 32c).

These results show that buffalo make physiological responses toward both high temperature and water restriction, by allowing body temperature to rise and by reducing evaporative cooling. However, the highest body temperatures observed in buffalo (40.5° C) are still low compared with those of other tropical ruminants, which can attain rectal temperatures as high as 46° C (Taylor 1970b). It appears, therefore, that when the buffalo's body temperature reaches its maximum of around 40° C the animal has to respond by seeking cooler environments either in shade or in wallows if it is to avoid high rates of cutaneous evaporation.

Clearly, shade would alleviate heat stress to some degree. Wallowing, although it took place during the hot time of day, would be of benefit to males only. Wallows were invariably in open areas, and so when making use of them these males would also be exposed to solar radiation. The only direct measurements of body temperature of animals exposed to solar radiation or allowed to wallow or stand in shade were obtained by Moran (1973) on the Asian water buffalo. The rectal temperature of those compelled to stand in the sun rose to a maximum of 40.2° C at 1400 h, whereas those allowed to wallow reached body temperatures of 38.8° C and those in shade showed no increase during the day, remaining at 38.0° C. Similar measurements taken after a 40-min exercise period at 1000 h showed an immediate rise in body temperature to 40.3–40.8° C. This remained above 40° C in those exposed to radiation but dropped to 38.3° C in those in wallows or shade. Subsequently the temperature of those in wallows rose to 38.7° C. Therefore it appears that lying in water, although of some benefit, was less satisfactory for temperature regulation than shade-seeking. Since wallowing is far less common in the African buffalo than in the water buffalo, where both sexes wallow, the benefits in terms of temperature regulation may be of only moderate importance. But aspects of social behavior are also involved in wallowing, and these I shall discuss in chapter 6.

DAILY MOVEMENT

One of the noticeable differences between the old bachelor males that live permanently away from the herds and those animals in herds lies in the size of their home ranges. A number of well-known old males remained within a range of 3–4 km² for at least four years. Daily movement amounted to no more than 2 km, and often it was only 1 km. The herds, on the other hand, had ranges that could be 30 km from end to end (fig. 44).

I measured daily movements of herd animals during 1972 and 1973, through radiotelemetry. I located the females carrying transmitters by using aircraft. One transmitter was placed in each of two adjacent herds, and daily records were obtained in samples of 7–10 days at intervals through the year. On occasions two or three records were obtained each day, and over one 36-h period the complete movement pattern was recorded. These more frequent records let me apply a correction factor to the minimum distance recorded from single sightings on consecutive days. The minimum distances underestimated the real distance traveled, and the errors may have been large, especially when herds moved along a circular route during the night and returned close to where they had started the previous day.

Distances traveled from day to day appeared highly variable, and this was not due entirely to errors of measurement. Herds would commonly remain in an area for three or four days, then move overnight as far as 10 or 15 km away and settle down for a few more days. The reasons for such movements were not obvious—certainly there were no special signs of predation, for example, on the nights movement occurred. The only times when there seemed to be an obvious reason for movement were at the beginning of the rains when scattered thunderstorms occurred. Then the herds would move long distances to reach the area receiving the rain. This was mentioned earlier in connection with herds' moving into the hills in the southern study area between 1967 and 1969. In 1972, with different herds under study, there was scattered rainfall in January, and larger than average movements occurred at this time (fig. 33). Similar conditions did not occur in 1973. For the other months the mean minimum daily movement remained more or less the same over both wet and dry seasons, which was perhaps unexpected. The only difference noted between the seasons was that the herds tended to move along the rivers in the dry season, whereas they often moved away from the rivers during the rains, which supports the findings on habitat selection reported in the previous chapter. The average minimum daily movement over the year was 2.75 km. The correction factor derived from the more frequent observations suggested that the minimum figure should be at least doubled for an estimate of the amount of

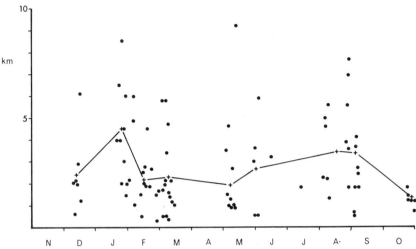

Fig. 33. The minimum daily movement of a herd shows great variability. The mean values (*crosses*) for each sampling period show no noticeable change with season.

movement during the 24 h. This gives an estimate of 5.5 km/day, but it may average as high as 8 km/day.

Taylor (1973) has developed empirical formulas relating the energy cost of movement in four-legged mammals to their body weight. Buffalo move at approximately 3 km/h, and they spend an average of only 1.84 h/day walking. However, they are active a considerable proportion of the day while grazing, although they are hardly covering much distance. Taylor's formulas also let us calculate the energy cost of this kind of activity which, as he points out, is 1.7 times that predicted from the standard metabolism by Kleiber's (1961) equation.

Taylor (1973) shows that the oxygen consumption of an animal (VO_2ml/g/h), given its body weight in kg (W) and velocity in km/h (V), is $VO_2 = V(8.46.W^{-.40}) + 6.0\ (W^{-.25})$. The second term on the right gives the oxygen consumed by a stationary animal. When we convert to calories for a buffalo of mean body weight 424 kg, the stationary cost is 458 kcals/h. The cost of walking at 3 kms/h is 736 kcals/h. Since the animal walks for only 1.84 h/day, the total energy cost per day is 11,523 kcals, of which movement accounts for only 12%. Therefore, although herd animals move twice or even three times as far each day as the old males, the energy cost is increased by only 4 to 7%. However, the long periods of activity and movement together add up to a daily energy cost twice that predicted from the standard metabolism. These figures are also fairly close to the predicted maintenance costs of lactating females (8.99 Mcals/day) in chapter 7, based on the work of Flatt and Moe (1974).

SUMMARY

1. Activity measurements of bachelor males in both wet and dry seasons show that they do more grazing in the middle of the day in the dry season. Also, activity is concentrated into longer periods of grazing or ruminating in the dry season.

2. Old adults do not appear to compensate for their poor teeth by altering the rate or amount of chewing per food bolus during rumination relative to younger adults.

3. Herd animals are highly coordinated in their activity patterns. Old females in the herd do not spend longer grazing or ruminating than younger adults. But bachelor males may do so.

4. Subcutaneous body temperature can reach 40° C when buffalo graze in the sun, but then they cease grazing and move to shade. Heat stress therefore influences the activity pattern. Because buffalo graze more during the day in the dry season, their water requirements probably increase.

5. Daily movements measured by radiotelemetry show that herd animals move two or three times the distance covered by bachelor males. This difference means herd animals use 4–7% more energy.

6 Social Behavior

Social behavior must, of course, play some part in regulating the size of animal population, if only because most animals behave socially simply to live and reproduce. What has caused considerable controversy is the suggestion that various aspects of social behavior have evolved for the specific function of keeping the population size below the limits imposed by the food supply. The main proponent of this theory has been Wynne-Edwards (1962), who suggested that such social mechanisms involving altruist genes could have evolved through group (interdemic) selection. Wilson (1975) summarizes the conditions necessary for such selection. He points out that an altruist gene can evolve by pure interdemic selection under special conditions of severe population extinction, but that these conditions are improbable. Wilson (1975, p. 113) concludes, "most of the wide array of 'social conventions' hypothesised by Wynne-Edwards and other authors are probably not true." Nevertheless, since interdemic selection can take place, Wilson points out that it must be taken into consideration when discussing the function of social behavior. Alternative hypotheses suggest that this behavior has evolved through individual selection, or kin selection, or neither—the alternative to selection of any kind is that behavior has evolved through random processes. From observations one should be able to see whether behavioral elements benefit the individual, or if altruistic, whether those benefiting are closely related.

Bearing these hypotheses in mind, I shall describe various aspects of buffalo behavior, starting with those concerned with reproduction. Then I shall turn to the social behavior of individuals within groups, discussing first their agonistic interactions and the dominance hierarchy, then the formation of subgroups within the herd, especially the characteristics of bachelor males. After this I shall describe the behavior of groups, including their antipredator behavior, home range, and herd spacing. Finally I shall look at spacing on the finer scale of groups or individuals within the herd.

SEXUAL BEHAVIOR

In a large herd a female that comes into estrus is soon identified by one of the adult bulls: these males constantly examine all the adult females by licking the vulva, which stimulates the female to urinate. The male smells the urine and then displays the characteristic *flehmen* posture, with the head held horizontal, neck extended, nares distended, and the upper lip curled up to expose the upper gums (plate 16). *Flehmen* appears to be a response to olfactory stimuli. Although Dagg and Taub (1970) cast some doubt on the role of the vomeronasal or Jacobsen's organ in this process, Estes (1972) provides a convincing argument that excreted sex hormones can be detected by this organ. Estes (1972) suggests that *flehmen* closes the nares, thus allowing inspired air to pass through the "incisive ducts" which in the buffalo pass from the anterior roof of the mouth into the nasal cavity. Opening into these ducts is Jacobsen's organ, which is lined with sensory epithelium. *Flehmen* is sometimes exhibited immediately after a bull licks a female, and solitary males often display this behavior after smelling the grass in areas where a herd had previously rested.

When the bull detects a female approaching estrus he remains close to her for the next two or three days. If the female has a small calf it is usually tolerated, although the bull may nudge it out of the way if it gets between him and the cow when he is following close behind. Tending by a bull often acts as a signal to others; on several occasions I saw bulls approach from the other side of a large herd a hundred meters or more away, displace the previous bull, and take over the tending. Within half an hour I observed five bulls successively displacing each other at Ngurdoto Crater. Once displaced the males resumed normal grazing and apparently had no further interest in the female. On this particular occasion the fifth male remained with the female for the next two days, indicating that he was one of the dominant animals in the herd. Since the herd contained some 250 animals at this time, the rapidity with which the dominant animals took over the female indicated their efficiency in securing the females in estrus. The proestrous period when males first start following but before the female will accept them lasts as long as two days; so the top bulls in the social hierarchy have ample time to secure the females simply by watching the other males.

As the cow reaches full estrus the male spends more time tending her by licking her and resting his chin on her rump. This behavior usually causes the cow to run forward with a few quick steps; if she does not react he attempts to mount. When copulation occurs the female remains stationary and lifts her tail out a little. On the six occasions when I observed this the male copulated at least twice within half an hour. During this period the female sometimes solicited mounting by resting her chin on the bull's rump or pushing her head under his belly. During copulation other males in the herd become intensely excited. They run toward the copulating pair and fight among themselves.

On occasions females will mount others. As in cattle and water buffalo, those in estrus may exhibit this behavior or solicit it from others. Subadult males and subordinate adults make frequent attempts at mounting when the herd takes fright, bunches together, and stampedes away. In the initial stages of flight it is common to see these young males attempting to mount and riding along for a second or two before dropping down again. Mounting also occurs during periods of play fighting between subadult males. In general the type and sequence of sexual behavior elements differ little from those of cattle and other Bovini (Hafez, Schein, and Ewbank 1969; Frazer 1968).

The occurrences of sexual behavior is seasonal. The number of observations of bulls at Manyara and Ngurdoto exhibiting any of the elements of sexual behavior—*flehmen*, tending, chin-resting or mounting—recorded for each hour of observation of 100 herd animals is shown in figure 34, plotted against the time of year. A low degree of sexual activity occurs throughout the wet period December to May, but at the end of the rains in June this increases rapidly to a sharp peak before declining to almost zero for the dry season. The timing of the peak is similar to that for the peak of conceptions seen in the Serengeti population, described in the next chapter.

BIRTH AND MOTHER-YOUNG BEHAVIOR

Although I was never present when a birth took place, on two occasions I found females that had given birth just a few minutes before, and several other times I found calves only an hour or two old. These records suggest that births occur either during the afternoon or just before dawn, periods when buffalo are resting.

Wildebeest give birth during a much more restricted period of the day. Wildebeest births are largely confined to the two hours between 0800 h and 1000 h, and none were seen before 0700 h. I observed this

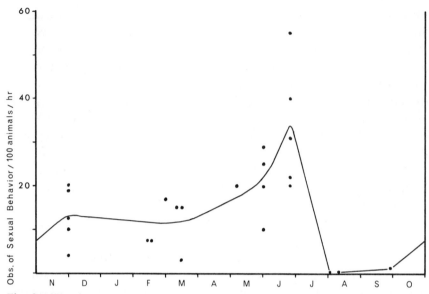

Fig. 34. The frequency of mating attempts (chin resting, mounting, or copulation) at different times of year. There is a peak toward the end of the long rains, followed by little activity during the dry season.

during February 1972 at the height of the birth season, watching female groups both at night and in the daytime. Some thirty records of the time of day when births took place were made, and the frequency distribution of these is shown in figure 35. Estes (1966) has also mentioned that births took place in the morning, and Alan Root, who spent many hours filming the calving of wildebeest, told me that the only birth he observed at another time was a malformed calf born during the afternoon, which subsequently died. The main time for births coincides with the time the wildebeest herds rest at the end of their early-morning grazing bout. Females with young calves and those about to give birth form closely packed maternity herds at this time.

For such a restricted birth time to have developed and be maintained in this species a strong selection pressure must be operating. As Kruuk (1972) points out, during the birth season of wildebeest, hyenas concentrate in large numbers to kill the newborn calves. At this time of year it is common to see hyenas with distended bellies basking in the early morning sun after their night's hunting. Kruuk (1972) describes the activity of hyenas as nocturnal, with a major peak just after dark and a smaller peak before dawn. His records of hyenas hunting at different times of day are reproduced in figure 35, and they suggest at least one reason why wildebeest give birth when they do. Births begin at a time when hyenas have normally ceased hunting. They probably are concentrated into such a short period to give them the longest possible time during the rest of the daylight hours to gain strength before the hyenas are active again ten hours later; it almost seems as if every minute counts.

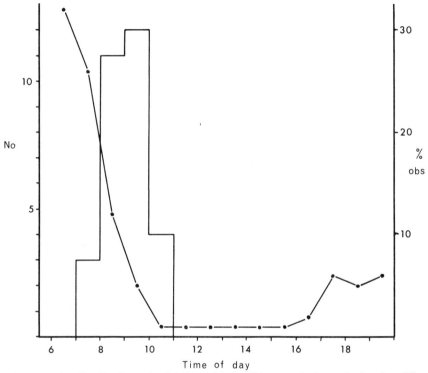

Fig. 35. The distribution of wildebeest births (*histogram*) through the day. The line shows the distribution of observations of hunting hyenas through the day, recorded as a percentage of the total by Kruuk (1972).

Other adaptations of wildebeest support this: calves can run 15 min after birth, and they can walk in as short a time as 5 min; moreover, the majority of calves, about a quarter of a million of them, are born within a mere three weeks in January and February. During the birth season the predators can capture the newborn calves with ease, and they eat as many as they can, for there is a superabundance of calves. But since the consumption capacity of the predators at any one time is limited, the overall proportion of calves that are killed is determined by the length of time they are available. By about a month after birth the calves can avoid the predators; so the shorter the birth season the smaller the proportion killed, and the smaller each individual's chance of being eaten. Hence predation would select for calves to be born at the same time, with the result that the predators become "swamped" (Kruuk 1972; Estes 1976).

By comparison, although hyenas do show an interest in newborn buffalo calves, the proportion they kill is considerably reduced. First, there were many fewer hyenas in the woodlands where buffalo lived than on the plains following the wildebeest. Second, tackling a buffalo herd to extract a newborn calf is a completely different proposition from chasing wildebeest, for buffalo are quite capable of defending themselves against a whole pack of hyenas. Lions are a different matter for the buffalo, but even these predators have difficulty when buffalo form a group defense. On the whole, predation seems to affect buffalo far less than wildebeest; there is much less need to give birth at restricted times of day.

Buffalo apparently give birth while the female is still part of the herd. The calf needs several hours to gain enough strength to follow the mother, in contrast to wildebeest, and so the mother is left behind when the herd moves off for the early-morning grazing period. On a number of occasions during the heat of the day females with their newborn calves have been seen hiding in small thickets. At this stage the mother shows a very strong attachment to her young. While catching animals for experiments to produce domesticated buffalo herds on one of the farms near Lake Manyara, I noticed that females with newborn calves would hide in thickets and emerge only to make short charges at the catching vehicles. Rarely would they abandon their calves to join the herd some distance away.

Sometime during the daylight hours following birth, the female gradually leads the calf back to the herd. I have seen this taking place through the middle of the day. The calf walks very slowly, stopping often, and the female has to return repeatedly. On these occasions she makes a low croaking noise lasting about two seconds. The calf usually makes no noise, although it may bleat if it loses contact with the mother. Although this movement takes place during the heat of the day, this is the time when predators are least active; the calf must be at its most vulnerable at this stage, being neither hidden, nor protected by the herd, nor capable of running. In normal circumstances the calf is never left hiding on its own.

During the first day the calf will follow any moving object, including vehicles and humans. In the course of rearing several abandoned calves found in the woodlands, we noticed that those less than a day old would follow humans immediately and accept milk. Those that were captured from herds and that were two or three weeks old showed considerable aggression toward their handlers until they could be encouraged to take their first drink of milk. After that first feeding they followed the person who gave the milk, but only gradually lost their fear of other humans. Newborn calves respond to an imitation of the mother's deep croak. Lost calves will approach stationary humans or vehicles emitting imitation croaks unless they also hear voices or engine noises. Since similar croaks are produced by adult members of a herd when following each other after an alarm, this sound appears to act as a contact call. Asian water buffalo make a short, high-pitched bleat in similar contexts, a noise quite different from that of the African buffalo.

For the first few weeks the calf is still very slow, running in a cumbersome and ungainly way. When the herds take flight the newborn calves drop to the rear and are sometimes left behind. The mothers stay with them, first running after the herd and then returning, and the calves bleat incessantly as they run. Their inability to run with the herd is in complete contrast to wildebeest and other savanna bovids, whose calves at this age can easily keep up with adults.

When the herd is grazing normally, the calf sleeps much of the time, only occasionally getting up to follow the mother if she has moved too far away. The calves suckle for periods of 3 to 10 min at intervals throughout the day. Normally the calf suckles with its head between its mother's hind legs; rarely does it suckle from the side, in contrast to calves of cattle (Hafez, Schein, and Ewbank 1969) and bison (McHugh 1958). If the female is lying down when the calf wants to suckle, it will nudge her hindquarters and rump until she stands up. Suckling is tolerated by the mother until the next calf is born, some fifteen months later. However it is unlikely that milk is obtained during all of this time, for lactation ceases when the female is seven months pregnant, when on an average the previous calf is ten months old in the Serengeti population. Longer periods of lactation may occur if the female is not pregnant or if there is a longer calving interval. Nevertheless suckling does seem to continue after milk has ceased to flow. My tame animals would suck my fingers at eighteen months although it had been almost a year since they were fed milk: in fact, when they were offered milk at fifteen months they rejected it. One can only speculate on the function of this post-weaning behavior, but one possibility is that it helps to maintain family bonds.

Once a new calf is born the previous calf is prevented from suckling, although it continues to try. The mother pushes the older calves away with sharp stabs of her horns. However, these yearlings remain close to their mothers until they are about two years old. At this age the male calves gradually become more independent and join males of similar age to form sub-adult groups.

Agonistic Behavior

A number of behavior elements are involved in the agonistic interactions of African buffalo, and different combinations of these indicate the intensity of aggression and avoidance. Although females display behavior patterns similar to those exhibited by males, a number of elements are missing and the frequency of interactions is lower. Threat behavior is shown most commonly in a stance with the head held high but with the nose pointing to the ground (fig. 36a). This position raises the horns and presents them to an opponent when facing head on. Buffalo also employ this head position side-on in a "lateral display" for it emphasizes the animal's size, the heavy shoulders and broad neck being clearly visible. The head-on threat position is shown by dominants when approaching groups of immature males; the lateral position is more frequently seen among adults more equal in rank. In both cases animals will also toss their heads up and down or make hooking motions in the air with one horn or the other. The position of the head when the animal is threatening does not resemble its position when charging or in a fight and is not suggestive of imminent attack. When a buffalo charges it stretches its head out with nose forward and parallel with the body and makes a deep growling noise. Just before it clashes with its opponent, it tucks its nose in under its neck and takes the impact on the boss of horn (fig. 37). The brief moment of impact constitutes the entire fight, for in that instant the winner is determined by who has the greatest speed and weight. Immediately one animal turns and flees, chased by the other, usually for not more than a hundred meters. Although the fight is short, the considerable impact that must be produced when two animals charge at each other from thirty meters distant and collide head on demonstrates the usefulness of the heavy shield of horn on the top of the head.

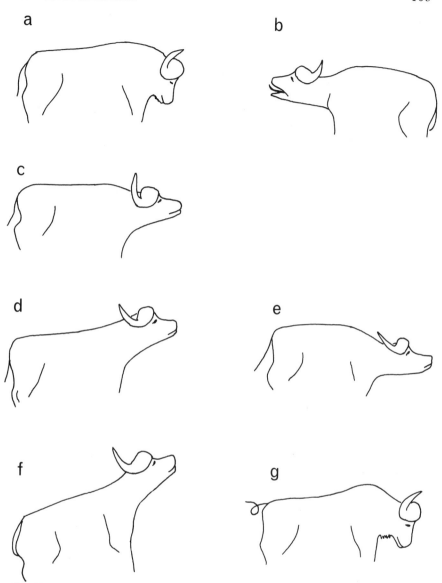

Fig. 36. Postures exhibited by buffalo: *a*, lateral threat; *b*, submissive; *c*, normal posture; *d*, alarm; *e*, suckling; *f*, intention flight after attack by conspecific; *g*, stretching.

Serious fights are very infrequent, but the preliminary threatening sequences are often seen. These bouts are initiated when a male, displaying his horns and tossing his head, approaches another which does not give way but returns the threat. The two animals, standing about twenty meters apart, will then assume a lateral display stance with much head-tossing. Often they will "circle" each other slowly for 10 or 15 min, breaking off to thrash their horns in nearby bushes or toss clods of earth into the air. Such bouts of "circling" usually end with one animal's giving up and walking away; only occasionally does a fight ensue.

Fig. 37. Mature males fighting. Note collision occurs on the bosses. Drawn from a photograph in Grzimek (1970).

Earth-tossing is clearly part of the threat display. It is most often seen when a male goes to a wallow, digs his horns into the bank, and throws clods of earth into the air. On these occasions the male also rolls in the mud, turning completely over onto his back. Then he rubs his chin and neck on the bank before horning it and may urinate into the mud. Only one male uses the wallow during this performance; the others vacate it when he arrives. Although not all these elements are displayed every time, they all appear to be parts of the threat behavior. On one occasion a bull followed this display by chasing another bull from the herd and kept him out for the rest of the day. On another occasion, M. Norton-Griffiths observed one of three old males in a bachelor group rolling in a wallow: the other two attacked the displaying male and gored him in the belly. The mud of wallows is strong-smelling, and probably this has some signal function for the dominant males that cover themselves with it. This, and its association with other displays, therefore, suggests that wallowing behavior has assumed a social function as well as any function related to temperature regulation or grooming.

In contrast to fighting, sparring by immature males and perhaps subordinate young adults is common (I have not seen dominant adults do this). The animals do not charge each other, and there appears to be very little pushing. A subadult male will initiate sparring by approaching another slowly, putting his horns down and waiting for the other to do likewise. On some occasions the initiator will rub his face and horns against the flanks of the second animal before moving round to the front. While sparring they twist their horns from side to side for several minutes (plate 17). They may break away, and one of the pair sometimes bucks and frolics in front of the other as small calves do, before the two lock horns. Sparring can occur between yearlings or between juveniles of different ages such as a yearling and a two-year old, and I have seen a calf only a few months old spar with its mother. In general the context is one of play rather than aggression.

Submission is indicated by a head position contrasting to that in threat, with head held low and parallel to the ground, horns lying flat and back sloping down to the hindquarters (fig. 36b). A submissive male in this position will actively approach a threatening male and place his nose under the belly of the dominant (fig. 38), sometimes under his neck or between his back legs. Immediately afterward the submissive male will turn and run, and at the same time emit a loud bellow. When bellowing the mouth is noticeably wide open (fig. 36b) with tongue protruding and curling up. Submissive males sometimes have their mouths open even before they have reached the dominant and are beginning to make their bellow, although at this stage it is no more than a low croak.

The actions of submissive animals resemble those of calves about to suckle (fig. 36e), especially when they place their muzzles between the hind legs of the dominant. This suggests that the posture of the subordinates and even the vocalization has developed from such suckling behavior and has assumed an appeasement function.

There is another posture adopted by a subordinate if he has been caught by surprise and horned by a nearby dominant: the subordinate runs two or three paces, making a short grunt, stops abruptly, and stands oriented away from the attacker but with head turned slightly to one side so as to watch him (fig. 36f). This stance is characterized by the nose pointing up in the air, back sloping down to the hindquarters, which are slightly bent, and the tail tucked between the legs. The position is an exaggerated form of that adopted by animals on the alert trying to scent danger with their noses in the air (fig. 36d). Since this testing of the wind usually precedes flight, it is possible that the stance adopted by the subordinate in an agonistic situation could have evolved from the alert position as a signal indicating an intention to flee if the dominant follows up his attack, with

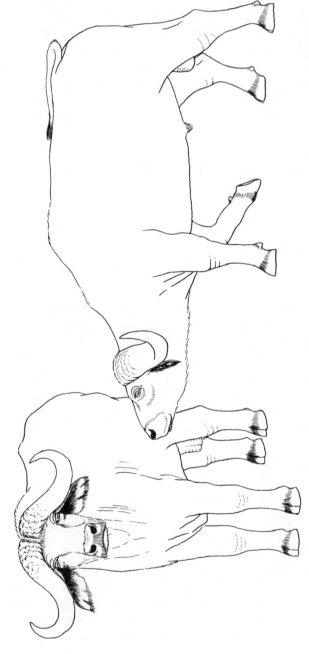

Fig. 38. A subordinate male (*right*) adopts a position with head low and outstretched when approaching a dominant male (*left*) who is displaying the lateral threat. The subordinate is about to place his muzzle under the belly of the dominant.

the exaggerated form appearing so as to emphasize the signal. Classical theories on the evolution of displays in conflict situations (Tinbergen 1964; Morris 1958) could explain the appearance of these two types of appeasement behavior in different situations.

Other Species of Bovini

The elements of agonistic behavior that can be readily identified are shown in table 6 for the nine species of Bovini. Information on the Asian water buffalo comes from Tulloch (1967) and personal observations, and that on *Bos taurus* is taken from the observations of Schloeth (1958, 1961) on Camargue feral cattle, and Hafez, Schein, and Ewbank (1969) on domestic cattle; that on banteng and kouprey comes from Wharton (1957), on gaur from Schaller (1967), on American bison (*Bison bison*) from McHugh (1958) and Lott (1974), and on wisent (*B. bonasus*) from incidental reports by the above authors, Krasinski (1967), and Krasinski and Raczynski (1967). The only information available on the yak (*Bos grunniens*) has been derived from Schaller (1976) and additional personal notes that he kindly provided.

All species in the Bovini group exhibit the head-up, nose-down presentation of horns and the lateral stance as threat displays. Water buffalo, however, have a special high-intensity threat, with the nose pointing high in the air and the head twisted slightly to the side where the opponent stands so that the backward-curling horns are visible. The head-up nose-down position appears to be a medium-intensity threat, and an animal displaying this toward an opponent displaying the nose-up position usually gives way in an encounter. Gentry (1967) has pointed out that in this species the balanced position of the head is with the nose held horizontal, whereas in the African buffalo the nose normally points toward the ground. Thus there may be a mechanical reason why water buffalo adopt the nose-high position in threat and other species cannot. In some species the lateral display is exaggerated through morphological developments in the male: bison, banteng, and more especially gaur have developed a pronounced dorsal ridge through the lengthening of the dorsal spines on the thoracic vertebrae, and this enhances the animal's apparent size; and kouprey and gaur have developed a large dewlap hanging in front of the brisket to provide the same effect. The submissive position with head down and nose horizontal is also common to all species, as are the behaviors of rubbing the head and chin on the ground, tossing earth into the air with the horns, and horning bushes.

Fighting among dominant males in species other than *Syncerus* involves a more prolonged pushing match, although an initial charge may be shown in some species, such as the American bison. None appear to have reduced the fight to this initial charge in the same way as has the *caffer* race of the African buffalo, nor have other species evolved the heavy boss. Schaller has remarked that *S. caffer* is more like sheep in this respect. It is intriguing to speculate on the form of fighting adopted by the small *nanus* race, which has almost no boss; it may well be that a pushing fight is also present in this race.

Pawing the ground with the front hooves before a fight is well known in cattle and is also present in banteng, gaur, and both bison species. Schaller remarks that he has not seen it in yak in situations when it might be expected. Water buffalo exhibit pawing only infrequently, and so far it has not been observed in the African buffalo. Equally noticeable, at least during the rut, is the bellowing or roaring made by dominant males of bison and all the cattle species. This appears to be directed at other males seen in the vicinity or in answer to other calls. Neither of the buffalo species produces any such calls in a similar context. These elements therefore make the cattle and bison groups more similar to each other than to the buffalo group.

Both bison species use areas of bare earth sometimes called wallows where the males roll in the dust or mud. This earth is often impregnated with urine and feces so that the resulting mixture sticking to the animals' coats has a strong odor. Of the American bison, Herrig and Haugen (1969) state, "Bulls urinated in a wallow while vigorously pawing the sand and then rolling, especially during the breeding season. The urine-wetted sand often stuck to their sides. Such behaviour was observed only when bulls were tending cows and being agonistic toward other bulls nearby." Similarly, McHugh (1958) writes of bison pawing a wallow, "The bull customarily moved a short distance backward with each pawing. He often unsheathed his penis and urinated a thin stream during the pawing and during and after the rolling. Such urination was quite typical of any hostile situation during the rut. The bull also dug his horns into the ground at times and rubbed his head in the earth after pawing." Wisent show similar behavior.

In the cattle group, only the yak commonly rolls in dust. Schaller tells me, "When free ranging they often have a dusty area, obviously used often before, where animals rest and take dust baths. Each animal has a scrape,, usually 25 to 50 ft from another. They defecate on the sites and horn them." Schaller also observed a large herd bull approach two dust wallows previously vacated by other bulls: he stopped, grunted, and then rubbed his face on the embankment. At the first wallow he ground his teeth, horned the ground and rolled over twice before going on to the second wallow, where he rubbed his face again. Schaller concludes, "Obviously these dust wallows have social significance." In many ways this behavior resembles that of bison and also the wildebeest in the Serengeti. Yak and bison differ from wildebeest in being nonterritorial. Wildebeest bulls set up small territories 20–30 m in diameter around each dust wallow and vigorously defend them. The wallow forms the center of the territory, and on it the animal defecates, urinates, horns the ground, and rolls. The territories are permanent (Estes 1969) in some areas or may be temporary, with the bull moving with the migratory female groups after only a day or two in one place.

Of the other cattle types, gaur occasionally roll over on dry, dusty spots, but it does not appear to be a common element of behavior. Of kouprey and banteng, Wharton (1957) noted that mud was confined to the top of the head and back, suggesting that it was thrown there by the horns. The hunters and guides accompanying him had never seen kouprey wallowing. He continues, "Muddy female kouprey were never observed, and neither male nor female banteng was seen with a mud-smeared side." Similarly Schloeth (1958) states that the Camargue cattle did not wallow either. In general, therefore, this behavior of rolling in dust or mud in an agonistic context was either absent or infrequent in the cattle group, except for the yak.

The two buffalo species, on the other hand, have taken this behavior to the other extreme. All water buffalo will wallow in deep water. Small wallows are turned into thick mud, and these are used frequently by the males. There is a tendency for dominant males to stay in the vicinity of one or two wallows and use them more often than neighboring wallows used by other males. On one occasion a group of grazing females with a large bull drifted into an area used by a lone bull. This animal immediately threatened the bull with the herd, using a lateral stance, and the two gesticulated at each other for four minutes. Without any further interaction the original bull with the herd then moved away slowly, followed closely for some thirty meters by the lone bull. Finally, the lone bull returned to the females and proceeded to test each one by sniffing the genital region. Clearly the lone bull was dominant in his own area and had priority with the females there. However, he did not exclude the other male from his area, only from consorting with the females. It appears from Tulloch (1967, 1969) that the areas adopted by lone water buffalo bulls are only temporary and that the bulls may move to join other female groups. This behavior is in contrast to that of African buffalo; these breeding bulls never become solitary during the rut and are not associated with any particular wallows, although they do use wallows in the immediate vicinity of the herd for displays of rolling and earth tossing. They will also lie in the mud, which becomes much fouled with urine and dung. Females never use these wallows. Thus immersing in deep mud appears to have a social function among males in the African buffalo and probably also in the Asian buffalo.

The circling of two bulls during the lateral display is conspicuous in African buffalo but appears not to be important in other species. It may occur in yak and gaur, is rare in cattle (V. Geist, personal communication), and is incipient in bison (Lott 1974). The submissive approach, orientation, and bellowing of African buffalo appear to be special features of this species. Water buffalo show some elements of this when two males threaten each other. The loser will move round behind the dominant, sometimes rubbing his neck on the dominant's hindquarters, at other times placing the head under the dominant's belly before moving away. However, this species does not show such an exaggerated submissive posture when approaching or make any vocalization during this performance. The only other specific behavior of note is the yak's habit of tooth-grinding as a form of threat, reported by Schaller (1976). No observations on this behavior have been reported for other species so far.

To conclude the comparison of the different behavioral elements among the species, it appears that *Bos* and *Bison* are more closely related to each other than either is to the buffalo species. The closest relative of the African buffalo would be the water buffalo, but there are large enough differences between them to suggest that evolutionary divergence was relatively early, a conclusion agreeing with the fossil evidence (Gentry 1967). Bison and cattle are very similar, showing most of the behavioral elements in table 6. One of the few differences is that bison roll in dust wallows, whereas the cattle group, except for the yak, do not. In this respect bison resemble the buffaloes. This may indicate that bison are more closely related to buffalo than are cattle. Of the cattle group, the yak may be the closest relative to bison.

The Dominance Hierarchy

So that I could investigate in greater detail the agonistic interactions between different sexes and age-groups, I differentiated the participants involved in each incident—termed an "attack" here whether it was a mild threat or a serious fight—into aggressors and recipients. As reported in Sinclair (1974e), an adult of either sex could be the aggressor, for only 2.5% of 358 interactions were initiated by immature animals, and these were all subadult males three to five years old attacking either subadults or two-year-olds.

The frequency distribution of attacks by these two groups is shown in figure 39 and compared with the number of attacks that would be expected if these adults directed their attacks randomly at other age-groups and sexes (calculated from the proportion of each age/sex class in the population). Clearly, males directed their aggression most often toward other adult males, less so but still significantly toward subadult males, only occasionally toward younger males, and never toward females. Adult females, although they showed some aggression toward two-year-old males, did so no more frequently than would be expected on a random basis, and toward subadult and adult males aggression was significantly reduced. However, against juvenile females of eighteen months and two years old attacks were considerably more frequent than expected by chance. These attacks occurred most frequently after the birth of the newborn calf and for the first few months of its life, when the penultimate offspring was still closely following the female, sometimes trying to suckle and generally getting in the way. The mothers would be constantly butting them away. In the interactions between adult females, there was a noticeable difference between those with calves and those without: single adults attacked females with calves significantly less often than expected ($p < 0.01$), but those with calves did not appear to make any distinction between other females.

From these observations it is apparent that rank hierarchies in the two sexes, if they occur, are independent of each other. In a small herd of 122 to 138 animals in Uganda, Grimsdell (1969) was able to identify a linear rank hierarchy of 14 dominant males from 96 interactions. Most of the interactions involved threats only, with very few resulting in fights and chasing. He found, as did Schloeth (1961) and

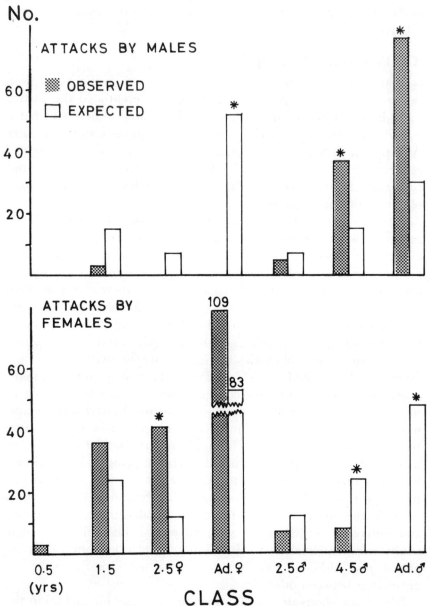

Fig. 39. The distribution of "attacks" by male and female buffalo against different age and sex classes. Shaded histogram is the observed distribution, open histogram is the expected distribution calculated from the known proportion of each class in the population.

Brantas (1968) in cattle, that overt aggression tended to be exhibited between individuals relatively far apart in rank, whereas those more equal confined their aggression to displays of threat. The rank hierarchy has also been described for American bison (McHugh 1958), and from the reports of Jaczewski (1958) it is also present in wisent. It probably occurs in water buffalo, but information is lacking for the other Bovini.

The hierarchy in African buffalo males appears to be confined to the larger adults, both size and age being important in determining rank. These males constitute 10% to 15% of the herd. In small herds, as in Uganda, the small number of individuals clearly can result in a well-defined system. The average herd size in the Serengeti is 350 animals, and many herds contain more than 1,000 individuals. This could result in more than 100 adult males being in the same herd, and the hierarchy in this situation is probably less well defined as a linear order. The subadult males and two-year-olds form groups among themselves and are subordinate to the adults. Among females Grimsdell (1969) found that although some were dominant over others, there was not enough information to show that there was a linear system. In cattle Schloeth (1961) found a linear hierarchy, but numbers (twelve females) were very small. Brantas (1968), with fifty animals, found triads within the linear system of dairy cows. So it is probable that in large herds of buffalo no linear system exists in females except perhaps within family subgroups.

The attainment of a dominant position in a hierarchy by males as opposed to females is clearly advantageous because dominant males perform most of the successful copulations (Grimsdell 1969). Similarly Schloeth (1961) observed in Camargue cattle that the two dominant bulls mated most often, as did the highest-ranking bull among the Chillingham feral cattle (Frazer 1968). But the maintenance of the hierarchy depends on the lower-ranking bulls' remaining within the herd and adopting submissive behavior toward the dominants; this suggests that there must be some advantage in staying with the herd rather than leaving to avoid the aggression of larger, dominant animals.

FAMILY RELATIONSHIPS IN THE HERD

The size of herds recorded in May 1968 in the Serengeti varied from 50 to more than 1,500 animals, and the frequency distribution of these groups is illustrated in figure 40. Many of the smaller groups were almost certainly only parts of a herd that had temporarily split up. The large herds appeared to be stable units and were not just

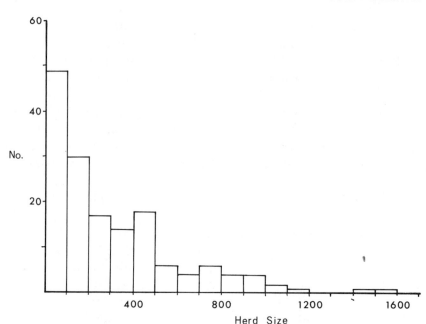

Fig. 40. The frequency distribution of herd sizes in the Serengeti population.

temporary aggregations of several herds: for example, one herd which lived on the Grumeti River near Klein's Camp and for 20 km downstream in the northeast of the park was recorded in every census from 1966 to 1973 as comprising between 1,300 and 1,750 animals. Thus such herds can maintain at least some degree of cohesion. The average herd size in the Serengeti was 350 animals, but in other parts of Africa herds become smaller as the vegetation becomes denser. On Mount Meru in montane forest, herds were about 50 animals, and in the denser lowland forests of the Congo they averaged about 20 animals (Sidney 1965).

I expect that the small herds of the forest are family groups with the individuals interrelated. However, within the larger herds there were no obvious divisions into subunits or families except the basic one of a female with a calf from the previous birth season and perhaps an older offspring of eighteen months. This is in contrast to the water buffalo herds of 30 and more in which family groups of 7 to 10 individuals can be distinguished: and such herds often break up into their basic families (Tulloch 1967). Nevertheless, in a herd of more than 100 African buffalo, Grimsdell (1969) noted that members always remained together even after mixing with and separating from adjacent herds; they were clearly able to identify their own group, perhaps through smell, even if they could not recognize each individual.

African buffalo ruminating in large herds typically rest in groups of up to 10 individuals. The animals in each group rest side by side, often lying against each other, and similar clumps form a few meters away (plate 18). A whole herd of 100 animals does not rest in one group, nor do all individuals rest alone, although a few—always adult or subadult males—may do so. At Ngurdoto Crater, where I could look down on a herd of about 300 animals, the sex and approximate age of the nearest neighbors of each resting animal were recorded. The frequency of these associations between the different sex- and age-classes (from 1,002 observations) was then compared with the expected distribution of associations obtained from the proportion of each class in the population. These results, reported in Sinclair (1974e), showed some definite groups. Juveniles less than two years old always stayed close to their mothers, more so than would be expected by chance. This was most pronounced with two-year-old females ($p < 0.001$), less so with two-year-old males ($p < 0.02$). By the time these males had become subadults (three to five years), they had left the females and were forming their own groups. They did, however, avoid the adult males, which formed their own subgroups within the herd. These adult males also associated with adult females, but only on a random basis. Females three years old and older remained together in a significant association ($p < 0.001$).

From all this emerges a picture of family cohesion that may continue into adult life among females but that ceases in males at approximately three years of age, the onset of puberty. The lack of any clear-cut subgroups within the herd apart from these associations indicates that once females reach maturity they lose contact with their mothers. Such a system is unlikely to produce a linear dominance hierarchy among females or a "herd leader" in large herds. Female leaders have been described in gaur (Schaller 1967; Ullrich 1968) and water buffalo (Tulloch 1967), the latter apparently having particular family groups leading others as well as having certain females leading each group. Leadership in dairy cattle has also been recognized in several situations (Hafez, Schein, and Ewbank 1969), and the leader is not always the most dominant female. When cattle are being forced to do something unpleasant the leader is of low rank, whereas the leaders of cattle performing voluntary movements are of high social rank (Beilharz and Mylrea 1963). Cattle also enter a milking parlor in a consistent order. This behavior could develop in small groups where all individuals know each other, as in cattle, gaur, and water buffalo, and would be unlikely to occur in large herds of African buffalo or American bison.

THE BACHELOR MALES

Although the degree to which buffalo aggregate in tightly knit herds is striking, it is equally apparent that old males and even some younger ones live away from the herd. I call these males bachelors because they do not consort with the females. The term, however, does not imply that all males in the herd are able to obtain copulations. A series of independent censuses (described in chap. 8) showed that in the wet season bachelor males made up some 5.7% of the population as a whole, which is 15% of the adult male population.

In the dry season, however, the number of bachelor males increased, owing largely to the appearance of groups of young adult males. In a small study area of 4 km² at Banagi that included an area used exclusively by bachelor males, the number of males was recorded from May 1967 until September 1969 (fig. 41a). Each dry season there was a considerable increase in the number of males, caused by the influx of young adults and some subadults. They usually formed groups of 5 or 10 animals, but the largest group of males recorded in the Serengeti contained 51 animals. Young male groups rarely mixed with the older animals, were more timid, and covered a greater range. One particular young male, identifiable by a malformed horn, was seen with a herd in the early dry season of 1969 at Moru Kopjes in the southern study area. A month later, in August, he was seen in the company of six other bachelor males, and only three weeks after that was back with the original herd. It seems that groups of young males tend to break away from herds and move farther afield during the dry season. This was supported by data from the northern study area: during monthly censuses the size of bachelor groups was recorded, and the mean size of these increased noticeably each dry season (fig. 41b), as did the total number in the area.

The timing of this movement of young adult males away from the herd coincided with the start of the dry season and with the fragmentation of the breeding herds into smaller groups (see below) as the available habitat of green riverine grassland became smaller. But it also coincided with the end of the rutting season, and the influence of these two factors could not be adequately sorted out. In the

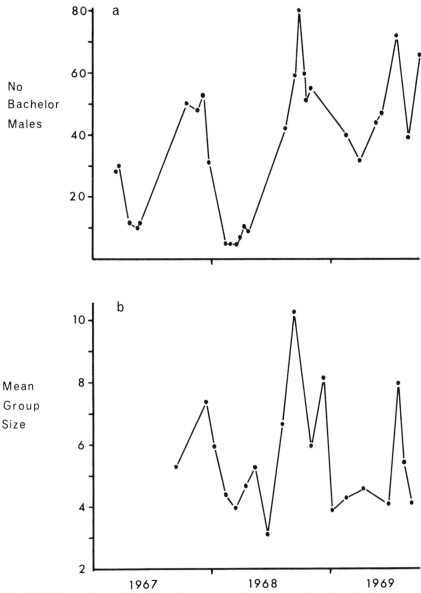

Fig. 41. The number of bachelor males (*a*) and the mean size of bachelor groups (*b*) at different seasons near Banagi. Bachelor numbers increase during each dry season. Redrawn from Sinclair (1974*e*).

somewhat smaller herds in Ruwenzori Park, Grimsdell (1969) noted that even the dominant males in the herd left for part of the dry season. When the rains started again in November, the males returned to the herd, and the first matings took place shortly afterward in December. Perhaps it would be more appropriate to suggest that the males move into the herd only during the rutting season, moving away to form their own groups when reproductive activity is at a low ebb.

This suggestion would also account for the behavior of the old males, who never return to the herds and hence cease reproduction. Grimsdell (1969) examined the testes of some old males, all of which were more than ten years old, and found a decrease in the functioning of the cells and an increase in the interstitial tissue. They were evidently showing signs of decreasing fertility. Not only were some of the males decrepit, suffering from arthritis and other difficulties, but some also showed symptoms of severe brucellosis, a disease which would ensure sterility even if old age did not. Some 20 of these old males were individually identifiable at Banagi, and during a period of three years many of them remained in a small home range of 1 km² for the whole time. Some were so familiar and constantly present that I have little doubt they did not return to a herd even for short periods. Apart from being incapable of such movements, these old animals were lighter and weaker than the dominant herd bulls and would have stood little chance of winning an encounter with one of them. I suggest, then, that as these males begin to lose their position in the dominance hierarchy from defeats in fights, they are either chased from the herd by the victors or kept on the periphery during the rutting season. As age overtakes them there is less tendency to return to the herd after each dry season, because of decline in sexual motivation and increasing difficulty of movement. Probably less harassment from dominants in their bachelor state also plays a part. One noticeable feature of these old bachelors was a very strong tendency for certain individuals to remain together and not associate with other groups.

Agonistic interactions continued among the members of each group of old males, but I never observed any between individuals of different groups, although presumably this occurred at times. Linear hierarchies were apparent within the group. Hence the grouping and behavior of these males was merely an extension of that seen in the herds. Within the very small home range of a group were a number of mud wallows which were visited most days in the wet season during the hot hours. These wallows were used only by one group, other groups of males having other ranges and wallows. No defense of an area was seen, and ranges overlapped considerably, although the overlaps did not contain wallows. Ranges of old males in the dry season always contained a small patch of green grass—the bank of a river, the edges of a spring, or a damp area where water seeped out from the base of rocks. In the wet season the bachelor males showed a tendency to spread out from permanent water to use the ephemeral pools as wallows.

On the whole, male groups differed little from the herds in terms of range and preferred habitats, as described earlier (chap. 4), and competition with herds was reduced because the bachelors chose small areas unsuitable for large herds. Certain areas of the Serengeti were favorite gathering points for bachelors, usually at a junction of rivers such as Banagi or around springs where there were patches of thicket in which to hide. Many of these places also had rangers or research camps, and there was some suggestion that buffalo were attracted to these. But more probably, human camps and buffalo tended to be in the same area because of the same need for permanent drinking water. This would be further enhanced by the fact that herds avoided human settlement, thus leaving an area where bachelor males could go without being harassed by herd bulls.

Thus the reasons old males live permanently away from the herd probably begin with the tendency for young males to leave the herds during the dry season, although always in groups. From the age determination of collected animals, males more than ten years old are not present in the Serengeti herds, and Grimsdell reports a similar situation in Uganda. Body weight declines in old age (chap. 7), beginning at approximately ten years old, and so dominant animals at this age would lose their position in the rank hierarchy and would be expelled or at least harassed. The decline in reproductive ability would also cause a reduction in the tendency to return to the herd at the start of the wet season. Finally, males live to an age of nineteen years or more, and progressive debility over this time would preclude a return. In the meantime, bachelors form their own groups and home ranges and find suitable feeding areas. Since the old animals contribute nothing to the survival of their offspring in the herds, there would be no selection for this behavior; it is merely an incidental feature resulting from the functioning of the rank hierarchy. Why then do they live so long? As I shall describe in chapter 8, although they suffer predation, some survive longer than any females. A possible cause of this could be the reduced energy expenditure discussed in chapter 5.

HERDING BEHAVIOR

Theoretical arguments for animals remaining in a closely packed group have developed along two main lines. One hypothesis suggests that herd animals avoid predation better than lone ones (Hamilton 1971). The second hypothesis suggests that animals, particularly inexperienced ones, learn essential features of their food supply by associating with others (Murton 1971). These features may vary in two ways. On the one hand, both the nature and the location of food may be highly variable. In this case experience is required to learn how to switch from one food type to the next and how to adopt a searching pattern to give an optimal rate of encounter with food. Young animals associating with any experienced adults would benefit in this situation. On the other hand, the food at difficult seasons may be reduced to a few permanent patches in a given home range, and animals must know the location of these at times of food shortage. In this case young animals must associate not only with adults, but the *same group* of adults over a period of time to learn this information.

However, the closer animals stay together and the larger the group, the more limited are the types of food they may eat. A large herd cannot be highly selective for scattered types of plants, for they would have to walk at an impossible rate to obtain enough food. Thus herding behavior is possible only if the food is locally abundant; and the degree of abundance could be critical. Even a slight decline could mean the difference between a maintenance and a submaintenance rate of intake. If food abundance declines in the last available habitats, the animals may respond in two ways: the herds may split up into smaller units, or individuals may space out from their neighbors. The following sections will examine these hypotheses.

Antipredator Behavior

The ages of buffalo killed by lions were determined from tooth measurements (see chap. 7). Since animals less than a year old were underrepresented, I considered only those older than one year. These records, combined with those of George Schaller (personal communication), produced a sample of 75 animals. In order to see whether lions killed buffalo of different ages in the same proportions as they died from other causes, I compared in table 7 the frequency distribution of the ages of killed animals with an expected distribution derived from life table data (tables 31 and 33). These expected distributions result from all causes of mortality combined. With the Kolmogorov-Smirnov test (Siegel 1956), the two distributions did not differ significantly.

Second, I examined whether lions were selecting particular age-groups from the population or merely taking them in proportion to their abundance. To do this I compared the kill data with the expected distribution from the live population (fig. 42, table 7). In males the two distributions differed significantly ($p < 0.01$), but no significant difference was found for the female distributions. Consequently, for males it appears that lions were selecting for old adults. They were not taking animals randomly from the live population of males. The peak of predation on males occurred between the ages of ten and thirteen years, the period when males normally leave the herd altogether and join the small groups of bachelor males. This suggests that younger age-groups are protected from predators in some way, perhaps by their remaining in the herd. Furthermore, females, which remain in the herd throughout life, do not suffer their main predation after ten years of age. The male and female kill distributions differed significantly ($p < 0.05$). In fact, it appears that lions killed age-groups of females in the same proportion as they occurred in the live population, and so were not selective. This evidence therefore supports the hypothesis that predators act selectively against animals not in herds. Young males experiencing such predator selection would have evolved the behavior of remaining with the herd as long as possible, and in order to do this they have to conform to the rank hierarchy. However, with old males this selection would have no effect since they are no longer reproducing or contributing to the survival of their offspring, and so there is no selection pressure to stop them from leaving the herd. Perhaps by staying in the herd they might even attract predators and so decrease the survival chances of their progeny.

Predation on the wildebeest was similar. Schaller (personal communication) collected 203 skulls of animals killed by lions. Approximate ages were determined by tooth wear, and the numbers in each age-class are shown in figure 43 and table 8, together with the numbers expected if lions had killed animals in the same proportions as in the living population. In the field there appeared to be no obvious

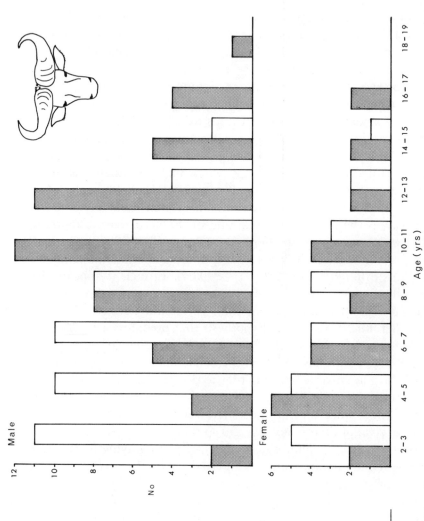

Fig. 42. The frequency distribution of ages of buffalo killed by lion in the Serengeti (*shaded histogram*) com- pared with the expected distribution based upon the pro- portion of each age-group in the living population.

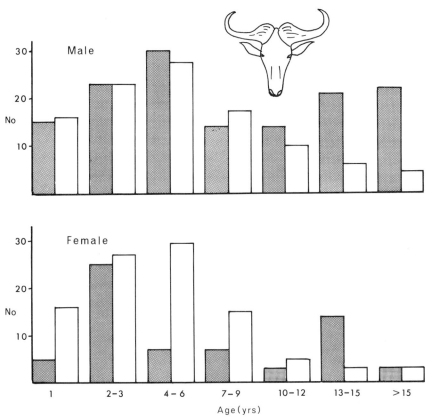

Fig. 43. The frequency distribution of ages of wildebeest killed by lion in the Serengeti (*shaded histogram*) compared with the expected distribution based upon the proportion of each age-group in the live population. Kill data from G. B. Schaller (personal communication).

bias in favor of either sex's being recorded as a lion kill. Since the sex ratio of adults in the living population was equal (measured from random ground transects run through the population when they were gathered on the plains in the wet season) one would expect an equal sex ratio of kills as a null hypothesis. From this argument lions killed significantly more male wildebeest than females ($p < 0.001$).

Male wildebeest are much less inclined to form herds, and after the age of four they become territorial for six months of the year. However, males also spend considerable time and energy fighting each other and rounding up females, so that they are less on the alert than females. Hence a higher predation rate in males may have resulted from a combination of factors including their more solitary existence. Both sexes suffered a higher predation rate than expected in old age, this being pronounced in old females, while the younger females were killed less often than expected. Younger males suffered the predation rate that would be expected if lions chose at random, but older males suffered an increasingly higher rate after they were about ten years old, when they were less likely to join large herds.

The data from buffalo and wildebeest predation rates, therefore, supports the suggestion that living in herds gives some protection from predators. Other studies also produce circumstantial evidence to support this: Hornocker (1970) found that mountain lions killed more solitary male elk and deer than herding females. Wright (1960), Mitchell, Skenton, and Uys, (1965) and Pienaar (1969) have all found that lions killed more ungulate males, including buffalo, than females. Estes (1976) has found that wildebeest calves living in large herds have a higher survival rate than those living in small herds, the main cause of death being hyena predation.

Although merely being in a herd may afford protection, buffalo also exhibit special behavior which appears to act as a defense. When separated from their mothers, calves make a long distress call, and older animals including adults make a short croaking call when separated from a herd. To investigate the response of a herd to the calf distress call, a tape-recording of it was made in the Serengeti, then played to a herd at Lake Manyara, where the animals are less timid. I played the call from downwind with the herd of 300 animals some 200 m away. Upon hearing the call they orientated to the direction from which it was coming, and after pausing for about 2 min, began to walk slowly toward the noise. The herd was compact, forming a phalanx some 50 m wide. Many of them made the same deep croaking call that a mother makes to her calf, or an adult makes when joining a herd; and both sexes made this noise. The herd moved through the bushes where the recording was being played initially, then surrounded the tree where it was played later; the extent of the response was quite unexpected in this first trial. An old solitary male also joined the herd, making the same croaking call. When the recording was switched off the herd ceased croaking, and after about 30 sec stampeded away. The recording was played again, and the herd returned. Two more trials were conducted on this herd and two on another herd, all producing the same response. A recording of a human talking was also used as a control to test whether the buffalo were responding to any noise being played. The only response on these occasions was that a few animals became alert, but none approached the noise.

Schaller (1972) has recounted incidents in which herd animals have attacked lions after one of the herd had been killed. He reports, "On one occasion, we came on four lionesses and a male lion in an acacia tree with about 200 milling buffalo below it. The lions had killed the buffalo, but they were unable to descend and eat until evening when the herd finally departed." On this occasion the victim was not so lucky, but Schaller mentions some attacks which fail because of the behavior of the herd: "A lioness first straddled a cow buffalo but then was thrown off and gored while attempting to hold on to the animal's neck with her forepaws. At that moment several bull buffalo attacked and drove the lioness and two others away" (Schaller 1972, p. 262). At Lake Manyara a lioness with three small cubs was attacked by a herd. The mother and two cubs managed to climb a tree, but the third was trampled to death (Schaller 1972). Grimsdell (1969) and Mitchell, Skenton, and Uys (1965) have also described herd members defending others from predators.

Hyenas (plate 20) are a much less formidable predator than lions but still present a threat to newborn calves. Kruuk (1972) writes: "I once saw a herd of buffalo walking slowly across an open plain come across two hyenas. The hyenas avoided the buffalo at about 15 m distance, but even so, two cows (one with a calf) charged at them with their heads low." As mentioned earlier, newborn calves of other herding ungulates, such as wildebeest, are extremely precocious and within a few hours can easily keep up with a herd of running adults. But buffalo are several weeks old before they can keep up with the herd. Clearly the calves are more vulnerable than those of many other species and so there would be a greater need for the adults to protect them more actively.

However, once the young buffalo have reached the age of two years they are capable of fending off packs of hyenas. One early morning in February 1967 I observed the following incident (see plate 21) during an exercise to immobilize an animal:

> A young male about 2 to 3 years old was cut out of the running herd with the Land Rover. When he was safely running alone a dart was fired into his rump to immobilize him for marking. The animal continued to run for the next 10 min, showing no sign that the drug was taking effect. We had dropped behind a little to load up for another shot when we noticed a group of hyenas converging on him and beginning to chase. I decided to watch what would happen. He was becoming tired and they caught up with him easily. He moved into some open woodland, and after about half a mile

stopped beside a fallen tree. The hyenas, eleven of them by now, surrounded him and tried to get hold of him at the rear. The buffalo, however, stood with his hind legs against the fallen tree. Although the tree was only about 18 in (35 cm) high, the hyenas found it difficult to climb over this obstacle to get at him. Nevertheless one did hold onto his hindquarters for a few seconds, but lost its grip and was thrown off when the buffalo whirled round. On several occasions the bull made short charges and one or two hyenas were tossed into the air. After 10 min the hyenas began to stand around a few yards off. The buffalo lay down, obviously exhausted. The hyenas moved in again, but he stood up and that was enough to deter them. After that they began to drift away and the bull lay down again.

In Ngorongoro Kruuk (1972) found no less than 69 hyenas feeding on the carcass of an old bull, and he thought they may have killed him. However, apart from unusual occasions like this, hyena probably do not kill adult buffalo. Very old males have occasionally been noted to show almost no resistance to predators. Schaller (1972) also observed this when lions attacked an old bull.

This evidence so far suggests that buffalo behave as a group to protect other members in distress. How did this behavior evolve? One suggestion is that it has developed through kin selection (Maynard-Smith 1964; Eberhard 1975), because the herds are discrete units with little exchange of individuals. However, Wilson (1975) states that this selection operates most effectively on groups of fewer than 100 animals, whereas buffalo herds, including the one I tested, are often much larger than this. It might suggest that interdemic selection is playing a part. Before accepting this, one should make sure that this group protection is purely altruistic and does not confer some individual advantage. For example, it may be advantageous to each individual to approach a predator to learn of its whereabouts and so prevent a surprise attack. This may be similar to the mobbing behavior of birds. Alternatively, most calves in a herd will be the direct offspring of one or two bulls, and it may be beneficial for these bulls to protect a calf in distress, since it is likely to be their own. Other animals may follow the bulls as a result of group cohesion.

Home Range

I have used the term "home range" in the sense employed by Jewell (1966), who defined it as "the area over which an animal normally travels in pursuit of its routine activities." A range was identified simply by drawing a line around all the points on a map where a known herd had been observed. Since herds traversed all areas within a range even if they did not utilize them equally, this method of identifying a home range seemed the most satisfactory. Initial studies on the movements and range of herds began in 1966. Herd members were immobilized and marked with ear tags (drugs used were initially succinylcholine chloride, which was unsuitable, and later etorphine hydrochloride (M.99)—4 mg mixed with 30 mg acetylpromazine per animal, which was satisfactory). Ear tags, however, were hard to see in large groups of animals, and I soon found that the animals had to be visible from aircraft in the wet season when they were inaccessible on the ground. Hence I placed collars in bright white, yellow, or red combinations (plate 22) on the animals, and these were visible from the air. Males shed the collars within a day, presumably by catching them on tree stumps, but females kept them on for 6 to 9 months. Females in one herd that lived around the Moru Kopjes and Lake Magadi in the southern study area were identified for a period of 20 months, and a marked animal in the adjacent herd in the Nyaraboro Hills immediately to the west was followed for some 12 months.

The effect of the collars on the behavior of the animals wearing them did not appear to be great, provided they were shepherded back to their own herd. However, on two occasions marked animals, while still partly drugged, wandered out of their normal range and joined another herd. Once a Moru animal joined the herd in the Nyaraboro Hills. The second animal at Seronera, wearing a radio transmitter and still very much sedated, wandered 15 km from its original group before meeting another group to which it attached itself. Those animals that were carefully coaxed back to their own groups were accepted fully and could be found on later occasions intermixing with the rest of the herd. However, the two that joined other herds were conspicuous because they always remained on the outside of the herd and were often attacked by other members. Perhaps it was not surprising, therefore, that one animal was eaten by lions three months later. Whether this was caused by its peripheral position, or because it was more conspicuous with a radio collar (these were brown), or perhaps because of more subtle effects such as debilitation from disturbed grazing and constant chivying remains unknown.

The observations on the Moru herd are summarized in figure 44a, details of which are given in Sinclair (1974e) for the cumulated sight-

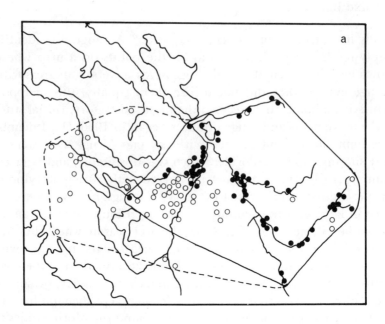

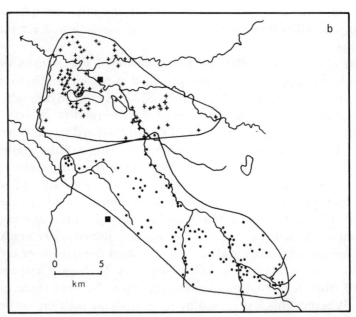

Fig. 44. Home ranges of buffalo herds: *a*, one herd at Moru Kopjes showing dry-season range *(solid line)*, which is included in the wet-season range *(broken line)*; *b*, annual range of two adjacent herds at Banagi and Seronera. Note the very small overlap in the two ranges.

ings of the herd over three years. As would be expected, the herd
remained close to the rivers in the dry season and wandered farther
afield during the rains. Nevertheless, there appeared to be a well-
defined area in which the herd remained. Since this herd lived on
the edge of the plains there were no other herds to the north, east,
or south of it, and only the Nyaraboro herd to the west. Observations
on this adjacent herd, although somewhat scanty, showed that in the
dry season there was very little overlap in the ranges of the two
herds. In the wet season, however, there was an overlap of approximately 42% for both herds, since their ranges were nearly equal in
size.

The searching time for visual markers was relatively high even
with aircraft, since it was necessary to find all herds and scrutinize
them carefully. This led me in 1971 to the use of radio transmitters,
with the help of Brian Bertram and Jack Inglis (plate 23).

> Two transmitters supplied by W. G. Cochran were attached to col-
> lars made of machine belting together with two sets of batteries
> (Mallory ZM12 in the first collar and TR232 in the second) and
> diodes, in case one set failed. The apparatus was then embedded in
> dental acrylic. The 30 cm antenna which lay against the outside of
> the collar was initally also embedded in acrylic. The weight of the
> acrylic, transmitter, and batteries was approximately 1.5 kg. This
> protection enabled the transmitter to continue operating after the
> first animal was killed by predators and even the belting was eaten.
> In the second collar the antenna was left exposed but was riveted
> to the belting. Range from the ground was approximately 3 km and
> from the air 15 km. The life of the first transmitter was 15 months,
> and the second was still operating after 13 months in August 1973
> when the study finished. Location was usually carried out from
> aircraft. The antenna system constructed by J. M. Inglis consisted
> of two yagis mounted pointing forward on the struts of the plane.
> They were connected to the receiver in such a way that a "null"
> was produced when receiving the signal from directly in front, with
> maximum signal coming either side of the null. This allowed
> greater directional accuracy and more efficient tracking. It was de-
> signed primarily for the tracking of long-distance movements of
> wildebeest by Jack Inglis and myself and was used for convenience
> with the buffalo on the same occasions.

An adult female in a herd to the east of Seronera was followed
from January to September 1972. After the range of this herd was

identified, a transmitter was placed on a female in the adjacent herd to the northwest at Banagi Hill in August 1972. Both herds were followed for a month until the first ceased transmitting. The second was followed for a complete year. As with the Moru herd, animals stayed closer to the rivers in the dry season. However, when all locations for both wet and dry seasons were plotted for the two herds (figure 44b), I found that in effect no overlap occurred in the ranges and that there appeared to be a boundary between them. This therefore differed from the earlier findings in which an overlap was seen in the wet season but not in the dry season. The later, more detailed work therefore suggests that these home ranges are mutually exclusive for each herd, and that only rare accidents of local rainfall cause transgressions.

Both the Seronera and Banagi herds, as well as the Moru herd, showed a preference for a certain small area within their home ranges, as judged from the concentration of observations. In the case of the Seronera herd this concentration centered on a small *Cyperus laevigatus* swamp, but they very rarely went into the swamp itself. The Banagi female preferred the slopes on the western end of Banagi Hill, whereas the Moru animals were found in stands of *Acacia seyal*, a tree with long thorns that could provide protection for the animals.

The size of herds in which the marked animals were found was estimated by eye or determined from photographs. The Banagi herd reached a maximum of around 800 animals, but such aggregations occurred rarely and only in the wet season. More frequently the animal with the transmitter was found in a smaller group. The mean size of group appeared to be related to certain localities. For example the mean group size in the most frequented area between Banagi Hill and the Orangi River to the north of the hill was 200, but in the area north of this river the mean group size was only 90 animals. Immediately south of the preferred area mean group size increased to 322, and to the east of the hill it was 428. Hence there was a gradient from small groups in the northwest, which occurred frequently, to very large groups in the east, which occurred only rarely. This may throw some light on the infrastructure of large herds; one possibility is that a large herd could be made up of subgroups of about 100 to 200 animals, each of which prefers certain parts of the complete range. Occasionally they may join other subgroups and move into other parts of their range. The farther they move, the more subgroups join in. This hypothesis explains why the marked female was always seen in large groups when she was farthest from her preferred area. It also explains why she was sometimes found in large groups in any part of the home range including her preferred area, because other groups had occasionally come over to join her group.

It seems therefore that a "herd" is a real entity in which the members can identify others as being of the same herd. How this is done remains unknown, but it probably involves smell. This "herd" is made up of subgroups, each of which has a "preferred" area that overlaps areas used by other groups. The combined areas of the subgroups then form the "home range" of the herd. Young animals in each subgroup first learn to identify other subgroups and their ranges through association with their mothers and thereafter reinforce this experience by remaining with the same group.

The present evidence indicates that the boundary of the "home range" is rarely transgressed but I have little idea how this comes about. No sign of aggression has been seen between herds. Even when herds have joined for a few hours, as observed by Grimsdell (1969) in Uganda, there was no aggression; yet both herds parted as they joined. At present I can only suggest that herds avoid areas unfamiliar to them or perhaps those containing smells of strange buffalo. Buffalo tend to defecate after a rest period, leaving behind dung that even humans can smell from a distance, and this could act as "signposts" for other buffalo. The fact that wallows contaminated by urine and feces are obviously used by males in agonistic displays suggests that the smell of dung or urine may act as a signal.

Why are buffalo ranges the size they are, and not smaller or larger? Why also is there such an apparently pronounced boundary with little overlap between herds? In other words, what are the evolutionary and behavioral functions of these phenomena? There is little evidence that the limits of a range are the maximum that animals can physically cover or learn: an individual wildebeest—comparable in size and physiology—has an annual range considerably larger than buffalo, as is shown in figure 45. One suggestion is that the difference between the two species lies in the nature of their food and its distribution. The preferred food of the wildebeest is short green grass, which changes geographically with season—the plains in the wet season, the western and northern areas with the green regrowth after burning and rainstorms in the dry season. But the buffalo prefers isolated pockets or thin strips of riverine grass, which are less in-

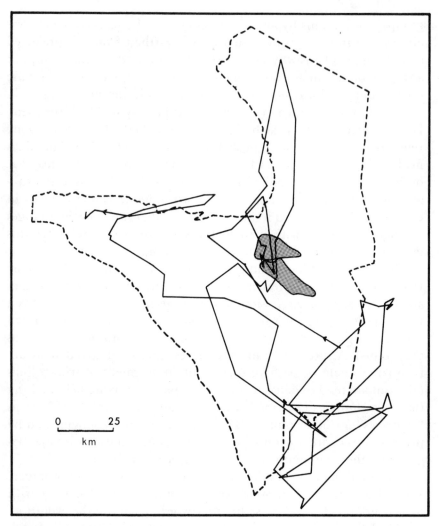

Fig. 45. The annual home range of a wildebeest female as indicated by its track, compared with the two buffalo herd ranges (*shaded*) shown in detail in figure 44*b*. Wildebeest data partly from J. M. Inglis (personal communication).

fluenced by accidents of rainfall. Whereas wildebeest can search for their food source by moving toward rainstorms, buffalo cannot. If the latter were to search for small pockets of food and water in the dry season by random movements and without prior knowledge of their location, the food supply would not be utilized efficiently; by chance some areas would be used by too many herds (to the detriment of those herds), while other areas would be missed. Consequently, random movements in search of other food patches merely exchange, at an energy cost, one area for another of equal value—or possibly worse if it is already occupied. In other words, the animals do better to stay in the same place, the home range.

When would this strategy of staying in the same place not occur? If patches of food were of unequal value and if the animals had a greater than even chance of finding a better patch by moving, then the strategy of moving should be adopted. In fact, this is the strategy exhibited by the migrating wildebeest. For this species the best patches of food in the dry season are formed immediately after a local rainstorm covering perhaps 10 km². There are poorer patches that have dried out and yet others that have been grazed. Hence there is a mosaic of good and poor patches that change in time and location. Any patch on which a wildebeest finds itself is deteriorating due to grazing by other members. By moving toward rainstorms the animal improves its nutritional intake substantially for a relatively small energy expenditure.

Answers to the question of why there is little or no overlap in home range must lie in the disadvantage of meeting other herds or using their range. Although there is no apparent aggression between herds, it was seen that marked animals that wandered out of their normal range and joined the wrong herd were not accepted and hence lost the possible protection that herds afford. Furthermore, they were presumably in an unfamiliar range with little knowledge of the location of essential resources. Reduction of overlap would reduce the chances of animals joining the wrong herd and becoming lost.

These hypotheses on the function of remaining within a discrete home range depend upon food and other resources being in short supply for a part of the year. If this is so one might expect the density of animals within each range to be correlated with the food supply. In chapter 3 (fig. 12) I have shown that food productivity is correlated with rainfall; so here I have used rainfall as an index of the food supply. The area of each home range, the number of buffalo within it, and the density are shown in table 9, for those ranges where information was available: besides the two in the southern study area, and the Banagi and Seronera areas, there were two in the northern study area identified largely by characteristic herd sizes. Grimsdell (1969) studied one in Uganda, and Vesey-Fitzgerald (personal communication) made detailed observations on a herd that lived between the two lakes at Momella near Mount Meru in Tanzania. In Tsavo, Kenya, Leuthold (1972) observed the movements of a herd for a few weeks only, and so the range there is almost certainly underestimated. Using this information, the density when plotted against mean annual rainfall for the area (fig. 46) shows a good positive relationship, even though the density for Tsavo is probably too high. This indicates that the number of buffalo in a range is related in some way to the amount of food within it, evidence that supports the hypothesis that home range behavior functions to optimize the location and use of limited food resources.

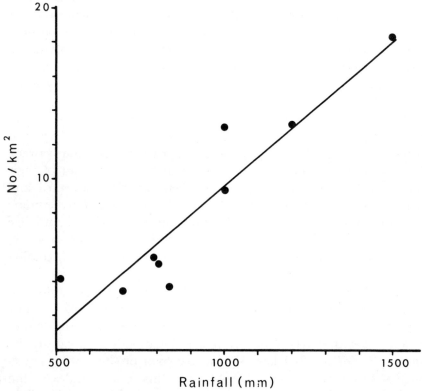

Fig. 46. The density of buffalo within the home range in different areas of East Africa is highly correlated with mean annual rainfall.

The area of a home range is highly variable. In general buffalo in the wetter regions have small home ranges and those in drier areas have large ranges. This relationship between rainfall and area may, however, be only an incidental result of the fact that herds are smaller in forested habitats in spite of high density.

If the herd is made up of subgroups that meet only occasionally, then as the herd gets larger, groups at each end of the range will meet less and less frequently until they drift apart to form different herds. This could explain how two herds and ranges develop with population increase and how the species might extend its distribution. One change in home range was observed during the study: a large herd in the northern study area included about 1,100 animals between 1967 and 1970. In 1971, however, about half of this herd began to use the northern end of the original range more and more often, and by 1972 they had become permanent residents of this area.

Seasonal Splitting in Herds

So far I have described observations indicating that herds sometimes split up into subgroups. Monthly censuses in the northern areas reveal that the splitting up has a seasonal regularity (fig. 47). During the wet season, animals lived in large groups but split up into smaller

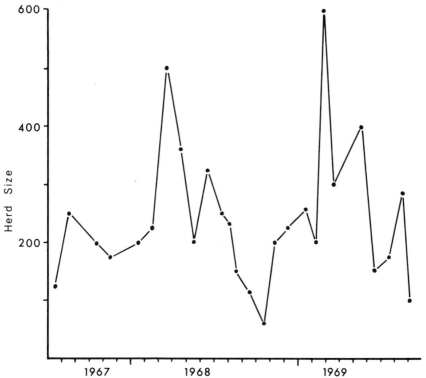

Fig. 47. The mean herd size in the northern study area reaches a peak in each wet season and a trough in each dry season. Redrawn from Sinclair (1974e).

groups during the dry season. These changes coincided with the movements of the younger bachelor males away from the herd. Since these males formed their own subgroups within a herd they were able to break away as cohesive units when the herd split up. Conversely, they returned to the herds at the start of the wet season, when the herds regrouped and the rut started.

There could be several reasons for these changes in herd size. First, splitting could be caused by a fragmentation of the preferred habitats into pockets too small for a large herd to use as one unit. Second, the rut may induce herds to form large groups in the wet season and when it ceases they may split up. Third, predation on the newborn may encourage groups to aggregate in the wet season as an antipredator mechanism. In the dry season the young may have grown large enough to reduce the importance of predation, thus allowing the herds to split up. However, survival of newborn calves as indicated by their proportion in the herds in May, during the peak of births, does not appear to be related to herd size (fig. 48), suggesting that predation may not be an important factor influencing herd size.

With respect to the influence of the rut, although some conceptions take place in December, most occur toward the end of the wet season between April and June (chap. 7), indicating that rutting activity in males does not become very prominent until that time (fig. 34). So although reproductive behavior may play a part in the aggregation of herds in the rains and their subsequent splitting up in the dry season, it is likely that the first alternative—changes in the distribution of food resources—also plays a part.

Herd Spacing

If herds avoid each other by forming discrete home ranges with little overlap, I would expect to find herds more spaced out than if they had been randomly distributed over the area with no interaction between them. The distribution of all groups of buffalo other than the bachelor males recorded during the wet- and dry-season surveys of 1968 were plotted on a map and distances to nearest neighboring herds of different sizes were measured. The frequency distribution of these distances was compared with the expected frequency distribution if the same number of herds had been randomly spaced in the same area using the formula of J. M. Cullen given in Patterson (1965). Figure 49 shows how the larger herds were distributed in the park area. During the wet season, when the whole area was suitable

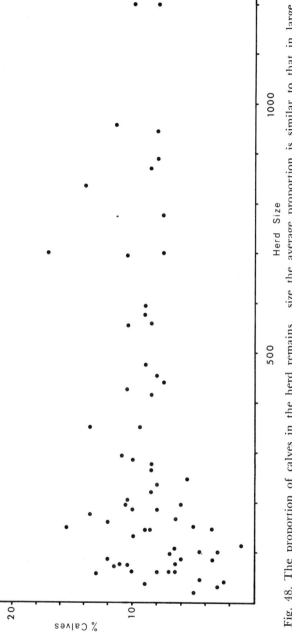

Fig. 48. The proportion of calves in the herd remains constant for different herd sizes above 200. Below this size the average proportion is similar to that in large herds but there is greater scatter. Data for May 1968.

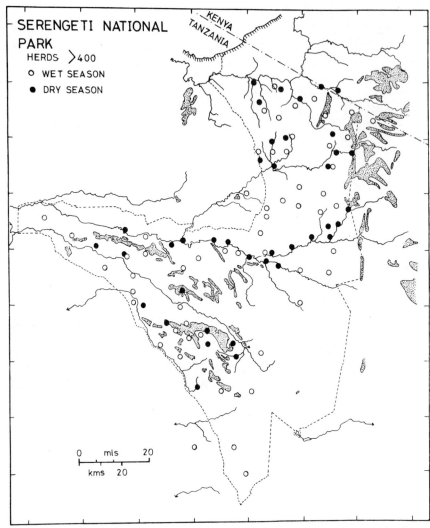

Fig. 49. The distribution of the larger buffalo herds (more than 400 animals) in 1968. The herds are spread over a larger area in the wet season (*open circles*) than in the dry season (*solid circles*).

for buffalo, the herds were spaced more evenly over the park, but in the dry season they concentrated along the rivers.

The northern half of the park was used in the first analysis because it was a relatively uniform area with no hills to disrupt the pattern of spacing. Taking all groups which could be reasonably distinguished as distinct herds—those larger than 400 animals—their frequency distribution of spacings (fig. 50*a, b*) was found to be signifi-

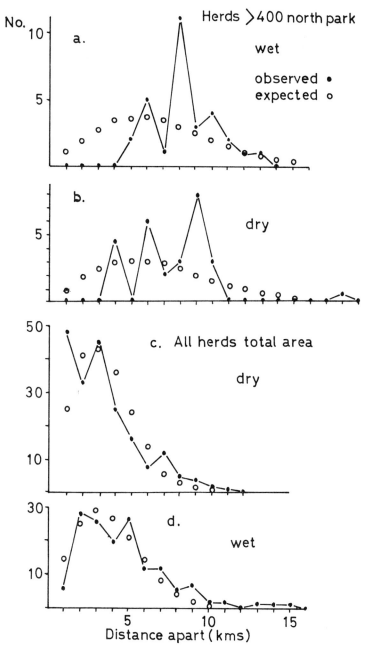

Fig. 50. The observed frequency distribution of nearest neighbor herd distances (*solid circles*) compared with an expected distribution from randomly spaced herds (*open circles*): a and b, for large herds, c and d, for herds of all sizes.

cantly more uniform (at about 8 km apart) than would be expected from a random distribution of these herds, in both seasons of the year ($p < 0.05$, Kolmogorov-Smirnov test; Siegel 1956). Thus, despite changes in seasons and habitats, the uniform spacing persisted, although it was somewhat more linear along the rivers in the dry season.

I have considered only larger herds here because some of the smaller ones are merely splinter groups from larger herds, and their inclusion confounds spacing patterns. Thus when all groups of any size are considered (fig. 50c, d), their frequency distribution of spacing does not differ from a random spacing of the same number in the same area. Since the observed spacing out of larger herds was not due to the mere distribution of suitable habitats in the wet season, it could have resulted from the home range behavior; at least it satisfies the predicted result of such behavior.

The Spacing of Individuals within Herds

In conjunction with J. M. Cullen, I used vertical aerial photographs to analyze the spacing of individuals within a herd. The laborious process of measuring the position of each animal and the direction it was facing was facilitated by the use of an automatic plotting machine (locally named "the mad monster") housed in the nuclear physics laboratory. This machine was normally used for plotting the tracks of particles in bubble chambers.

> An enlarged photograph was fixed to the plotting table and the cursor was then placed over each animal in turn. Each position of the cursor was then determined electromechanically and recorded automatically on punched tape. For each animal the position of head and tail was recorded, and from this was calculated the direction the animal was facing. Also calculated were the distances (in units of animal lengths) to the nearest neighbor of each class, these being adults or calves in high-level photographs and females, males, and subadult males in low-level photographs. The bearing of the nearest neighbor with respect to the facing direction of the reference animal was also calculated. Thus frequency distributions of nearest-neighbor spacings and their bearings were compiled. The frequency distribution of spacings was then compared (Kolmogorov-Smirnov test; Siegel 1956) with a possible expected distribution that would have occurred if the same number of animals had been randomly spaced out in the same area. This expected distribution was

calculated in the same way as for herd spacing above, using Cullen's formula as given in Patterson (1965).

High-level photographs were of herds grazing in the morning, and only adults and calves could be distinguished on the prints. The frequency distribution of nearest-neighbor spacings was calculated for adults in five separate herds. In all five the distribution had a higher than expected number of long distances between nearest neighbors, and an example of one such distribution of 153 adults is shown in figure 51a. In all five herds the observed distributions were signifi-

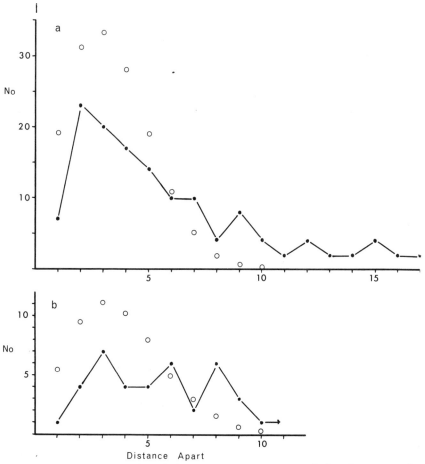

Fig. 51. The observed (*solid circles*) and expected (*open circles*) frequency distribution of distances apart (in animal lengths) of nearest neighbors within a herd: *a*, adults in a grazing herd, *b*, males in a compact running herd.

cantly different from the expected ($p < 0.01$). The mean nearest-neighbor distances, their standard deviations, and the mean bearings of nearest neighbors to each animal are given in table 10. These figures indicate that the animals are overdispersed, implying that there is a heterogeneity in the groupings of adults, with some animals being closer together than others and some scattered. For convenience, distances were measured in terms of animal lengths; since an average animal was approximately 2 m long, one can see that there were a few animals between 30 and 40 m away from any other.

Since calves stay close to their mothers when grazing, analysis of the spacings between them reflects the spacings of females with young. The same type of distribution of spacings was found as when all adults were considered. This suggests that females with young calves in a herd do not group together for protection when grazing, as do wildebeest, but rather appear to be dispersed among the others. For the analysis of other classes of animals, low-level photographs were used. Because the airplane flew low, the animals were disturbed, bunched together and running. The spacings between females, and similarly between males and subadult males under these conditions, again showed frequency distributions that indicated overdispersion. The distribution of spacings between males, for example, is shown in figure 51b. Hence all age- or sex-classes appear to show the same pattern—some in close groups and others spread apart. There is little evidence of any sort of uniformity of spacing between individuals within the herd. However, mean distances between individuals were greater than expected from a random distribution. More than one factor may have determined the spacing between individuals, and the combination of these could have produced the large variability in spacings.

Finally I examined the position of the neighbor nearest each reference animal. In the absence of any other information I expected that neighbors should be found with equal frequency in front, at the back, or at any angle to the side of an animal. Bearings to either side of the reference animal were lumped together, so that the distribution of bearings of nearest neighbors lay between 0° and 180° from in front of the animal. The distributions were grouped into nine equal segments of 20° (table 11). Calculating for each of five grazing herds the proportion of bearings that fall in each segment and then taking the mean of these over all herds, there is very little difference in these proportions from the expected 11.1% per segment.

In conclusion, therefore, it appears that although certain patterns of spacing of individuals within herds do appear, there is no consistency in the type of pattern adopted. There is little to suggest the type of pattern that had been reported for grazing sheep (Crofton 1958), where neighbors tend to be at about a 55° angle in front. Probably these patterns are related to specific situations, and until these are studied in much greater detail few generalizations can be made. Of these, one can perhaps say that adults are overdispersed within a herd—in other words, some animals form groups while others are scattered singly. Furthermore, females with calves show the same overdispersion and do not gather into maternity groups like wildebeest. Little can be said on the cause of the overdispersion—it may be due to family groups, some with many females, others just a mother and her calf, or it may be due to the mosaic of vegetation on which the animals were feeding. However, in the running herd this same overdispersion occurs, suggesting that some social grouping is playing a part.

Discussion and Conclusion

The evolution of social behavior in bovids has been discussed by Jarman (1974), Estes (1974), and Geist (1974b). These authors have all noted the general correlation between ecological parameters and the type of social organization a species exhibits. Thus Estes (1974) states that in African bovids, species living in closed habitats are generally solitary, small, and sedentary, and they hide from danger. Open-country species are mostly gregarious, medium to large in size, and mobile, and they run from danger. Jarman (1974) goes into these aspects in some detail. He points out that there is a correlation between body size and several ecological and behavioral characters such as food type and dispersion, feeding methods, the size of groups formed by each species, and methods of avoiding predators. Geist (1974b) expands on this theme, suggesting sixteen ways in which ecological parameters could explain the behavior and social organization of ungulates.

There is a problem, however, in deciding from these sets of correlations between ecology and behavior what selection pressures actually determine a specific character such as body size in a particular species. Most of the above variables are interrelated, and there is a danger of circularity in the argument. Thus one hypothesis could be that interspecific competition leads species to select certain types of

food, which in turn determine body size and hence social groupings
and antipredator behavior. However, it is just as easy to argue the
other way and suppose that predation has caused some species (e.g.,
buffalo) to become very large to outgrow the predator while others
such as dik-dik (*Madoqua kirki*) have become very small and thus
fall below the normal prey size of predators like lions. Body size so
determined results in certain food preferences and social organization. In other words, this same result can be obtained through two
different processes. At present it remains a matter of opinion whether
predation, competition, or some other factor is most important as a
selection pressure determining social behavior. The general hypotheses can only say that both predation and competition are important, but to an unknown extent. It seems reasonable to suggest
that for some species predation is the major selection pressure and
that all other ecological and behavioral correlates result from this,
whereas for other species competition is the most important. Therefore, when discussing which selection pressure is influencing which
behavior pattern, we must consider each species separately.

In this instance I ask: What are the selection pressures that produce the various elements of social organization of African buffalo?
To what extent are these elements produced by individual selection,
kin selection, intergroup selection, or merely chance events? First I
examine the agonistic interactions between individuals, and the resulting dominance hierarchy. This hierarchy is strongly developed in
males but not in females; and males, at the top of the hierarchy obtain most matings, a clear indication of sexual selection acting on the
individual. Equally, there is no need for females to have such a system, since all appear to have the same probability of mating.

Why, however, do the subordinate males stay in the herd and for-
feit their right to mate instead of adopting another system such as
setting up territories and taking females with them as do wildebeest?
First, females tend to form a few large herds rather than many small
ones, so that the males must go where the females are; second, by remaining in the herd subordinates may achieve an occasional mating,
whereas they obtain none by leaving; and third, there is a disadvantage from predation if males leave the herd when too young. After
the age of ten years males become progressively infertile, so that there
is less selective advantage in a behavior that keeps them in the herd;
these males in fact leave the herd altogether and do suffer an increased rate of predation compared with females of the same age that

stay in the herd. The annual rate of predation will be discussed in chapter 9; but, briefly, it is found that about 30% of the total mortality of adults is accounted for by lion predation. This, then, provides a strong selection pressure for females and young to stay in herds and also for males during their reproductive lives.

One special feature of buffalo herds, however, is that individuals stay in the same group and there is little interchange between groups. In wildebeest, on the other hand, individuals constantly move from group to group. Theoretically, some form of group is all that is needed to provide some protection against predators (Hamilton 1971). But wildebeest can run fast, their calves are precocious at birth and can keep up with the herd within a few hours, and running is this species' main response to predator attacks. Newborn buffalo, however, can hardly run for several weeks; so running by the herd would be a disadvantage to its calves. They in fact show a group behavior by approaching calves in distress, and they even attack predators.

Since the members of a herd are likely to be more closely related to each other than to members of other herds, unlike wildebeest, it is also possible that such behavior has evolved through kin selection (Maynard-Smith 1964; Wiens 1966; Eberhard 1975; Wilson 1975). Significantly, when wildebeest calves are caught by predators, only the mother comes to help; and even this happens only occasionally. Because buffalo remain within a home range that has little overlap with that of other herds, the only calves in distress they are likely to hear are from their own herd. However, the problem with suggesting kin selection for the evolution of this protective behavior is that the herds are large and hence genetic similarity may be too low. Therefore, one must also consider whether the individual benefits from approaching a predator in a group, much like the mobbing behavior of birds, so as to frustrate a potential attack. Alternatively, intergroup selection may play a part. In conclusion, predation pressure may also produce the group protection behavior and explain the cohesiveness of individuals in the same herd.

The size of home ranges, however, is related to habitat, with small ranges occurring in forested or high-rainfall regions and large ranges in open, drier areas. The density of animals within the ranges is closely related to the amount of food which occurs in patches along riverbanks, around swamps, or in forest glades. Theoretically, individuals in genetically related groups have a greater chance of surviving in times of stress and producing more offspring by remaining near a few known patches than by searching at random; it is a more efficient way of utilizing resources, and consequently animals have a better chance of survival with this strategy. But to learn the location of these resources young animals would need to follow the same adults for a relatively long period of time—well beyond weaning. Thus resource limitation would select for animals that adopt a home range, remain in the same herd, and maintain postweaning bonds with their mothers.

My observations show that the movements of individual wildebeest in the Serengeti conform to the same principle, but on a much larger scale. The main migratory population of three-quarters of a million animals acts like one enormous herd, with individuals showing no particular attachment to any subgroup. In fact, the evidence suggests that there are no well-defined subgroups, (except for the mother, her calf, and for a brief period her penultimate calf). At times in the wet season they may all combine into one herd (plate 3). The home range of this herd is approximately shown by the movements of the female in figure 45. Their preferred habitat and food are two patches of short green grass in the woodlands and plains that are contained within the range. There are also adjacent, partly overlapping, home ranges belonging to other much smaller herds, one in the west of the Serengeti at Ndabaka, others to the north on the Loita plains, and east both at Loliondo and at Ngorongoro Crater. Although the animals meet, there is very little interbreeding between the herds, for their rutting seasons take place at different times of year and normally the herds are geographically separated. The wildebeest calf could learn the range by following its mother through the annual cycle. As in buffalo, individuals also show preferences for certain areas within the home range.

Finally, there remains the question of why male buffalo leave the herd if predation selects for animals that stay with the herd. Males from about four years old, and occasionally even two-year-olds, show an increasing tendency to leave the herd, until in old age they remain permanently separated from it. Furthermore, despite predation, some males live to a very old age. These males prefer habitats and food that are essentially the same as those chosen by herd animals, but because they live in groups of only three or four they can utilize patches of habitat too small for the herds. Hence by living in smaller groups they have access to extra resources. In fact, this behavior appears as merely an extension of the way herds split up in the dry season, perhaps as the preferred habitat fragments into small patches, and could have evolved to reduce undernutrition. Since young males form their own subgroups within the herd, they break away as all-male groups when the herds split up. Thus the old males merely continue this behavior into old age. They are kept out of the herd by the dominant males.

That social behavior is a compromise between different selection pressures is also shown in herding behavior. To minimize predation, buffalo form compact herds; but by doing so they are restricted to food which is very abundant—necessarily some form of grass. But as I shall describe later (chap. 9), grass is very poor food in the dry season compared with leaves of herbs and bushes. Because the buffalo is so large, it must eat long, rank grass near water, which becomes patchily distributed in the dry season. Competing for food with wildebeest (chap. 10) would be one selection pressure maintaining this food selection, and to alleviate the resulting undernutrition the herds must break up in the dry season. But if these groups become too small they again become vulnerable to predation. Thus a compromise behavior results from interspecific and intraspecific competition and from predation. The old males' deviation illustrates how this norm is not optimal with respect to certain requirements. For example, buffalo would get more food if they dispersed and did not form herds. But then the danger of predation would increase.

Tinbergen (1965) has pointed out that very small selective advantages can be sufficient to produce evolutionary change. In view of the crude nature of the measurements of predation rates on animals in and out of the herd, and of the intensity of interspecific competition (chap. 10), a selection pressure must be powerful before one can detect it; sufficient, perhaps, to maintain observed behavior in the population and to have evolved it in the past. In general, the circumstantial evidence suggests at present that most aspects of the social behavior of African buffalo have evolved through individual selection or kin selection. But for a better understanding of those aspects of group behavior such as home range and protection from predators, we need more data on the degree to which animals move between herds and whether there are characteristic gene frequencies for each herd.

SUMMARY

1. The self-regulation hypothesis suggests that social behavior functions to keep a population below the level permitted by resources. The social behavior of buffalo is therefore described with a view to understanding its behavioral and evolutionary function.

2. The sexual behavior of males is described. The dominant males are proficient at securing the females in estrus by observing other males and then displacing them.

3. The newborn buffalo calf is underdeveloped compared with the calves of other grazing ungulates, and it is several weeks before it can keep up with a running herd. There is a strong following response, and the mother is aggressive in her protection.

4. There are a number of agonistic displays in males which result in the formation and maintenance of a dominance hierarchy. Comparing these displays with those of other Bovini shows that this species is relatively distant from the others genetically and supports the findings of taxonomists. Dominant males obtain most of the matings.

5. Analysis of association between herd members shows that the basic family unit is mother, calf, and penultimate calf. Males break away from this unit at two years of age to form all-male subgroups, but females may stay in the family until they produce their first young, and perhaps even longer. There is little evidence of a rank hierarchy in females or of leadership in large herds.

6. From about four years of age males leave the herd in bachelor groups during the dry season but return during the rains. This is associated with the splitting up of herds as a response to fragmentation of habitat. Old males (more than ten years old) remain permanently separated from the herd. Many are decrepit. They form their own bachelor groups of 3–4 animals and like the herd males show a rank hierarchy and have a home range.

7. Males living out of the herd suffer greater predation than animals in herds, which show group protection behavior. Predation pressure may have selected for this behavior since herd members are probably genetically related, but further information is needed.

8. Herds have a home range which overlaps little with those of adjacent herds. The size of the range is related to habitat, and the density of animals within it is related to food. Home range appears to result from the restricted availability of essential resources in the dry season. To learn the locality of these resources, young animals

need to remain with the same adults in the same herd. Because resources become localized in the dry season, the large herds break up to use the small patches of food. To ameliorate resource limitation, herds space out to utilize available resources efficiently.

9. Within the herd, animals of all ages and either sex are over-dispersed; that is, there appears to be clumping of some animals, while others are scattered singly. Although spacing is not random, it is also not uniform.

10. The features of social behavior are therefore a compromise resulting from the opposing selection pressures of predation and competition for food resources (both inter- and intraspecific). All could have evolved through natural selection or kin selection, but the advantages of group protection behavior need further elucidation. Intergroup selection appears to be unnecessary. None of the behavioral features appear to hold the population below the level imposed by food resources.

7 Reproduction and Growth

Changes in populations take place through variation in reproduction, mortality, and migration, and there has been much debate over which contributes most toward population regulation. Reproduction, together with the growth of individuals, forms the production of a population during the annual cycle. In this chapter I shall describe the characteristics of reproduction and growth and collate the known information on different populations in Africa (Pienaar 1969; Grimsdell 1969, 1973b; Sinclair 1974b), making comparisons with other bovid species. I shall discuss how these characteristics may be affected by changes in population density and environment.

Since for most aspects of this study buffalo had to be identified by sex and age, I shall first detail the various methods I used. Grimsdell (1973a) has described the sequence of tooth eruption and interpreted the lines seen in the cementum of molar roots, and both he and Pienaar (1969) have suggested field criteria.

Methods of Determining Sex and Age

Determination of Sex

Adult male buffalo have a heavy shield of horn, the boss, which covers the whole top of the head above the eyes. This is formed in the immature male by a gradual thickening of the base of the horn where the bone core leaves the head (fig. 52). The thickening grows inward as the animal becomes older until the two bosses meet at the midline of the head (plate 28). At the same time the bones above the eye form a pronounced ridge to support this boss. The ridge can be seen in the skulls of animals as young as eighteen months, although in the live animals it is usually not noticeable until two years old, when the males begin to lose the hair over the bosses.

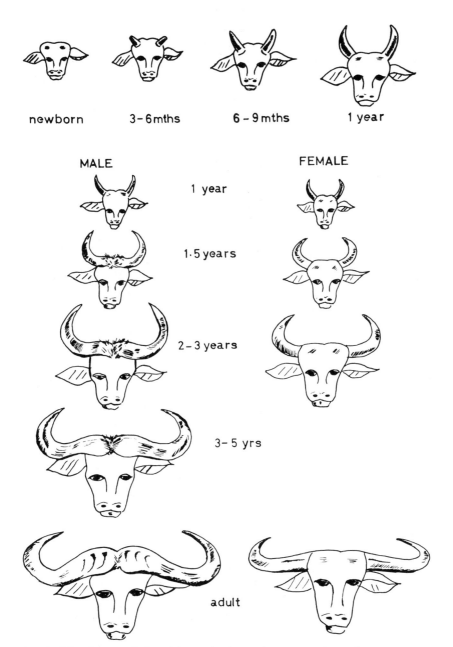

newborn   3 – 6 mths   6 – 9 mths   1 year

MALE   FEMALE

1 year

1·5 years

2 – 3 years

3 – 5 yrs

adult

Fig. 52. The shape and size of horns in the various age and sex classes.

The adult female does not grow a boss, the horn layer beginning at the base of the bone core. Females' horns are also narrower than males', and the forehead ridge is absent. This makes the female's head look flat in profile. In aerial photographs (plate 26) the boss of males appears white and contrasts with the animal's black hair while females' horns are dark and narrow. The differences between the sexes can be distinguished only on photographs of animals two years old and older.

Age-Determination of Fetuses

Huggett and Widdas (1951) found a relationship between a fetus's weight (W) and its age in days from conception (t), such that $W^{\frac{1}{3}} = a(t - to)$ where to is the intercept of the linear growth line with the time axis, which in large mammals approximates 20% of the gestation time (fig. 53), and a is a constant called the specific fetal growth velocity. If the gestation time (tg) and mean birth weight (Wg) are known, then $a = Wg^{\frac{1}{3}} / (tg - to)$. Since for small fetuses below 170 g these formulas do not hold, ages were estimated from the curves shown by Grimsdell (1973b), which he obtained by extrapolation from cattle data (fig. 53).

Age-Determination of Young Animals by Tooth-Eruption Sequence

With young animals the sequence of eruption of teeth was used to determine age in skulls or occasionally in live animals. The dental formula is 2 (i^0_3, c^0_1, pm^3_3) = 20, for the deciduous dentition, and 2 (I^0_3, C^0_1, PM^3_3, M^3_3) = 32 for the permanent dentition.

Grimsdell (1973a) established the sequence of eruption by reference to nine known-age animals. Additional known-age data has been accumulated from observations on two captive juveniles in the Serengeti, a three-year-old female at Nairobi, and the tooth array of a four-year-male described by P. Hemingway (personal communication). These records confirmed the ages allocated to the eruption pattern by Grimsdell, which is set out for the lower jaw in table 12. The eruption of premolars and molars in the upper jaw is delayed by 1–3 months compared with the lower jaw. This pattern is similar to that of the Asian water buffalo (Rollinson 1974), in which eruption age for each tooth varies by approximately six months, and Grimsdell considered that this is also true with the African buffalo. The last stage, in which there is a full complement of teeth, was recorded only

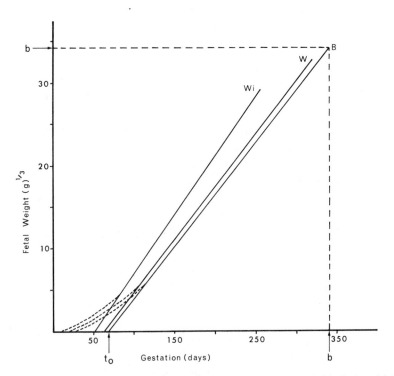

Fig. 53. The relationship between fetal weight and age up to birth for African buffalo (*B*), water buffalo (*W*), and wildebeest (*Wi*). Calculated from Huggett and Widdas (1951).

when no wear was visible on the canine, which acts as the fourth incisor.

Age-Determination from Cementum Lines and Tooth Wear

Since the eruption sequence was suitable only for animals less than five years old, other methods had to be used for older animals. Where teeth could be examined in skulls of dead animals, measurements of wear or counts of cementum lines were used.

Both dentine and cementum are laid down in layers in the tooth roots as the animal grows older. By sectioning the roots and counting these layers, age can be determined. This has been done for a number of different ruminant species in temperate regions including, for example, deer (Ransom 1966) and caribou (McEwan 1963). In tropical species, cementum lines have been observed in waterbuck (Spinage 1967), and Grimsdell (1973a) used this technique with buffalo. Sagittal sections of the first molar root were cut and decalcified. The cementum lines were counted, and their number was correlated with the height of the enamel on the buccal side of the tooth. This enamel extends from the base of the root to the top of the cusp and wears away with age in a curvilinear way. The first molar was used because it occupies a central position in the jaw and wears away to a greater extent and more consistently than the other teeth. For practical reasons it was also useful in the field because incisors and premolars were often missing from the weathered skulls of animals that had died of natural causes; the molars were usually present. It was also relatively easy to remove these teeth to take back to the laboratory for measurement and sectioning.

Cementum layers appear under the microscope as alternate light and dark bands. Spinage (1967) found that these layers were deposited annually and were related to season, the dark lines representing periods of arrested growth and restricted deposition. He suggested that this might occur during the dry season. Grimsdell (1973a) pointed out that cementum is formed first as uncalcified tissue composed of collagen and mucopolysaccharides and only later becomes calcified with calcium phosphate. Therefore the formation of cementum could be influenced by the availability of protein and other nutrients as well as by calcium and phosphates: and the dry season is the period when protein is least available.

In Uganda, Grimsdell found from known-age animals that there were two dark layers per year and suggested that this could be because there are two dry seasons each year in that area. He also found that the first year of life was not recorded in the cementum, since the first molar did not erupt until one year of age. Therefore age in years was calculated as one plus half the number of cementum lines. There was no apparent difference between males and females.

The number of cementum lines was plotted by Grimsdell (1973a) against the mean crown heights of both the maxillary and mandibular first molars. Mean heights were obtained by measuring to the nearest half millimeter with calipers the heights of the enamel on the two buccal cusps for each of the two upper and lower first molars. Thus four measurements of upper and lower teeth were recorded from which the means could be calculated. This eliminated the effects of asymmetric wear. Grimsdell found the relationship of cementum line number (Y) to mean crown height (X) to be curvilinear for both upper (fig. 54) and lower teeth. He gave the regression formulas as maxillary M1 $Y = 32.155 - 0.883X + 0.00285\ X^2$; man-

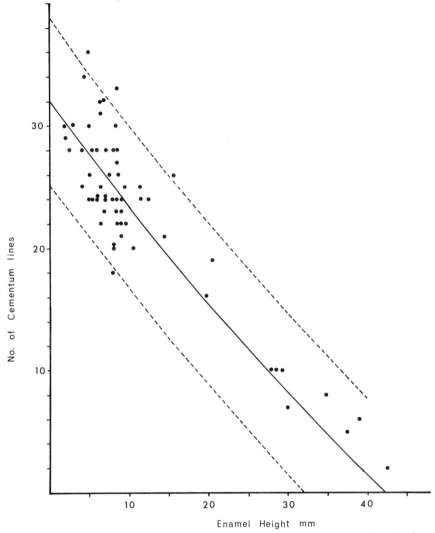

Fig. 54. The relationship between the number of cementum lines in the first maxillary molar and the mean enamel height on the buccal cusps of both first molars. The points are from the Serengeti, and they fall along the regression curve redrawn from Grimsdell (1973a) for Uganda animals.

dibular M1 $Y = 36.283 - 1.191 X + 0.00900 X^2$; of which the first equation was not significantly different from the linear regression. Sample sizes were 85 for the former and 102 for the latter.

There was some doubt whether methods of age-determination based on rates of wear developed in one area could be applied to other areas: rates of wear could be different because of different food and perhaps more important, because of different soils. Sandy soils inadvertantly eaten with the food could cause greater wear than less sandy soils. Consequently, I felt it necessary to check whether rates of wear in the Serengeti were similar to those found by Grimsdell.

A sagittal cut was made through the tooth root with a hacksaw, making sure that part of the pulp cavity and the base of the root were present. I used the method of decalcification suggested by Reimers and Nordby (1968) because it is relatively quick, taking no more than 48 h. The segments of root were decalcified in 5% nitric acid for 24 h, then washed for 24 h. The material was then frozen on a microtome freezing stage, and sagittal sections were cut at 30 μm, using a base sledge microtome. Slides were cleaned with an ultrasonic agitator, dipped in gelatin solution, and allowed to dry. Sections were placed on the slides and left for 10 min in formalin vapor to fix. They were then placed in a mordent of 4% iron alum for 20 min, stained in Ehrlich's hematoxylin for 10 min, differentiated in acid alcohol, and then blued in tap water for 10 min.

The best areas of the section for counting the rings were the root base and tip, where the rings were more spread apart. Inaccuracies occurred in the teeth of old animals, where resorbtion of cementum may have been taking place: this took the form of pitting in the root surface. If a number of sections were made the pits could be accounted for by comparing sections. The cementum of younger animals, however, is not resorbed because the tissue of the outer surface resists resorbtion (Grimsdell 1973a).

A total of ninety-one teeth were sectioned in this way. Most were from old animals whose teeth were too worn to measure, but a number were from younger animals. Examination of the sections showed that the dark lines were present in pairs (plate 24) separated by a narrow space which I interpreted as representing the short rains, the wider space representing the long rains. In some teeth the lines were well defined, whereas in others they were too faint to be of use, and in some parts of the sections the dark lines fused, whereas in other places they were spread out. However, by searching the sections and following the lines it was possible to tell whether or not they were paired. An example of these paired lines can be seen in plate 24, which is from the root base of an eighteen-year-old animal. Finally, the number of paired cementum lines plus one was plotted against the mean height of the first maxillary molar, and this distribution was compared with the curve and 95% confidence limits calculated by Grimsdell (fig. 54). The points fall within the area delimited by the 95% confidence limits of the Uganda measurements, indicating a similar rate of wear and variation in the Serengeti region.

Grimsdell checked the method by comparing the number of lines with the eruption sequence in juvenile animals and found it accurate to within ± 1 yr. For older animals, he compared the number of cementum lines with the tooth wear on cattle incisors of known age and counted more lines than expected, but he considered that this was due to the inaccuracy in aging from the criteria on cattle incisor wear. The mean number of extra lines was only 0.5. The scatter on the cementum-line/molar-wear graph gave the accuracy of aging as ± 2 yr for animals six to fourteen years old. For these ages the wear method was adopted, and the age was read from the graph. For older animals the wear method was too inaccurate, and so the teeth of these buffalo were sectioned to count the lines directly.

Age-Determination from Horn Shape

The above methods were satisfactory only for dead animals. I also needed to obtain the age of live animals in the field and of animals in aerial photographs. The horns of female buffalo continue to grow until four years of age and those of males until they are five years old. At the same time the shape of the horns changes and the overall size of the animal increases (plate 25). Using these criteria it was possible to pick out the age-groups shown in figure 52. Absolute ages were assigned to these groups by use of the tooth formula. Pienaar (1969) gives a series of front- and side-view photographs of animals of these age-groups, and they agree reasonably well with the drawings presented here. Animals less than one year old are classified as "calves," those between one and two years old are termed "yearlings," and those between two and three years old are called "two-year-olds."

"Subadult" animals are between three and five years old, and "adults" are over five years old. "Juvenile" is a general term for those under five years old.

Most of these age-groups can be distinguished on aerial photographs (plates 26, 27). From a number of near-vertical photographs, the length of all animals was measured using a graduated scale mounted in a binocular microscope. A number of distinct size classes were found, whose frequency distribution agreed with the subjective estimates based on shape and size taken from the same photographs. Since direct measurements were difficult and time-consuming, the subjective method was used thereafter. Also, it was probably more accurate than direct measurements because three criteria instead of one were being used—horn shape, horn size, and body size—and, moreover, a slight change in angle on an oblique photograph caused large changes in an animal's apparent length. The eye can compensate for this and make use of the other two criteria as well.

Age-Determination of Males in the Field

At two years old males begin to develop a boss that can be seen in the field. This boss is covered with skin and hair, and the whole horn is covered with a light-colored outer layer. The skin and hair on the boss progressively disappear as the horn grows toward the middle of the head. Two-year-old males have horn halfway to the center (plate 28), and subadult males of three to five years (fig. 52) have horn over most of the boss, but with skin and hair in the region of the central division; and they still have an outer covering on the horn.

Young adult males have very little, if any, hair left between the bosses, and the outer covering of the horn has flaked off. The general appearance is of clean, sharp-tipped, and unridged horns (plate 28). These animals also are covered with hair, have few scars, and have not developed the thick neck. This category covers approximately the ages of five to seven years. The middle-aged animals (about eight to ten years) are distinguished by the ridges of horn that have grown on the bosses, although these remain relatively unworn; the face does not have many scars and the body is still covered with hair. By this age they have developed the bull neck and thickening of the brisket and forequarters (plate 28). Old males, estimated at older than ten years, show signs of considerable wear on the horns and scarring and loss of hair both on the face and on the body. Many very old animals have broken horns (plate 29) and suffer from other injuries.

On a number of occasions adult males were immobilized and Plasticine impressions were obtained of their incisors. The wear on these teeth was compared with a set of diagrams published by Cornevin and Lesbre (1894) for different ages of cattle and supplied by J. Grimsdell (personal communication), who found that they adequately described the pattern of incisor wear in buffalo. Ages estimated from the wear pattern agreed with those described above.

REPRODUCTION

Collection of Material

In the Serengeti, material was collected in three main samples, each at a different season, between 1967 and 1969. The animals were shot from the same herd and care was taken to avoid bias with respect to age- and sex-classes. Each day·a group of ten to fifteen animals was killed, then weighed, measured, dissected, and examined in the field. Animals were weighed either whole or in pieces on a large spring balance attached to a tree. If the animal had to be cut up before weighing a correction of 3% of this weight was added to account for fluid loss, as recommended by Sachs (1967). The weight of the gravid uterus was subtracted to obtain the basic weight of the animal. Teams of veterinarians and assistants from the Veterinary Investigation Centre at Arusha carried out autopsies for analysis of diseases. In the course of these, the state of the reproductive organs was recorded, and fetuses, ovaries, and testes were measured and weighed. The ovaries were preserved and later cut into 1 mm sections for the measurement of follicles.

Characteristics of the Estrous Cycle and Gestation Period

The estrous cycle in African buffalo lasts 23 days on average (Pienaar 1969). This is similar to cattle—22 days with a range of 17–24 days (Braden and Baker 1973)—and European bison (18–22 days [Krasinski and Raczynski 1967]). In Asia the water buffalo has a cycle of 21 days (Bhattacharya 1974), but in northern Australia the cycle is apparently much longer and more variable—32–50 days (D. G. Tulloch, personal communication). According to Pienaar (1969), the female African buffalo is in estrus for 5 to 6 days, which seems a long time compared with the 1–1½ days for Asian water buffalo (Bhattacharya 1974) or the 1–3 days of bison (Krasinski and Raczynski 1967), or the mere 13 h of tropical zebu cattle (Braden and Baker 1973). However, it is not clear whether the same criteria for identifying estrus were being used by the different authors.

A corpus luteum occurred in the right ovary on 19 occasions against 12 in the left. Implantation was found in the right horn of the uterus in 25 animals, in the left in 17. Neither of these distributions differed significantly from parity. However, implantation occurred in the right horn in 46 out of 71 animals from Ruwenzori Park and in 60 out of 91 animals from northern Uganda (Grimsdell 1969). The figures combined over all areas—131 (64%) in the right horn versus 73 (36%) in the left horn—showed that the right-side bias, present in all samples, was indeed significant ($p < 0.01$). This bias is similar in cattle, where two-thirds of the ovulations are produced from the right ovary (Braden and Baker 1973), and a similar trend is apparent in water buffalo. In African buffalo implantation usually took place in the uterine horn on the same side as the ovary giving rise to the fertilized ovum. In only 2 out of 28 animals was a crossover found, one from right ovary to left horn and one in the other direction. Grimsdell (1969) recorded 5 out of 71 cases of crossover, in four of which the embryo migrated from left ovary to right horn. The placenta is cotyledonary, discrete areas of the maternal uterine epithelium fusing with small areas of the fetal chorion.

In cattle only one egg is ovulated at each estrus, and the incidence of twins is as low as 0.4% in beef cattle. Twins are extremely rare in African buffalo: Pienaar (1969) found two pairs of embryos, one in each horn, in a sample of 17 pregnant females, and in one pair one embryo was degenerating. So far twins have not been found in other populations. In both the American and European bison twins are reported as very rare. Geist (1974a) has suggested that large ungulates should have an overall greater chance of reproductive success from single births than from multiple births.

The gestation period for African buffalo has been measured by Vidler et al. (1963) as 343 days and as 346 days. They also quote a previous published record of 330 days, giving a mean of 340 days for the three records. This is therefore the longest gestation period found in the Bovini: that for water buffalo is 310–30 days (Mason 1974; Kay 1974; Bhattacharya 1974), American bison 270–300 days (McHugh 1958), European bison 254–72 (Krasinski and Raczynski 1967), yak 258 days (Jaczewski 1958), and cattle 283 days on average (Braden and Baker 1973). Despite their size, bison are very similar to cattle in this respect. The long gestation period of African buffalo takes al-

most a whole year (11.5 months) which suggests that the much larger
fossil buffalo in Africa may have had even longer periods, lasting
more than one year, and consequently they may have suffered from
the problems of low reproductive rates through breeding only every
two years.

The birth weight of calves has been reported from a number of
populations (table 13). Most weights fall within the range 35–50 kg.
Some variation is due to the fact that calves lose weight shortly after
birth as they dry out. A full-term fetus weighs several kilograms more
than a day-old calf. In calculating conception and birth dates from
fetus weights Grimsdell (1973b) used 45 kg as the theoretical birth
weight, and I have used the same figure for the Serengeti data to
make the calculations comparable.

Puberty and Sexual Maturity

Puberty is the age when reproduction first becomes possible, and
sexual maturity is the age when the animal reaches its full reproductive capacity (Asdell 1965; Joubert 1963). In the female bovid, therefore, puberty is the age when estrus is first recorded. Grimsdell (1969)
considered that ovulation in the African buffalo was imminent when
follicles were greater than 12 mm, and the same criterion has been
used for the Serengeti population. In the small sample of females
less than three years old (table 14), none were ovulating. Between
three and four years of age 62.5% were ovulating, and all were doing
so by the time they were four and one-half years old. In the Ruwenzori Park, where larger samples were collected, Grimsdell (1969)
found one-thirteenth ovulating at eighteen months and one-sixth
(14%) ovulating at two and one-half years old. In northern Uganda
ovulation did not start until animals reached three years. The age at
which 50% of the animals were ovulating was close to three and one-
half years in both the Serengeti and Ruwenzori populations and four
years in those from northern Uganda. There is considerable evidence
now that puberty occurs when animals reach a certain size or body
weight rather than a certain age. Consequently, slow-growing animals reach puberty later than fast-growing animals (Joubert 1963).

Sexual maturity was taken to be the age when females first conceived. In the Serengeti only one-eighth (12%) conceived at three
and one-half years (table 15), and Grimsdell (1969) did not record
any pregnancies at this age in Uganda. Pienaar (1969) commented
that conception probably occurred at this age in the Kruger Park. At

older ages the proportion pregnant in the Serengeti population increased from 28% at four years to 91% at five and one-half years, and similar proportions were found in Uganda. The age at which 50% of the animals were pregnant was five years in the Uganda and Serengeti animals. It appears from this that sexual development was very similar in these different areas. For the Serengeti females the mean ovary weight was 2.3 g when immature (nonovulating), 3.0 g when pubertal, 2.9 g when mature but not pregnant, and 4.7 g when pregnant.

In mature females, five to nine years old, 83% were pregnant (N=42), but of those older than ten years only 66% were pregnant (N=12). Although this is not a significant difference because of the small sample, Grimsdell (1969) also found a similar difference, so that it may suggest that old animals produce fewer offspring. Similar observations have been made on the American bison (Fuller 1961).

Grimsdell (1973b) has examined sexual development in males. Puberty, judged by the presence of spermatozoa in the epididymis, occurs between two and three years of age. Grimsdell considered that sexual maturity was attained when the combined testis and epididymis weight reached the minimum observed for adults, which was about 300 g. At the age of four and one-half years 50% of the animals had reached this testis and epididymis weight, and by six years old all had done so.

The Pregnancy Rate of Adults

The pregnancy rate is the proportion of the total number of adult females that are pregnant. Three main samples were collected during different stages in the breeding cycle (table 16), that is during early pregnancy (August), midpregnancy (October), and late pregnancy (March). In the latter sample those that had recently given birth were classified as pregnant for the past season. An overall pregnancy rate of 75% was found for the Serengeti. This allows the "incidence of pregnancy" to be calculated as $0.75 \times t/$gestation time, where t is 365 days (Davis and Golley 1963). This came to 0.80 calves/female/ year.

Calving Interval and Lactation Anestrus

The calving interval is the average time between successive births and can be calculated from the gestation time/pregnancy rate. For the Serengeti this was 15.1 months (455 days), with a 95% confidence

interval of 13.3–17.5 months. Similar calculations for the Ruwenzori
Park and northern Uganda were 18.0 (15.6–21.3) months and 24.6
(19.2–34.3) months respectively. From data on Kruger Park buffaloes
(Pienaar 1969), the pregnancy rate was calculated as 74.5%, giving a
calving interval of 15.2 (14.1–16.1) months. Thus populations in the
Kruger, Serengeti, and Ruwenzori parks had similar calving intervals. That in northern Uganda had a longer interval than the Serengeti population.

The variability in calving interval is due to the postpartum anestrus, which can be as short as 3.6 (2.0–6.2) months in the Serengeti
or as long as 13.3 (7.9–23.0) months in northern Uganda. In the former area conception can take place within the same wet season as
the birth (see later), in the latter a whole year must pass before conception occurs. It is known that in cattle anestrus is influenced by
the length of the suckling period, and it is often referred to as "lactation anestrus." If calves are removed within three days of birth,
estrus occurs within five weeks, and if the calves remain with their
mother for two weeks, estrus occurs within seven weeks. But if suckling is allowed to continue for several months, estrus does not reappear until three to five months postpartum. In buffalo, as in cattle,
conception can occur while the female is lactating, but it is possible
that lactation causes a longer anestrus: in a sample of adult females
that had experienced at least one previous pregnancy, collected in
August 1969 after the rutting season had ended, the mean weight of
the fetuses in lactating animals (286 g), was lower than that in nonlactating females (720 g). This indicates that the average date of conception in nonlactating animals was about 20 March whereas those
in lactating females would not have been conceived until a month
later, around 22 April. A result of this possible relation between lactation and conception is that heavy mortality among newborn calves
in a herd could result in earlier calving the next year. This would
give the mothers a longer period on good food to enable them to
suckle the young, and consequently the calves might have an above-
average chance of survival. This would tend to compensate for the
previous year's heavy mortality.

Sex Ratio of Newborns

Of the fetuses from the Serengeti 26 were males and 21 females.
These combined with other published records (table 17) give a total
of 86 males and 85 females. A small sample of 20 calves between six

months and one year old also had an equal sex ratio. In other Bovini, for example, both species of bison, the sex ratio of fetuses does not deviate significantly from parity (Fuller 1961: Krasinski and Raczynski 1967). In a sample of 1,618 newborn wildebeest that had drowned while trying to swim across Lake Lagarja in the Serengeti in February 1973 (plate 36), there were 784 females and 834 males, a ratio which is also not significantly different from unity. A sample of 84 fetuses from water buffalo in northern Australia contained 40 females and 44 males. However, from the very large number of records (approximately 20,000) on the Asian water buffalo summarized by Bhattacharya (1974) males make up 51–53% of births, and this is a significant deviation from parity. Such a small deviation, if it occurs in African buffalo, would not be detectable with the present samples, and so I have assumed an equal sex ratio at birth.

Changes in Population Fertility

The fertility estimated from the shot samples was only a single mean figure covering the years 1967–69, and it gave no indication of how fertility changed from year to year. But it was impractical to collect such samples each year. However, by observing the rate at which the proportion of newborn calves declines through mortality after the peak of calving, it is possible to extrapolate backward in time and estimate the proportion of calves as they entered the population. This method was developed from one devised by Richards and Waloff (1954) for grasshopper populations. The proportion of calves that enter the population is of course the population fecundity. The difference between fertility (the proportion conceiving) and fecundity would be due to resorbtion or abortion. Examination of ovaries for regressing corpora lutea or distended uteri suggested that very little resorbtion or abortion occurred. The one disease that could have caused this, brucellosis, is known to be of low incidence and probably does not cause abortion in these animals (see chap. 9). Consequently, fertility can be equated with fecundity.

Aerial photographic samples were taken from several herds in the two study areas at intervals of one month or less between 1967 and 1973 (excepting 1970). Initially, between 1967 and 1969 three herds or groups of herds were sampled to record the seasonal pattern of reproduction and mortality. Herds in study area B in the north made up the first group. Herds in the western half of the southern study area A formed the second group. A single herd in the eastern half of this study area was treated as a third group, for it lived along the watercourses on the plains and much of its range was marginal habitat. After 1969 study of the third group was discontinued. I considered that samples from the first two groups more nearly represented the changes in the fertility of the population. Since data from these two groups were very similar, they were combined for samples up to 1969. Thereafter only herds in the northern area were sampled and these were taken to represent the population. For each sampling occasion calves born in the previous birth season were recorded as the number of calves per 100 adult females. The results from the northern study area are shown in figure 55 to show the sequence of events.

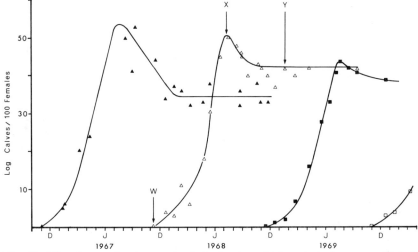

Fig. 55. The changes in the proportion of calves during their first year. *W* indicates the point when calves for that year group were first observed, *X* the point where deaths begin to exceed births, and *Y* the time when the mortality of newborn calves lessens. From Sinclair (1974*b*), with permission of Blackwell Scientific Publications, Ltd.

The first calves were recorded in December or January at the beginning of the rains, and from this time the proportion of calves increased steadily, reaching a peak in July. Thereafter, a decline in the proportion of calves occurred as the newborn mortality began to exceed the births, the decline continuing until sometime between October and December, when the dry season was drawing to a close (*Y* in fig. 55): at this time the juvenile mortality eased and the proportion of calves thereafter remained more constant. It was the data during this initial decline (between *X* and *Y*, fig. 55) that was used in calculating the proportion of pregnant females. For each year, the proportion of calves in the samples that were collected during this decline was transformed to logs, and these were plotted against time (fig. 56) measured from the point (*W*), when newborn calves were first observed in the population. A regression equation of log proportion of calves against time was calculated as shown diagrammatically in figure 56, and from this the log proportion of calves at point *W* could be deduced. This was equivalent to the log proportion of pregnant adult females in the population.

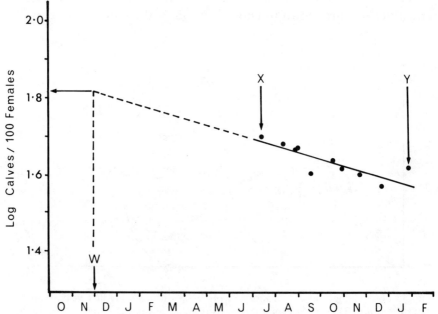

Fig. 56. The method of estimating fertility. The points *W*, *X*, and *Y* are explained in fig. 55. Redrawn from Sinclair (1974*b*), with permission of Blackwell Scientific Publications, Ltd.

The above method of fertility estimation relies on the assumption that mortality rates remain constant over the period of births and the initial decline. Pronounced and well-defined breeding seasons obviously must have some survival value, which implies that animals born outside this period are liable to suffer higher rates of mortality. But since the actual number of individuals involved is small, the error due to the higher mortality rate will also be small. The assumption of a constant mortality rate, in fact, results in a slight underestimate of the number of calves born. An error in the opposite direction, however, is produced by transforming the data to logs. The residual error therefore is likely to be small. An indication of the size of this error was obtained by comparing the results from this method with those from the independent samples of animals shot. The mean fertility for herds in study areas A and B from the method using photographic samples over the period when the shot sample was collected, was 69.6% ± 9.6% (95% confidence limits). This included the subadult age-groups of three to four and four to five years old which could not be identified on the photographs, but as I have described above, both of these had fertility rates lower than that of adults. The proportions of these age-groups in the female population could be calculated from the life table (chap. 8), and these, together with their contribution to the calf total, could be subtracted from the photographic counts, so that the fertility for the mature adults alone could be estimated. This was found to be 73.0% ± 12.5% and was very close to the 75.0% adult fertility found from the shot samples. A further check on the method was obtained from the wildebeest population with similar results (Sinclair 1970). Therefore it would appear that the errors were small, and since they would be similar from year to year, they would not affect the results with respect to the changes in fertility that were of interest in this analysis.

The samples obtained during the initial decline due to newborn mortality (XY, fig. 55) were used to obtain the estimates of population fertility for each group (table 18). Fertility varied not only from year to year but also from one area to the next. The three herds, however, did not show any consistent trends. I considered the third herd to be atypical and felt it did not represent the population. The mean fertility for this herd over the first three years was much lower than that of the other two, both of which showed means close to each other (70.0% and 69.3%). The population fertility estimates (table 18) derived from the latter two groups varied from 79% in 1967 to 64% in 1968, with those in later years being intermediate. Such fluctuations show clearly that populations living in different areas cannot be compared meaningfully with respect to their reproduction characteristics simply by collecting single samples from each.

The fluctuations in fertility in the Serengeti population showed no significant correlation with either population size or rainfall, possibly because of insufficient data. In other species, for example, elephant (Laws 1969; Laws, Parker, and Johnstone 1975), there does appear to be a good relationship between fertility and environmental conditions, and I expect that in due course this will be found for buffalo. But this is not to imply that fluctuations in fertility regulate the population; they may only cause fluctuations in population size. Indeed, Phillipson (1975) has suggested for Tsavo Park elephant that mortality of juveniles may be regulating. Alternatively, if fertility changes in ungulates show a delayed density-dependent response, then cyclical population phenomena could result. At present further analysis is required of most species' populations to determine whether fertility changes regulate or disturb the population.

GROWTH

Growth was measured by obtaining weights of animals at different ages in the population. Weights were measured for the most part from shot animals, using a large spring balance. A close relationship is known to exist between thoracic girth and weight in several animals, and the same has been found for African buffalo. Grimsdell (1969), using 80 males and 118 females, calculated curves to predict live weight (y) from girth (x): for males $y = 84.36 - 2.346x + 0.02338x^2$; for females $y = -109.79 + 0.774x + 0.01131x^2$. Because data from the Serengeti followed these curves with the confidence limits that were published ($\pm 10\%$ of the estimated weight), I did not consider that new curves were needed for this population. Using these data the weight of a number of immobilized bull buffalo was estimated.

Mean weights for each age-group with their 95% confidence intervals (where possible) for the two sexes are shown in figure 57 and tables 19 and 20. Similar data published for Kruger Park (Pienaar 1969) and Ruwenzori Park buffalo (Grimsdell 1969) are included for comparison. In both sexes the Serengeti and Kruger animals were similar in their growth curves and attainment of maximum weight. The animals in the Ruwenzori population are quite clearly smaller, indicating the influence of the forest races of buffalo which merge with the *caffer* subspecies in this area.

Growth rates up to the age of three and one-half years measured as kg/animal/yr are very similar in the four populations so far studied—Kruger, Serengeti, Ruwenzori, and northern Uganda—with Kruger highest at 108 for females, 113 for males, and Ruwenzori lowest at 92 for females, 103 for males, the other two being intermediate with Serengeti animals at 99 and 103, and northern Uganda at 100 for females and 105 for males. Because the confidence intervals overlap,

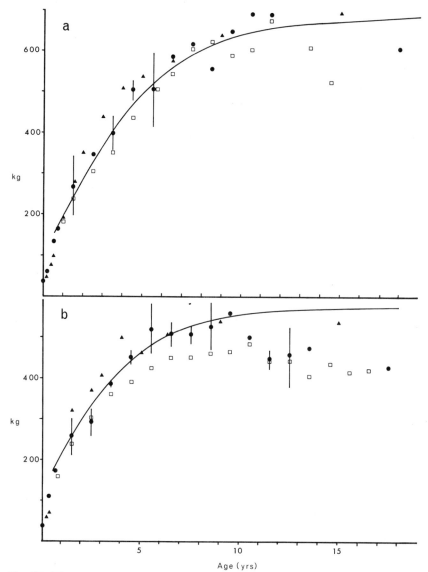

Fig. 57. The growth curves of *a*, male, and *b*, female, buffalo. The circles (with 95% confidence limits for the mean) are for the Serengeti, triangles for the Kruger Park, and squares for the Ruwenzori Park animals.

I assume little difference exists between the populations. Since age of puberty depends upon the rate of growth (Joubert 1963), these figures explain the similarity in the populations for the age when puberty is attained.

Old age produces a decline in weight in both sexes. This is seen quite clearly in the data from Ruwenzori and Serengeti (fig. 57). The decline begins sometime between the ages of ten and twelve years and continues until death. Pienaar (1969) extrapolates his curves for males as an increasing weight and for females as a steady weight, but I think the evidence obtained from the other populations suggests that these extrapolations should be revised.

I have fitted a theoretical growth curve to the Serengeti data, using the von Bertalanffy growth equation given in Beverton and Holt (1957): $Wt = W\infty (1 - [\exp - K (t - to)])^3$, where Wt is the weight at t years, $W\infty$ is the asymptote of the growth curve, K is a physiological constant, and to is the age at which the animal has zero weight with the observed growth rate. Such curves have also been fitted to data on Uganda buffalo (Grimsdell 1969), wildebeest (Watson 1967), and elephant (Hanks 1972). Growth in young animals still suckling did not obey the curve; so this was drawn in by eye: neither could old animals losing weight be included. Consequently, only the ages 1.5–10.5 years were used to calculate the curve. The asymptote $(W\infty)$ was calculated by plotting the cube root of the weight of one age-group on the ordinate against that of the previous age-group on the abscissa. The intersection where the regression line through these points cuts the 45° line is taken to be the cube root of the asymptotic weight.

To estimate to and K, the difference between the cube root of the asymptotic weight and that of each age-group is plotted as the natural log; i.e., $\log_e (W\infty^{\frac{1}{3}} - Wt^{\frac{1}{3}})$, on the ordinate against age (t) on the abscissa. The regression line through the points is then extrapolated back to the time when the line reaches $W\infty^{\frac{1}{3}}$, this time being to, and is negative. K is the slope of the regression line. The rationale and the details of this procedure are outlined in Beverton and Holt (1957). Hanks (1972) illustrates the method and points out some important limitations.

The female and male values of K were -0.36 and -0.30, those for to were -2.45 and -2.60, and those for the asymptotic weight were 575.9 kg and 686.1 kg respectively. The equivalent weights for the Ruwenzori Park are 475 kg and 659 kg. These weights are close to the maximum observed weights. However since the von Bertalanffy equation takes into account only part of the growth and ignores weight losses, I suggest it is only of marginal value for ecological work on wild populations: it may be more useful in studies of growth rates in animal husbandry or in physiological studies.

SEASONALITY OF BREEDING AND THE LUNAR CYCLE

The dates of conception and birth were estimated for each of the 49 fetuses collected in the Serengeti. The number of births per month is shown in figure 58 and table 21, together with the mean monthly rainfall. There was one birth peak, during the long rainy season. The number of births per month was correlated with the months of highest mean rainfall ($p < 0.05$). It appears that very few births occurred during the short rains in the western areas of the Serengeti where the samples were collected. However, in the higher-rainfall northern area newborn calves were usually observed by the beginning of December, and I have occasionally seen one or two in the months of September-November. These dry-season births are rare and form only a small proportion of the total number of births. The two rain periods of Uganda produced two birth peaks (Grimsdell 1973a), in either the early or the middle part of the wet season. Both Pienaar (1969) and Fairall (1968) have reported that in the Kruger Park a peak of buffalo calving coincides with the period of grass growth.

Conceptions in the Serengeti buffalo occurred toward the end of the rains, as they also did in Uganda. However, once the dry season had set in, conceptions appeared to cease. This suggests that births in particular, but also conceptions, must occur during a period of food abundance in the rains. I shall discuss this further in the next section, but here we face the problem that if births are to occur at a certain time of year, conceptions must be triggered by an external stimulus nearly a year earlier. So far there is little to suggest what this may be.

The problem is highlighted to a greater extent by the highly synchronized breeding of the wildebeest (fig. 59). In this species gestation lasts about 8.5 months or 255 days (Watson 1967), and birth weight is about 25 kg. The same methods of calculation (fig. 53) were used with a sample of 33 fetuses obtained during 1971; 87% were born within a period of 20 days toward the end of January and the beginning of February on the plains, similar to results obtained by Watson (1967) for the years 1963–66. Clearly, the births occur in the middle of the rainy season on the eastern plains, when the females are eating good-quality food. But for this to happen, the whole adult population has to synchronize its mating activities so that conceptions can occur within a similarly short period. This conception period occurs toward the end of May and varies from year to year by

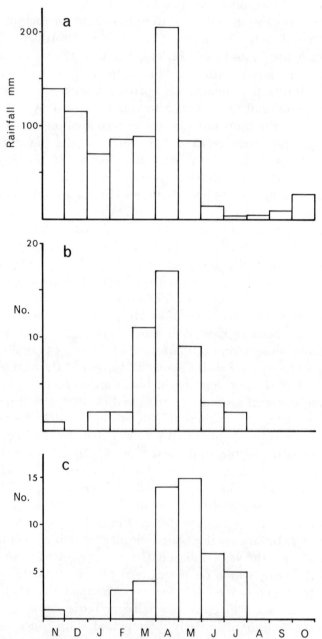

Fig. 58. The seasonality of reproduction in buffalo of the western Serengeti: *a*, mean monthly rainfall at Handajega; *b*, births; *c*, conceptions. Redrawn from Sinclair (1974*b*) with permission of Blackwell Scientific Publications, Ltd.

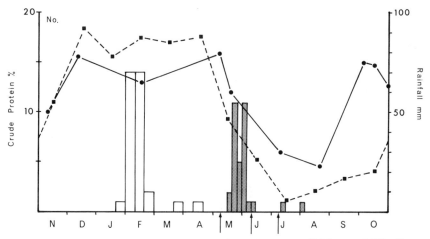

Fig. 59. Seasonality of reproduction in the migratory wildebeest, 1971. Open histogram (10-day blocks) shows the distribution of births; shaded histogram (5-day blocks) illustrates that of conceptions. Note the two peaks of conceptions 15 days apart, indicating two synchronized estrous cycles. Arrows point to date of full moon. The crude protein quality of food eaten (*solid circles*) in 1971 was declining during the conception period. The ten-year mean monthly rainfall (*squares*) shows this decline is normal during the rut.

only a month either way. At the time of conception the rainfall on the plains is declining, the quality of the food is dropping (fig. 59), and the population is usually in the process of leaving the plains and moving into the woodlands. These changing features of the environment may act in a general and imprecise way as a cue to the females to commence the estrous cycle, but they cannot produce the exact synchrony of conceptions seen in this species. In South Africa wildebeest calve in early summer at the beginning of the rains and conceive in autumn over a longer two-month period (Fairall 1968). Skinner, Van Zyl, and Van Heerden (1973) consider that this species, as well as the black wildebeest (*Connochaetes gnou*) and a number of other Alcelaphini, are entrained in their synchrony of breeding by the photoperiod. Whereas this may be important in the higher latitudes of South Africa, there is some doubt that it can be predominant near the equator.

Some suggestion as to the mechanism of synchrony of conceptions in tropical ruminants comes from information on the water buffalo in northern Australia (12° S). The species may be regarded as being in an experimental situation, for although it experiences the monsoonal climate similar to its normal range in Asia, it suffers almost no natural predation selecting against calves, and food supply is abundant for eight months of the year. The fetal growth curve is shown in figure 53, taking gestation time as 320 days and birth weight as 35 kg. A sample of 90 fetuses collected in September 1974 from culled animals at Mudginberry abattoir east of Darwin showed a relatively widespread distribution of births through the year (fig. 60a). The

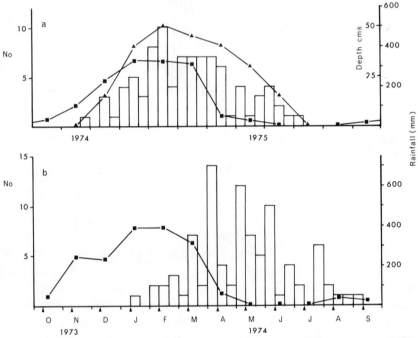

Fig. 60. The seasonality of reproduction in the water buffalo of northern Australia: *a*, the distribution of births (*histogram 10-day blocks*) calculated from fetuses collected in September 1974. Squares show the ten-year mean monthly rainfall, and triangles show the flood levels for one year, 1970. *b*, the distribution of conceptions grouped in 10-day blocks starting after full moon (*arrows*). Squares show the monthly rainfall for that area in 1973–74.

ten-year mean rainfall for Mudginberry (1964–73) supplied by the Australian Bureau of Meteorology is included in figure 60a to show that the peak of births coincides with the average peak of rainfall. However, rainfall in this area is not the best indicator of food conditions, for floodwaters remain some time after the rain has ceased. Indeed floodwater heights published by Tulloch (1970) for the relatively close Carmor Plain do show a better correlation with the distribution of births in figure 60a than do the rainfall figures. In general it seems that the breeding season of water buffalo is correlated with certain features of the water regime and presumably the food supply.

The distribution of conceptions as they occurred through 1973–74 is also shown, together with the rainfall for the same months (fig. 60*b*). As with the African species, conceptions reach a peak at a time of declining rainfall and drying out of their swamp pastures. This drying out causes the sedges to lose their nutrients and die back.

In calculating the dates of conception for these fetuses I noticed that many of them occurred over the full-moon period. With this in mind, I grouped conceptions into three periods of 10 days—one before and including full moon, one after full moon, and the third covering the new moon. With this grouping I found that 44 out of 90 conceptions (49%) occurred in the 10 days before the full moon (fig. 60*b*), and this was significant to $p < 0.02$. The other two periods had equal numbers of 23 conceptions. I had no a priori hypothesis for thinking that this result should emerge. But having found this, I reexamined the wildebeest conception dates in relation to the lunar cycle (fig. 59): it was immediately apparent that 82% (27 out of 33) of them occurred in the 14 days before and including the full moon, and they stopped abruptly on that date. Examination of conception peaks for the years 1956 to 1971 shows a very good correlation between the peak and the lunar cycle. This material is still in preparation and will be published elsewhere.

The data for the African buffalo was spread over a period of three years and was therefore quite insufficient to detect whether synchronized conceptions were occurring. The estrous cycle of water buffalo in northern Australia is of approximately the same period as the lunar cycle. If females were able to synchronize their conceptions, then a polymodal distribution could result, with periods of about a month, and this would automatically show a high correlation with the lunar cycle, although it may have no causal significance. However, in wildebeest the evidence indicates that the peak of conceptions shifts each year by the same number of days as does the occurrence of the full moon, suggesting that there is a lunar influence.

The one feature that is clear from this analysis is that conceptions are synchronized in both water buffalo and wildebeest. The data for African buffalo are inconclusive. The cause of this synchrony remains obscure, but there must be some external stimulus initiating the process, because it occurs at the same time each year. It could be some feature of illumination in the lunar cycle acting directly upon ovulation or indirectly through the mating behavior of males. Alternatively, the external stimulus may be some feature other than the lunar cycle. The lunar cycle could work in the same way as does day length in higher latitudes by inducing a physiological or behavioral response at some critical photosensitive period in the animals' circadian rhythm (Follett 1973). But whereas day length has an annual rhythm, thus ensuring breeding at the same time each year, this does not hold for the lunar cycle, and consequently it would have to be tied in with another environmental variable which has an annual rhythm. Such a variable could be rainfall or nutrition or both.

Since these environmental variables are far from constant in their intensity of effect between years, they cannot by themselves explain the relatively sharp onset of mating seen particularly in the wildebeest. They could, however, act as a coarse modulator setting the animals in the right physiological state to initiate mating. A declining nutritional plane of feeding lasts several months, and so the precise timing of onset of mating must be a variable with a more constant effect. The lunar period could possibly provide this and act as a fine modulator. Its effect would operate only during the time of year when there is a high plane of nutrition or a declining plane from a high level. This could explain the double breeding of African buffalo in Uganda, because there are two periods when nutrition drops from a high level. The hypothesis could also explain the variability in onset of wildebeest mating in the Serengeti; the rut varies by about one month between years, which is similar to the variation in the occurrence of the full moon during the calendar month in different years.

In wildebeest a further factor is evident: since all females conceive together the effect of suckling clearly does not influence the anestrous period, for about half the females would have lost their young at an early stage while the rest continue suckling. In the buffaloes lactation appears to be delaying estrus so that females start their cycle at different times, thus producing several peaks and covering several lunar periods. This could produce the polymodal peak of conceptions seen in water buffalo. Potentially, in wildebeest the following lunar cycle may be equally suitable for conceptions, but since 95% of all females have already conceived within one lunar cycle, a negligible number remain for the second cycle. Complex though this hypothesis may appear, it does not involve mechanisms which have not already been suggested for other animals, mainly birds. It may simply involve a photosensitive physiological oscillator with a circadian rhythm operating only above a certain nutritional threshold and triggered by some aspect of an external stimulus such as the lunar cycle.

Alternatively, the lunar cycle may simply affect male activity patterns: females may ovulate at any time in the lunar cycle but conception may be more probable in the pre–full moon period because more copulations may take place in the early part of the night when there is moonlight. Observations of copulatory activity are insufficient to allow any decision on this. Further, this hypothesis leaves unanswered the question of what triggers the synchronized ovulations of the wildebeest at one particular time of the year. Sadleir (1969) comments that although the extra light available during the full-moon phases might have a stimulating effect on reproduction in nocturnal and crepuscular species because it allows longer activity times, as yet no evidence is available to support this. Erkert (1974) has found that activity patterns of nocturnal monkeys and bats are influenced by the lunar cycle.

NUTRITION AND REPRODUCTION

Lactation

It is evident that in a number of ungulates the birth season occurs during the rainy season when there is high productivity in the grasslands (Sinclair 1975). This applies invariably for the ungulates in the East African savanna areas. But it follows from this that the mating period and hence conception cannot always occur in the wet season, for in some species the gestation time is too short. For example, waterbuck conceive in the dry season in Uganda (Spinage 1969), and the same must be true for many of the smaller bovids; species with long gestation periods, such as the buffalo, may be able to fit the conception period into the previous wet season. From this we may infer that the high nutritional demands of the full-term fetus and of lactation act as a selection pressure to produce young at times when most food is available for the mother. This same selection pressure must also influence the females' ability to conceive at times of declining or low available nutrition.

Some indication of the nutritional stresses imposed on the mother during reproduction and lactation can be obtained from measurements on domestic ruminants. Cattle and sheep given the same food show no significant difference in their ability to obtain energy from the food (Blaxter 1962). These two species, from different subfamilies, illustrate the general phenomenon that herbivores are similar in their ability to digest similar food. Thus Abrams (1968, p. 53) is able to remark, "The relative absence of data for the less familiar herbivora is thus perhaps not so unfortunate as might have been the case. For all but the most mature fodders which not even the adult ruminant digest very efficiently alone, one may safely assume comparable digestibility coefficients for herbivora generally."

From the many different systems for expressing energy requirements I have used the net energy of lactating cows (NE lact.) system described by Flatt and Moe (1974). Net energy is that which is used by the animal for maintenance and production, whether for milk, pregnancy, growth, or work. Each of these tends to be slightly different. The NE for lactating cows can be calculated from the sum of the maintenance requirement and the energy in the milk. Flatt and Moe (1974) use the following equation: Milk energy (kcal/kg) = 353 + 96 (% milk fat). The fat content of water buffalo milk is given in Jenness (1974) as 7.4%, which is probably similar to that for African buffalo, for most bovids have milk of about this fat content. Hence, 1 kg of milk contains 1.06 Mcals. I have assumed the rate of milk production to be as low as 5 kg/day. It may well be higher, for Jenness (1974) states that available data on milk production in twenty-two widely different species indicate a daily milk yield of 0.126 ± 0.0169 kg/kg$^{0.75}$ body weight, which predicts 13 kg for buffalo. Flatt and Moe (1974) have calculated that the maintenance requirement for lactating cows is 0.085 Mcal NE lact./kg $^{0.75}$ body weight. Thus, for a 500-kg lactating buffalo, daily maintenance costs 8.99 Mcal net energy.

The energy in food that becomes net energy can be calculated from the various equations in Flatt and Moe (1974), the main one being NE lact. (Mcal/kg Dry Matter) = 0.84 DE(Mcal/kg Dry Matter) − 0.77, where DE is the digestible energy found from digestibility trials. Typical values of NE lact. for native grasses in hot tropical or arid areas would be 1.37 Mcals/kg Dry Matter for young growing grass shoots, 1.14 for long green grass, 0.75 for mature, poor-quality dry hay (Weston and Hogan 1973; Flatt and Moe 1974). The quantity of grass eaten per day by a 500-kg adult buffalo is approximately 2% of the body weight, or 10 kg, as calculated in chapter 9, and this agrees well with the published figures for cattle (Flatt and Moe 1974; National Research Council 1970).

The relationship between energy requirement and the different levels of food quality is shown diagrammatically in figure 61. Lactation lasts about eleven months in the Serengeti, and I have assumed that the energy demands fall off at a constant rate, starting with a

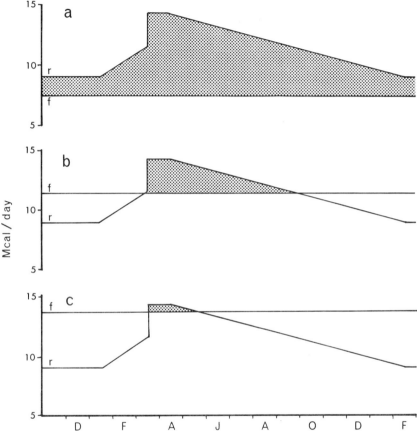

Fig. 61. Diagrammatic representation of the energy requirements of a female African buffalo (*r*) through the breeding cycle compared with energy available (*f*) at three different levels: *a*, low; *b*, intermediate; and *c*, high. Shaded area indicates the extent and time when requirements exceed availability.

maximum at birth in March or April. The last two months of fetal development also cause energy demand to increase from 8.99 to 11.6 Mcals/day (Flatt and Moe 1974). The lowest energy level of food at 7.5 Mcals/day, which would occur at the height of the dry season, is clearly insufficient not only for lactation but also for maintenance. With long green grass, energy is adequate for maintenance but in-

sufficient for the lactation demands. Only with the younger green
grass does the energy intake (13.7 Mcal/day) approach the needs of
lactation. These diagrams suggest that lactation should be occurring
during the period of new growth. In figure 62 I have put this infor-

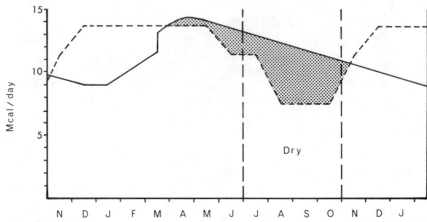

Fig. 62. Model comparing the energy requirements of a reproducing female
buffalo (*solid line*) in the Serengeti with the energy available (*broken line*). Requirements are in excess of available energy (*shaded area*) throughout the dry
season.

mation together to fit in with the rainfall pattern. Kay (1974) has
published the lactation curve for water buffalo, and this shows that
the peak of milk production is not at birth but some five weeks later;
i.e., 11% of the way through the lactation period. Production at birth
is approximately 85% of that of the peak. I have used this curve for
African buffalo in figure 62. Again, this is diagrammatic and can be
considered only as an approximate model of events. Nevertheless, it
does show up two important points: that lactation, on average in the
population, occurs only toward the end of the good period, and that
lactation continues throughout the dry period, during which the female experiences a large energy deficit. What is probably happening
is that during the early part of the good nutritional period, December–February, the female is building up fat reserves in order to cover
the dry season. Grimsdell (1973*b*) calculated a body condition index
using the omentum weight as a percentage of live weight. In females,
but not in males, this index increased either before or during the
peak of births and declined rapidly after this, which is in agreement
with the energy calculations.

A similar energy budget diagram can be constructed for the female wildebeest (fig. 63). Daily fasting metabolism has been measured by Rogerson (1968) as 104.3 kcal/kg W $^{0.73}$, which for a 130-kg adult female is 3.64 Mcal/day. This rate is some 30% higher than for cattle of the same weight under the same conditions. Taylor (1973) found that the maintenance energy of a standing animal is approximately 1.7 times higher than that calculated for standard based metabolism of cattle (see chap. 5). Blaxter (1964) produces evidence that estimates of maintenance requirements of cows grazing under natural conditions are 1.87 times the estimates obtained from indoor experiments. Consequently, for wildebeest I have assumed that maintenance energy is 1.7 times that of basal metabolism. This gives a maintenance energy of 6.19 Mcals/adult female/day. A second estimate was obtained by extrapolating from Flatt and Moe's (1974) figures for net energy of maintenance in lactating cows, as described for buffalo, and this gave a figure of 5.2 Mcals/day. The mean of the two is 5.70 Mcals/day.

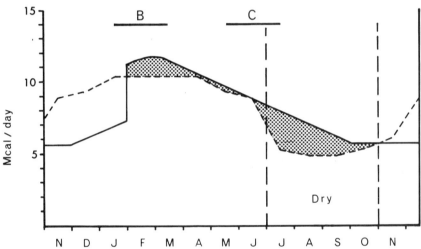

Fig. 63. Model comparing the energy requirements of a reproducing female wildebeest in the Serengeti (*solid line*) with the energy available (*broken line*). The lines *B* and *C* indicate the period of births and conceptions for the population. Shaded area shows the extent and time when requirement exceeds available energy.

Milk production was calculated in two ways. Blaxter (1970) gives the equation of Payne and Wheeler (1968), derived from a range of mammal species, relating energy secreted as milk to the maternal body weight (W) in grams: Milk energy (kcals/day) $= 0.88\ W^{0.75}$. For a 130-kg wildebeest this gives a daily lactation cost of 6.02 Mcals. Alternatively, the milk-yield formula of Jenness (1974) predicts 4.85 kg/day. Milk fat content is taken to be 10% because eland and greater kudu have milk at this level (Jenness 1974). Consequently the milk energy can be calculated, in the same way as with buffalo, to be 6.37 Mcals/day. The mean of the two estimates is 6.20 Mcals/day. The total energy requirement at the peak of lactation is therefore 11.90 Mcals/day. By extrapolating from cattle, the total energy required during the last two months of pregnancy is estimated as 7.35 Mcals/day.

Voluntary food intake of cattle can be increased from 2% to 3% of the body weight per day under good feeding conditions. For wildebeest, the equivalent intakes would be 2.4% of body weight in the dry season, increasing to 4% in the wet season. Energy levels of grass used for maintenance (NEm) can be estimated approximately from the crude protein content (CP) by the formula of Armstrong, Blaxter, and Waite (1964), $NEm = 1.30 + 0.056CP$. Therefore, using the crude protein values of the food consumed as shown in figure 59 and the above estimates of amounts eaten, we can calculate the ingested net energy for maintenance. Since the net energy in the food available for lactation is less than that for maintenance, these calculations of available energy are overestimates. Figure 63 shows the relationship between energy intake and energy demand. Lactation starts at the end of January and ceases sometime during September or October as judged from samples of animals collected during this period. Again the lactation energy curve has been derived from that of water buffalo (Kay 1974). An energy deficit appears to occur in early lactation and during the dry season. At the time of the rut in May–June, however, requirements approximately equal the available energy.

In 1971 the condition of females, males, and young wildebeest was measured at intervals through the year using two indexes—the kidney index (100× weight of kidney fat/weight of kidney) and the bone-marrow fat content. Sinclair and Duncan (1972) have shown that bone-marrow fat is the last fat deposit in the animal to be mobilized during periods of shortage and the first to be replaced. The kidney index, on the other hand, indicates fluctuations of body fat at levels above that at which bone-marrow fat is mobilized. Figures 64 and 65 show how these two indexes changed during the year in fe-

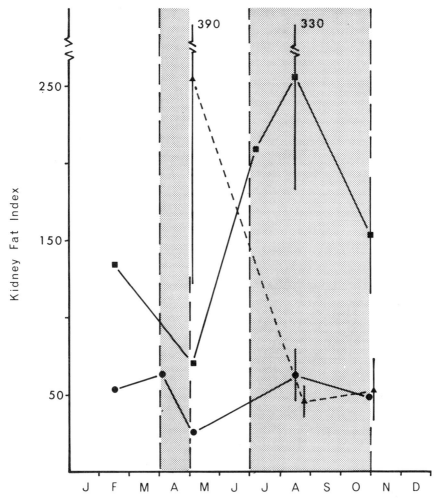

Fig. 64. Changes in the kidney fat index through the year for wildebeest males (*triangles*), lactating females (*circles*), and nonlactating females (*squares*). Dry periods are shaded.

males and males. In 1971 rainfall on the plains was low during April and the wildebeest had to move west into the woodlands. Later rain fell at regular intervals from June to August, thus producing a rather late wet season and shortening the dry season to the two months of September and October.

In February 1971, just after the birth period, lactating wildebeest females already had a low kidney index which declined still further through the dry spell of April (fig. 64). More important, bone-marrow fat also declined to a very low level (fig. 65): Clearly, the abnormal

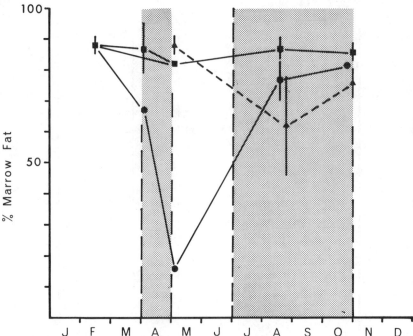

Fig. 65. Seasonal changes in femur marrow fat for wildebeest males (*triangles*), lactating females (*circles*), and nonlactating females (squares). Dry periods are shaded.

dry spell (April is usually the highest rainfall month) came at a time of maximum energy demands on the mother, so that she had to mobilize her very last reserves. Obviously, if the dry spell had continued any longer there would have been a heavy mortality of calves and perhaps of females as well. But this abnormal weather highlights, as a natural experiment, the necessity of having the lactation period at a time of normally good nutrition. In fact, when rain did fall from May onward, the females regained their marrow fat, although they did not manage to put on any excess body fat. They maintained this state through the dry season.

In direct contrast to lactating wildebeest females, the nonlactating animals—those that had lost their calves immediately after birth in February or were two-year-olds not yet pregnant—maintained a very good marrow fat throughout the year. Their kidney index dropped through April, but the subsequent wet period allowed them to put on large amounts of excess fat in the body tissues. This was partially lost through the dry season.

Sexually mature wildebeest males showed a pattern very different from that of the females. By the end of April their condition was very good, with large amounts of body fat (fig. 64). Clearly they had built this up throughout the preceding wet months and maintained it despite the dry April. In the following two months the adult males took part in the rut, a period of several weeks in which the males have little time for eating. They indulge in constant chases, fights, and rounding up of females. In this period they use up their large fat deposits, which it appears were specially laid down for the purpose. As a result, the adult males enter the dry season in the same moderate condition as that of the lactating females.

This evidence, therefore, shows that fat deposits can be laid down in preparation for periods of excessive energy demands—lactation in the female and the rut in wildebeest males—and the early wet season is normally a time when this can be done. Nevertheless, the animals cannot avoid every period of nutritional stress; their strategy can only be one of minimizing this stress.

Conception

With lactation imposing a heavy energy demand, how is conception affected by the availability of food? As I mentioned earlier, in cattle there is a correlation between the length of the "lactational anestrus" and the length of the suckling period: this is particularly pronounced in cows in poor body condition, and if condition is very low estrus will not reappear until some degree of recovery is effected, which may take a year (Baker 1969). At the same time Baker (1969) also showed that zebu cattle, provided they did not have unduly low body weight, commenced estrus between 90 and 140 days postpartum irrespective of when the calves were weaned at varied periods between 95 and 188 days. From this it appears that the condition of the female before calving determines whether estrus occurs.

Energy rather than protein determines the length of anestrus and ovarian activity, according to Wiltbank et al. (1962). These authors also conducted an experiment on cows fed a high- or low-energy level of rations before or after calving and examined the result of these treatments on the occurrence of estrus and the conception rate. They found that the level of feeding before calving appeared to be the most important factor, for a higher proportion of cows exhibited estrus and the anestrus period was shorter in those receiving high-energy food before calving. The response to the level of energy provided them after calving was determined by the precalving level: little effect of postcalving energy was found in those on precalving

high-energy foods, but it had a marked effect on cows fed low-energy
foods before calving. The majority of cows fed continuously on the
low plane failed to show estrus, whereas most of the cows that were
moved to the high plane after calving had exhibited estrus by 90 days
later. Conception rates were affected in a similar way. The rate of
energy intake did not appear to be the only effect in those groups
with a low precalving energy plane. Half of the group on a continuously low plane was put onto a high level at 90 days postpartum
and the animals showed estrus—but not until energy had been used
to put on body weight. The main conclusion from these experiments,
therefore, is that a high level of energy intake resulting in good
body condition before calving is the most important factor influencing estrus and conception: if body condition is good, conception
rates are good irrespective of the nutritional conditions after calving.
Similar conclusions were reached by Lamond (1970).

These experiments suggest why the mating period of African
bovids can take place at times of declining or even very low nutrition,
and why one need not assume that these conditions have a direct
effect on conception rates. On the other hand, these experiments also
show the importance of the precalving period; for if body condition
is not restored to a high level at this time the conception rates later
will indeed be affected. This provides a possible explanation for why
births, lactation, and conceptions take place in the latter half of the
period of good nutrition experienced by buffalo and wildebeest,
since they utilize the first half of this period to build up their body
condition, and this need appears to be an important selection pressure determining the timing of the breeding season. Of course, other
factors such as the availability of calcium may also be important
(Kreulen 1975).

Growth and Puberty

Since conception takes place toward the end of the rains, a considerable proportion of the gestation period occurs during the time when
there is nutritional stress on the mother. With buffalo and wildebeest, only the very early and late pregnancy periods are likely to
occur in good conditions, and this depends on whether the rainy seasons are late or early: the timing of these seasons in fact varies by one
or two months from year to year.

Everitt (1968) and Tassell (1967) have presented evidence from
studies of domestic ruminants that undernutrition of the mother had

permanent subsequent effects on the newborn animal, impairing its survival. Incipient undernutrition in early pregnancy allowed implantation but limited placental size, and this in turn limited fetal food in late pregnancy. This led to early termination of pregnancy, small calves, and high mortality. Everitt stated that the earlier in developmental life nutritional stress was applied the more permanent was the result. The effect of poor nutrition in impairing fetal development, lactation, and postpartum survival in ruminants under natural conditions has been described by Murphy and Coates (1966) and by Short et al. (1969). Verme (1963) found that fawns born to deer fed on a submaintenance diet during pregnancy averaged 54% of the normal weight. In the Serengeti, the normal birth weight of buffalo lay between 38 and 45 kg. The weights of three newborn calves less than 24 hr old that had been abandoned in the Serengeti were found to be 45% (18 kg), 62% (25 kg), and 75% (30 kg) of the normal birth weight. All three died subsequently. These weights were too low to have resulted from the abandonment and starvation in the short period since their birth. Thus there is evidence that calves are born underweight.

Since the time of maximum fetal demand on the buffalo mother in late pregnancy usually occurs in the rains, the incidence of poor nutrition at this time is likely to be low. Abnormally late rains could have an immediate effect on the growth of the fetus and survival of the newborn. Mortality of calves, however, immediately takes a burden off the female, thus giving her a better chance to gain body condition and conceive in the same season: it compensates for the mortality.

There is little direct evidence concerning the effect of nutrition on growth in buffalo. Observations indicated that some but not all calves became very thin during their first dry season when they were about six months old. For wildebeest there is better evidence. Figure 66 shows the bone-marrow fat content and kidney index in calves ranging from newborn to eighteen months. Fat content increased steadily from birth in February until August. There followed a significant decline coinciding with the dry season and with weaning. Growing animals already have a high protein and energy demand, and any decline in intake of these must have an effect on survival. Once the dry season is past the animals build up marrow fat until at eighteen months they reach levels similar to those of adults. In the first year of life the kidney index is very low, indicating that calves

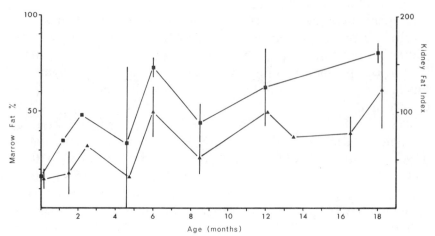

Fig. 66. The increase of kidney fat *(triangles)* and marrow fat *(squares)* of young wildebeest. Fat reserves are very low during the first year of life.

do not, and probably cannot, create a fat store. These animals are therefore very vulnerable to environmental fluctuations.`

Since puberty is determined by growth rate, as was discussed earlier (Joubert 1963; Sadleir 1969), the age of first ovulation and conception must inevitably be influenced by the nutritional conditions prevailing in the first year or two of life. Consequently, nutrition will have a delayed effect on the fertility of young animals. However, because the three- and four-year old females together make up only 15% of the total female population and their contribution to the total production of female offspring is only 6.8% (chap. 8, tables 30, 31), even changes as high as 50% in the fertility of these age-groups will cause only a 3.4% change in total population fertility.

SUMMARY

1. The methods for determining sex and age are described. Field identification of sex is possible in animals two years old and older. Age of fetuses is found from their weight, that of juvenile animals from the tooth eruption pattern or body size and horn shape. Age of adults can be determined with reasonable accuracy only from measurements of tooth wear or counts of cementum layers in the tooth root. Rough age categories for live males are based upon wear of horns.

2. The estrous cycle lasts approximately 23 days. There is a right-side bias for implantation, and only one fetus is produced at each

pregnancy. The gestation period is approximately 340 days. Mean birth weight is 40 kg.

3. Fifty percent of animals were pubertal by three and one-half years old and 50% conceived by five years old. These figures are similar in different populations. The mean prevalence of pregnancy for Serengeti adults was 75%. The calving interval was about fifteen months. This is similar to some populations in Uganda and South Africa but differs from others. There was an equal sex ratio at birth.

4. Population fertility changed from year to year, but there was no consistent trend in different herds. There was little correlation between fertility and either population density or environmental variables.

5. From body weights at different ages, growth curves for the two sexes in the Serengeti are constructed. Up to three and one-half years of age growth rates in different African populations were similar. Adults in Uganda are smaller than those in the Serengeti or South Africa, due to the influence of the smaller forest race.

6. Births take place during the latter half of the rains, and conceptions occur at the end of the rains during the period of declining available food. Conceptions cease in the dry season when conditions are poor. A double breeding season occurs in Uganda, where there are two wet-dry periods. In Serengeti wildebeest and Australian water buffalo births also occur in the wet period, and conceptions occur when conditions are drying out. In both of these species conceptions are synchronized, producing peaks at regular intervals which are correlated with the lunar cycle. The data for African buffalo suggest a similar relationship. Since the estrous cycles of these species are similar to or are multiples of the lunar cycle, the latter may not be directly synchronizing conceptions. Since an external stimulus is necessary for conceptions to occur at the same time each year, a mechanism is suggested whereby the lunar cycle could act as a synchronizer.

7. Using data from domestic animals, models are constructed to show that lactation imposes nutritional stress upon the female. These models also show that least stress is experienced by both buffalo and wildebeest if lactation occurs during the rains.

8. Other evidence from domestic ruminants shows that conception rates are determined by the plane of nutrition before calving, which must be high to maintain good body condition postpartum so that

conception can occur. Low body condition inhibits conception. Therefore it is suggested that lactation cannot take place in the early rain period, for this time is used to build up body reserves. This may be the main factor determining the timing of the breeding season.

9. Age of puberty is determined by body weight, which in turn is determined by growth rate. This is influenced by periods of poor nutrition in the dry season. Fluctuations in conception rates of young animals cause little change in total population fertility, however.

8 Population Trends and Mortality

Buffalo populations occur at different densities in different areas of eastern Africa. In the Serengeti the population has been increasing over the past decade. In this chapter I shall examine these differences in density to see whether regulation is taking place. I shall also examine mortality rates in the Serengeti population to see how these change with time and with the age-distribution of the population.

Density in Different Areas

Over the past several decades much theoretical discussion has centered on whether animal populations can exist in tolerable environments both with and without some sort of negative feedback mechanism operating at some stage in the life history of the animal. Reddingius (1971) has shown from a theoretical point of view that the presence and the absence of regulation are both likely possibilities for any one persisting population. In a continuously varying environment, mortality rarely equals natality simply by chance. However, in the absence of regulation any one population may remain within relatively narrow limits. But it is extremely unlikely that the mean densities of several such nonregulated populations would show any correlation with an environmental factor if they are discrete and do not exchange migrants. Thus Reddingius (1971, p. 93) comments on theoretical populations that are not regulated: "If populations in different areas fluctuate independently of one another, and conditions in the areas are different, then in some areas the density will decline and in others it will increase to very high levels (disregarding random fluctuations). There would be a relationship between area chosen and density, but the whole thing would not last long."

Weather factors should not be considered wholly density-independent any more than they should be thought of as wholly density-dependent. The distinction is perhaps more obvious if one says that most aspects of weather can have an indirect density-dependent effect

197

by altering resources, whereas their direct effects on the animals are usually density-independent (but may be density-dependent if the animals have a social response to the weather). Therefore, a correlation between density in different areas and an environmental factor shows that the populations under study are being regulated provided that this weather factor can be shown to be an important influence limiting essential resources for the animals. In other words, the environmental factor here can be considered as an index of some resource productivity it is influencing.

In chapter 3 (fig. 12) I showed that grass productivity in the Serengeti is significantly related to the amount of rain in the previous month, and this applies to the type of grass eaten by buffalo on the lower parts of the catena. This relationship holds in other areas of tropical Africa, for example on Mount Meru, but a few exceptions may be seen. These occur in the vicinity of lakes, where groundwater is available for growth of forage, in addition to rainfall, as can be seen at Lake Manyara, Tanzania. Other areas are characterized by very tall "elephant grass," which buffalo eat in the young stages after a fire but not when it is mature. In these areas, for example, Murchison Falls Park in Uganda, rain influences food availability positively only part of the time, later producing a negative relationship.

Considering for the moment only those areas where rainfall is the main positive influence on food availability, I have taken estimates of crude density—that is, density over all habitats—measured in this study or published in the literature for different areas and plotted these against mean annual rainfall (fig. 67, table 22). The calculated regression is significant to $p < 0.001$. From this it appears that rainfall, acting through the food supply, determines the equilibrium level of buffalo crude density in eastern Africa, which indicates that the populations are regulated.

This conclusion is valid only if the populations are close to their equilibrium densities. Because all the areas under consideration are protected as parks or reserves, human interference has been kept to a minimum. In some, such as at Ruwenzori Park, Mount Meru, and Tarangire, the populations are stable; in other areas, such as the Mara, Serengeti, and Manyara, they have been increasing but are now reaching equilibrium, and in these I have used the highest figures available. In some areas the trends remain unknown. For these populations the most important influence would have been the eradication

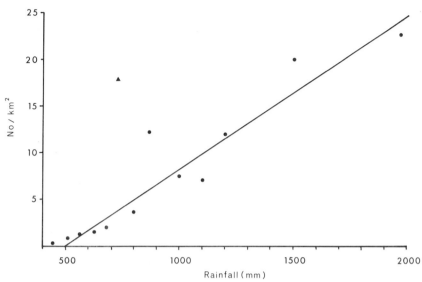

Fig. 67. The relationship between mean crude density in different areas of eastern Africa and mean annual rainfall. The regression line is for the data excluding that of Lake Manyara (*triangle*).

of rinderpest disease which took place in most areas in the early 1950s (I shall discuss this in detail in chap. 9). By the time the measurements of density were made these populations would have already reached some relatively stable population size. This probably applies to the Virunga Park, Zaire, which is close to the known stable population of the Ruwenzori Park, to Tsavo, Mkomasi, and Ruaha areas also. At present, therefore, I think most of these figures are representative of populations close to their equilibrium densities.

The populations that do not fit the curve in figure 67 are irregular because the index I have used to measure resources—namely, rainfall —is inappropriate in these cases. Thus the density for Lake Manyara Park (fig. 67) is exceptionally high compared with other areas with similar rainfall. This is because the park contains a number of permanently flowing springs as well as extensive swamps and lakeshore alkaline grasslands which increase the food available to the buffalo beyond that produced through rainfall. At the other extreme, Murchison Falls Park in Uganda has lower than average buffalo densities for the rainfall of the area. In this area of high rainfall the grasses are tall (2 m high) and coarse, and the buffalo can eat only the leaves, picking them off one by one. Thus only a small part of the plant is edible. Hence rainfall here has a different relationship to resources than in the areas with shorter grasslands. If food productivity could be measured directly these areas would probably fall into the same pattern shown by the other areas.

Although the regression equation predicts that zero buffalo density occurs at about 500 mm mean annual rainfall (fig. 67), Stewart and Stewart (1963) stated that buffalo could be found in areas with annual rainfall as low as 250 mm but not less. In these areas of desert scrub the animals could be found only near rivers. Therefore the amount of permanent water available in the dry season may explain some of the variability in figure 67.

I tested the effect of permanent water supplies by comparing the wet- and dry-season densities in different areas of the Serengeti with the length of permanent river in the same area and the total and dry season rainfall, using simple and partial regression analysis (Sinclair 1974d). The regression coefficients are given in table 23. Over these small areas none of the simple regression coefficients were significant, nor were there significant partial regressions with either total annual rainfall or dry-season rainfall when river length was held constant. However, the partial regressions of dry-season density on river length were significant when rainfall was held constant. Hence this analysis supports the suggestion that local variations in density were determined by the extent of permanent water in the dry season. Since these permanent water supplies determined the extent of the riverine habitats that were preferred by the buffalo (chap. 4), the local variations in density could be explained by variations in the extent of these habitats. Thus mean annual rainfall, the extent of permanent water in the dry season, and perhaps soil moisture are three factors that determine the mean crude density of buffalo in eastern Africa. All could do so by influencing the availability of food resources.

POPULATION TRENDS

The Serengeti Population

If regulation is occurring as I have suggested above, the next question is, "What mechanism brings this about?" Some section of the population must be sensitive to density so that mortality is affected by it. To understand at what stage or stages of the life cycle this density-dependent response occurs I examined the data from the Serengeti population which has accumulated on a regular basis since 1965.

1. Censuses

Buffalo. Since details of the methods and the corrections for errors are given in Sinclair (1973*a*) for counts of the breeding herds, I shall give only a brief description here. The area under study (see figs. 9 and 68) was the woodlands within the national park, excluding the Lamai triangle north of the Mara River (although in some years this and the Mara Park were also counted). Included as part of the population were the animals in the Ikoma triangle between the Grumeti and Orangi rivers to the west of the northern extension. The population was restricted by barriers of human cultivation to the west and south. The plains extending north to Loliondo formed a natural boundary in the east. In fact, censuses showed that few herds lived outside the eastern boundary of the park; so this was taken as the boundary of study. The only artificial boundary was therefore in the north—the Sand River continuing as the Mara river until cultivation was reached at the western boundary (see fig. 4). The Mara River formed an obstacle that herds did not often cross, as judged from my studies in the northern study areas, but the Sand River was easily crossed. Since herds were fairly sedentary (see chap. 6), movements over the Sand River were confined to a few known herds that were accounted for by extending the survey north of the river a few kilometers.

Methods

The complete population, which covered an area of approximately 10,000 km², was censused in the years 1965–68 and 1970. For 1969 and 1971 onward only the northern woodlands were censused and the results were extrapolated to the total area by comparison with the figures for the same areas in May 1970. These northern woodlands were to the north and east of the road that ran from Seronera to the junction of the Orangi and Grumeti rivers. In 1968 two censuses of the whole area were carried out, one during the wet season in May (the time when censuses in the other years were conducted), and one in the dry-season month of September. For each census, the area to be surveyed was divided into blocks, and each of these was searched by one aircraft. The boundaries of these blocks were easily observable rivers and roads, and the total area was covered in 3 to 4 days. Each aircraft had a pilot and observer and both had maps of the block. The block was searched in regular strips at a height of 500 to 800 ft. The flight lines were determined by the observer, and usually

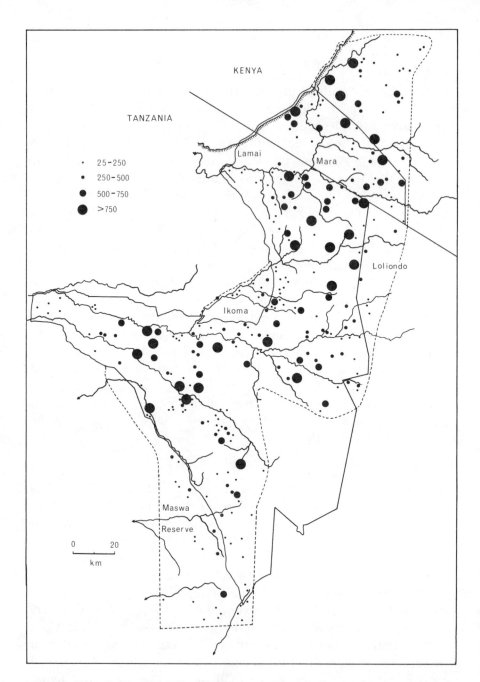

Fig. 68. The distribution of buffalo herds of different sizes in the wet season of 1970. Names refer to areas discussed in the text. The dotted line indicates the boundary of the survey area when not coincident with the Serengeti Park boundary.

they were placed transversely to the long axis of the block, which made it easier for the observer to follow his position on the map. Counts of a block took from 2 to 6 h and when possible were done in the morning when the animals were grazing in the open.

Both pilot and observer were required to take part in observing. When a herd had been seen, it was photographed and its position on the map noted by a group number. On the data sheet the group number, number of photographs taken of the herd, and an estimate of its size were recorded. This last was carried out as a safeguard in case of photographic failure. Large herds required several overlapping frames to cover them, and these were usually made with the aircraft taking a straight course past the herd.

The width of the strips searched varied from 1.5 to 3 km according to the terrain. Buffalo herds could be seen up to 1.5 km on either side of the aircraft and on occasion up to 3 km, because of their black color and their compactness. In 1968, quarter-mile (400 m) markers were laid out on the airstrip to give observers a more accurate idea of distance at the altitude of normal searching before the census. From 1968 onward detailed topographic maps of a scale 1:100,000 and 1:250,000 were used. In earlier years rather less accurate maps were used.

The boundaries of the blocks between days were designed to be as short as possible. All searching extended 2 km into other blocks, thus giving a 4 km overlap, in 1968 and later. In this overlap zone, both teams recorded all the animals they saw. Later, when the results were plotted on a map, it was possible to detect herds that had been double counted by the similarity in herd size and position on the map. The purpose of this zone was to minimize the effect of herds crossing over block boundaries. It also enabled a check of the observers' efficiency.

The herds were counted from the photographs at a later date. The overlap on the prints in the cases where several frames were taken was easily detectable and was demarcated with a chinagraph pencil. Each animal within the outlined area on the photograph was pin-pricked to prevent missing animals or double counting, and a hand counter was used for the counting.

Single males or small bachelor groups were not adequately counted by these methods. But since most of the males had rejoined the herds by May, the number away from the herds was small and was taken to be a constant. This was estimated by intensively searching subsamples of the area and calculating the total from these samples (Sinclair 1972).

Before I could rely on the results of the censuses I had to assess the errors involved. These have already been treated in detail elsewhere (Sinclair 1973a). Because sampling error can cause the estimate to be above or below the true total in different counts, information on population trends would be confounded unless this error was very small. The total count is essentially a 100% sample, and so this type of error is avoided. However, there still remain the bias errors: if they are small, their fluctuation will be of little importance; if they are large but constant, consecutive counts are directly comparable; but if they are large and variable, they must be determined for each count separately and appropriate corrections made before counts are compared.

The main error during the early censuses or surveys made in 1958 by Darling (1960) in the Mara reserve and in 1961 by Stewart and Talbot (1962) in the Serengeti-Mara region occurred because the areas were undersearched. I could deduce this from the total time taken to conduct the census, which I found from later experience was considerably less than the time needed to conduct a complete search of the area. Probably the flight lines were spaced too far apart so that there were gaps between them in which some herds were missed. I found from trials that searching rates should not be less than 25 min/ 100 km^2 for that type of wooded grassland.

A second serious error was due to failure in photography. Hardly a census took place without one film's being poorly exposed, lost, or otherwise rendered unusable. To circumvent this problem observers were asked to make a visual guess or "eye estimate" of the herd size and record it. With some consistency observers underestimated the actual number by 20%–40%; by comparing estimates and photographic counts for each observer on each day, corrections could be made for photographic failures. In 1972 and 1973 I gave the observers a short period of precensus training in visual estimating by using color slides, and the accuracy of their estimates improved (Sinclair 1973 a).

Other errors were due to undercounts from poor photographs and hidden newborn calves. Both could be assessed, but in neither case was the error large. Potential errors due to movements over boundaries were avoided by overlapping the blocks surveyed. Undercounting of the small bachelor male groups, however, could not be assessed directly from these methods of survey, and so separate sample censuses for these groups had to be carried out.

During 1968 seven sample blocks were searched intensively for bachelor males, the total area covering about 10% of the population's range. This led to a crude estimate of 4,000 males. In 1969 an independent estimate was obtained by using the ratio of bachelor males to breeding herds in the northern study area, then assuming that this ratio was the same for all herds: 199 bachelor males and 2,968 breeding animals were counted in this sample area. Hence for the total breeding population the estimate of bachelor males was 3,518. This figure was supported by a further independent estimate obtained from a stratified sample count in 1971, which I have described elsewhere (Sinclair 1972). The estimate over the same area came to 3,097, with a 95% confidence interval of 2,424–3,766 males. Thus, from the last two estimates a mean of approximately 3,300 bachelor males was taken to be present in 1968. In May of that year, during the total count, 583 males were recorded: only 18% of the bachelor males were seen in the total count, but the error in undercounting the total population was only 4.9%. Since the number of bachelor males must be proportional to the size of the total breeding population which was estimated in the total count, I have considered this error a constant for all counts.

Initial results have been published in Sinclair (1973a). Since then, counting of the 1970 census that covered both the Mara and Serengeti parks (fig. 68) has been completed: previously only the northern woodlands had been counted. Also the 1973 census had been counted and the 1967 and 1968 May censuses recounted to correct errors in undercounting areas at the southern extremity of the park in 1967 and outside the park along the Grumeti River in 1968. The 1970 figures are used to extrapolate the results from the northern woodlands censused in 1969 and 1971–73. Since increases in population have been similar in the southern and northern halves of the park, these extrapolations are considered reasonable.

The results of these corrected censuses are summarized in table 24 and shown in figure 69. They were accumulated from the following surveys:

1958: Darling (1960) conducted an aerial survey flight in the dry season of 1958 with experienced observers, in order to estimate herbivore numbers. In one flight of 5.8 h the flight paths included an

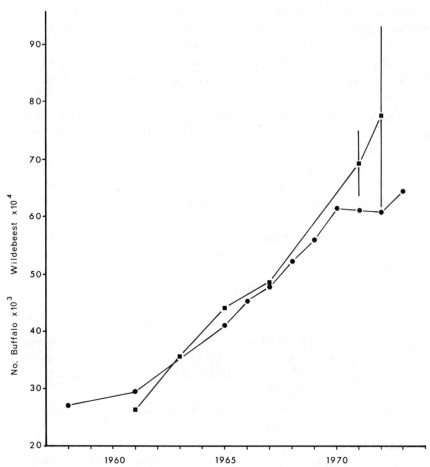

Fig. 69. The population increase of buffalo (*circles*) and wildebeest (*squares*) between 1958 and 1973. Vertical lines indicate the 95% confidence limits of the total.

area of some 2,600 km², and a total of 3,400 buffalo was estimated. Correcting for underestimating and undersearching the area, I calculate the probable number as 9,150. Stewart and Talbot (1962) gave a figure of 5,934 buffalo in the Mara region and 15,898 in the Serengeti in 1961. Using the same ratio for 1958 I estimate that there were approximately 24,000 in the Serengeti. In 1970 the ratio of 18,200 in the Mara area compared with 61,620 in the Serengeti predicts about 30,000 in 1958. Consequently I have taken a mean of 27,000 for that period.

1961: From the flight times published by Stewart and Talbot (1962) it is clear that the area was undersearched. Correcting for this and photographic counting error I estimate that there were about 29,500 animals in 1961.

1965–68, 1970: Methods for these censuses are described above. Apart from the Serengeti Park other adjoining areas have also been censused on occasion. The Kenya Mara Park was censused in 1970. This produced a total of 11,254 buffalo with another 6,946 to the north of the park along the Mara River and in its associated forest. Other buffalo are known to occur to the west of this above the Isuria escarpment in Kenya, where the area is forested, with open glades produced by frequent burning. On the Tanzania side above the escarpment heavy settlement and cultivation by the Wakuria tribe keep out buffalo or other wildlife. Furthermore, this tribe poaches in the Lamai area of the Serengeti, which lies between the Mara River and the escarpment. Only 340 buffalo were counted in this area in 1970, compared with 3,216 in an identical area between the Mara River and the escarpment on the Kenya side of the international boundary (fig. 68). The vigilance of the Kenyan Masai-Mara Park rangers deters poachers from crossing the boundary here. I shall say more about poaching as a mortality factor in the next chapter.

To the east of the Serengeti as far as Loliondo, 873 buffalo were counted in 1967, 834 in 1968, and about 800 in 1970, although this last census was only a brief survey and the population was probably higher. The Maswa Game Reserve lies to the southwest of the Serengeti (fig. 67). An attempt to survey this rocky country in 1967 failed when one of the two planes searching the area crashed on takeoff from an overgrown temporary landing strip. The occupants of the plane, unhurt, were rescued by the second plane, which happened to pass by not five minutes later. This incident also caused a small undercount of the southernmost corner of the park, which I have corrected by comparison with the census of 1968. A brief survey in that year tallied 960 animals in the Maswa Reserve, but a thorough search in 1970 revealed 3,795 animals. The Maswa Game Reserve, supposedly protected from settlement and poaching, has in recent years been completely neglected by the Game Department. In 1971 a survey showed that about one-third of the area had already been cultivated and settled, and snareline fences were common and appeared to rapidly be spreading eastward. Consequently one must expect the surviving animals originally living in this area to be pushed steadily into higher densities in the southern corner of the Serengeti Park. Because of these events in the Maswa Reserve I have considered only those buffalo occurring within the park boundary in the southern part of the park.

1969, 1971–73: In these years only the northern sector of the woodlands was searched. The figures given in table 24 were then extrapolated to the whole area using the results from the most recent census of the park in 1970.

Wildebeest. Since 1961 the migratory wildebeest population has also been monitored, although less systematically than that of the buffalo because of the considerable practical difficulties of censusing such large numbers. Nevertheless censuses have taken place in 1961 (Talbot and Talbot 1963), 1963, 1965 (Watson 1967), and 1967, also by Watson. In 1971 I conducted a total count (Sinclair 1973*a*) while Norton-Griffiths (1973) carried out a sample count at the same time, a technique he repeated in the following year. Consequently there is some data with which to compare the trends in the buffalo population. A total count of the wildebeest can be done only when the population congregates on the treeless Serengeti Plains during the wet season between February and June. Occasionally during this period they form into a few very dense herds, and it becomes possible to carry out a total photographic census; this was done in May 1971. The method was essentially similar to that of previous workers such as Talbot and Talbot (1963) and Watson (1967).

Methods

The distribution of the population was defined by an initial systematic survey which extended far beyond the last wildebeest seen. The area covered by the distribution was divided into blocks, and these were searched systematically by aircraft, as described for buffalo. The searching height was 800 to 1,000 ft. Two planes (Cessnas 180 and 182) were used to cover the main concentration on the first day and outlying groups on the second day. The animals were not migrating, and there was negligible crossing over between blocks.

Two motor-Nikon 35 mm cameras with cassettes containing 250 frames were used because of the large number of photographs needed. The lenses were of 55 mm focal length, and the film was Plus X exposed at f 5.6, 1/1,000 sec. A large herd was photographed with overlapping runs of oblique photographs, and each run in turn comprised overlapping photographs—the longest run contained fifty frames. The overlaps, both between frames on the same run and between runs, were detected using cues such as the shape of groups of animals and the pattern of the vegetation. The overlaps were demarcated on the prints (size 8 x 12 cm) with a chinagraph pencil. The prints were searched with the naked eye, and the animals counted in the same way as for buffalo. In all, 2,770 frames were counted, by a number of different people.

In order to estimate the error in counting, a sample of 98 frames was chosen randomly, reprinted, and counted again under a binocular microscope of $\times$ 5 magnification. At the same time as these frames were counted the proportion of that year's calves was estimated. This proportion was then compared with an independent estimate from ground transects randomly placed through the whole population and run immediately after the aerial count. This was considered necessary because the small calves may have been obscured on the prints. These corrections were then combined to produce a final estimate (P) from an equation formulated by G. M. Jolly (personal communication), which is given in Sinclair (1973a).

Details of the wildebeest counts can be found in that paper and in Norton-Griffiths (1973). The results are summarized in table 25. The censuses were:

1961: Two censuses were conducted in this year, one by the Royal Air Force, the other by Talbot and Talbot (1963). They produced similar results, which after corrections for counting errors, produced a total of 263,362 animals.

1963, 1965: These censuses conducted by Watson (1967) were corrected in the same way as that for 1971 described above. A census in the woodlands in 1966 was of a dispersed population, and the errors involved were not comparable to those of other censuses, all of which were on the plains. Consequently, I have not included the results of this in the comparison of buffalo and wildebeest.

1967: The photographic count reached a total of 390,000, with an estimated 20,000 remaining (R. H. V. Bell, personal communication). After corrections a total population of 483,292 animals was calculated.

1971: Two censuses were conducted at approximately the same time. One, a total count, produced an estimate of 692,777, which when

corrected for undercounting of calves on the photographs produced
a total of 720,769. The first figure is used to compare with earlier
censuses, for they incorporated similar errors in undercounting
calves. The second figure can be used to compare with the sample
count of Norton-Griffiths (1973) which produced an estimate of
754,028. The two combined produced a mean of 737,399 $\pm$ 43,600
as 95% confidence limits.

1972: The sample count for this year estimated 841,359 $\pm$ 153,389
animals (Norton-Griffiths 1973), the widely scattered population
causing the large confidence interval. Since these sample counts min-
imized the error of undercounting calves, I used the ratio of the two
estimates in 1971 (692,777/754,028) to give the figure of 773,014 for
1972, which I have used to compare with previous counts.

To summarize these results, the censuses indicate that there has
been an increase in buffalo in the 1960s followed by a leveling off in
the early 1970s (figure 69). There is some indication of a new increase
beginning after May 1972, for the figures for 1973 were higher than
those for earlier years. Furthermore, Grimsdell (1975), continuing
the monitoring of the northern population, reports an even higher
figure of 40,828, which gives an estimated 67,927 for the whole
population, based on the 1970 census.

For wildebeest, not only did an increase occur during the same
time period as that of buffalo, but the rate of increase was remark-
ably similar, as can be seen from the two curves in figure 69. The
census for 1972 had such wide confidence limits that it is not possible
to say whether or not an increase occurred after 1971, and further
censuses are needed for this population.

2. Recruitment and Yearling Mortality of Buffalo

Recruitment was measured as the number of animals between one
and two years old (yearlings) per 100 adult females. Because mortality after two years old was small and relatively constant, the yearling proportion in the population was an index of the proportion
that would reach sexual maturity. Animals were counted from aerial
photographic samples taken between February and May in the northern and southern areas between 1965 and 1969, and thereafter in the
northern areas only. Table 26 gives the number of yearlings/100
adult females and their proportion of the total population. For some
years there were not enough samples to determine the standard error,

but where it was calculated it was small enough to suggest that the observed figures were not too inaccurate. Figure 70 shows the similarity in the fluctuations between the two areas. Since they were more than 100 km apart, this similarity suggests that the factors determining recruitment were similar over the whole population.

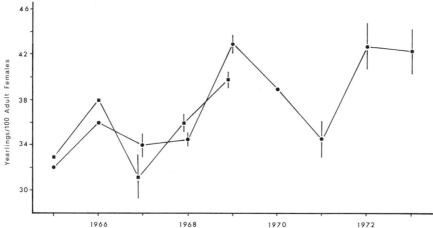

Fig. 70. The proportion of yearlings present between February and May each year in two study areas—south (*squares*) and north (*circles*). Vertical lines indicate 95% confidence limits. Note the similarity in fluctuation between the areas. Reproduced from Sinclair (1974*b*) with permission of Blackwell Scientific Publications, Ltd.

The proportion of yearlings in the population did not show any correlation with the size of the population; for instance, recruitment was as high in 1972 as it was in 1969. In the southern study area recruitment did show a correlation ($p < 0.05$) with the rainfall in the previous January to December. This period covered the latter half of pregnancy, lactation, and newborn mortality experienced by these yearlings. However, this relationship was not found for the northern study area.

Mortality during the first year of life was calculated from the differences between the number born in one year and the number surviving at the May census a year later, these figures being obtained from the measurements of fertility described in the previous chapter and those of recruitment. The numbers that died each year are given in table 27. They are also expressed in the same table as a proportion of the number of animals in the total population alive at the start of the mortality, which I have taken to be June each year. These proportions, plotted against population size in figure 71, show little relationship between the two. Some relatively large changes in mortality did take place from year to year.

3. Adult Mortality of Buffalo

For this analysis I have counted all those over one year old as adults. The numbers in this category that died each year were calculated from the difference between the adults plus yearlings alive in May one year and the adults alone alive in the following May. (The yearlings in the previous May move into the adult class. If none in this category died, the adults in the following May would equal the sum of adults and yearlings in the previous year). These figures for adult mortality are given in table 27 and are also presented as a proportion of the population before mortality. Although fewer than half as many adults as juveniles die, the percentage of mortality due to adults does appear to show a positive relationship to the size of the population, as indicated by the regression line in figure 71. This, therefore, indicates a density-dependent relationship which I shall now examine in greater detail.

4. Analysis for Regulation and Buffalo Population Models

The models. I have used the method of Varley and Gradwell (1968) to detect the stage of the life cycle at which regulation is occurring (Sinclair 1973*b*, *c*). The new census data now permit a new analysis. Although this approach may have certain drawbacks, mainly statistical, as has been pointed out by a number of authors (e.g., Ito 1972; Kuno 1973), the method does allow one to examine different stages of the life cycle. The information on when regulation may be occurring in this cycle helps to focus the search for the cause of the regulating mortality: it does not of course identify this mortality, but it does shorten the search. The method, moreover, is not used here to prove or disprove the occurrence of regulation itself, which was approached using other evidence described earlier in this chapter.

The information needed for the analysis has been compiled from the estimates of fertility, recruitment, and the annual census. Using this, it is possible to identify three reductions in population each year. The first is due to the decrease in fertility relative to the potential maximum, the second and third are due to the mortality of calves under one year old (juvenile mortality) and animals over one year

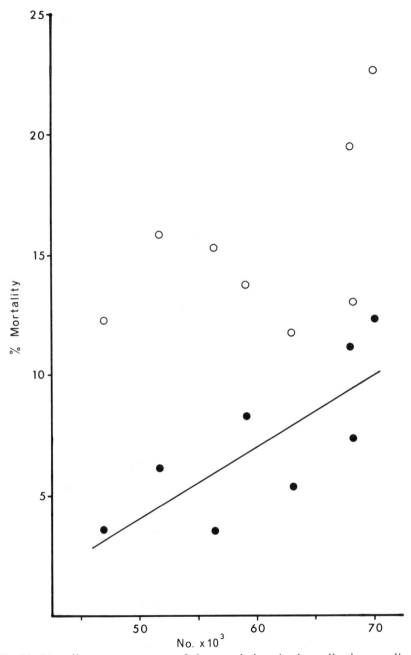

Fig. 71. Mortality as a percentage of the population size immediately preceding it in June. The regression line is for mortality of adults (*solid circles*). Open circles illustrate juvenile mortality.

old (adult mortality) as described above. Changes in fertility are measured as the difference between the number of calves born if all mature females produced calves and that which would occur with the observed pregnancy. The proportion of mature females in the population over one year old was estimated from random aerial photographic samples and found to be 42.5% ± 1.8% (S.E.). By measuring these three reductions I was able to calculate a life table which showed the actual number of animals present after each reduction had taken place in each year: for simplification, the reductions were calculated as taking place consecutively in the order fertility loss, juvenile mortality, and adult mortality, although the period of adult mortality tended to overlap that of juvenile mortality; but the simplification did not radically alter the results. Each reduction was analyzed with respect to how it changed from year to year as the population changed. In particular, it was necessary to find whether or not any reduction increased proportionately as the population increased so that it could act as a negative feedback mechanism regulating the population.

Each reduction can be expressed as a proportion in terms of the initial (I) and final (F) population before and after that reduction has occurred, in the form $\log (I/F)$. This has been termed the k value by Varley and Gradwell (1970), and it is plotted against $\log I$ in order to see if a positive relationship exists. Since I appears on both axes, any significant positive relationship formed must be subjected to further analysis. Varley and Gradwell (1968) state that formal proof of a positive relation between k and $\log I$ can only be acceptable if both of the regression slopes of $\log I/\log F$ and $\log F/\log I$ are significantly different from a slope of unity and lie on the same side of this slope.

The sum of the k values (K) is the total reduction in population during the year. Thus for the Serengeti buffalo $K = ka + kj + kf$, where ka represents adult mortality, kj, juvenile mortality, and kf, the reduction in fertility.

The changes taking place due to natality and mortality each year from 1965 to 1973 have been compiled as a life table and are shown in table 28. From these figures the k values were calculated and plotted against the log population before each reduction (fig. 72). In fact, all three k values were plotted against the log population in June when all the newborn calves had appeared, for it was after this that both juvenile and adult mortality took place, and it was also the

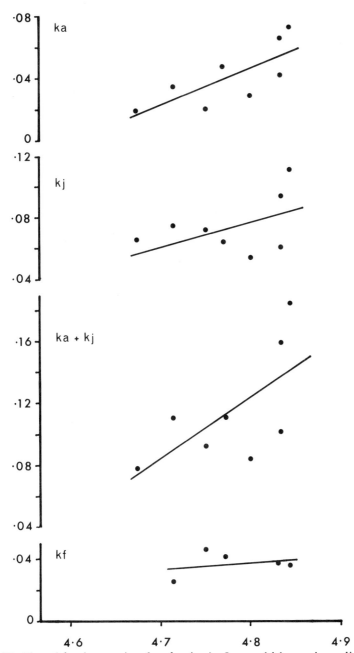

Fig. 72. Plot of *k*-values against log density in June, which was immediately before the mortality. The slope for *ka* was the only one significantly different from
zero; *ka* represents adult mortality, *kj*, juvenile mortality, and *kf*, reduction of
fertility.

time when conceptions occurred. The only reduction which showed a significant positive slope with log density was ka ($b = 0.2357$, $p < 0.05$). The points for kj showed so much scatter that no significant relationship could be found, although the regression line showed a positive slope ($b = 0.1575$). Because of this scatter the combined figures for ka and kj also produced a regression line of positive slope ($b = 0.3932$) when plotted against density, but this was not significant. The regression line for kf ($b = 0.0449$) was very close to zero, suggesting that fertility remained relatively constant as the population increased.

The population estimates, before and after the adult and juvenile mortalities, were transformed to logs and tested by the methods described above. Only the estimates for adult mortality produced regression slopes significantly different from unity (log F/log I, $p < 0.002$; log I/log F, $p < 0.05$), and on the same side of this slope. Consequently I consider that adult mortality is the only reduction which appears to be acting in a density-dependent manner.

This conclusion by itself, however, does not necessarily mean that the population is regulated by adult mortality alone. This regulating effect may be too weak, for example, and there may be some part of the juvenile mortality which is also density-dependent but which is obscured by errors in data collection or by large random mortalities. To examine these possibilities I constructed two models and compared them with the existing census data (Sinclair 1973b). The new information covering the years 1965–73 now allows a reanalysis and permits new models to be made, the parameters of which are given in table 29.

In the first model adult mortality acted as a negative feedback mechanism, the rate being that of the slope of the regression line of ka against log population size, and reduction in fertility and juvenile mortality were held at a constant proportion by using their mean k values. Thus the population was started with the log adult plus yearling population as it was known from the census in 1965. This was increased by a constant proportion (log P) which represented the calves that would have been born if all females had been fertile. This was reduced first by a constant proportion due to reduction in fertility (kf). Then a reduction due to the adult mortality was made, this being calculated for the appropriate density from the regression equation (ka on log population of adults and newborn). Finally, a constant juvenile mortality (kj) was subtracted to give the new total of log adults and yearlings. Thus if the population was started with $\log N_0$ adults and yearlings, then the following year's population of adults and yearlings ($\log N_1$) was found by

$$\log N_1 = \log N_0 + \log P - \overline{kf} - ka - \overline{kj} , \qquad (1)$$

and ka is given by the regression equation as

$$ka = b_1 (\log N_0 + \log P - \overline{kf}) + a_1 , \qquad (2)$$

where b_1 is the slope and a_1 the intercept of the regression line. This model was investigated first because adult mortality seemed the one most likely to be regulating the population.

The second model assumed that juvenile mortality was also regulating the population, and so the slope of the regression line of the combined adult and juvenile mortalities ($ka + kj$ plotted against log population size) was used in the computations while reduction in fertility was kept as a constant proportion. So with an initial population of N_0', $\log P$ was added and the constant mean kf subtracted. Then ($ka + kj$) was calculated for the existing population of adults, yearlings, and newborn. Thus

$$\log N_1' = \log N_0 + \log P - \overline{kf} - (ka + kj) \qquad (3)$$

and

$$(ka + kj) = b_2 (\log N_0' + \log P - \overline{kf}) + a_2 , \qquad (4)$$

where b_2 and a_2 are the slope and intercept of the regression line.

From these formulas the equilibrium population can also be calculated. Thus for model 1 the equilibrium level of adults and yearlings (x_1) occurs when the density-dependent adult mortality (ka) equals the increment due to conception less the average fertility loss and newborn mortality, i.e., when

$$ka = \log P - \overline{kf} - \overline{kj} . \qquad (5)$$

Also from equation (2), at equilibrium,

$$ka = b_1 (\log x_1 + \log P - \overline{kf}) + a_1 . \qquad (6)$$

By substituting into equation (5) and rearranging,

$$\log x_1 = \frac{(\log P - \overline{kf} - \overline{kj} - a_1)}{b_1} - \log P + \overline{kf} . \qquad (7)$$

The equilibrium level (x_2) from model 2 can be derived in a similar way, so that

$$\log x_2 = \frac{(\log P - \overline{kf} - a_2)}{b_2} - \log P + \overline{kf} \,. \qquad (8)$$

Both models were also used to extrapolate back in time from the starting census of 1965.

Regulation and disturbance. The results of the extrapolations for the two models are shown in figure 73, together with the observed popu-

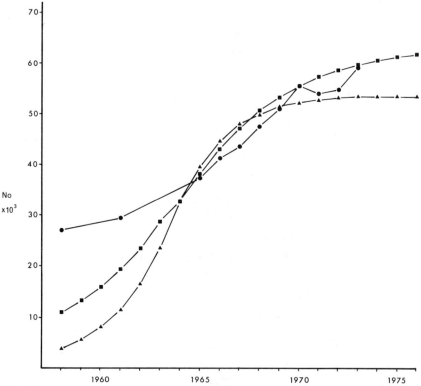

Fig. 73. Population models, starting with the observed number of adults and yearlings in May 1965 and extrapolating forward and backward. Model with *ka* alone regulating (*squares*), that with the sum of *ka* and *kj* regulating (*triangles*), compared with the observed data (*circles*).

lation of adults and yearlings. Model 1 shows the closest fit to the observed data, and it predicts 60,770 adults and yearlings for the year 1974. From the count of the northern woodlands in early June 1974 (Grimsdell 1975), I estimate 67,927 for the whole park at that time. Assuming that this total contained 10% newborn calves (since all previous years' censuses showed 9–10% newborn at this time), the total of adults and yearlings would be 61,134, which is reasonably close to the predicted population. The model also predicts an equilibrium population of 63,570 adults and yearlings.

The forward extrapolation of model 2 results in a lower asymptote, the equilibrium population of adults and yearlings being 53,650. This is lower than any of the census figures since 1970, and consequently this model must be rejected. This means that the apparent density-dependent result for juvenile mortality (indicated by the positive regression slope of kj against log numbers of adults and yearlings) is spurious.

Juvenile mortality, therefore, is probably density-independent and results from one or several randomly fluctuating environmental variables. However, because of the very sensitivity of the young animals to random causes of mortality this stage of the life cycle produces the fluctuations in population from year to year. A mortality behaving in such a way has been called a "key factor" (Varley and Gradwell 1960) and has been defined as that which contributes most to the fluctuations in the total annual reduction (K). This can be observed graphically by plotting the successive values of K and comparing their changes with those of each of the separate reducions (k values). When I did this for the buffalo data, juvenile mortality was clearly the most important contributor to K (Sinclair 1973b). Recently this data has been reanalysed by Podoler and Rogers (1975) by plotting each k value against K. Their conclusions confirmed that juvenile mortality was the "key factor." The main point, therefore, is that juvenile mortality appears to cause the fluctuations in population and adult mortality compensates for these disturbances in a density-dependent way, tending to dampen the fluctuations.

Changes in fertility probably have little effect in regulating the population, for this reduction remained almost constant while the population was increasing and leveling out. This does not mean that large changes in fertility do not occur; first, failure of the rains, particularly in the first half of the wet season when females are building up body stores, could cause large changes in fertility, as was discussed in the previous chapter. Such changes, however, would act more to disturb the population further from equilibrium than to regulate it. Second, different populations do appear to have differences in their mean fertility levels, as can be seen in the comparison of the northern Uganda and Serengeti populations.

The rinderpest perturbation. The backward extrapolation of both models shows that neither agrees with the population estimates of 1961 and 1958, although model 1 is still a closer fit than model 2 (fig. 73). In effect, the models developed from data during the years 1965–73 showed a faster increase than was actually exhibited by the population during the years 1958–65. The models are based on the assumption that the regulating effect was linear. If this is correct, we can conclude, first, that conditions acting upon the population were different before 1965 than after that date: second, that those conditions must have changed at some period between 1961 and 1965, since the models do not fit the 1961 figure: and, third, that those conditions before 1965 must have resulted in either a reduction in fertility or an increase in some mortality compared with conditions after 1965, in order to have produced the slower increase. Alternatively, the regulating effect of adult mortality (ka on log density) may have been curvilinear in a concave way such that there could have been a positive regulating effect at low density, thus producing a slow initial increase. At present the k value data do not allow a distinction between linear and curvilinear regressions, and so I have assumed the former for the models.

The exotic disease rinderpest, which had been introduced to Africa through human activities, caused repeated die-offs of buffalo and wildebeest in the Serengeti up to 1963, mainly through juvenile mortality. Through the efforts of veterinarians the disease disappeared entirely by 1964 (see fig. 81), and it has not reappeared in the ensuing twelve years. In the next chapter I shall describe the evidence for this series of events.

Both the presence of rinderpest and its removal can be regarded as an artificial perturbation, the effects of which have allowed the above analysis for regulation in the population. The question is, therefore, Was it the removal of rinderpest that resulted in the change in rate of increase between 1961 and 1965? To test for this I estimated the juvenile mortality that would have occurred had rinderpest been operating and inserted this into my first model population (fig. 74). The mortality of buffalo due to rinderpest has not been measured, but that for wildebeest has (Talbot and Talbot 1963). Since the population dynamics of these two species are so similar, and since their causes of mortality, including rinderpest, are comparable, I consider that mortality rates for wildebeest can be extrapolated to buffalo for the purposes of the model. When rinderpest was acting

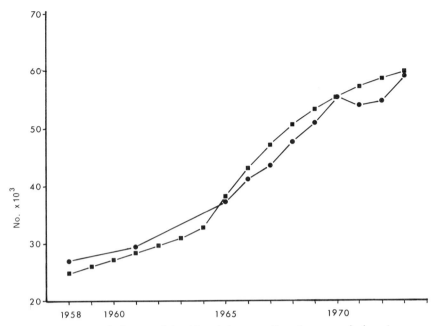

Fig. 74. The population model with adult mortality alone regulating (*squares*, see fig. 73), adjusted for a constant proportional mortality due to rinderpest before 1964, compared with the observed number of adults and yearlings (*circles*).

1.73 times more yearling wildebeest died than when it was absent. Consequently, I increased the mean juvenile buffalo mortality by the same amount. Taking the population model in which adult mortality alone was regulating, I extrapolated backward from 1965 to 1964 using the same parameters as those for the post-1965 model. Then for 1963 and earlier years I inserted the higher juvenile mortality due to rinderpest, as a constant, and continued the extrapolation back to 1958, when the first population estimates were made. As can be seen from figure 74, this extra mortality was sufficient to produce a reasonable fit with the observed estimates of 1961 and 1958. I should point out that this mortality was considered merely as a constant, and I have made no assumptions that it regulated the population. However, when large but constant mortalities such as rinderpest are present, rates of increase are small, and the population takes a long time to regain equilibrium if disturbed. Moreover, when regulating mortalities are weak, chance variations due to weather play a more conspicuous part. If this is what occurred, then low buffalo populations in the late 1950s could have remained at a low level and increased only very slowly if they suffered recurrent juvenile rinderpest mortality, as the evidence suggests they did.

This leads to the question, How did the population reach such a low level in the first place? As I have outlined above, the historical evidence for rinderpest is that it appears in epizootic form. The partly successful inoculation campaigns by the veterinarians in the 1940s and 1950s resulted in quiescent periods. During such periods the animal populations build up a relatively large proportion of susceptible individuals—this need take only two or three years—and reappearance of the disease then causes a large reduction. It is in fact an artificial result of human activities. This type of reduction appears to have taken place in both Serengeti wildebeest and buffalo and in Lake Manyara buffalo in the late 1950s. Thereafter rinderpest remained in the area and continued to affect juveniles until it was artificially removed. In conclusion, therefore, the evidence suggests that rinderpest could have acted to perturb the population, and its removal could have allowed the population to increase in a way similar to that observed.

The Lake Manyara and Tarangire Populations

The events I have described for the Serengeti population have been closely paralleled in another population at Lake Manyara, where rinderpest was also present until the early 1960s. Apart from this the habitats, weather, and predators differed between the two areas, adding to the probability that rinderpest was the cause of the changes.

At intervals of four or five years the buffalo in Lake Manyara Park have been censured. The first census was done in April 1965 by Watson and Turner (1965), and 1,507 animals were counted. The second I carried out in May 1969, counting 1,548, and the third I conducted in March 1973, counting 1,793 animals.

The presence of the lake provides year-round grazing for the animals, thus allowing a much higher density than in the Serengeti. However, lions are also much denser at Manyara, and they concentrate their depredations on the buffalo (Schaller 1972). The Manyara buffalo are restricted by human cultivation to the north and south and above the escarpment on the western side. To the east lies the lake. Between 1958 and 1965 the area of the park was about 102 km², according to I. Douglas-Hamilton (personal communication). However, between 1965 and 1968 the level of the lake rose as a result of heavy rainfall (especially in 1967 and 1968), falling on surrounding areas draining into the lake, which has no outflow. Consequently the area of the park was decreased to 87 km² (plate 30). Much of the inundated area consisted of the *Cyperus-Sporobolus* pasture preferred by the buffalo in the dry season (Vesey-Fitzgerald 1969).

The density of buffalo before the lake level rose was 14.8 animals/km², that after the rise in level was 17.8/km², and that in 1973 was 20.6/km². The increase of density in Manyara between 1965 and 1969 was 16% that of the former year, while in the Serengeti it was 15%. Between 1969 and 1973 the increase was 20% in Manyara and 36% in the Serengeti. So it appears there has also been an increase in density in this small area of Manyara similar to that in the Serengeti 200 km to the west.

The changes in population at Manyara are important because they parallel those in the Serengeti after a similar perturbation, the die-offs due to rinderpest in the late 1950s (see next chapter). Equally important is a population in the Tarangire Park, Tanzania, which did not show such increases in density but which also did not suffer the large die-offs due to rinderpest at the time the Serengeti and Manyara populations were experiencing them. The Tarangire population, of course, did suffer from rinderpest at one time, but the disease was eradicated at an earlier stage in the campaign by the veterinarians—probably sometime in the 1950s—so that the population may have already completed its increase.

The Tarangire Park lies 60 km southeast of Lake Manyara in relatively flat and dry (600 mm rain p.a.) *Acacia* woodland. A description of the area, including the vegetation, is given in Lamprey (1963*b*). In 1961 Lamprey (1963*b*) counted approximately 1,100 animals, these being confined to the floodplains on each side of the Tarangire River in the southern part, with a few occurring in the Sangaiwe Hills on the western boundary. Twelve years later, in March 1973, Hugh Lamprey and I counted 1,148 buffalo in the same areas as those observed by Lamprey earlier. From these results it appears that little change in the buffalo population had occurred.

In the 1973 census of Tarangire we also counted elephants. Our searching efficiency for this species was poor because of the thick woodland and the scattered nature of the elephant herds. However, we did see 513 elephants, estimating that only half the area was searched, since there were strips between the transects that were too far away to search properly. Consequently I estimated that there were at least 1,000 elephants in the park in 1973. In the early 1960s Lamprey (1963a, 1964) records only about one-quarter of this number. At the time of the 1973 census the vegetation was very green, with abundant water both inside and outside the park; so the animals were not concentrating for lack of these resources. The reasons for this rise in elephant density within the park appear to be an increase in hunting and expansion of cultivation in the surrounding areas.

The impact of the elephant population on the numbers of buffalo, however, did not appear to be of any great importance. This observation is relevant to the Serengeti, where elephants may have been immigrating and reducing the tree density during the time when buffalo were increasing (Lamprey et al. 1967). Although the events related to elephants are disputed by several workers (e.g., Watson and Bell 1969), they may have caused the increase in buffalo population, or at any rate have confounded the effects due to the removal of rinderpest. The observation at Tarangire that large changes in elephant population, with its consequent effects on habitat, produce no noticeable effect on the buffalo, suggests that the elephants of the Serengeti have not been the cause of the increase in buffalo there.

Finally, in Ngorongoro Crater there has been an increase over the past decade in the number of buffalo that graze the crater floor (Rose 1975). However, this increase is partly due to immigration from the surrounding forests, and so it is not possible to say whether a numerical change in population has taken place.

To sum up this comparison of buffalo populations, it appears that the two which experienced heavy rinderpest mortality in the late 1950s showed a subsequent increase in population after the removal of the disease, while a third population at Tarangire, which also suffered less from rinderpest, showed no such increase. On the other hand the Tarangire area did experience a large increase in elephant density, suggesting that this species has little effect on buffalo numbers.

AGE-SPECIFIC SURVIVAL AND MORTALITY

I have constructed composite life tables showing the probability of surviving to different ages for the Serengeti population as it was in the years 1965–69. The information for these tables has been derived from two sources. The skulls of animals two years of age and older were found in the field. These animals had died of causes other than shooting or large-scale snaring by humans. From the tooth eruption pattern or from measurements on the upper first molar teeth of these skulls, the age at death of the animals was calculated by the methods described in chapter 7. The skulls of animals younger than two years were underrepresented in the field collections because they disintegrated easily from weathering or were broken up by predators. Mortality for these ages was therefore calculated from the survival measurements obtained from the low-level photographic samples which I have described in the previous chapter. Of the potentially fertile females 69.5% produced calves, and on average only 36 of these calves per 100 females remained a year later, which indicates a 48.5% mortality. Measurements of animals in the second year of life, although subject to greater errors from identification, ranged between 25 and 30, with a mean of about 27 two-year-olds per 100 adult females. This gives a mortality of 9 two-year-olds/100 adult females, or 12.9% of the original newborn number, in the second year. (In Sinclair [1974c] an error in tabulation resulted in the first-year mortality's being placed in the second-year age group.) Since at two years of age the sex ratio was still approximately equal as judged from ground counts of the population, the same probabilities of survival and death have been used for both sexes up to these ages. Separate life tables were constructed for the two sexes. For the males, the sample was large enough to divide into those from northern and southern halves of the Serengeti, to investigate whether there were any differences between the two areas.

In a sample of 584 skulls collected in the field, 246 were of females and 155 and 183 were of northern and southern males respectively. The frequency distributions of ages of these samples are given in the second columns of tables 30, 32, and 33. These distributions have been increased proportionately to produce a total sample of $k = 1,000$ for each sex, these distributions being termed kd_x'. Until recently the life table (kl_x) has been calculated directly from the kd_x' distribution (e.g., Quick 1963). Caughley and Birch (1971) have pointed out, however, that this procedure is valid only if the population rate of increase is zero and has been so for long enough to produce a stationary age-distribution. For most populations—including that of the Serengeti buffalo—these conditions either do not prevail or are unknown. Before a life table can be produced the rate of increase must be calculated from census data. The rate of increase (r) was calculated as the slope of the regression of $\log_e$ May census on time for the years 1965–69, which was the period when the skull samples were collected. This gave $r = 0.077$. The number in each age group of the $kd_x{'}$ was then multipled by e^{rx} to produce column (4), and this in turn was brought back to a total sample of 1,000, to give the true kd_x. Then the kl_x was produced by starting with 1,000 newborns and subtracting the mortality of successive age groups. Finally kq_x (the probability at age x of dying before age $x + 1$) was calculated by the ratio kd_x/kl_x at each age. In table 30 m_x is also shown, this being the number of female young produced per female per year for each age group. This information was obtained from the fertility data in chapter 7.

It is of practical interest in much wildlife research to know what difference there is in the survivorship curves if one calculates kl_x assuming $r = 0$, when in fact r may be of some other value. In figure 75 I show the two curves produced from the same data on Serengeti females but using $r = 0.077$ in one case and assuming $r = 0$ in the

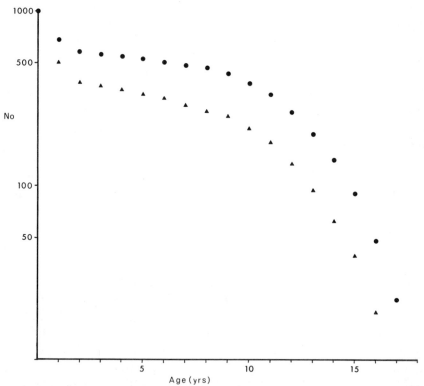

Fig. 75. Survivorship curves for Serengeti female buffalo. Figures calculated with the known rate of increase (*circles*) are compared with those calculated assuming zero rate of increase (*triangles*).

other. The figures are given in table 31. The greatest difference in terms of numbers occurs in the first two age groups, with age-specific mortality (kq_x) being 30–45% lower relative to kq_x' $(r = 0)$ when r is 0.077. Furthermore, for the first half of life this mortality remains about 37% lower than the assumed rate. In the latter half of life this discrepancy declines to zero, giving a mean error for this period of only 13%. Although very few comparisons of mortality rates at different rates of increase have so far been calculated (see Caughley 1976 for a discussion of this), it may be possible in due course to provide a rough estimate of errors involved when life tables are constructed assuming $r = 0$.

The survival rates for the two sexes in the Serengeti were essentially similar to each other and to those in Uganda (Grimsdell 1969). However, with the method of construction of these kd_x and kl_x columns, a sampling error in one age-group is then carried on into the calculations for other age-groups, so that survivorship in different populations is difficult to compare (Caughley 1966). This difficulty is avoided in the calculation of age-specific mortality rate, which is shown for the female and two male samples in figure 76. For females the fishhook shape of the curve is similar to the curves for most mammals as discussed by Caughley (1966). The greatest rates of mortality were in the first year of life and in animals fourteen years old and older. For all populations, after the initial calf mortality, there was a period of approximately six years when the rate was very low, less than 10% of the age-group. Until ten years of age the age-specific mortality continued to remain relatively low at less than 15%. Thereafter, for females age-specific mortality increased steadily until eighteen years old, when all died. Both male populations showed a similar accelerating rate of mortality until sixteen years old. After this age there appeared to be a drop in mortality rate which could be due to chance fluctuations in the very small samples involved. However, there is some evidence from the Uganda populations (Grimsdell 1969) which shows that males live longer than females there as they do in the Serengeti and that males have a lower mortality rate for a period in old age. Similarly, in the Serengeti (Watson 1967) wildebeest males live longer than females and experience a drop in mortality in the older age groups. Thus, although the evidence remains inconclusive, there may be some mortality factor which acts upon the sexes differently in old age, so that males benefit relative to females.

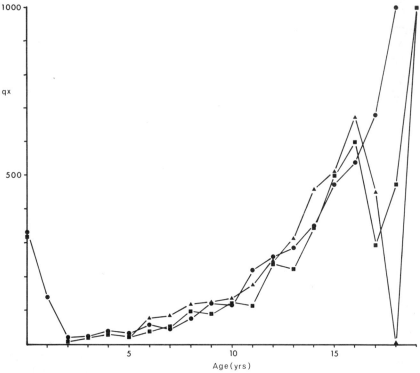

Fig. 76. Age-specific mortality for female buffalo (*circles*), northern males (*squares*), and southern males (*triangles*).

SUMMARY

1. Buffalo crude density from separate populations in eastern Africa is positively correlated with rainfall, and hence with food supply. This indicates that these populations are regulated.

2. In the Serengeti both the buffalo and the wildebeest populations have increased since 1961 at similar rates.

3. Analysis of the dynamics of the buffalo population indicated that adult mortality showed a proportional increase with density. Fertility remained constant and juvenile mortality showed large fluctuations. This effect of adult mortality indicates that the population was tending toward an equilibrium level.

4. By the construction of population models, it could be shown that: (*a*) adult mortality alone could regulate the population in a way similar to the observed census figures; (*b*) juvenile mortality produced the fluctuations in population from year to year and was there-

fore the "key factor"; and (c) fertility changes had very little regulating effect.

5. The models assumed that there was a linear regulating effect upon the population. If this is correct, they indicate that before 1965 another mortality factor was acting upon the population which later disappeared. Alternatively the regulating effect may have been curvilinear, or a combination of this and changes in causes of mortality may have been operating.

6. The effect of rinderpest, which disappeared in 1963, was incorporated into the population model before this date. The resulting model followed closely all the observed census figures. This indicates that rinderpest, and its removal by veterinarians, was the artificial perturbation which caused the increase in population and allowed the analysis for regulation.

7. Comparing populations in the Serengeti and at Lake Manyara showed that both had increased in a similar way and had experienced heavy rinderpest mortality before the increase. A third population, at Tarangire, showed no increase but also suffered less rinderpest mortality. This supports the conclusion from the models that rinderpest was a major cause of population increase in the Serengeti.

8. Age-specific survival and mortality rates for Serengeti female and northern and southern male buffalo were calculated after correcting for the rate of increase (r). Differences in the survivorship curves with different r values are discussed.

9 Causes of Mortality

From the previous chapter it appears that the two processes of regulation and disturbance acting upon the Serengeti population take place through adult mortality and juvenile mortality, respectively. I shall now consider the information on the possible causes of this mortality. There are three main external causes—undernutrition, disease, and predation—and one internal cause—social stress—which appear as possible agents for regulation and disturbance.

UNDERNUTRITION

Undernutrition can be thought of as a shortage of any one of the main constituents of diet—protein, energy, vitamins, or minerals—relative to the minimum requirements for body maintenance. The evidence presented here, in fact, deals mainly with protein.

The Food Supply

1. The Serengeti

For most animals the available food supply is difficult if not impossible to measure, for the researcher is required both to detect and to select food items in the same way as the species he is investigating. Consequently, measurements of food derived from this approach are usually overestimates because the human observer includes as food items that the animals would reject; I assume the animals are better adapted to selecting their own food than the researcher. This approach, then, is probably valid only if the food is simple, undiversified, and easy for humans to find.

One method of estimating available forage which overcomes these difficulties is measuring ingested food. Here the animal does its own searching and selecting. This approach was used to estimate the quality of the food eaten by buffalo in the Serengeti. The quality was measured in terms of crude protein, but since this is positively correlated with the energy content of the grass (Armstrong, Blaxter, and

Waite 1964), changes in one parameter reflect changes in the other. Crude protein measured directly from rumen samples provided inaccurate information of food values because other nitrogenous compounds were present in the stomach. Therefore the crude protein values of the standing grass were first determined for the different parts of the grass being eaten by the animals. Then these were multiplied by the proportions of the same parts that occurred in the diet, which were known from the rumen analysis (chap. 4). For example, in March grass leaf had a crude protein value of 12.7%, and this component made up about 56% of the diet. Therefore leaf provided 7.15 g of crude protein for every 100 g dry weight of food. These computations for leaf, stem, and leaf sheath are shown by month in table 34. Their sum gives the total protein value in the diet. This information allowed comparisons not only between different times of year but also between different age- and sex-classes. Chemical analysis was carried out by members of the East African Agricultural and Forestry Research Organisation at Nairobi, using the Kjeldahl method for nitrogen and multiplying the result by the standard constant 6.25 to obtain the crude protein percentage.

The calculated percentages of crude protein in the diet of the animals at different times of year are shown in figure 77, with the 95% confidence limits for the three large samples. The quality remained high between November and June when there was an abundance of green leaf. However, the quality of food eaten declined steadily as the dry season progressed from July until October. This was due to the decreasing proportion of leaf and the increasing proportion of stem in the diet during this season, combined with an overall decline in protein content of all components. The quality of the most nutritious component, grass leaf, changed from 12.7% crude protein in March to 4.0% in October while the proportion in the diet also declined from 56% to 13%. The grass stem quality also dropped over the same time period from 5.2% to 1.6% crude protein, but this poor-quality component increased proportionately in the diet from 11% to 42%. These trends were present in all age-groups and both sexes. A random sample of animals collected at the end of the dry season showed they consumed a diet consisting of only 2.18% crude protein.

French, Glover, and Duthie (1957) and Glover and Duthie (1958) have shown that the digestibility of crude protein is similar for both ruminants and nonruminants. Abrams (1968) has stated that digest-

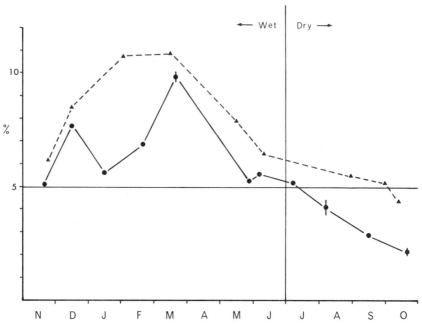

Fig. 77. The percentage of crude protein eaten by buffalo in the Serengeti declines below the 5% minimum maintenance level in the dry season. Figures corrected from rumen analysis are indicated by the solid line, those calculated from
fecal analysis by the broken line (see fig. 78). Vertical lines represent 95% confidence limits of the mean.

ibility results obtained from domestic ruminants can be extrapolated
to wild ruminants. Consequently I have used data from cattle to calculate the minimum maintenance requirements for crude protein in
buffalo. Bredon, Harker, and Marshall (1963) show that the digestibility coefficient (DC) is related to the crude protein percentage
(CP) in the diet of cattle by $DC = 100.89 \log CP - 44.45$. This predicts a zero digestibility at 2.76% crude protein in the diet. However,
the activity of the ruminal microflora is inhibited at crude protein and energy levels below about 5% crude protein (Chalmers
1961). This figure is approximately the minimum level of crude protein needed to maintain body weight in tropical cattle. Several measurements of the minimum requirement have been reported, and
most lie between 4% and 8% crude protein values (French 1957;
Plowes 1957; French, Glover, and Duthie 1957; Bredon and Wilson
1963; Bredon, Harker, and Marshall 1963; Agricultural Research
Council 1965; Milford and Minson 1966; National Research Council
1970). Below this minimum level, animals lose weight because they

are utilizing their own body reserves to make up for the nutritional shortage. I have used the 5% crude protein level in figure 77 to indicate the probable minimum maintenance level for buffalo.

Throughout the dry season the quality of the diet remained below the minimum maintenance level, and by October the crude protein values fell below even the theoretical zero digestibility level. Since these results were obtained from samples of the population covering the period 1967–72, they represent the changes in the mean level of diet quality for the whole population through the year.

The information from a random sample of a herd, collected in the late dry season, was divided into diet quality eaten by pregnant females, bachelor males, adult herd males, and two juvenile age groups (table 35). There was no difference in the diets consumed by any of these groups. This information therefore suggests that no particular class of animals is experiencing undernutrition as a result of social factors—for example, by being excluded from the herd—in order to leave a superabundance of good-quality food for the others. Rather, it reflects a real shortage of the good-quality grass leaf which affects all sections of the population. The information also supports the models for energy budgets of pregnant females described in chapter 7, where I suggest that they experience an energy deficit in the dry season.

I have also approached the problem of measuring the quality of ingested food by a second independent method. Nitrogen excreted in the feces is positively related to the nitrogen ingested down to the minimum level for nitrogen balance. If nitrogen intake falls below this level, it is not reflected in the feces because metabolic breakdown products continue to be removed irrespective of intake. Consequently, fecal nitrogen remains at approximately the same level when the animal's diet is at or below the minimum maintenance level, but it does predict nitrogen intake when levels are above the minimum.

Bredon, Harker, and Marshall (1963) have found for cattle that dietary crude protein (CP) is related to fecal crude protein (FP) by $CP = 1.677\ FP - 6.93$. This regression is shown in figure 78. I have included in this figure the few measurements of buffalo feces plotted against the quality of the food they were eating at the time. They show an approximate agreement to the regression line from cattle, which is to be expected (P. Arman, personal communication). Measurements for wildebeest are included in figure 78 to show that the regression line is slightly different for these data, the equation being

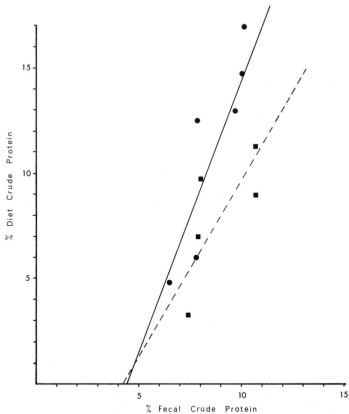

Fig. 78. The relationship between the percentage of crude protein in the diet and that in the feces for buffalo (*squares*) and wildebeest (*circles* and *solid regression line*). The broken regression line is for tropical zebu cattle given by Bredon, Harker, and Marshall (1963).

$CP = 2.61\ FP - 11.90$. The higher nitrogen content in the feces for this species compared with cattle is in agreement with results for digestibility trials on alcelaphines by P. Arman (personal communication).

Using this regression equation for cattle, I estimated crude protein intake of buffalo from samples collected during 1970–73 (fig. 75). The results were similar to those from the rumen analysis in that protein intake declined in the dry season to a level equal to or below that required for body maintenance. Buffalo, however, are not the only animals to suffer a food depletion in the dry season. Wildebeest also experience this. The diet quality for wildebeest males in the relatively mild year of 1971 was estimated from an analysis of green grass leaves in the areas where the animals were grazing. The animals were able to obtain a diet higher in protein content than the mean for the available grass, indicating that they were selecting their food (Sinclair 1975). Nevertheless, the protein in the diet fell to the minimum necessary for body maintenance during the dry season (fig. 79) even though conditions were mild.

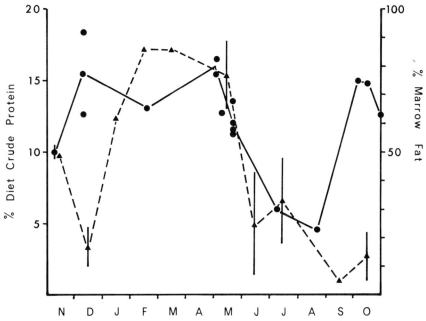

Fig. 79. The seasonal change in the marrow fat content of dead wildebeest (*triangles*) is highly correlated with the changes in the percentage of crude protein in their diet. Vertical bars indicate 95% confidence limits of the mean.

In the dry season wildebeest eat, for the most part, short green regrowth (greenflush). I measured the quantity of this available to the animals in the areas where wildebeest concentrated in the northern Serengeti during the years 1968 and 1969. Both of these seasons were drier than 1971. Three wire exclosure cages (5 x 2 m) were set up in three localities (plate 31). Samples of 1 m² were cut at the beginning of the dry season and then monthly thereafter both inside and outside the cages. This allowed an estimate of both available growth and offtake.

The mean density of wildebeest in this area was calculated from aerial photographic surveys at intervals of ten days or two weeks.

Numbers built up from a few in June to a maximum in August, after which they fluctuated according to the distribution of the local rainstorms. The mean density was calculated for the period during which growth measurements were made. The dry weight food requirements were estimated at between 2.1% and 4.5% of an animal's body weight per day (chap. 7), since wildebeest metabolic activity is 30% higher than that of cattle (Rogerson 1968). In the two months August and September 1968, the mean population requirement was 2.3–4.6 kg dry wt/hectare/day. However, mean growth over this period was only 0.82 kg dry wt/hectare/day, indicating that the needs of the population were greater than what was produced. Similarly, in July-August 1969 the population requirement was 3.0–6.1 kg dry wt/ hectare/day, and growth was 2.20 ± 0.76 (S.E.) kg dry wt/hectare/ day. The wildebeest also ate the few stems and bases of plants which were of poor quality. The amount they ate was 6.1 kg/hectare/day in 1968 and 4.8 kg/hectare/day in 1969. They effectively removed the small amount of standing crop in the first month and then subsisted on what grew in the following months. Even in the unburned poor-quality long-grass areas I found from transects and sample plots in 1969 that 32.0%, 70.5%, and 92.5% of the initial standing crop in June was removed successively in the months July to September. What remained in October was trampled and decomposing litter. In effect, they ate all their food. The mean crude protein of this long dry grass was 2.17%, and a diet of this probably resulted in a negative nitrogen balance (Bredon, Harker, and Marshall 1963). Consequently it appears that the population needed more good-quality food during these years than was available to them.

2. Mount Meru

The montane pasture on Mount Meru presents one of the few situations where food supply can be measured directly. These pastures on exposed ridges and edaphic glades are maintained as a permanent short greensward by buffalo. D. Vesey-Fitzgerald (personal communication) demonstrated this by preventing animals from grazing in a sample area (plate 32). Within the protected plots the grass grew to heights of 50–70 cm, and cut samples showed a standing crop of 10,000 kg/hectare, a value similar to those obtained in the Serengeti. On Mount Meru the buffalo is the only grazer, the other ungulates being browsers. The short greensward is maintained in a state where there are few stems and many leaf shoots, the preferred food component for the buffalo. Since the quality of this food rarely if ever fell below the minimum maintenance quality, I had to measure the available quantity of food as well.

The grass production on this sward was measured by temporary exclosure plots, with the help of D. Vesey-Fitzgerald. Ten 1m² plots were placed on montane pasture at 1,800 m altitude, each being set up 1 wk after the previous one. They were each left for 10 wk, then clipped and reset for a similar period. This allowed a continuous measurement of growth throughout the year. Unprotected sample plots were also clipped for comparison with the protected plots to calculate offtake. Since clipping grass does not resemble the grazing mechanism, I adopted a conservative approach by arranging that plots should be cut to a level below that maintained by the buffalo. Normally they would not graze the sward lower than about 3 cm. By clipping in this way I ensured that measurements of available food were always biased on the high side. Similar plots were set up lower down the mountain near a swamp, for the animals retreated to this area during the cold season when growth ceased higher up. The grass growth measurements are shown in figure 80 for both mountain and swamp pasture. Because standing crop was so low, growth represented the only food available, and when growth stopped, as it did on the mountain pasture, the available food declined to zero.

The population of buffalo in this area was isolated by barriers of human cultivation. The numbers were estimated from both ground and aerial censuses and the density was calculated at 51/km² of pasture. The quality of the food remained relatively constant throughout the year at between 8% and 10% crude protein. This quality was probably sufficient for their needs. The minimum quantity requirements of food of this quality was calculated from information on cattle and confirmed by grazing measurements of tame buffalo. The minimum quantity of food cattle must eat for maintenance has been estimated at between 1.5% and 3.0% of the animal's body weight per day, with most estimates lying between 2% and 3% (Klapp 1960; Agricultural Research Council 1965; National Research Council 1970). In making measurements on buffalo, the animal was allowed to graze a given area of grass for a given length of time, and the actual time of grazing was recorded by an observer. Before the grazing period, a sample strip of grass had been cut, dried, and weighed to determine the standing crop available. At the end of the day the animal was removed and the remaining grass was cut and

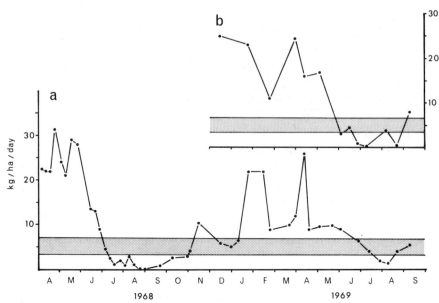

Fig. 80. Grass food production on Mount Meru slopes (*a*) and lower swamp pasture (*b*), compared with the amount needed per day (*shaded bar*) by the buffalo population. Each dry season growth falls below requirements. Reproduced from Sinclair (1974*d*) with permission of Blackwell Scientific Publications, Ltd.

measured. From the grazing rate the amount eaten by the animal in a 9 h grazing day was calculated to be 2.2% of the body weight per day.

The minimum requirement for the population was estimated from the crude density of animals and the intake range of 1.5%–3.0% of body weight, and this is shown as a band in figure 80. It can be seen that in both sample sites where measurements were made, the available growth was less than the requirement of the population during the dry seasons of 1968 and 1969. This suggests that even in areas such as Mount Meru, where quality remains high, the overall nutrient intake is reduced to below the maintenance needs for a part of each year. Resource limitation, therefore, may be generally experienced by buffalo in eastern Africa.

Condition

An index of the condition of animals was calculated from their fat reserves. Smith (1970) showed that a reliable index for total body fat in African ungulates was the ratio of kidney fat weight to kidney

weight, and Anderson, Medin, and Ochs (1968) came to similar conclusions for North American ruminants. However, the amount of
bone-marrow fat was not investigated by Smith (1970) and it has
since been found that this declines after the rest of the body fat has
been utilized (Sinclair and Duncan 1972). Consequently a decline in
bone-marrow fat reflects a relatively severe depletion of energy reserves. I examined the bone marrow of animals found dead in the
field to see if such an energy depletion was occurring at death. The
smaller changes due to incipient depletion, reflected in the kidney
index, would not be detected from the bone marrow, of course. However, the bone marrow does show whether a major decline in body
condition occurs under natural conditions.

Initially the fat content of the central section of femur marrow was
obtained by Soxhlet extraction, but it was then found that the proportion of fat was closely related to the dry weight of the marrow as
a proportion of its fresh weight by: % marrow fat $= 1.0045 \times$ % dry
weight $- 3.42$ for buffalo, and % marrow fat $= 1.0442 \times$ % dry weight
$- 7.28$ for wildebeest. These formulas were used for later samples.
On some occasions in the field, samples were described merely on the
basis of color and texture, a method which is reliable for identifying
whether an animal was in good or poor condition (Sinclair and Duncan 1972). For example, the marrow of those in good condition may
contain 98% fat and appears solid, white, and waxy. Marrow from
those in poor condition may have as little as 1% fat, the rest being
made up by water, and looks yellow, translucent, and gelatinous. If
an animal was found with marrow in very poor condition—usually
less than 10% fat—then undernutrition was considered to be at least
partly responsible for death, although secondary agents such as predators or disease may have actually killed it. The animal's weak condition could have enabled a predator to capture it or allowed potential pathogens to cause disease.

In buffalo dying from natural causes, marrow from 19 animals less
than ten years of age contained more than 20% fat, but of 16 animals
over this age, 15 possessed marrow with less than 10% fat. Consequently there was a significant inverse relation between age at death
and an animal's energy reserves. Most old animals died during the
dry season (plates 33, 34, 35), whereas young adults died in small
numbers throughout the year. Observation of the marrow from the
shot samples showed that those between two and ten years of age
were in good condition in the dry season. Those less than two years

old and old adults showed some but not extreme depletion of bone marrow fat. Old adults made up only a small proportion of the live population, although most of the adults found dead were old. Therefore it appears that old adults suffer a depletion of energy reserves during the dry season when there is a shortage of food (plates 33, 34) and some of them die, whereas younger animals maintain their energy reserves and few of them die.

The evidence on the body condition of wildebeest is similar to that of buffalo and more extensive (fig. 79). In males, for example, those I found dead in the wet season were in good condition, those found in the dry season were in poor condition, and this pattern follows closely that seen for diet quality (fig. 77). The condition of animals in a random sample of the live population remained moderately high throughout the year, as can be seen in fig. 63 and 64. This shows more clearly that if animals reach a state of low energy reserves they are liable to die as a result. From this evidence I suggest therefore that because this population experienced a shortage of good-quality food during the dry season, the animals were compelled to utilize their fat reserves, and for some the reserves were insufficient for survival.

PARASITISM AND DISEASE

Information concerning disease in the Serengeti was obtained for the most part from the samples of animals collected between 1967 and 1969. Teams of veterinarians performed autopsies to look for signs of disease and to collect samples for later analysis. Blood samples were obtained as soon as the animals were shot. The large numbers of animals that had to be processed in the short time available precluded any intensive study of worm burdens, but a few young animals were examined for this. Furthermore, R. Sachs and his coworkers had carried out intensive studies of helminths in the same region during previous years (Sachs and Sachs 1968). Serum was sent to the Veterinary Investigation Centre, Arusha, the Central Veterinary Laboratory, Dar es Salaam, and the East African Veterinary Research Organisation, Nairobi, for analysis. The majority of the serum analyses have now been published. In this section I have drawn together as much of this information as I can find and discussed it in terms of its relevance to the population dynamics of buffalo and to ecology in general.

Helminths, Pentastomids, and Ticks

A number of authors have now published species lists of helminths found in buffalo in various areas of Africa (Round 1968; Bwangamoi 1968, 1970; Graber 1969; Sachs and Sachs 1968; Sachs, Frank, and Bindernagel 1969; Basson et al. 1970), and these are summarized in table 36. I have little doubt that more species can be added to this list. Some twenty species of trematodes, six species of cestodes, and twenty-eight species of nematodes have been recorded, together with three species of pentastomids (Sachs, Rack, and Woodford 1973), giving a total of at least fifty-seven species of endoparasites. Although not all of these are found in buffalo in the same area (approximately one-third of these have so far been recorded for Tanzania), it is clear that buffalo are host to a large number of parasite species. In table 36 I have listed the species according to the number of hosts in which they have been found, as documented by Round (1968). In each group of helminths there are a few such as *Cotylophoron cotylophoron, Avitellina centripunctata, Haemonchus contortus*, and *H. bedfordi* which occur in many different hosts and are ubiquitous. About 30% of the species have been described from the buffalo only, but this is probably due to a lack of information on other hosts. The true proportion of host-specific parasites is probably smaller than this. In general buffalo are constantly exposed to a challenge by those species found in many hosts, for these hosts will be egesting a supply of eggs and larvae irrespective of the level of the parasite population in the buffalo itself. For example, several of the ubiquitous parasite species are found in wildebeest as well as buffalo (table 37), and these two hosts often graze in the same grasslands, thus allowing parasites to be transferred.

The prevalence—that is the proportion of a population infected— varies for different parasites and also for the same parasite in different populations. Thus in Uganda the proportion infected by *Cysticercus gonyamae* was only 5% (Woodford and Sachs 1973), whereas the proportion infected by *Ashworthius lerouxi* may be as high as 73% (Bindernagel and Todd 1972). Yet this latter species was absent in another population in Uganda. It is perhaps significant that in the population where *A. lerouxi* was prevalent another nematode, *Haemonchus contortus*, was of low prevalence (16%), and *H. contortus* was prevalent (68%) where *A. lerouxi* was absent (Bindernagel and Todd 1972). Both of these nematodes inhabit the abomasum, and this suggests that there may be competition for susceptible hosts. Other figures for prevalence are listed in table 36 (Dinnick et al. 1963; Basson et al. 1970; Bindernagel 1971, 1972 a,b; Sachs, Rack, and Woodford 1973).

The mean numbers of worms per host individual also varies considerably. In the Serengeti *Cooperia* species normally number a few hundred per host, but in one thin calf a total of 5,800 was estimated. In Uganda *Haemonchus contortus* numbers varied from 1 to 2,756 (Bindernagel and Todd 1972). Similarly, Pester and Laurence (1974) report for wildebeest total nematode burdens varying from 0 to 7,726. Both the prevalence and numbers per individual vary in some cases with the age of the host. Bindernagel (1971, 1972b) suggested that the nematode *Thelazia rhodesi* was more prevalent in old animals than in younger ones. However, with *A. lerouxi* the number of nematodes per infection in yearling animals was almost twice as high as in any older age groups (Bindernagel and Todd 1972). On the other hand, a survey of helminths, ticks, and mites in 100 randomly selected animals from the Kruger Park indicated no relation between prevalence and age (Basson et al. 1970).

Of the ectoparasites, ticks occur on all animals, both young and old. Seventeen species of ticks have been recorded on buffalo (table 36), and at least ten of these have been found in the Serengeti. Several are known to transmit blood parasites. Sarcoptic mange occasionally occurs on young calves in the Serengeti. In the Kruger Park the prevalence of mange is 10% (Basson et al. 1970). Several species of biting flies attack buffalo in the Serengeti, the most noticeable of which is the tsetse fly (*Glossina*). Apart from their bloodsucking effect these flies, together with mosquitoes and biting midges (culicoides), act as vectors for various parasites and viruses. For example, *Glossina* is the vector for *Trypanosoma*.

The main point that appears from this is that in the host population, although the majority of animals may contain only moderate or low populations of parasites, there is a small proportion of hosts which contain a high number of parasites. This latter group might be more susceptible to changes in environment and stress because of their heavy worm burdens and poor body condition. I shall return to this later in the chapter.

Protozoa, Bacteria, and Viruses

Information on the diseases I consider important for Serengeti buffalo is summarized in table 38.

Theileriases. One species of the blood protozoan *Theileria* causes in cattle the disease known as East Coast fever, and a similar species has been described for buffalo and wildebeest (Brocklesby and Vidler 1961, 1966). One type was identified from two calves in the Mara Park. One of these calves, only a month old, was weak after an attack by lions and showed a heavy infection of 57 piroplasms/1,000 red blood cells (Brocklesby 1965). Of four buffalo calves experimentally infected with *Theileria* originally obtained from other buffalo, 1 died and the other 3 became sick but recovered (Brocklesby and Barnett 1966).

In the Serengeti the prevalence of *Theileria* in buffalo was 74% (20/27) as judged from serum antibody tests. A. S. Young (personal communication), however, found the parasite in 90% (36/40) of the blood slides that he examined. These covered all age-groups from two months to fifteen years·of age. Young et al. (1973) were able to transfer the *Theileria* found in my two tame buffalo calves to cattle and produce a highly pathogenic infection using the tick *Rhipicephalus appendiculatus*. Piroplasmic parasitemias in the buffalo calves varied from 0.9% to 1.4%.

The prevalence of *Theileria* in Uganda has been recorded as 88% (37/42 blood slides), similar to that in the Serengeti (Dinnik et al. 1963), and in the Kruger Park it is 97% (Basson et al. 1970). In wildebeest equally high figures have been found—70% in the Mara area and 86% at Ngorongoro (Brocklesby and Vidler 1966). In general the *Theileria* parasite infects the host at an early age through ticks and then reaches an equilibrium population in the host. It can be pathogenic to young buffalo, especially those in poor condition. In cattle, endemic *Theileria* affects susceptible calves (McCulloch et al. 1968).

Allerton-type herpes virus. In December 1969, following a year of mediocre rains and a severe dry season, an outbreak of disease, associated with an appreciable mortality, occurred in the buffaloes of the northern Serengeti (Plowright and Jessett 1971). When diseased animals were examined an Allerton-type herpes virus was recovered. This was the first time such a virus had been isolated from wild ruminants in East Africa. However, when these authors conducted antibody neutralization tests on other serum collected in previous years during this Serengeti study, they found that the buffalo population showed a 100% prevalence of antibody in 1967 and 1969. Similar tests on buffalo sera from the Ruwenzori Park, Uganda, showed positive reactions in 58 out of 60 animals, and antibodies were present in three widely separated populations in Kenya. Evidently infection with this virus was extremely common despite the lack of overt signs of its presence in the populations.

Plowright and Jessett (1971) noted that it was the animals over one year old that were serologically positive and that the disease predominantly killed animals six to twelve months old. Their survey of other species showed that sera from Serengeti wildebeest during 1965–68 were negative, and only 1% were positive in Kenya. Positive results from other species were waterbuck 29%, giraffe 15%, and impala 3%. Cattle in areas surrounding the Serengeti showed a prevalence of 60–85%. These authors suggest that the widespread prevalence of infection in buffalo probably means that the virus has been present in this species for a long time and is not a recent introduction to Africa. This finding underlines the fact that some prevalent organisms and diseases can be overlooked by human observers. Thus Plowright and Jessett (1971) remark, "It could hardly have been foreseen that about 85–95% of cattle more than 2 years of age would show evidence of past infection in vast areas of E. Africa . . . , and that the infection was never absent in any locality tested." Clearly, diseases can have subtle effects on populations.

Because the previous incidence of this disease was so high in Serengeti buffalo, these authors conclude, "It therefore seemed to be highly unlikely that the virus was a primary cause of the severe morbidity and mortality observed in 1969." Some other factor must have caused the virus to become pathogenic. On the possible vectors of the virus, ticks and lice were observed in large numbers on the sick animals, but these species may have responded to the poor health of the hosts. The biting fly *Biomyia faeciata* may be involved, because the virus was isolated from this species six days after it had been feeding on infected cattle. Although Plowright and Jessett (1971) state that no other overt signs of the disease have been noticed apart from the 1969 outbreak, I have notes of sick calves in both the 1967 and the 1968 dry seasons showing similar signs of disease, and these were from the same herds as those suffering from the 1969 outbreak. It is quite likely, therefore, that this disease has been playing an important role in juvenile mortality for these three years, and probably for much longer. I should point out that although about 10,000 calves die each year in the Serengeti, very few are ever found in a moribund state suitable for veterinary examination. Therefore, lack of evidence does not mean that this disease has not been operating. That signs of disease have been observed either during or immediately following the dry season suggests that nutritional stress leading to poor condition of the host could have been the primary reason the disease became pathogenic.

Foot-and-mouth disease (FMD). Of twenty serum samples collected from the Serengeti buffalo in 1967, 12 (60%) were positive for this disease. In Uganda, serum samples from two populations were 45% positive in one case, 21% in the other (Hedger, Forman, and Woodford 1973). An extensive survey covering Zambia to South Africa, done by Condy, Herniman, and Hedger (1969), showed that serum-neutralizing antibodies were present in 66% of the buffalo and 21% of the wildebeest. From the Chobe National Park, Botswana, Hedger (1972) found FMD virus in 35 of 62 buffalo sampled (56%). However, in the Kruger Park no positive results were obtained from 97 buffalo (Basson et al. 1970). In general, therefore, in the areas of eastern and southern Africa where FMD virus occurs, approximately half the buffalo appears to have been infected.

Hedger (1972) found no clinical signs of disease. His examinations suggested that young calves obtain immunity from their mothers. After this wanes calves become susceptible to the several virus types present. He writes, "The higher virus titers found in animals one to three years old suggests that active infection with the current virus types occurs at this age. Thereafter, animals remained carriers, excreting virus of one or more types." In this way calves may be continually reinfected. However, Hedger stresses that transference of virus from buffalo to the domestic animal population may occur only rarely in Botswana because of the transient nature of buffalo/cattle contact and also because of vaccination.

The only type of FMD so far recorded in the Serengeti is type O. During an outbreak in the severe dry season of 1968 Rweyemamu (1970) recorded type SAT2 fairly frequently and type A rarely in domestic stock of other areas of Tanzania. In both Uganda and southern Africa types SAT1, SAT2 and SAT3 have been recorded.

Brucellosis. The microorganism *Brucella abortus* can cause abortions in domestic stock and possibly could have an effect on the reproductive capacity of related wild ruminants. In the Serengeti one isolation of the organism has been obtained and described as Biotype 3, the usual one for cattle (Kaliner and Staak 1973). Serum agglutination titers at dilutions of 1:40 or greater have been considered positive for present or past infection of Serengeti buffalo by Sachs, Staak, and Groocock (1968), and dilutions between 1:20 and 1:40 were regarded as suspicious. However, Staak, Sachs, and Groocock (1968) obtained an isolation from a buffalo with an agglutination titer of only 1:20, which may confirm these suspicions. Since other authors have used various dilution levels to signify a positive result, I have adjusted all available information to compare with the results of Sachs, Staak, and Groocock (1968).These authors tested buffalo serum collected in the Serengeti from 1964 to 1967 and found none positive and only 2/23 (9%) suspicious. In the following two years, during this study, 5/96 (5%) were positive and 11/96 (11%) were suspicious. Consequently brucellosis cannot be regarded as an important cause of fetal mortality for the Serengeti population. The cattle herds outside the park had similar rates of 15% positive antibody titers.

Reports from other areas of Africa agree in general with the results from the Serengeti. In Rhodesia 2/43 (5%) were positive (Roth 1967), in the Kruger Park 28/253 (11%) were positive (de Vos and van Niekerk 1969), and in Botswana 40/233 (17%) were positive (Cooper and Carmichael 1974). A small sample of 15 from Uganda showed 2 animals positive (Rollinson 1962). The results for wildebeest appear more variable, ranging from a 10% prevalence in the Serengeti to zero in South Africa and Botswana. This disease must be regarded as of low prevalence relative to others.

Trypanosomiasis. Blood slides examined by A. S. Young (personal communication) from 40 Serengeti buffalo showed that 17% contained *Trypanosoma,* and most of these were young animals. The buffalo is one of the preferred hosts of the tsetse fly—the vector for the disease—and so animals come under constant attack (Lamprey et al. 1962). Young examined the gut content of these flies and found up to 30% of them contained *Trypanosoma.* From this he concluded that in view of the constant challenge through the tsetse fly, the low incidence of *Trypanosoma* in adults must be due to an acquired immunity. Young buffalo do become infected. For other mammals in the Serengeti Baker, Sachs, and Laufer (1967) report *Trypanosoma* infection in 27% of wildebeest and between 20% and 30% of topi and kongoni.

Corynebacterium pyogenes. This bacterium is ubiquitous and usually becomes pathogenic only when the host is otherwise weakened. It was the terminal cause of death for one old male buffalo in the Serengeti. In May 1969 at Lake Manyara a number of calves under six months old showed extreme swelling of the parotid glands. Autopsies by C. Staak and D. Protz (personal communication) showed that *C. pyogenes* caused the swelling, but they thought the primary cause of the infection was the poor nutritional conditions at that time. In one herd 50% (5/10) of the calves had this infection, and in another 70% (10/14). Unlike other buffalo herds in East Africa, those in Manyara were easy to approach in a vehicle. This closer examination may explain why I observed this infection in Manyara and not elsewhere. Calves over six months of age did not show signs of the disease.

Other diseases. In the Serengeti a number of other diseases have been investigated. Serum antibodies for *Babesia* were found in 78% (21/27) of the samples. Despite this the protozoan was not definitely identified in blood slides, and little has been reported about this parasite in other wildlife populations. Antibodies for *Anaplasma* were also detected in 78% (21/27) of the serum samples, and A. S. Young identified the organism in five blood slides. This disease organism transmitted by ticks, causes anemia and high fever in cattle. Kuttler (1965) found that 4/38 (10%) wildebeest showed positive antibody titers. Blood tested serologically for virus diarrhea was positive in 30% of the cases, these being mostly adults. Again it appears that young animals contract the disease and build up immunity as adults.

Rweyamamu's 1974 analysis of the serum from the Serengeti for infectious bovine rhinotracheitis (IBR) has shown a high prevalence of antibody (76%). Antibody was also present at a lower rate in wildebeest (18%) and in cattle (23%) in the surrounding areas. This disease usually causes a mild or subclinical infection, but Rweyamamu suggests that in conjunction with foot-and-mouth disease it could be severe. He also suggests it is endemic and is not a recent introduction.

Malignant catarrh fever (MCF) is a virus disease of cattle. This virus has been found in a small proportion of Serengeti wildebeest (7–16%; Plowright 1965). It has also been isolated from a wildebeest fetus, indicating a transplacental infection. All the animals from which virus was isolated were one year old or younger. In the first three months of life the prevalence of infection was 31%, but this declined to 7% by nine months and 2% by one year of age (Plowright 1965). No antibody was found in 25 buffalo serum samples, which was consistent with the finding that buffalo could not be infected experimentally with the virus.

Negative results for contagious bovine pleuropneumonia (CBPP) using complement fixation tests were found for 98 serum samples from the Serengeti. However, buffalo can be infected experimentally with the organism (*Mycoplasma mycoides*). Furthermore, water buffalo, cattle, yak, and bison are all susceptible to the disease (Shifrine, Stone, and Staak 1970). But samples from buffalo collected elsewhere have also been found negative (Shifrine and Dommermuth 1967). According to Hammond and Branagan (1965), CBPP has been endemic in the cattle populations adjacent to the Serengeti for most of this century. In the 1940s an epidemic spread through the cattle population in the Mara and Loliondo regions close to the northern Serengeti buffalo. Consequently the absence of CBPP in buffalo indicates that transmission rarely occurs and that buffalo do not appear to be affected or to act as a reservoir for the disease.

Anthrax is endemic in the Serengeti region. One buffalo probably died of this in the Ikoma area, and I have found wildebeest that had died from the disease on the Serengeti plains. This occurred regularly each year. Anthrax also killed Thomson's and Grant's gazelle and presumably other herbivores. Although its prevalence was low, potentially it could still be an important mortality agent because of the long life of spores in the soil. Given the right conditions it could cause local epizootics. Its presence in the area therefore creates a serious problem for the schemes to crop the Serengeti ungulates for human consumption since the disease can be transmitted to humans. Anthrax has also been reported killing buffalo in the Kruger Park (McConnell, Tustin, and de Vos 1972).

Tuberculosis was reported in old buffalo in the Ruwenzori Park, Uganda (Guilbride et al. 1963). These authors point out that this buffalo population occurs in an area notable for the incidence of tuberculosis in cattle (approximately 17%), and they suggest that cattle may have initially introduced the disease into buffalo. Examination of more than 100 buffalo in the Serengeti has not shown tuberculosis in this population.

This list of endemic diseases is not intended to be exhaustive; others are known—for example, blue-tongue disease in the Kruger

Park—and probably there are more that I have overlooked or that
have yet to be described. I have tried to present a spectrum of the
better-known diseases about which there is some information and to
illustrate how they might act as mortality agents for the buffalo
population.

Disease, Nutrition, and Immunity

Scrimshaw, Taylor, and Jordan (1968) have reviewed the widely
scattered but considerable literature pertaining to the interaction of
disease and nutrition in mammal populations, including man, and I
consider their conclusions particularly relevant here. They reviewed
482 studies dealing with how nutritional status conditions the host to
infectious disease. They recorded whether poor nutrition increased
infection (synergism), decreased it (antagonism), or had no effect.

The published evidence demonstrates conclusively that protein
malnutrition has a profound effect on resistance to infection. Of 86
studies, protein undernutrition was found to increase the effects of
disease in 72% of the cases, and antagonism was recorded in only
14% of the cases. Similarly, of 29 studies involving multiple nutritional deficiencies, 83% showed that the disease response was synergistic, 14% showed it was antagonistic. Simple limitation of food, or
inanition, also resulted in synergism in 18/30 (60%) of cases studied,
whereas antagonism was found in 30% of cases.

Synergism is characteristic of certain types of infection. For example, with bacterial infections, 158 studies were recorded involving
synergistic interactions, and antagonism was seen in only 13 cases.
Antagonism is relatively common with organisms that are highly dependent upon the metabolism of the host, as are, for example, systemic protozoa and helminths or viruses which are intracellular.
These cases of antagonism usually occur when the deficiency is a
specific amino acid, vitamin, or mineral (Scrimshaw et al. 1968).
When the deficiency is protein, an interaction, if it occurs, is synergistic in most types of disease. In 94 cases where helminths were involved, malnutrition of the host caused heavier parasitism in 80%,
lower infection in 16%; and synergism was most pronounced with
intestinal helminths.

In their turn, diseases have an adverse effect on the nutritional
status of the host. For example, Scrimshaw et al. (1968) noted that
even trivial infections resulted in increased loss of nitrogen in the
urine. Infections also contributed to protein and other nutrient deficiencies by decreasing appetite and diminishing tolerance for food.

Acute diarrhea, characteristic of most intestinal and some systemic infections, decreases nitrogen absorption. Severe helminthic disease also reduces nitrogen absorption, even in the absence of diarrhea. Symons (1969) has reviewed some of the effects on the host that result from gastrointestinal helminthiases. These may include anemia due to the parasites' ingestion of blood, poor growth rate in young animals, and even weight loss; loss of appetite and hence reduced food intake; diarrhea, often associated with derangement of digestion and absorption, which could be responsible for weight loss through dehydration and be accompanied by a salt loss; edema or accumulations of fluid in the body cavities; disorders of the nervous system and the brain. Specific examples of some of these effects in ruminants are reported by Vercoe and Springell (1969), Roseby (1973), and Reveron et al. (1974). In humans the disease known as kwashiorkor is precipitated by acute diarrheal disease or some other infection superimposed on a diet dangerously low in protein or calories. The conclusion is clear, therefore, that malnutrition can cause a disease organism to become pathogenic, which in turn further reduces the nutritional status of the host. Such a positive feedback system must result in a rapid decline in host condition and could result in death.

It is well documented that the mechanism producing the malnutrition–disease synergistic interaction lies in the impairment of the host's immune system (Scrimshaw et al. 1968). These authors suggest that the interaction of host and disease organism depends on the genotypes of the two. With the extreme cases of host resistance and disease virulence the outcome is usually determined by genotype alone. For example, high virulence often results in death irrespective of host resistance, and low virulence usually results in host survival. However, Scrimshaw et al. (1968) argue by means of a model of the frequency distributions of these extreme cases that they are likely to occur in fewer than 10% of interactions. By far the majority of interactions—nearly 50% in their model—involve intermediate resistance and virulence, and in these cases a third factor, the nutritional state of the host, plays an important part in determining death or survival. Scrimshaw et al. (1968) write, "On theoretical grounds, the deduction clearly follows that the nutritional state of an organism is often the deciding factor in a particular infection." They conclude, "In the ecologically balanced populations characteristically present in nature, the situation is an intermediate level of both virulence of agent and resistance of host, with the result that diet often determines the outcome. Dietary factors thus have greater significance in nature and in public health practice than some laboratory experiments suggest." An example of the balance between nutrition and parasitism in ruminants can be seen in Reveron and Topps (1970). These authors found that the effects of gastrointestinal nematodes on sheep were greater when the plane of nutrition was low at 6% crude protein than when it was high at 18%. Lack of protein and vitamin A caused the greatest changes in parasitism.

Malnutrition can interfere with any mechanism that defends the body against infectious agents. These agents stimulate the production of specific antibodies, which are normally composed of protein. If protein deficiency is severe enough, normal antibody response is inhibited. For example, antibody response in humans with a negative nitrogen balance was poor compared with that in those receiving an adequate diet. Antibody production is also impaired in children suffering from kwashiorkor and in many persons with debilitating illnesses (Scrimshaw et al. 1968). Phagocytosis by leukocytes can also be impaired by nutritional deficiences, particularly of protein, vitamin A, and ascorbic acid. Experiments by Aschkenasy (1974) have shown that foreign lymphocytes injected into rats induce a lowered defense reaction in hosts fed protein-free diets compared with those on normal diets.

Several forms of malnutrition alter the gastrointestinal flora, and there is some evidence that this results in decreased resistance to intestinal infections. Endocrine activity is also altered by nutritional deficiencies of protein. Starvation by itself produces a stress reaction, thereby altering the endocrine balance. This balance in turn affects the various forms of the immune response (Scrimshaw et al. 1968). All these mechanisms therefore play a subtle but important part in the interaction between food supply, population, and disease.

One further question that needs to be considered in this context is, How do parasites continue to live in a healthy host that has developed immunity toward them? This question is important because it is the very presence of the parasites within the host that enables them to respond rapidly to changes in nutrition and hence the immune reaction of the host. The problem was considered in a symposium of the Ciba Foundation (1974). The published conclusions, representing the general consensus of the symposium, point to several possible mechanisms of parasite survival. These include antigenic variation of the surface of the parasite; suppression of the host's immune system; uptake of host antigens; the production of soluble antigens; and mechanisms for surviving within macrophages. In conclusion, it appears that an uninfected host is susceptible to infection. After infection an immunity develops which does not kill the parasites already present but allows only a low level of multiplication or further infection by parasites of that species. Thus a balance develops which under circumstances of adequate nutrition is not detrimental to the host. However, the balance is upset when host nutrition drops to a submaintenance level.

Circumstantial evidence of this disturbance in parasite equilibrium through nutritional changes can be seen in some of the diseases of buffalo. For example, mortality attributed to Allerton-type herpes virus was observed only after a long dry season; yet it was present at other times without causing an epizootic. Ticks and lice appeared in larger numbers on the sick animals than on healthy animals in good condition. Mange in the Serengeti wildebeest and buffalo calves was seen commonly in the severe dry seasons of 1968 and 1969 but was not observed in the mild seasons of 1971 and 1972. These examples indicate that it was the poor condition of the host which led to the proliferation of the organism causing the disease.

The Exotic Disease Rinderpest

As I explained in chapter 1, this virus is probably an exotic disease in Africa. It affects ungulates such as cattle, buffalo, eland, and wildebeest severely, others such as giraffe less so, and young cattle are possible carriers (Atang and Plowright 1969). Branagan and Hammond (1965) argue that although rinderpest had periodically invaded Egypt before the panzootic of 1890, extensions of the disease had not occurred because there was little cattle traffic with areas south of the Sahara. Even if rinderpest had been in East Africa before 1889, it would have been only at very infrequent intervals, and it was certainly not endemic, for the panzootic at the end of last century showed up a complete lack of immunity in the cattle population.

Branagan and Hammond (1965) have reviewed the history of the disease in Tanzania. The virus was introduced to Somalia in 1889 through cattle from Arabia or India brought in during an Italian military expedition. It was panzootic in East Africa by 1890 and had reached Malawi by 1892. Thereafter it was widespread through Tanzania. During the First World War it was out of control, and only in 1917 were efforts begun to contain the disease. By 1927 rinderpest was present throughout Kenya and northern Tanzania, but it had been eliminated in the southern half of the latter country. However, control was tenuous, and repeated epizootics swept southward through the 1930s. For example, between 1929 and 1931 the disease spread through the Mara area of Tanzania and was specifically noticed in the Serengeti wildebeest. The severity of the disease can be judged by records of mortality in cattle herds approaching 80% or even 100%. The next epizootic started in 1933, was recorded in buffalo, and was present in the Serengeti region. At that time wildlife was considered an important carrier of the disease. It was present in every year between 1933 and 1942. This epizootic stimulated an intensive inoculation campaign which for a time controlled the disease in all areas except in the Mara and the Serengeti. These measures were only partly successful because outbreaks continued in various areas, and by 1945 another epizootic was under way. In 1946 outbreaks in Maswa were believed to have originated in the Serengeti, where young wildebeest had been dying in large numbers, and buffalo were also known to be affected. Once again rinderpest recurred annually throughout northern Tanzania.

Eventually in 1950 veterinary authorities changed their methods of control from tackling each outbreak as it occurred to adopting mass inoculations of all susceptible cattle, particularly in areas where there was wildlife-cattle contact. This policy proved very successful and quickly confined rinderpest to the Serengeti region, Ngorongoro, Manyara, and a few other areas. In 1952 buffalo at Loliondo just to the east of the Serengeti were suffering from the disease, and during 1953–54 there were isolated outbreaks in other areas near the Serengeti. In 1956 there were no confirmed reports of the disease for the first time since 1919. The early 1950s, therefore, appear to be a period of relative quiescence. But it did not last long, for in the dry season of the following year, 1957, wildebeest as old as two and one-half years of age were dying in the western and northern areas of the Serengeti. The fact that such age-groups were dying confirms there was a previous period free of disease and also that mortality must have removed a large proportion of the population, possibly as much as 20%, judging from age-distributions calculated in chapter 8. Similar heavy mortalities were reported for buffalo in the Ngorongoro highlands and at Manyara in January 1959. Branagan and Hammond (1965) write of the Lake Manyara buffalo, "Though all ages were affected, the majority of the estimated 1,000 deaths were among

young buffalo." They describe this outbreak as due to a "very viru-
lent rinderpest." Such a mortality at Manyara could have removed
more than 50% of the population, since even in 1973, after ten years
without the disease, the population was only about 1,800 animals.
There is strong circumstantial evidence, therefore, that Serengeti and
Manyara populations of buffalo and wildebeest suffered unusually
heavy mortalities in the late 1950s.

Between 1958 and 1961 rinderpest was observed every year in
yearling wildebeest (Talbot and Talbot 1963). Stewart (1964) mentions that it occurred in calves of this species up to 1962, and it was
also recorded in buffalo in the Kenya Mara area. Plowright (1963)
found that a high proportion (65%) of Serengeti wildebeest had
antibodies to rinderpest virus during the years 1959–61 and concluded that the disease recurred annually over this period by affecting the calves, for this age-group had no detectable antibody.

For buffalo I collected serum in 1967 and 1969, and this was tested
for neutralizing antibody by W. Plowright (personal communication).
I calculated the age of these animals and the few collected by Taylor
and Watson (1967) and assigned them to the approximate year when
they were born. Then I calculated the proportion of each year-group
that showed immunity to the disease (table 39). Figure 81 shows this
proportion plotted against year of birth. It demonstrates quite clearly
that animals born in and before 1963 suffered from the disease and
the survivors had developed an immunity to it. Those born in 1964
and later have never experienced this disease. This has been confirmed by similar investigations of wildebeest in the Serengeti region
(Plowright and McCulloch 1967; Taylor and Watson 1967). The
only difference with wildebeest is that rinderpest may have died out
a year earlier, in 1962. Thus Atang and Plowright (1969) conclude,
"The position with respect to wild ungulates in Tanzania and Kenya
has been clarified by continuous serological investigations commenc-
ing in the Serengeti region in 1960 and continuing to date. There
has been no evidence of significant rinderpest infection in any wild
species including buffalo, eland and wildebeest since 1962 or, at the
latest, early 1963." There has been no evidence of a recurrence up to
1976. The reason for its sudden disappearance appears to have been
an intensive campaign to inoculate cattle in the areas surrounding
the Serengeti. The wild animals do not seem to have evolved a state
where they can be carriers: they either die or become immune noncarriers. Consequently, when the immune ring of cattle was created,

Fig. 81. The percentage of Serengeti buffalo found with rinderpest antibody. No animals born in 1964 or later have been exposed to this disease.

the wild ungulates were protected from reinfection by the cattle, which are carriers. Contrary to earlier opinion, the wildlife species were not foci of infection.

Rinderpest disappeared by 1964, at a time when the buffalo population began a rapid increase. These events are a plausible explanation for the initiation of the observed population increases of buffalo and wildebeest in the Serengeti and of buffalo at Manyara. Rinderpest may not be the only cause, but it is the only one I have identified that reasonably satisfies the observations.

PREDATION

The event of predation usually draws the attention of casual observers. Nevertheless, it is difficult to measure its contribution to the total annual mortality of the population. When buffalo were found dead in the field, very often only the skeleton remained, and I found it impossible to tell whether a predator had killed the animal or whether it had died of other causes and had subsequently been scavenged. Few dead animals were allowed to remain intact for long in these areas, for vultures were soon on the scene, followed by hyenas and lions. In relatively intact carcasses I recorded predation if claw and tooth marks were found, particularly on the muzzle or neck, or if there were clear signs of a struggle. Although I have commented (chap. 6) that some old buffalo accept predation passively, the more general rule is a vigorous struggle. Frequent large scars on the backs of both males and females (2–3% of some herds) are a clear indication of injury caused by a lion jumping up and being shaken off. I also examined bone-marrow condition to see if predators were killing healthy or unhealthy prey.

Lions are the only important predators of buffalo over one year old in the Serengeti; no other predator species was known to have killed buffalo. Kruuk (1972) also states that hyenas have little effect on adult buffalo. Lions in the Kafue Park, Zambia, and in the Kruger Park, South Africa, were known to be present on 99.5% and 98%, respectively, of the occasions when predation could have occurred (Mitchell, Skenton, and Uys 1965; Pienaar 1969). Lions also killed many more adult males than females. At Lake Manyara they killed 44 males as opposed to 6 females, 6 calves, and 6 unsexed (Schaller 1972) from a population which did not have an excess of males.

Schaller's (1972) studies on the quantity of food eaten by lions allowed him to estimate the total amount of prey that the Serengeti lion population would eat annually. Of this total buffalo made up 15% and wildebeest 20–25%. On average the edible part of a buffalo would weigh 300 kg, that of wildebeest 100 kg. Consequently, the number of buffalo killed was roughly 2,468–2,961 each year. Since the mean number dying annually over the period of Schaller's study was 10,593, lion predation accounted for approximately 23–28% of the total mortality. Similar measurements from the wildebeest population showed that lions accounted for only 7–11% of the total mortality. However, hyenas were also important predators of wildebeest. From figures published by Kruuk (1972), I calculated that hyenas accounted for 6–10% of the total mortality, giving a total proportion caused by predation of 13–21%. Since many of the animals killed by predators were known to have been suffering from undernutrition as well, predation as a primary cause of death would have accounted for an even smaller proportion of the total mortality. Thus, over 70% of the annual mortality of buffalo and wildebeest must be accounted for by some other factor.

The effect of predation on buffalo calf mortality could be assessed only at Lake Manyara, where there were few scavengers and a high chance that a kill would be recorded. Calves amounted to only 11%

of all kills, whereas total calf mortality made up approximately 50% of annual population mortality. Again predation appears to be only a minor factor in buffalo calf mortality at Manyara; and in the Serengeti this proportion may well have been much smaller, for the lion density was much lower in this region than at Manyara (Schaller 1972).

SOCIAL STRESS

Stress usually causes endocrine imbalance (Christian and Davis 1964; Christian, Lloyd, and Davis 1965), which in turn can directly cause death or can permit disease organisms to become pathogenic, or may result in a reduction of fecundity. Stress itself can be caused by many factors, including malnutrition, disease, weather extremes, and socially induced aggression from conspecifics. It is this last factor which produces "social stress." But aggression can be defined as causing "social stress" only if it is not itself initiated by some other cause such as malnutrition. If undernutrition affecting the whole population alters aggressive behavior, the ensuing stress is due primarily to resource limitation.

Few cases in Serengeti ungulates were recorded in which the animal was apparently in good condition at death but was not killed by predators. Old buffalo males that have left the herd do suffer increased predation, which may be interpreted as resulting from social influences, but overall mortality rates show that these males survive at least as long as females, if not longer. On the whole, there is little evidence that social stress is a primary cause of mortality in Serengeti ungulates.

POACHING

Poaching, the illicit capture of animals by humans, is becoming increasingly important in the Serengeti as human population densities build up and encroach on the Maswa Game Reserve in the southwest and along the western and northern boundaries of the park. As I described in chapter 8, buffalo numbers in the Lamai sector (see fig. 67) are now very low compared with a similar area on the Kenya side of the border. Similar low numbers are found in the northwest corner south of the Mara River. In both of these areas the park wardens and I have observed the results of organized large-scale hunting operations.

The usual method of capture involves wire snares, sometimes several hundred of them, set along the edges of riverine thickets. Then perhaps fifty hunters spread out and drive a herd into the snares. Some of the men stand to act as wings, others move behind the herd. Often they have to drive the herd several kilometers. Up to 200 animals may be killed, and usually much of the meat is wasted because the poachers are in a hurry to move out. Strings of porters carry dried meat and hides up to 30 km back to their villages up on the Isuria escarpment. They have staging posts on the way where they lie up during the day. Vultures are the curse of the poachers, for they concentrate in large numbers, circling in the air and perching on the surrounding treetops, and this attracts the attention of the park rangers. To avoid attracting vultures, the poachers burn the buffalo heads and other remains at night and then cover them with branches (plate 37). While collecting skulls, I was able to identify animals killed by poachers because the skulls were found in characteristic piles and often the braincases had been neatly sliced open.

Mortalities as high as 200 from even large herds of 400 to 500 animals need only occur once a year to eliminate a population within a few years, and I know such large-scale kills happen more than once each year. There is a lucrative market for the meat among the local populace, and snare wire is easy to obtain. Although the overculling this mortality represents is not important at present for the major part of the Serengeti population, it could easily cause a serious decline if allowed to spread. The availability of snare wire makes this type of hunting a modern phenomenon, and it bears no resemblance to the traditional hunting with poisoned arrows, which is dying out. Similarly, in the western sector of the Serengeti poachers shoot with rifles from vehicles at night. Neither of these activities can be regarded as part of the natural system.

SUMMARY

1. In the dry season the quality of food eaten by Serengeti buffalo fell below the minimum necessary for animals to maintain their body weight. This drop in quality was due to a diminishing quantity of available grass leaf, this component being the most nutritious and their preferred food. All age and sex groups were affected in the same way. Similar changes were found in the wildebeest food supply. Measurements of the quantity of buffalo food at Mount Meru demonstrated that buffalo encountered a deficit in the dry season.

2. The animals' condition was judged by the fat content of their bone marrow. This fat is the last to be utilized and consequently reflects whether or not severe energy depletion is taking place. Fat reserves of dead buffalo and wildebeest decline to a low level in the dry season, correlated with the poor food intake at this time. Some live animals remain in good condition all year. It appears that in some animals, usually old ones, insufficient food leads to depletion of reserves and eventually death.

3. Buffalo are known to be hosts to at least 57 species of endoparasites, including trematodes, cestodes, nematodes, and pentastomids. They are also hosts to 17 species of ticks and some mites and lice. Not all of these occur in one area, but there are enough to ensure that all host animals harbor parasites to some degree. Some helminths infest several host species, and these ensure a constant challenge to the buffalo.

4. There is a range of endemic hematozoan parasites, bacteria, and viruses. Almost all affect calves, causing mortality, whereas adults have developed immunity. Some diseases such as Allerton-type herpes virus are ubiquitous; yet their action as a mortality agent has remained unnoticed until recently.

5. Published work by other authors has demonstrated a causal link between the poor nutritional condition of a host, the breakdown of the immune system, and the pathogenicity of disease. Evidence from the Serengeti populations supports this. Consequently, only a moderate depletion of energy reserves in the host is needed to break down the host's immune system and cause pathogenic infection. Since the host is already harboring a large number of potential agents this reaction to poor nutrition can come very quickly.

6. Rinderpest, an exotic disease lethal to buffalo, was present in Tanzania for the first sixty years of this century. It affected the Serengeti buffalo and wildebeest for most of this time. It caused heavy mortality of Serengeti and Manyara buffalo in the late 1950s and subsequently recurred until 1963 in the Serengeti. By 1964 it had disappeared entirely and has not since reappeared. This disappearance was due to the inoculation against the disease of cattle, which previously acted as carriers, reinfecting the buffalo.

7. Predation, although conspicuous to humans, does not account for more than 30% of the total mortality each year, and as a primary agent this proportion is much less. Lions are the only important predators in the Serengeti.

8. Social stress does not appear to be an important primary agent causing mortality in buffalo.

9. Poaching has resulted in overkilling of buffalo in some areas. If this spreads it could become a serious threat to the population.

10 Resource Limitation through Competition

In this chapter I shall develop a hypothesis on population regulation to account for the observations I have described in the preceding chapters. Then I shall discuss this in the context of other hypotheses that have been published on this subject.

INTRASPECIFIC COMPETITION

Regulation and Disturbance

It is appropriate at this point to return to the two basic questions I asked in chapter 1—namely, Is the Serengeti buffalo population regulated? and if so, What are the causes of this regulation?

I approached the first question in two ways (chap. 8). Mean crude density of buffalo in various different areas of eastern and southern Africa is positively correlated with the mean annual rainfall of those areas. Since rainfall also determines the amount of grass growth, it follows that buffalo density is also correlated with grass production. A relationship between an external factor and density measured from separate populations not influenced by migration indicates that regulation is taking place, since in an environment exhibiting random variations, their effect on mortality and reproduction will also vary randomly, sometimes resulting in greater mortality than reproduction and sometimes the reverse. Although any one population can remain within relatively narrow limits without regulating factors playing a part, it is extremely improbable that several independent populations can do this and also show mean densities that are correlated with some environmental factor (Reddingius 1971). In other words, without regulation there should be no correlation between density in different populations and environmental conditions. If, however, mortality or reproduction is also responsive to the density of the population relative to some resource, then this response will counteract disturbances in density which have resulted from past

261

random variations in weather. This is regulation. In this case one should expect to find a correlation between density in separate populations and a resource or the weather factor influencing the resource. Such a correlation between buffalo density and rainfall suggests that regulation is taking place.

The evidence from the analysis of changes in the Serengeti population supports this conclusion. Adult mortality was positively correlated with the population density before that mortality. Consequently, it could act as a negative feedback response to changes in density. However, this by itself did not mean that the observed population regulation was due to adult mortality alone. For example, there could be other undetected responses owing to juvenile mortality. So population models were constructed to test whether adult mortality or juvenile mortality or both combined could regulate the population in a way similar to the observed changes. This process was not merely one of putting the same observed data into a model and getting the same answer out again, for there were several possible answers. Assuming a positive linear relationship between mortality rate and density, it turned out that adult mortality alone was sufficient to regulate a model population in a way similar to the observed Serengeti population during the period 1965 to 1974. When I assumed juvenile mortality was also density-dependent, then the regulatory response became too strong and this model reached an asymptote, or equilibrium level, lower than the observed population. This result suggested that juvenile mortality was unlikely to be a regulating response. Juvenile mortality, however, produced the greatest changes in population and was the most sensitive to changes in the external environment, thus acting to disturb the population from its potential equilibrium.

Why should adult mortality regulate when juvenile mortality does not? One reason can be found in the change in age-structure of the population as it approaches the equilibrium level. The increasing population has a relatively high proportion of juveniles and a low proportion of old adults. As the population increases in density and approaches a stationary age-distribution, there is a proportional increase of old adults and hence a proportional increase in adults susceptible to environmental mortality factors. In other words, a density-dependent mortality would occur. On the other hand, since the proportion of juveniles decreases under these conditions, mortality in this group has a smaller effect as a regulating factor, although remaining susceptible to random environmental factors.

Extrapolating the models backward in time demonstrated that neither agreed with the population estimate of 1961 and that they agreed even less with that of 1958. The models assumed that the population would increase in a symmetrical sigmoid way between 1965 and 1973. If this assumption is correct it suggests that the population dynamics changed sometime between 1961 and 1965 in such a way that the population increased faster after 1965 than before. The slower rate of increase before 1965 could have been due to a higher mortality rate or a lower reproductive rate during that period, and the cause of this would have disappeared between 1961 and 1965. Alternatively, the assumptions of the model could be wrong. For example, instead of a linear regulating effect producing a symmetrical sigmoid population growth curve, there may be other factors which would produce an asymmetrical growth curve to describe the whole period 1958 to 1973.

Concerning the causes of the population increase, the most noticeable and profound change in environmental conditions was the artificial removal of the exotic disease rinderpest during 1963 through inoculation of cattle in surrounding areas. The wild ungulates did not appear to be carriers for the disease, perhaps because it was only recently introduced to Africa through cattle. So wild animals either died of it or developed an immunity as noncarriers. In fact, yearling cattle are now considered to be the carriers (Atang and Plowright 1969), and these animals probably continually reinfected the wildlife before the inoculation campaigns. The initial low numbers of buffalo may have been produced by an unusually heavy mortality due to rinderpest, which is known to have occurred in the late 1950s in both the Serengeti and the Manyara populations. Attempts by veterinarians to control the disease produced a short period in the early 1950s when the populations were not exposed to it, thus allowing a significant proportion of susceptible animals to build up. The subsequent rinderpest epizootic would have killed many of these animals and could have reduced the population by as much as 50%. In fact, the populations of Manyara buffalo and Serengeti wildebeest and buffalo have all increased at approximately the same rate in the second half of the 1960s. On the other hand, the buffalo population at Tarangire Park has not increased over this period. Consequently, the increases were probably not due to some universal factor such as weather.

In conclusion, there is evidence that the initial low numbers of buffalo and their subsequent increase can both be attributed to the effects of rinderpest and its artificial manipulation by veterinarians. Although protection from rinderpest may not have been the only factor causing the buffalo to increase, at present I think it is the most important, for evidence on other factors does not agree with the observed sequence of events. For example, the only noticeable change in weather patterns has occurred since 1971, consistent with global changes (Kukla and Kukla 1974), and no trend in rainfall was apparent in the 1960s. Changes in population due to other species such as wildebeest and elephant are possible alternatives. But since wildebeest have increased at approximately the same rate and over the same time period as buffalo, this suggests a common cause, rather than that wildebeest facilitated an increase in buffalo by improving the buffalo habitat. If anything, buffalo improve the wildebeest grazing areas rather than the other way around. But the difference in the absolute size of the two populations means that the facilitative effect of buffalo on wildebeest is very small. Censuses of elephants conducted on the same occasions as those on buffalo between 1965 and 1973 have shown no obvious increase. Over this period the number of *Acacia* trees has been declining slowly, and much of this decline is thought to be caused by elephant (D. Herlocker, personal communication). The possible increase in area or change in type of grasslands due to the tree changes would have only a small effect on buffalo, for their most important habitat in the dry season—riverine grassland and forest (chap. 4)—has been little affected by elephant. The *Acacia* and *Terminalia* trees occur in habitats that buffalo use mainly in the wet season when there is a superabundance of food anyway (Sinclair 1975), and so changes in these habitats would probably have little effect.

Murdoch (1970) has pointed out the difficulty of distinguishing between a population returning to an unknown equilibrium and one following a changing equilibrium. One way of testing between the two, he suggested, is to manipulate the population experimentally. In effect this is just what has probably occurred in the Serengeti and Manyara populations through the removal of rinderpest. Such manipulation, although unintentional, allowed an analysis of the population changes. This showed that the population has been increasing toward an equilibrium from an initial low point, through the negative feedback response of adult mortality. This situation has also provided an opportunity to observe the present causes of the adult mortality.

Causes of Regulation

I have considered causes of mortality according to whether they initiate the sequence of events leading to death (primary causes) or participate at some stage after the initial cause but do not themselves initiate the mortality (secondary causes). For example, rinderpest was clearly a primary cause, for it killed nonimmune adults and calves even if they were healthy and in good condition. This disease, of course, was not playing a part in the regulation of the population after 1965.

Measurements of the quality and quantity of food available to all classes of the population showed that a period of undernutrition occurs during the dry season. Animals dying at this time had very low fat reserves, indicating that the food shortage was having a primay effect as a mortality agent in some animals. However, members of the live population—particularly that of wildebeest—on average showed only a moderate decline in fat reserves during this season. Severe inanition resulting in "walking skeletons" was almost never observed.

This raises the question, How does incipient or moderate undernutrition result in rapid death? In simple starvation it can take many months before death occurs. If inanition was the only process, the response of the population to food limitation would be very slow, creating time lags and therefore fluctuations in population and resource. Clearly some process occurs which acts as an amplifier to speed up death initiated by undernutrition. An amplifier of this kind must be sensitive to small changes in the condition of individuals. There are various diseases which show just such a sensitive response. In the Serengeti the Allerton-type herpes virus, for example, was ubiquitous but in some individuals became pathogenic after a period of resource restriction (chap. 9). Normally individuals in low body condition are juveniles or old animals. Juveniles have no initial immune response, and so the pathogenicity of the disease in this age-group is high irrespective of condition. Old animals do have immunity to the disease when they are in good condition. There is now considerable published evidence from both human and other mammal populations which shows that undernutrition impairs the immune response and affects the endocrine system, which in turn allows existing diseases to become pathogenic (chap. 9). The immune system appears to be impaired through protein restriction, which prevents the production of specific antibodies and also phagocytes (Scrimshaw, Taylor, and Gordon 1968; Aschkenasy 1974). Although energy restriction may also be important, the present evidence on the immune system does suggest one way protein can operate as a limiting resource. Consequently, adult animals can become susceptible to disease—older ones first, but even younger adults if the resource restriction is severe enough. Thus there is a possible causal relationship between the degree of undernutrition and the proportion of the population susceptible to disease, and hence the degree of mortality. Apart from Allerton-type herpes virus, there are other diseases such as theileriasis, foot-and-mouth disease, trypanosomiasis, and helminthiasis which can act in this manner. In fact there is such a wide range of helminths, protozoa, bacteria, and viruses already living in the buffalo hosts that the chances of one of these disease organisms' becoming pathogenic the moment there is any impairment of the immune system must be very high. Exactly which disease predominates may depend upon the balance already existing in the host, and different host individuals may die from different diseases although all may have been initiated by the same undernutrition. Another factor important in maintaining a constant disease challenge is that many species of parasites live in several hosts, so that their populations are dependent not upon the buffalo population itself but upon the overall density of ungulates in the region. For example the blood-sucking intestinal nematodes *Haemonchus contortus* and *H. bedfordi* must present a constant challenge to buffalo irrespective of fluctuations in the buffalo population, because they also live in most of the other Serengeti bovids, whose populations maintain the output of parasite eggs.

The behavioral response of predators (as opposed to their reproductive response) may be sensitive enough to take advantage of incipient undernutrition in some species of bovids. In buffalo and wildebeest, predation probably is a contributory secondary cause but not as sensitive as disease to the changes in the condition of prey. The amplifying action of disease is seen in its effect on the nutritional status of the hosts. Various reviews (e.g., Scrimshaw, Taylor, and Gordon 1968; Symons 1969) have noted that diseases contribute to protein and other nutrient deficiencies through loss of appetite, decreased nitrogen absorbtion, increased nitrogen demand, and increased nitrogen excretion (chap. 9). Thus a positive feedback system is produced through undernutrition leading to disease, which in turn leads to further undernutrition. So from small beginnings a host can be rapidly reduced to poor condition and eventually to death. The only way this cycle can be broken naturally is through a return to good food conditions. This hypothesis can explain how the food limitation recorded in this study could lead to the observed poor condition of those buffalo and wildebeest found dead in the dry season.

The essential feature of this nutrition hypothesis is that it requires at least two factors acting in sequence. A primary lack of available food leads to incipient undernutrition and impaired immunity to disease, then by a secondary response diseases become pathogenic, which in turn reduces the host's condition to a low level and results in death. This causal pathway may therefore be subtle, inconspicuous, and easily overlooked by human observers.

Causes of Disturbances in Population

Juvenile mortality appears to produce the main disturbance in population density. Virtually every potential cause of mortality affects animals under one year old. Because calves spend most of their protein and energy intake on growth they do not build up energy reserves (chap. 7). Consequently, in periods of food shortage (chap. 9) they probably succumb quickly to undernutrition. Most of the diseases recorded in table 38 affect this age-group of buffalo. Death has been induced experimentally in juveniles using *Theileria*. Mortality has been observed in calves showing signs of Allerton-type herpes virus when they were living under natural conditions in the Serengeti. Similarly, foot-and-mouth diseases, trypanosomiasis, sarcoptic mange, and some helminths, among other diseases, affect this age-group particularly. In general these animals are susceptible because of their lack of immunity. Rinderpest is known to affect calves for the same reason. Calves are also probably more susceptible to predators than are adults. Although predation probably has only a minor effect on buffalo, with wildebeest it is clearly an important factor during the calving season. Weather may also contribute to mortality through exposure and cold, or waterlogged ground may cause footrot. So far these effects of weather on buffalo have not been very noticeable. However, there were catastrophic mass drownings of wildebeest calves at Lake Lagarja in February 1969 and 1973 as a result of unusually high lake levels (plate 36).

Most of these causes operate irrespective of the condition of the calves, and some can produce heavy mortalities. Their action is often fast. Consequently the sensitivity of calves to all causes of death results in large random mortalities. They are perhaps too sensitive to produce a density-dependent mortality. Potentially they could produce an overcompensating density-dependent mortality, which could become evident during a population decline, but this remains speculative at present.

Causes of Food Limitation

If food shortage ultimately results in the density-dependent adult mortality as I propose above, the question arises, What causes the food shortage in the first place?

Essentially there appear to be two factors that determine the amount of food—the environment and the density of herbivores. Rainfall determines the amount of grass growth and hence the amount of buffalo food, for buffalo are entirely grass feeders in the Serengeti (chap. 4). Buffalo crude density in various areas of Africa is correlated with mean annual rainfall. This result, apart from indicating that regulaton is taking place, also shows that rainfall is one environmental factor that determines the position of the equilibrium level. Analyses of data from within the Serengeti show that in this area the extent of permanent water supplies in the dry season is also correlated with the mean density. Another factor which seems important is soil moisture, for example, near alkaline lakes, where grasses or sedges grow even when there is no rain. The structure of the grass plant also affects food availability, for some species when mature are too tall and coarse to be eaten by buffalo and are grazed only at an early stage of growth. Rainfall and soil moisture determine the amount of food directly, whereas permanent water determines the preferred dry season habitat of buffalo, the riverine grassland strips and forest. All three ultimately determine the amount of food and can be regarded as limiting factors. It is possible that in other areas of Africa temperature and humidity may also act as limiting factors.

These limiting factors cannot, of course, regulate the population. This must come from the impact on the food by the herbivores themselves. Buffalo prefer grass leaf over other components of the plant, and they actively select for this when feeding (chap. 4). In the wet season, when green growing grass is superabundant, the animals find little difficulty in selecting for this part. But in the dry season green leaf suitable for buffalo is more or less confined to the riverine habitats, and even here growth is very limited. To maintain body weight buffalo must find food of high enough quality at a certain rate—approximately 850 g/hr (calculated from mean daily grazing times and daily dry weight food requirements). In the dry season sufficient quality would be achieved only if the animals selected grass leaf entirely (chap. 4). However, as the dry season progresses this selection reduces the amount of available grass leaf to a point where the time spent searching for leaf would cause the intake rate to drop below the animals' minimum food requirements. In order to maintain their rate of intake they are forced to be less selective and to eat lower-quality forage such as grass stems. Although this strategy of becoming less selective may save searching time and may maintain a higher rate of intake, the quality of the food still drops below the minimum necessary for body maintenance. The more animals there are the lower the amount of leaf available and the greater the drop in diet quality below the minimum maintenance requirements. Finally, the lower the diet quality, the faster the animals will use up their fat reserves and the greater the proportion of the population that will die. In other words, this is the effect of density producing the regulating mortality.

The effects of food selection on depleting grass leaf are accentuated because buffalo live in compact herds. Each individual is removing grass and leaving less in the immediate vicinity of the next animal. To counteract this effect of being in a herd they could behave in a number of ways: they could move faster and so cover a greater area, or they could spread themselves farther apart, or they could split up into smaller groups. Herds do not appear to show greater daily movements in the dry season than in the wet season (chap. 5). Changes in individual spacing have not been studied, but the splitting up of herds in the dry season (chap. 6) may be a response to the changing availability of food.

The Effects of Social Behavior

Since undernutrition, predation, and diseases are all mortality agents, they therefore act as selection pressures that could shape the behavior and physiology of the species. In chapter 6 I suggested that social behavior has evolved to reduce the effects of these mortality agents, although of course it cannot counteract them entirely. Thus food selection, habitat selection, the maintenance of a group home range, and changes in group size all seem to optimize the use of available resources. Herd formation and group protection behavior could reduce predation. The dominance hierarchy in males may be as much associated with obtaining copulations as with avoiding mortality. On the physiological side, the development of fat stores delays the effects of undernutrition and, of course, the immune system counteracts disease.

Since I found undernutrition in all sections of the population, it does not appear that social behavior prevents such a condition from occurring at all. The behavior appears to have evolved to minimize mortality and results in relatively stable population densities and low rates of increase. In the terminology of r and K selection (Pianka 1974), this species appears to be one of the more extreme K-strategists.

INTERSPECIFIC COMPETITION

So far I have considered only the effects of the buffalo population on its own food supply. However, there are a number of other herbivore species which do eat at least a small proportion of same riverine grass leaf. Consequently their depredations must not only contribute to resource limitation, but act also as a selection pressure on the buffalo to improve their methods of resource selection relative to other species feeding on the same resource. Other ungulate species that occassionally feed on riverine grasses in the dry season are zebra, topi, kongoni, waterbuck, hippopotamus, and wildebeest (plate 38). Zebra move into this habitat in large numbers. They eat more grass stem than do other species, but they still eat the leaf that buffalo prefer (Gwynne and Bell 1968). Furthermore, they trample a significant proportion of the grass, which then becomes inedible. Topi and kongoni appear to be highly selective for grass leaves when they utilize these habitats in the dry season (P. Duncan, personal communication). Similarly, wildebeest select for short green grass leaves, but when they pass through riverine habitats to drink or to move to grazing areas beyond, they eat some of the grass and trample much of the rest (plate 40).

Interspecific competition is generally defined as occurring when two species require the same resource and there is not enough for both (e.g., Klomp 1961). However, competition can still take place if the resource is limiting for only one of the species and the other species eats it, perhaps by chance and probably inefficiently, while passing through the habitat. In this case the first species is competing with the second but not the reverse. Such a situation appeared to be occurring between buffalo and wildebeest, and a measure of the proportion of buffalo food removed by wildebeest has been made (Sinclair 1974d). Samples of buffalo and wildebeest were collected from the same area at approximately the same time of year. Both buffalo and wildebeest eat grass almost exclusively, and they eat the available grass species in similar proportions, so that those eaten most by buffalo are also eaten most by wildebeest. Gwynne and Bell (1968) analyzed rumen samples from wildebeest and found they contained 17% grass leaf. The buffalo rumen samples contained 11% grass leaf (Sinclair and Gwynne 1972), showing that they were eating relatively similar proportions of the different grass parts in the dry season.

In chapter 4 I showed that a small but significant association was found between wildebeest and one of the preferred buffalo habitats, riverine grassland. Thus in the dry season some wildebeest were feeding in the same habitats as buffalo and on the same food. Since this food was insufficient for even the buffalo population, the buffalo were competing with the wildebeest for their limited resources.

The proportion of the wildebeest population that was observed in the riverine grassland, as calculated from aerial censuses, amounted to only 7.1%. This was a mean figure for the dry seasons of 1967–69. Although it was only a small proportion, the large size of the wildebeest population relative to that of the buffalo meant that absolute numbers were high. Thus an approximate mean of 1,030 wildebeest were in the riverine grassland at any one time. The mean buffalo population in the same area was 2,380 (Sinclair 1974d). Taking into account metabolic body size, the amount of grass these wildebeest could have been eating was equivalent to that which would have been eaten by 472 buffalo. This number represents about 18% of the sum of 472 and 2,380, the approximate maximum buffalo population. Because of the difference in absolute numbers of the wildebeest and buffalo populations, the reverse impact of buffalo removing potential wildebeest food must be regarded as negligible.

At this point it is appropriate to mention a report by Eltringham (1974) describing an interaction between hippopotamus and buffalo in one particular area of Ruwenzori National Park, Uganda. In 1957 a high density of hippopotamus was artificially reduced to very low numbers and then maintained at this level until 1967. Buffalo, which were originally in low numbers, increased sixfold by 1968, probably through both reproduction and immigration. Eltringham thinks this happened because vegetation cover, and hence buffalo food, increased threefold when the hippopotamus were removed. Other areas of the park unaffected by hippopotamus did not exhibit such changes in vegetation or in buffalo numbers. This approximates an experimental elucidation of interspecific competition.

Not all of the buffalo habitat in the Serengeti is invaded by wildebeest. Wildebeest completely avoid riverine forest, whereas buffalo prefer it. Similarly, topi, kongoni, and hippopotamus all avoid forest, and zebra enter only at the edges. Thus there is one area which buffalo can use as an "ecological refuge" from these potential competitors. Conversely, the short "greenflush" is the refuge for wildebeest, for the grass is too short for buffalo to graze. Long, dry *Themeda* grassland is grazed somewhat infrequently by both species (plate 39). Thus this habitat and the riverine grassland become the overlap areas for these two species (and probably several others), where competition probably takes place and where a dynamic balance may be achieved.

Waterbuck, on the other hand, do use the forest and graze the grasses in it. In fact, the similarity of diet between buffalo and waterbuck has been remarked upon by Field (1968*b*), who found very little difference between these two in the Ruwenzori Park, Uganda. In general, ecological differences between species have been considered either in terms of space (that is, habitats) or in terms of food preferences. However, there are also differences in the rate of food intake that each species needs to maintain because of differences in body size. Although a small animal needs relatively larger amounts of food than a large animal because of its higher metabolic activity, in absolute terms it still eats less. This can be seen in figure 82, where rates of intake for different herbivores are plotted against body size. Rates of food intake for these species were estimated from their approximate daily food requirements, which I have calculated elsewhere (Sinclair 1975), and from studies of daily grazing activity. Apart from the measurements of total grazing time per day for buffalo given in chapter 5, I also measured those for wildebeest and kongoni, and P. Duncan (personal communication) provided me with information on topi. Grazing times have also been reported for waterbuck (Spinage 1968), impala (Jarman and Jarman 1973), and Thomson's gazelle

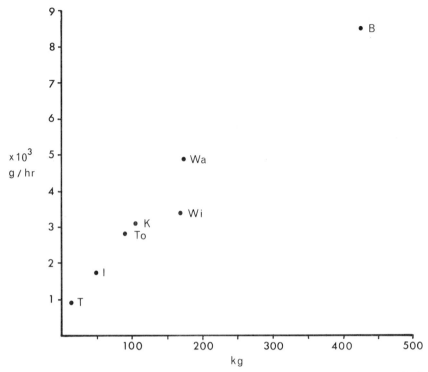

Fig. 82. The relationship between the rate of food intake and the mean body weight of buffalo (*B*), waterbuck (*Wa*), wildebeest (*Wi*), kongoni (*K*), topi (*To*), impala (*I*), and Thomson's gazelle (*T*).

(Walther 1973). What is indicated from figure 82 is that two species can coexist eating identical food provided this food is differently dispersed. Thus buffalo may eat the same food as waterbuck, but only where it is sufficiently abundant for the buffalo to maintain their high rate of intake. In such areas buffalo can probably succeed in competition with waterbuck. However, because waterbuck eat less they can exist in areas where food is more widely scattered. Such areas can be those already grazed and depleted by the buffalo themselves. In other words, buffalo potentially could be creating a habitat for waterbuck. In fact, this may be an example of the facilitation between species originally suggested by Vesey-Fitzgerald and elaborated by Bell (1969). In conclusion, buffalo could be both facilitating and competing with waterbuck. This and similar interactions between other herbivores would be interesting to study in greater detail.

This discussion illustrates the complexity of the possible interactions between the different species in an ecosystem. I have suggested (Sinclair 1975) that the whole herbivore trophic level can be food-limited, and that competition may be occurring not only between different ungulate species but also between different groups of organisms such as orthoptera and ungulates. Despite this, it is conceivable that predators could be regulating the smaller populations of kongoni or waterbuck, for example. The predator populations could be maintained by the large populations of wildebeest and zebra. For part of the year this migrating prey is unavailable and the predators have to switch for a short time to other species. This time period would be short enough to depress a small population of prey but not that of the predator, which switches again to some other species. So far this merely remains a suggestion for further investigation, and there is little evidence for it.

A summary of the processes of regulation and disturbance of the Serengeti buffalo population is perhaps best expressed as a model in figure 83.

NATURAL SELECTION, REGULATION, AND ALTERNATE THEORIES

If food shortage ultimately results in death, as I suggest it does, then it also acts as a selection pressure so that buffalo evolve behavioral and physiological mechanisms to minimize the mortality. I have already described some of these mechanisms. If this selection pressure took effect only infrequently, then in the intervening periods the normal genetic variability within the population would produce individuals poorly adapted behaviorally and physiologically. Consequently, when food limitation recurs this more extreme proportion will die off, causing a relatively large mortality. If this selection pressure operated more frequently there would be less time for extreme individuals to enter the population before they were eliminated, and as a result the mortality would be smaller and less conspicuous. Logically, therefore, the more constant the selection pressure, the better adapted the individuals are to counteract the selecting agent, the smaller the mortality rate, and the less conspicuous the action of the selection pressure. One might almost say that this argument produces the paradox that if a mortality cause appears to be absent it may well be present. The paradox exists only if one looks at population processes too superficially.

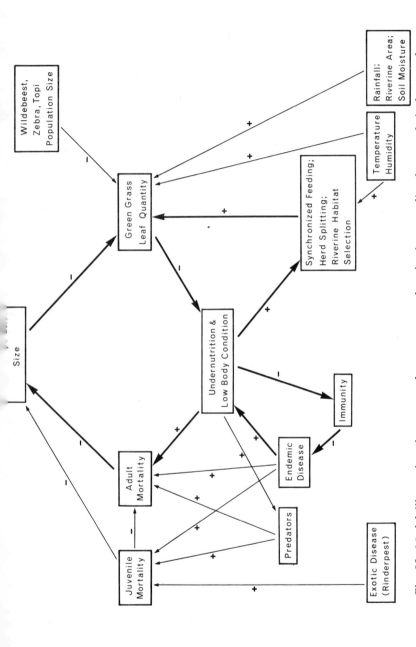

Fig. 83. Model illustrating the suggested processes of regulation and disturbance in the Serengeti buffalo population, with the main pathways shown as thicker lines. Minus signs indicate that higher values in the preceding box result in lower values in the succeeding box, while plus signs result in higher values.

This argument may be better understood by turning to an analogous situation. There are some cryptic forms of caterpillars which, to the human eye, perfectly resemble the twigs upon which they rest. At one time it was suggested that natural selection through bird predation could never have produced such crypsis, since birds could not see these insects well enough to have much influence on their morphology, and also because previous, less perfect stages would all have been seen and eliminated. De Ruiter (1952) conducted experiments on these caterpillars using bird predators and showed that once the birds had found one insect they were indeed able to distinguish their food from the inedible twigs. So not only could birds act as a selection pressure to maintain crypsis in the insects, but they must be doing so all the time for the crypsis to have reached such a high degree of perfection. The actual proportion of the population in any one generation suffering this mortality may be very small, however, and consequently under natural conditions it would hardly be noticed by human observers.

Therefore I suggest that the very presence of efficient behavioral and physiological mechanisms in animal populations to detect and avoid food shortages implies that food shortages may be constantly causing mortality or inhibiting reproduction. Some of the effects of nutritional stress on populations may be very subtle, as has now been described for red grouse (*Lagopus lagopus*) in Scotland (Moss, Watson and Parr 1975), for example, and these effects may be easily overlooked if the nutritional physiology of the animals is not studied in detail.

One major problem with all theories concerned with regulating animal populations is that they have to make the assumption that animals are more or less well adapted to their environment—that they are not at some intermediate stage of evolution where they are poorly adapted. This assumption is almost impossible to test, for with populations one cannot produce an experimental situation where the animals are better adapted to their environment than are those found in nature, as can be done, for example, in the analogous situation where an especially strong stimulus is presented to an animal in a behavioral test. The difficulty arises because the components of the biotic environment of a species—the plant food, the diseases, and the predators—are themselves all adapted to the species under study. One would have to manipulate the genetic constitution of a whole ecosystem.

However, there have been a few occasions where this has happened accidentally. These have occurred when a species has been introduced into a new land that has never had its ecological equivalents. Such a situation exists with the water buffalo in northern Australia. This species was introduced in 1839 and has since spread in a wild state over much of the floodplains along the rivers in the area. This race is similar to the wild form in Asia. The regular tropical monsoon climate is like that in the areas where water buffalo are normally found in their wild state. However, the floodplain sedges are quite unadapted to grazing pressure, for Australia has no indigenous grazers of this type of vegetation (there are magpie geese which eat the bulbs rather than the leaves). There are also no serious natural predators. Similarly, the introduced animals arrived without many of their diseases. Thus water buffaloes in northern Australia have only eleven species of helminths (M. Bainbridge, personal communication), whereas in Asia as many as seventy-seven species have been recorded (Griffiths 1974). Consequently, in Australia the water buffalo is living in a suitable climate, eating plants which are not adapted to grazing pressures, and the animals hardly suffer from any disease or predator. This situation should lead to the prediction that, since there is little adaptation of the biotic environment to the buffalo, the normal regulatory processes through nutrition and disease are of a rather crude nature. One should expect the population to be insensitive to incipient undernutrition, for there are almost no diseases to respond to the poor body condition; the food supply should be depleted to an obvious extent; the animals should show signs of extreme starvation and there should be large die-offs followed by rapid increases. In short, this population should show large fluctuations relative to the more balanced populations in Africa.

My observations on the Australian buffalo, although only qualitative, indicate that some of these features do occur. Thus in some areas there is so great an impact on the black-soil plains that nothing but bare ground remains in the dry season. Tulloch (1970) reports die-offs in 1961 and 1965. In 1972 a large die-off (plate 41) was observed in areas east of Darwin, apparently as a result of a high population and dry conditions, and many emaciated animals were observed at the time (R. H. Barrett, personal communication). By

1974 my measurements showed that the population was increasing relatively fast, with a recruitment of 20%, a proportion much higher than that observed in the African buffalo of the Serengeti. Consequently there is some evidence that this introduced population is responding to the environment through large fluctuations. Unfortunately, even this situation could be unsatisfactory as a test of natural regulatory processes, for farther south in central Australia erratic weather conditions produce superficially similar fluctuations in indigenous populations. However, since rainfall variability is less than 20% of the annual mean in the Darwin area, as opposed to more than 30% in central Australia (Davidson 1972), it should be possible to account for the effects of weather in future analyses.

I have suggested from observations on African buffalo that resource limitation can regulate a population through competition and that in well-adapted species undernutrition occurs at frequent intervals but that the resulting mortality is small. This is because the species has developed behavioral and physiological mechanisms which can detect the resource limitation at an early stage and hence allow individuals to respond appropriately. Wynne-Edwards (1965, p. 173) has stated, "It is readily apparent that, although food is generally the commodity that ultimately limits the carrying capacity of the habitat, the population dependent on it must not be allowed simply to increase until further growth in numbers is chronically held in check by general starvation. Famine is a catastrophe especially likely to damage the resource and lead to its permanent depletion." The reason why excessive damage to the resource is not normally seen is that the population, as the rate of increase slows down, has a change in age-structure, with an increased proportion of old animals. These animals are sensitive to the first signs of resource depletion through impaired immunity and increased endocrine stress. This results in increased mortality from disease. In some species endocrine stress leads to increased aggression, leading to both decreased reproduction and increased mortality. In essence these secondary steps, which can all be initiated by incipient undernutrition, accelerate the process of death so that further resource depletion does not normally occur. Therefore it seems unnecessary to introduce complex behavioral mechanisms which have the specific purpose of limiting the size of populations (Wynne-Edwards 1965), especially since it is difficult to account for the evolution of such mechanisms (Wilson 1975).

The concepts of Andrewartha and Birch (1954) were developed in an environment where the disturbing influences of weather are so much more conspicuous than possible regulating processes that the latter were overlooked. This does not mean they were not present. Attention was focused on the rapid increases at times of superabundance and the equally rapid declines when conditions returned to the normal low. Little attention was paid to why this low level was so similar after each increase. The similarity of the low points in several fluctuating Australian populations is illustrated in Varley, Gradwell, and Hassell (1973). As with the Wynne-Edwards hypothesis, some of the differences appear to be a matter of semantics. Thus Andrewartha (1961) suggests that the effect of weather is density-dependent because populations which are too large for the available cover at times of inclement weather show density-dependent mortality. The density-dependent school would say that this was competition for space as a resource, and that weather was the limiting factor, not the regulating factor.

Lack (1966) concluded that food supplies regulated populations through density-dependent mortality and argued against the Wynne-Edwards hypothesis that populations experienced a permanent super-abundance of food. Lack paid much less attention to the secondary processes taking place between food shortage and the resulting mortality.

In conclusion, much of the polemics in the argument concerned with the limitation of animal numbers appears to have resulted because early theories were too simplistic. Thus Reddingius (1971) has shown that stochastic processes operate in population dynamics, and Chitty (1960, 1967) has argued that populations are composed of individuals of different genotypes whose responses to environmental effects may be different. These are concepts which were not appreciated previously. I also consider that the concept of food and its effects on a population has so far been treated in a naive way. The main conclusion from this work on buffalo, therefore, is that the mechanisms whereby food shortages lead to mortality are subtle and complex, and that the need to reduce this mortality has led to a variety of adaptations in the animals. The mechanisms have thus been overlooked by human observers in some cases, and this may have contributed to the arguments concerning the regulation of populations.

11 Practical Implications

In this chapter I shall first consider the implications of this present work for the management of buffalo and wildebeest in the Serengeti and other areas. Then I shall discuss the relevance of some more general scientific ideas to the national parks in East Africa. These concepts, now common knowledge in North America, have only recently been considered in the context of parks in developing countries.

THE SERENGETI BUFFALO AND WILDEBEEST POPULATIONS

The present evidence suggests that the buffalo population is returning to an equilibrium point as a result of the removal of rinderpest in the early 1960s. Since there appears to be no large-scale damage to the vegetation, there does not seem to be any immediate need for management by the park authorities to counteract overgrazing or overtrampling. The wildebeest population appears to be responding in the same way as the buffalo. Similarly, there is no evidence of overgrazing, such as areas of bare soil and erosion. There have been suggestions of an increase in unpalatable plants on the plains, but at present there is little hard evidence on this. Even if this is occurring it should be regarded as part of the natural and normal vegetation response toward grazing. Since it results in a negative feedback regulating the grazing pressure so that plant cover is maintained and soil erosion is avoided, from the national parks standpoint of maintaining natural ecosystems the increase of relatively unpalatable species in the vegetation should be considered as a normal and perhaps desirable response to heavy grazing. So at the present time there is also little need to consider management of the wildebeest population. However, since both the buffalo and the wildebeest populations are only now approaching equilibrium, it is necessary to continue monitoring the population dynamics through censuses and estimates of recruitment to observe whether an equilibrium is maintained.

In chapter 9 I pointed out that poachers have seriously reduced the buffalo population in the northern sector of the park, particularly in the Lamai wedge and along the south bank of the Mara River. Judging by the very low numbers of topi, kongoni, and other ungulates in these regions, compared with either the Kenya Mara Park or farther south on the Grumeti watershed, it appears that poachers are also affecting these animals. Consequently, if poachers are allowed to expand their activities, particularly the use of snare lines and vehicles at night, it may cause serious declines in the populations. I recommend that management to prevent inroads of poaching be continued. Snare lines and the temporary poachers huts in the riverine forest can be seen from the air, and regular reconnaissance flights at random intervals about a week apart would help considerably toward limiting this type of poaching.

The cropping of buffalo and wildebeest for commercial exploitation is of course not relevant to the Serengeti National Park, since the park and its populations should be maintained as a natural ecosystem as far as possible. However, there are other areas in Tanzania where these species could be exploited on a sustained-yield basis. The estimation of the maximum sustained yield is calculated from the maximum rate of growth the population can achieve in a given environment. To determine this, censuses are required over a period of time to observe rates of increase or to estimate the equilibrium density. These should be conducted before culling takes place, and it is important that censuses be continued as a monitoring procedure after culling has commenced.

There are considerable logistical difficulties in capturing the kill quota efficiently. Methods of doing this for buffalo and wildebeest have been developed in Australia and South Africa (Densham 1974). For example water buffalo in northern Australia are rounded up with a helicopter and driven into yards using hessian-lined wings to direct them to the yard opening. Thereafter they are transported to an abattoir where the animals are inspected by veterinarians both before and after slaughter. This procedure meets the requirements for the export of buffalo meat from Australia. In Africa, because foot-and-mouth disease is endemic, export over national boundaries will prob-

ably be difficult, but since the meat will normally be for local consumption this may not be a problem. There remains the question
whether wild populations can be harvested economically enough for
the local populace to be able to buy the meat. This aspect is beyond
the scope of my work and requires study by agricultural economists.

OVERCROWDING AND HABITAT ALTERATIONS IN NATIONAL PARKS

It is a truism that any herbivore population, when introduced into a
new habitat, will alter that habitat by reducing the vegetation biomass (Caughley 1976). The herbivore may even alter the community
structure and the diversity of the vegetation. Theoretically, in a sufficiently diverse community, the herbivore population will reach an
equilibrium point and the vegetation will do likewise (Caughley
1976). Houston (1971) has pointed out that there is circumstantial
evidence for this equilibrium in several of the North American
parks. The present studies on buffalo provide evidence that the
herbivores are achieving such an equilibrium without any direct
interference from man, and for this to happen the vegetation the
buffalo depend on must also be reaching an equilibrium. The point
is that it is quite possible for populations in national parks to reach
their own equilibrium levels without catastrophic damage to their
habitat. This requires a sufficient array of disease organisms and
predators to promote a fast response to changes in vegetation.

The changes in vegetation that elephants cause in some East African national parks, although more conspicuous to the human observer, seem no different in principle from changes caused by other
species. The present evidence on buffalo, together with the theoretical work of Caughley (1976) suggests that perturbations in vegetation owing to an artificial buildup in elephants will eventually
smooth out, resulting in an equilibrium between elephants and vegetation. This is only one of several possible hypotheses, but it can be
tested objectively by collecting annual population data and developing models along the same lines as has been done with African buffalo, in order to predict whether an equilibrium will be achieved. If
an equilibrium does not seem possible, this allows an objective argument for human interference through culling.

An important misconception concerning ecosystem dynamics has
been pointed out by both Houston (1971) and Caughley (1976). Tra-
ditionally trained range managers are concerned with obtaining the
maximum production of cattle from a given pasture. This maximum

sustained yield is usually achieved when the cattle population is about half that when it is allowed to remain unexploited. In both the exploited and unexploited situations an equilibrium population can be achieved. Equally, the vegetation also reaches two different equilibriums with a higher vegetation biomass present when cattle are exploited than when they are not. The latter vegetation equilibrium is achieved when it supports herbivores at "carrying capacity"—a term often used by wildlife ecologists. To a range manager the vegetation at carrying capacity appears "overgrazed," which from his point of view of maximizing the culling rate is valid; to the wildlife ecologist the vegetation is not overgrazed, which from his point of view of maintaining an unexploited, balanced ecosystem is equally valid. These two ways of looking at vegetation, because of the two different objectives, have often led to confusion and are probably still doing so. When a range manager is asked to advise, as an "expert," on management of wildlife parks and reserves, his training and experience are often unsuited to the objectives of such wildlife reserves. It is not surprising, therefore, that many wildlife authorities in Africa, North America, and elsewhere support culling operations on the grounds that the herbivores are overgrazing their habitats. In small areas without the normal array of species that should be present, a balanced system may not be possible and culling may be valid, but there must be many larger wildlife reserves where management has been based upon the sort of misconceptions that Caughley (1976) has pointed out.

NATIONAL PARKS AS ENVIRONMENTAL BASELINES

Up to this point I have talked about national parks as areas where material exploitation does not take place. The International Union for the Conservation of Nature defines a national park as "an . . . area where one or several ecosystems are not materially altered by human exploitation and occupation" (Myers 1973). The above scientific discussion really depends upon this definition of parks; yet it begs the question, "Why do we want to set up unexploited areas in the first place?"

To answer this question I would like first to mention briefly the historical background to the conservation movement in East Africa. During the first quarter of this century, and particularly during the First World War, the white colonists slaughtered the abundant wildlife that had previously been left unharmed by the African peoples.

In many areas the fauna was exterminated and some races became extinct. The story is only too familiar. By the 1930s there was a reaction to this wanton extermination, and preservationists started calling for refuges to be set aside. The conflict between the ranchers who wanted to remove the wildlife and the preservationists forced the latter into adopting an extreme position where no interference with the animals was condoned.

The preservationist movement gained impetus over the next thirty years, and by the 1960s they were a dominant force in the conservation area. By this time many national parks had been set up, and the initial emotional justification against killing had been transformed into an argument for the preservation of esthetic values. Thus Russell (1968) in discussing management policy for the Tanzania National Parks, considered with certain qualifications that a National Park should be "an area set aside where Man can enjoy, as a privileged visitor, the plants and animals that are indigenous to that environment under conditions as little affected by his presence as possible; the Trustees of the Park hold it in trust for the benefit of future generations as well as for the present" (Owen 1972). Philosophically this sounds reasonable to those who follow Western ethics. But to the local African on the boundary of the park, being told that he is merely a privileged visitor is quite incomprehensible.

An offshoot of the preservationist movement developed in the early sixties with the idea that wildlife stood a better chance of survival if it could be shown that it was of some commercial value as food for the local population. The history of this group is described by Curry-Lindahl (1974). Their approach is essentially a pragmatic one that advocates material exploitation of wildlife. Of course, this can be done and is done outside the national parks. However, in recent years there has been a growing feeling that the preservationist philosophy is becoming out of touch with local political attitudes and that the only way to rectify this is to introduce material exploitation to national parks systems. Thus Myers (1973, p. 131) states, "Policy for the United States parks concentrates on the aesthetic, as opposed to the economic, factors of park values. It suggests that if you once let commercial considerations into a park, the place stops being a park: to which one might retort that, in Africa, *unless* you let commercial considerations into a park, it will stop being a park." Since this practice would no longer meet the definitions of a national park, it is actually advocating the disbanding of national parks in East Africa.

So the pendulum has now swung to the other equally extreme position.

Both Curry-Lindahl (1974) and Myers (1973) make some good points concerning the integration of national parks as one form of land use with surrounding agricultural areas so as to form a multiple land use unit. This integration requires that national parks provide some direct benefit to the surrounding populace. It also requires that the adjacent agricultural practices be consistent with the continuing viability of the park, practices for example, which prevent the destruction of trees, erosion, and the silting up of rivers that flow into the park.

If the only reason for the existence of national parks is the emotional and esthetic one, then parks managers are faced with choosing between the preservationists and the exploiters. However, there is another reason for the continued existence of national parks as they are at present, of direct long-term benefit to the African countries, which has not been considered by the exploiters, and hardly thought about by the preservationists. It is this: every country needs to set aside a small proportion of its natural areas to act as baselines against which to measure changes imposed on surrounding areas by human activities. This concept, discussed in some detail by Jenkins and Bedford (1973) and mentioned by Owen (1972), has a sound logical and scientific basis. For the African countries it is an ecological necessity, not a luxury as are the esthetic reasons.

Ecosystems are composed of a series of highly complex and intertwined processes. These processes, consisting of organisms interacting with their environments, have evolved over a long period of time through natural selection. When humans introduce perturbations through exploitation and pollution, they are usually so extensive and rapid that the delicate natural balance may not be able to adjust or accommodate to them. As Jenkins and Bedford (1973) point out, "Such events can disrupt the internal cohesion of the entire system and destroy the very processes which our intrusion was intended to maintain. The results can be seen in the history of past civilizations and the deserts and dust-bowls which have so frequently been created." The recent famine in the Sahel zone of West Africa, generated in part by the misguided introduction of artificial watering places, thus causing overstocking, is a good example (de Vos 1975). That human interference partly generated this situation was demonstrated when a space satellite photographed an area that was surviving the famine better than its surroundings. Closer examination of this area in Niger showed it to be a fenced-off state-owned ranch properly managed and protected from nomadic incursions (Council on Environmental Quality 1974). This example not only shows that human interference with ecosystems can lead to catastrophe but also illustrates the advantage of having control areas protected from this interference, to which one can turn for information on why things went wrong outside.

It is an unfortunate fact that the damaging results of human activities are often subtle and inconspicuous and consequently are not perceived until it is too late to do anything about them. Some deleterious effects, for example, those caused by pesticides, build up slowly and have important consequences only when they reach a certain threshold. Furthermore, humans become accustomed to slowly changing but degrading conditions and so do not notice the impending danger, as has happened in West Africa. The standard scientific way to detect these changes caused by human actions is to have control or "baseline" areas where human interference is absent or at a minimum. Use of controls is the standard technique in studies of crops in agriculture and of drugs in medicine, and obviously it must be applied to ecosystems as a whole.

Jenkins and Bedford (1973) have suggested that natural areas including national parks and reserves should be used to establish environmental baselines so that we can detect changes in similar ecosystems that are being exploited by man. Since knowledge on how undisturbed ecosystems function is minimal, the first step must be a detailed fundamental study of them, such as is being conducted by members of the Serengeti Research Institute. One often-expressed criticism is that there are almost no areas left which have not felt the impact of men, for example, through pollution or burning. Jenkins and Bedford (1973) comment, "The idea still has merit relative to many less-altered parameters such as some soil conditions, vegetation associations, animal populations, etc. A somewhat unnatural baseline is probably better than no baseline at all." They define the baseline as "an accurate description of the status and working of an ecosystem in the absence of human disruptions." Since ecosystems are constantly changing as world climates change, one should perhaps emphasize that monitoring is essential subsequent to the initial description.

Since many environmental factors vary considerably between different regions, the protection of several natural areas representing the different regions or biomes is necessary to establish the required range of baselines. For example, data from *Acacia* savanna areas in northern Tanzania and Kenya are not applicable to the *Brachystegia* woodlands in southern Tanzania. These regions need separate studies. It is obvious that the present national parks and reserves in East Africa constitute ideal ecological control areas. Present management policies of minimum interference are correct for the purpose of maintaining baselines. But the inclusion of culling for commercial exploitation of populations that are supposed to be protected by national parks, as was initiated in 1974 with Serengeti wildebeest, will prevent those areas from being used as baseline areas and others will have to be established. From the purely logistic point of view it would be better to keep the habitats and animal populations of national parks free of material exploitation and to allow commercial culling in the extensive areas that are not part of the national park ecosystems. The establishment of unexploited baseline or control areas is an insurance policy for the ecological viability of a country. The lessons from events in West Africa and Ethiopia should not be forgotten. The baseline areas eventually should become part of a global monitoring system like that suggested by Dasmann (1972) and Jenkins and Bedford (1973).

EXTINCTION RATES AND NATIONAL PARKS

Following from the discussion on the need to preserve unexploited areas, one meets the problem of how the natural diversity of such areas can be maintained in the face of extinctions. Natural systems are in a state of dynamic equilibrium, with some species evolving and expanding their range while others are becoming extinct. However, the former process takes a very long time in human terms—perhaps thousands of years—while the latter has no such constraints; extinctions can occur at any pace, and where humans have altered ecosystems extinctions generally occur very rapidly. Fundamental studies on extinction rates in natural ecosystems have been based upon island biogeography (MacArthur and Wilson 1963; Terborgh 1974; Diamond 1975). National Parks and reserves, Terborgh (1974) points out, will become islands surrounded by a landscape inhospitable to the fauna and flora of the reserves. This is already occurring in many areas of the world.

Islands which have been cut off from the mainland by the rise in sea level after the Pleistocene have lost part of their original complement of species in proportion to the area of the island. Thus small islands have lost more species over the past 10,000 years than have large islands (Terborgh 1974), since small areas can contain fewer species than larger areas because they lack suitable diversification of niches large enough to maintain viable populations. National park "islands" are probably affected in a similar way with respect to large mammals and other forms that cannot migrate across cultivated or urban areas.

Terborgh (1974) reviews the types of extinction-prone species and suggests the size of reserve necessary to prevent extinction. The first group includes the large mammals and birds, such as lions, wildebeest, and eagles, which require large amounts of living space because of their dispersed food and high metabolic demand. These animals may require several thousand square kilometers. For some animals that migrate or range widely, such as birds of prey, protection within park boundaries is not sufficient. Other groups of extinction-prone species include those with poor dispersal or colonizing ability, and continental endemics. These often have well-defined and restricted distributions, and a number of small reserves may suffice (de Vos 1975, p. 144). In many areas, including Africa, it is the lack of knowledge of these species' distributions that has prevented conservation measures from being effective. A national inventory of biological resources (including species of birds which migrate across continents) should be a high priority for wildlife authorities. Myers (1976) discusses the advantages to mankind of preserving the rare endemics, particularly those in the tropics. He concludes that conservation will only succeed if there is international coordination.

INTERACTIONS BETWEEN WILDLIFE AND HUMAN POPULATIONS

Given the need to maintain wildlife areas in East Africa, there is a growing problem concerning the conflict between wildlife and human interests, particularly on the boundaries of natural reserves. Large ungulates encroach upon and plunder cultivation, and large predators constitute a threat to the safety of the human population and its livestock.

Furthermore, wildlife species carry a number of disease organisms which affect man or his stock. Several species of trypanosomes, morphologically indistinguishable from those affecting domestic stock, are known to be carried in Serengeti animals (Schindler et al. 1969). On types of foot-and-mouth disease these same authors state, "In

Africa, besides the more common global types, there are others, specific to the continent, known as SAT strains. Thus one may reasonably assume that foot-and-mouth disease caused by the latter is not of exotic origin like rinderpest but indigenous to Africa and capable of maintaining itself in wild hosts even in the absence of cattle." However, it should be noted that transference of this disease from wild animals to domestic stock has yet to be proved. Young et al. (1973) have demonstrated experimentally that buffalo in the Serengeti harbor a *Theileria* organism which when transferred to cattle can cause a disease with symptoms similar to East Coast fever. Buffalo probably act as foci for the disease, since they also carry the *Rhipicephalus* ticks which can act as vectors. Malignant catarrhal fever in East Africa is usually caused by a virus which is enzootic in wildebeest and is not known in other wild species. The virus is either nonpathogenic or of very low pathogenicity for wildebeest, but the disease is fatal for cattle (Plowright 1963).

With these few but important examples it is clear that even at this stage the government and wildlife administrators must give thought to integrating national parks land use with other forms in the surrounding areas. For this to occur the local populace should receive some direct benefit to compensate for the drawbacks. Parks apparently attract substantial foreign exchange from tourism (Thresher 1972). At present, most goes directly to the government and very little goes to the local peoples. Obviously, they should benefit by obtaining a greater share of this revenue, as do the people that run the Masai-Mara and Amboseli reserves. Buffer zones around natural reserves could be set up, which could be used for grazing livestock or for licensed hunting by the local inhabitants. The logistical problems of arranging this may be great, but this is all the more reason for applied research and development at an early stage.

APPENDIXES

A. Scientific and Common Names of Mammal, Bird, and Plant Species Mentioned in the Text

MAMMALS

Order Primates

Cercopithecus aethiops (Linnaeus)	Vervet monkey
Papio anubis Fischer	Olive baboon

Order Lagomorpha

Lepus capensis Linnaeus	Hare
Lepus crawshayi De Winton	Hare

Order Rodentia

Hystrix cristata L.	Porcupine
Pedetes capensis (Forster)	Springhare
Arvicanthis niloticus (Desmarest)	Grass rat

Order Carnivora

Lycaon pictus (Temminck)	Wild dog
Canis mesomelas Schreber	Black-backed jackal
Canis aureus Linnaeus	Golden jackal
Otocyon megalotis (Desmarest)	Bat-eared fox
Crocuta crocuta (Erxleben)	Spotted hyena
Felis serval Schreber	Serval
Felis libyca Forster	Wild cat
Panthera pardus (Linnaeus)	Leopard
Panthera leo (Linnaeus)	Lion
Acinonyx jubatus (Schreber)	Cheetah

Order Proboscidia

Loxodonta africana (Blumenbach)	African elephant

293

Order Hyracoidea

Procavia johnstoni Thomas   Rock hyrax
Heterohyrax brucei (Gray)   Tree Hyrax

Order Perissodactyla

Equus burchelli Gray   Zebra
Diceros bicornis (Linnaeus)   Black rhinoceros

Order Artiodactyla

Hylochoerus meinertzhageni Thomas   Giant forest hog
Potamochoerus porcus (Linnaeus)   Bushpig
Phacochoerus aethiopicus (Pallas)   Warthog
Hippopotamus amphibius Linnaeus   Hippopotamus
Giraffa camelopardalis (Linnaeus)   Giraffe
Rangifer tarandus Linnaeus   Caribou
Cervus canadensis Erxleben   Elk
Odocoileus virginianus (Zimmermann)   Whitetail deer
Tragelaphus strepsiceros (Pallas)   Greater kudu
Tragelaphus scriptus (Pallas)   Bushbuck
Taurotragus oryx (Pallas)   Eland
Syncerus caffer (Sparrman)   African buffalo
Bubalus bubalis Linnaeus   Asian water buffalo
Bison bison (Linnaeus)   American bison
Bison bonasus Linnaeus   European bison
Bos gaurus H. Smith   Gaur
Bos banteng Wagner   Banteng
Bos sauveli (Urbain)   Kouprey
Bos grunniens Linnaeus   Yak
Sylvicapra grimmia (Linnaeus)   Gray duiker
Cephalophus natalensis A. Smith   Red forest duiker
Kobus defassa (Rüppell)   Waterbuck
Redunca redunca (Pallas)   Bohor reedbuck
Aepyceros melampus (Lichtenstein)   Impala
Hippotragus equinus Desmarest   Roan antelope
Oryx beisa Rüppell   Oryx
Damaliscus korrigum (Ogilby)   Topi
Alcelaphus buselaphus (Pallas)   Kongoni, Coke's
                                               hartebeest

Connochaetes taurinus (Burchell)   Wildebeest (blue)
Connochaetes gnou (Zimmermann)   Black wildebeest

Oreotragus oreotragus (Zimmermann)	Klipspringer
Nesotragus moschatus Von Dueben	Suni antelope
Madoqua kirki (Günther)	Dik-dik
Raphicerus campestris (Thunberg)	Steinbuck
Ourebia ourebi (Zimmermann)	Oribi
Gazella thomsoni Günther	Thomson's gazelle
Gazella granti Brooke	Grant's gazelle
Ovibos moschatus Zimmermann	Muskox

BIRDS

Anseranas semipalmata (Latham)	Magpie goose
Ardea melanocephala Vigors & Children	Black-headed heron
Elanus caeruleus (Desfontaines)	Black-shouldered kite
Lagopus lagopus Linnaeus	Red grouse
Lophoaetus occipitalis (Daudin)	Long-crested hawk eagle

PLANTS

Trees and Shrubs

Acacia brevispica Harms
A. clavigera E. Mey.
A. drepanolobium Harms. ex Sjostedt
A. gerrardii Benth.
A. hockii De Willd.
A. mellifera (Vahl.) Benth.
A. senegal (L.) Willd.
A. seyal Del.
A. tortilis (Forsk.) Hayne
A. xanthophloea Benth.
Albizia harveyi Fourn
Balanites aegyptiaca (L.) Del.
Capparis tomentosa Lam.
Combretum molle R. Br. ex G. Dom.
Commiphora trothae Engl.
Cordia ovalis R. Br.
Croton dichogamus Pax.
Euclea divinorum Hiern.
Grewia bicolor Juss.
Harrisonia abyssinica Oliv.
Heeria mucronata Bernh.
Juniperus procera Hochst. ex Endl.

Ormocarpum trichocarpum (Taub.) Harms.
Pappea capensis (Spreng.) Eck & Zey.
Podocarpus usambarensis Pilg.
Rhus natalensis Bernh.
Sesbania sesban L.
Tabernaemontana usambarensis K. Schum.
Teclea nobilis Del.
Terminalia mollis M. Laws. in Oliver
Trichelia roka (Forsk) Chiov.
Ziziphus mucronata Willd.

Herbs

Indigofera basiflora Gillett.
Pluchea ovalis DC.
Solanum incanum L.

Grasses

Andropogon greenwayi Napper
Aristida stenostachys W. D. Clayton
Brachiaria brizantha (A. Rich.) Stapf.
Cenchrus ciliaris L.
Chloris gayana Kunth.
C. pycnothrix Trin.
Cymbopogon excavatus (Hochst.) Stapf.
Cynodon dactylon (L.) Pers.
C. plectostachyus (K. Schum.) Pilg.
Digitaria macroblephora (Hack.) Stapf.
Eleusine jaegeri Pilger
Eragrostis cilianensis (All) Lutati
E. usambarensis Napper
Eustachys paspaloides (Vahl) Lanzr. & Matte
Harpachne schimperi A. Rich.
Heteropogon contortus (L.) R. & S.
Hyparrhenia filipendula (Hochst.) Stapf.
Imperata cylindrica (L.) Beauv.
Leersia hexandra Swartz
Loudetia kagerensis (K. Schum.) Hutch.
Odyssea jaegeri (Pilg.) Hubb.
Panicum coloratum L.

P. infestum Anders
P. maximum Jacg.
Pennisetum clandestinum Chiov.
P. mezianum Leeke
Poa leptoclada A. Rich.
Setaria chevalieri Stapf.
S. sphacelata (Schumach) Moss
Sporobolus consimilis Fres.
S. greenwayi Napper
S. marginatus A. Rich.
S. pellucidus Hochst.
S. pyramidalis Beauv.
S. spicatus (Vahl.) Kunth.
Themeda triandra Forsk.

Sedges

Cyperus laevigatus L.
C. obtusiflorus Vahl.
C. teneriffae Poir
Kyllinga alba Nees
Mariscus mollipes C. B. Cl.

B.   METHOD OF CALCULATING THE ASSOCIATION COEFFICIENTS OF BUFFALO FOR DIFFERENT VEGETATION TYPES

This method has been adapted from that of Cole (1949), who was considering the association between two species of animals. He pointed out that since the frequency distributions of organisms in samples normally differ widely from a random distribution, standard correlation techniques cannot be used. In this case the buffalo do not distribute themselves randomly over the landscape. Cole therefore devised a method of measuring association with values ranging from $+1$ to -1, the maximum possible positive and negative associations. Zero represents random association. In the statistical sense Cole defines association as "the amount of co-occurrence in excess of that to be expected if two categories are independently distributed."

In the present case the association was one-way in that buffalo distribute themselves with respect to the vegetation, but the reverse does not occur. The total number of squares containing each vegetation type in each of the two study areas was counted. Then for each survey occasion the following categories were calculated by subtracting from the total: a = number of squares with buffalo present, vegetation type present; b = number of squares with buffalo present, vegetation type absent; c = number of squares with buffalo absent, vegetation type present; d = number of squares with both buffalo and vegetation type absent. These categories were then segregated into the accompanying 2 x 2 table.

Habitat Type

		+	−	
Animal	+	a	b	
Species	−	c	d	
				N

The rarer of the two categories (either total number of squares containing buffalo observations or the total number of squares with vegetation type) must be on the left side of the 2 x 2 table. The coefficient of association (C), its standard error, and the chi-square value were calculated according to the formulas given in Cole (1949).

C. VEGETATION TYPES DISTINGUISHED IN THE ANALYSIS FOR HABITAT SELECTION

RIVERINE VEGETATION TYPES

Riverine Grasslands

This long rank grassland is made up of grasses growing to some 2m in height on impeded drainage soils along the edges of rivers and swamps (plate 12). Such soils remain damp long after those higher up the catena have dried out, and during the wet season they are frequently inundated, although not for long enough to allow swamp vegetation to grow. In fact, the undulating topography in the Serengeti allows few swamps to develop. The tall grasses are mainly *Panicum maximum* or, on more alkaline soils, *P. coloratum*. On the sandbanks at the edge of permanent rivers the short creeping grass *Cynodon dactylon* is common. The southern area includes a number of small permanently flowing streams originating in the Serengeti Plains, and these support the riverine grassland. In the north this grassland occurs in small patches between stretches of forest.

Riverine Vegetation

This category includes the vegetation in the northern area along the banks of the numerous permanently flowing tributaries of the Mara River. Although the Mara (plate 6) itself is the largest river in the Serengeti ecosystem (50–100 m wide), the banks are steep, with little riverine grassland and almost no forest. The tributaries, however, are lined by a dense forest, in parts several hundred meters wide, with small openings and glades containing riverine grassland (plate 13). The grass species of the latter are those mentioned above.

Forest

The trees of this part of the northern riverine vegetation form a closed canopy near the rivers (plate 6). Outside this is a layer of dense thicket of *Teclea nobilis* and *Croton dichogamus*. Long, coarse shade grasses such as *Setaria chevalieri* and *Panicum infestum* are grazed within the forest. Buffalo also use the forest for shade during the middle of the day, and they gain protection from predators by standing in the densest parts of the vegetation to prevent predators from attacking their flanks and rear while they present their horns. The use of thicket by a young male being attacked by lions is described by Schaller (1972).

Wet-Season Watercourses

In both areas there are numerous small gullies, creeks, or watercourses a few meters wide at the most that contain water in the wet season but are otherwise dry. They support a thin line of bushes and thicket along the banks but few riverine grasses. The thicket provides a modicum of shade and is sometimes used as a midday resting place for bachelor males, but it is too sparse for herds. Similarly, it offers these males a potential refuge against predators.

Seepage Lines

Contouring the slopes of the shallow valleys in the north, a narrow seepage line is apparent where the water table comes to the surface. A thin band of green grass and sedges a few meters wide grows along this line. Small springs flow down the slope for a short distance before being absorbed or drying out. These seepage lines occur after heavy rains, as in 1968 when they remained throughout the dry season. Grass fires in that year burned off all the grass above and below this line but left the distinctive narrow band of green grass which can be seen in plate 9. Not surprisingly, buffalo, particularly the small groups of bachelor males, graze these strips and also trample out wallows in the wetter patches. Most of this line dried up in the 1969 dry season after the previous very light rains.

NONRIVERINE WOODLANDS

Gall-Tree Stands

On depressions in the southern area where there are impeded drainage and black silt soils, pure stands of the gall trees *Acacia seyal* and *Acacia drepanolobium*—so named because of their ant galls—are found. Both species are small, relatively thin-stemmed trees between 3 and 5 m high. Their foliage is thin and provides scant shade, although it is used by buffalo herds when nothing else is available. *Acacia seyal* is found in slightly more waterlogged soils than *A. drepanolobium*. Grasses growing among these stands are dominated by the coarse *Pennisetum mezianum*. In the dry season the soil under both these vegetation types dries out, becoming hard and cracked, and the grass dies off, leaving a mat of thick coarse material which is invariably burned.

Acacia Woodland

This typical woodland in the southern area is characterized by the umbrella trees *Acacia tortilis* and *Balanites aegyptiaca* (plate 14); the former provides good shade, but both are very scattered. Grasses are mostly *Themeda triandra* and *P. mezianum*. They produce almost no green growth in the dry season, and consequently fires burn through much of the area.

Terminalia Woodland

This type consists of the nonriverine woodland in the northern area. It covers the top half of the ridges, the lower limit being formed by the seepage line (plate 9). The broad-leaved tree *Terminalia mollis* is found on the rockier ridge tops, with *Acacia clavigera* taking over lower down (plate 7). Both are good shade trees. Dominant grasses on the thin stony soils are *Loudetia kagerensis* and the tall *Hyparrhenia filipendula*.

Hills

The western part of the southern area includes part of a range of hills rising 200–300 m above the *Acacia* woodland and plains to the east (plate 5). The vegetation is similar to the *Acacia* woodland, with *Commiphora trothae* appearing more commonly and *Combretum molle* bushes forming small clumps on the stonier areas. The grasses are a mixture of *Themeda triandra* and *Loudetia kagerensis* growing on thin soils. Because the hills attract rain, they invariably receive the first showers at the beginning of the rains in November.

NONRIVERINE GRASSLANDS

Plains

The eastern half of the southern study area is mostly treeless plains dominated by *Themeda triandra* and *Pennisetum mezianum* (plate 3), similar to the *Acacia woodland*. In the dry season they are desolate, with few ungulates, little green growth, and no shade.

Open Grassland

In the northern area this grassland is found on the lower slopes between the seepage line and the riverine forest (plate 9). Few trees grow in the area. The grass species are similar to those on the plains in the southern area but are strikingly different from the association of grasses immediately above the seepage line.

Greenflush

This term is applied to the short green regrowth that occurs on burned ground after a local rainstorm in the dry season. It can take place on any of the nonriverine woodlands and grasslands. Usually the grass leaves grow only to about 7 cm. I found that the old males could sometimes eat this grass by picking the scattered longer leaf blades, but rarely did I see herds grazing on it.

D. TABLES

TABLE 1

Approximate Numbers and Density of Large Ungulates in the
Serengeti Ecosystem, (1971–72)

Animal	Number	Density (No./km^2)
Wildebeest	750,000	37.5
Thomson's gazelle	500,000	33.0
Zebra	200,000	10.0
Buffalo	68,000	6.8
Impala	57,000	6.0
Grant's gazelle	30,000	2.0
Topi	27,000	2.9
Eland	18,000	0.9
Warthog	17,000	1.7
Kongoni	9,000	1.0
Giraffe	7,000	0.8
Elephant	2,500	0.3
Rhinoceros	1,000	0.1
Waterbuck	1,300	0.1
Oryx	400	0.04
Roan antelope	300	0.03

TABLE 2

The Potential Dry Season Requirements of Buffalo Provided by Different Vegetation Types in the Serengeti Study Areas

Vegetation Type	Green Food	Water	Predator Protection	Shade
Riverine				
Riverine grassland	+	+		
Seepage line	(M)	(M)		
Forest	+	+	+	+
Wet-season watercourse			(M)	+
Nonriverine woodland				
A. seyal, A. drepanolobium				+
Acacia woodland				+
Terminalia woodland				+
Hills				+
Nonriverine grassland				
Open grassland				
Plains				
Greenflush	(M)			

NOTE: (+) indicates presence for herds and bachelors, (M) for bachelors only.

TABLE 3

Mean Monthly Rainfall (mm) in the Two Serengeti Study Areas, October 1966–September 1969

Month	Southern Area		Northern Area
	Plains	Hills	
January	61	65	91
February	98	83	91
March	104	83	131
April	101	71	180
May	58	80	122
June	24	22	63
July	1	1	12
August	4	7	48
September	15	11	68
October	20	13	59
November	65	54	167
December	95	104	199

TABLE 4

Correlation Coefficients (r) of Habitat Association with Mean Monthly Rainfall

Vegetation Type	Rain Same Month	Association Coefficient Correlated With	
		1 Month Before	2 Months Before
Riverine			
Riverine grassland (south)	—0.69x	—0.81x	—0.82x
Riverine vegetation (north)	—0.28	—0.70x	—
Forest	—0.65x	—0.77x	—
Riverine grassland (north)	—0.43	—	—
Wet-season watercourse (south)	0.24	0.04	0.03
Wet-season watercourse (north)	—0.41	—0.02	—
Seepage line	—0.27	—0.66x	—
Nonriverine woodland			
Terminalia woodland	0.17	—	—
Acacia woodland	0.52	0.64x	0.71x
Hills	0.78x	0.72x	0.30
Nonriverine grassland			
Plains (south)	0.17	0.36	0.34
Open grassland (north)	0.37	0.33	0.52
Greenflush (north)	0.33	0.14	0.28

NOTE: x = p <0.05; N = 12 months.

TABLE 5

Grass and Sedge Species Commonly Eaten by African Buffalo in Eastern Africa

Species	Dry		Savanna		Wet	Forest	
	Tarangire (1)	Tsavo (2)	Serengeti (3)	Manyara (4)	Ruwenzori (5)	Congo (6)	Mount Meru (7)
Cyperus laevigatus				x			x
Sporobolus spicatus				x			
Panicum coloratum		x	x				
Cynodon dactylon	x		x	x	x		x
Panicum maximum		x	x				
Cenchrus ciliaris	x						
Sporobolus pyramidalis				x	x	x	
Pennisetum mezianum			x				
Cynodon plectostachyus	x			x			
Digitaria macroblephora		x	x				
Hyparrhenia filipendula					x	x	
Hyparrhenia spp.						x	
Pennisetum clandestinum							x
Chloris gayana					x		
Bothriochloa spp.					x	x	
Eragrostis spp.	x	x					
Themeda triandra			x		x	x	

SOURCES: (1) Lamprey 1963*a*; (2) Leuthold 1972; (3) this study; (4) Vesey-Fitzgerald 1969; (5) Field 1968*b,c;* (6) Bourliere and Verschuren 1960; (7) this study.

TABLE 6

Elements of Agonistic Behavior in Different Species of Bovini

Behavior	Buffalo		(Bison) (Bison)		Cattle (Bos)				
	Syncerus	Bubalus	bison	bonasus	grunniens	gaurus	banteng	sauveli	taurus
Head up, present horns threat	+	+	+	+	+	+	+	+	+
Lateral display	+	+	+	+	+	+	+	+	+
Rubbing face in earth	+	+	+	+	+	+	+	+	+
Earth tossing	+	+	+	+	+	+	+	+	+
Horning bushes	+	+	+	+	+	+	+	+	+
Pawing	−	+	+	+	−	+	+	+	+
Pushing fight	−	+	+	+	?	+	+	+	+
Aggressive roaring/ calling	−	−	+	?	+	+	+	+	+
Rolling in mud/dust	+	+	+	+	+	+	−	−	−
Circling	+	?	−	?	?	+	?	?	−
Wallowing in deep mud	+	+	−	−	−	−	−	−	−
Submissive bellow	+	−	−	−	?	−	−	−	−
Nose-up threat	−	+	−	−	−	−	−	−	−
Suckling from behind	+	+	−	−	?	−	?	?	−
Suckling from the side	−	−	+	+	?	+	?	?	+

TABLE 7

Age-distribution of Buffalo Killed by Lion in the Serengeti

Age (years)	Males			Females		
	Observed	Expected Death Distrib.	Expected Live Distrib.	Observed	Expected Death Distrib.	Expected Live Distrib.
2–3	2	2	11	2	2	5
4–5	3	3	10	6	2	5
6–7	5	10	10	4	3	4
8–9	8	10	8	2	4	4
10–11	12	9	6	4	5	3
12–13	11	9	4	2	4	2
14–15	5	6	2	2	3	1
16–17	4	2	0	2	1	0
18–19	1	0	0	0	0	0
Total	51	51	51	24	24	24

TABLE 8

Age Distribution of Wildebeest Killed by Lion

Approx. Age (years)	Male		Female	
	Observed	Expected	Observed	Expected
1	15	16.0	5	16.0
2–3	23	23.0	25	26.8
4–6	30	27.5	7	29.5
7–9	14	17.5	7	14.8
10–12	14	9.9	3	5.1
13–15	21	5.8	14	3.2
> 15	22	4.4	3	3.1
Total	139	104.1	64	98.5

SOURCE: Observed data from G. Schaller.

TABLE 9

Home Range Areas and Density of Buffalo within Them

	Area (km²)	Number	Density (No./km²)	Mean Annual Rainfall (mm)
Serengeti				
Moru (Herd 3)	271.4	900	3.31	700
Nyaraboro (Herd 2)	296.3	1,500	5.06	800
Banagi	143.8	800	5.56	787
Seronera	178.4	700	3.92	840
Northern (Herd 1)	83.5	1,100	13.17	1,000
Northern (Herd 4)	53.0	500	9.43	1,000
Ruwenzori, Uganda	10.5	138	13.14	1,200
Momella lakes	10.9	200	18.34	1,500
Voi Lodge, Tsavo	85	350	4.1	510

SOURCE: Authors cited in the text.

TABLE 10

Mean Distances and Bearings of Neighbors in Five Grazing Buffalo Herds

(units in animal lengths)

Herd	N	Mean Distance	S.D.	Mean Bearing
1	237	2.30	1.84	104o
2	77	4.57	3.30	51o
3	153	7.59	7.90	83o
4	99	5.84	5.10	102o
5	109	5.69	5.22	89o

TABLE 11

Distribution of Nearest Neighbors According to Bearing from the Reference Animal, in Grazing Buffalo Herds

Segment	Herd 1		Herd 2		Herd 3		Herd 4		Herd 5		Mean %
	N	%	N	%	N	%	N	%	N	%	
0-20o	12	5.1	15	19.5	36	23.5	15	15.2	2	1.8	13.02
21-40o	13	5.5	21	27.3	18	11.8	5	5.1	10	9.2	11.78
41-60o	24	10.1	18	23.4	15	9.8	6	6.1	16	14.7	12.82
61-80o	34	14.3	10	13.0	10	6.5	7	7.1	19	17.4	11.66
81-100o	28	11.8	6	7.8	8	5.2	10	10.1	22	20.2	11.02
101-20o	25	10.5	4	5.2	10	6.5	11	11.1	12	11.0	8.86
121-40o	32	13.5	1	1.3	18	11.8	12	12.1	9	8.3	9.40
141-60o	42	17.7	2	2.6	15	9.8	12	12.1	14	12.8	11.00
161-80o	27	11.4	0	0	23	15.0	21	21.2	5	4.6	10.44
Total	237	100	77	100	153	100	99	100	109	100	100

TABLE 12

Tooth Eruption Sequence for African Buffalo

Age	I_1	I_2	I_3	C	PM_2	PM_3	PM_4	M_1	M_2	M_3
1 wk	(D)	(D)	(D)	—	(D)	(D)	(D)	—	—	—
4 mo	D	D	D	D	D	D	D	—	—	—
6–9 mo	D	D	D	D	D	D	D	(P)	—	—
12 mo	D	D	D	D	D	D	D	P		
18–21 mo	D	D	D	D	D	D	D	P	(P)	—
24 mo	D	D	D	D	D	D	D	P	P	([P])
33 mo	P	D	D	D	D	D	D	P	P	(P)
36 mo	P	D	D	D	D	D	D	P	P	P
42–44 mo	P	D/P	D	D	(P)	(P)	D	P	P	P
4 yr	P	P	D/P	D	P	P	(P)	P	P	P
4½ yr	P	P	P	D	P	P	P	P	P	P
5 yr	P	P	P	P	P	P	P	P	P	P

SOURCE: Grimsdell 1973a.
NOTE: D = deciduous tooth. P = permanent tooth. ( ) indicates tooth erupting and, with molars, both cusps visible above bone. ([ ]) indicates only one cusp visible above bone.

TABLE 13
Birth Weights of African Buffalo

Place	Weight (kg)	Source
Serengeti	40.2, 38.5, 36.4	This study
Uganda	45, 38.5, 38.1, 33.6	Grimsdell 1969
Kenya	53.6, 50.0, 36.4	Vidler et al. 1963
Kruger	35.8, 36.0, 38.1, 40.8	Pienaar 1969
Rhodesia	38.6	Dassman and Mossman 1962

Mean = 42.8

TABLE 14
Age-Specific Rate of Ovulation in Serengeti Buffalo

Age	Number Ovulating	Total	%
1.5 yr	0	2	0
2.5 yr	0	2	0
3.5 yr	5	8	62.5
4.5 yr	18	18	100

Mean age of ovulation = 3.5 yr

TABLE 15
Age-Specific Rate of Conceptions in Serengeti Buffalo

Age	Number Conceiving	Total	%
2.5 yr	0	4	0
3.5 yr	1	8	12.5
4.5 yr	5	18	28.0
5.5 yr	10	11	91.0
6.5 yr	10	10	100.0

Mean age of conception (sexual maturity) = 4.8 yr

TABLE 16

Pregnancy Rate of Adult Buffalo in the Serengeti

Month	Pregnant	Nonpregnant	Total	%
August	18	13	31	58
October	20	1	21	95
March	12	5	17	71

Mean $p_p = 0.75$, S.E. $= p_p (1 - p_p)/N = \pm 0.052$

TABLE 17

Sex Ratio of Buffalo Fetuses

Place	Number Males	Number Females	Source
Serengeti Park	26	21	This study
Ruwenzori Park	36	32	Grimsdell 1969
North Uganda	10	18	Grimsdell 1969
West Uganda	9	11	Bourliere and Verschuren 1960
Kruger Park	5	3	Pienaar 1969
Total	86	85	
Ratio	101	100	

TABLE 18

Annual Population Fertility Estimates for Serengeti Buffalo

Herd	Year	Time of First Calving	% Fertility
1	1967	December	85.1
	1968	December	65.3
	1969	December	59.6
	Mean		70.0
2	1967	January	72.4
	1968	January	63.1
	1969	January	72.4
	Mean		69.3
3	1967	January	72.4
	1968	March	57.5
	1969	January	58.8
	Mean		62.9
Mean for 1 and 2	1967		78.8
	1968		64.2
	1969		66.0
	1971		70.3
	1972		68.0

TABLE 19

Observed and Calculated Age-Specific Weights of Serengeti Female Buffalo

Sample Size	Age	Mean Weight (kg)	95% Limits of Mean	Calculated Weight (kg)
3	1.5 yr	256	43.5	252
4	2.5 yr	290	32.5	331
10	3.5 yr	385	7.5	396
18	4.5 yr	450	17.5	446
11	5.5 yr	520	60.0	483
10	6.5 yr	507	30.5	510
8	7.5 yr	506	44.0	529
9	8.5 yr	528	59.0	543
2	9.5 yr	544	—	553
2	10.5 yr	500	—	560
4	11.5 yr	446	23.5	565
4	12.5 yr	454	—	568
1	13.5 yr	472	—	570
1	17.5 yr	423	—	575

TABLE 20

Observed and Calculated Age-Specific Weights of Serengeti Male Buffalo

Sample Size	Age	Mean Weight (kg)	95% Limits of Mean	Calculated Weight (kg)
1	2 mo	60	—	—
5	6 mo	133	—	152
1	9 mo	163	—	—
3	1.5 yr	269	72	243
2	2.5 yr	343	—	330
7	3.5 yr	398	40	406
4	4.5 yr	503	25	469
3	5.5 yr	505	90	520
3	6.5 yr	587	134	560
2	7.5 yr	614	—	591
1	8.5 yr	557	—	615
2	9.5 yr	648	—	633
2	10.5 yr	690	—	646
2	11.5 yr	690	—	656
1	16.5 yr	605	—	679

TABLE 21

Seasonality of Breeding Estimated from Fetuses in the Serengeti

	J	F	M	A	M	J	J	A	S	O	N	D
Births	3	3	11	17	9	3	2	0	0	0	1	0
Conceptions	0	3	4	14	15	7	5	0	0	0	1	0
Mean rain	69	86	88	205	84	16	4	5	10	28	138	115

TABLE 22

Mean Crude Density of Buffalo and Annual Rainfall in Different Areas of Eastern Africa

Area	Mean Crude Density/km²	Mean Annual Rainfall (mm)	Source
Mount Meru, Tanzania	22.8	1,968	
Ngurdoto, Tanzania	20.0	1,524	
Manyara, Tanzania	17.8	725	
Virunga Park, Zaire	12.3	863	Bourliere 1965
Ruwenzori Park, Uganda	12.0	1,200	Eltringham and Woodford 1973
Mara Reserve, Kenya	7.0	1,100	
Serengeti, North	7.4	1,000	
Serengeti, South	3.6	800	
Tarangire Park, Tanzania	1.9	678	
Ruaha Park, Tanzania	1.4	625	Norton-Griffiths 1975
Zambezi Valley	1.2	560	Jarman 1968
Tsavo Park, Kenya	1.0	510	Leuthold and Leuthold 1976
Mkomasi Reserve, Tanzania	0.23	445	Harris 1972

TABLE 23

Regression Coefficients for Buffalo Density Plotted against Rainfall and River Length in the Serengeti

Simple Regression of dry season density against:	Regression Coefficient (b)
Annual rainfall	−0.17
Dry season rainfall	−0.005
River length	0.19
Simple regression of wet season density against:	
Annual rainfall	0.16
River length	0.57
Partial regression of dry season density against:	
River length (annual rainfall constant)	9.8*
River length (dry season rainfall constant)	10.9*
Annual rainfall (river length constant)	−3.5
Dry season rainfall (river length constant)	−0.64

*$p < 0.05$.

TABLE 24

Censuses of Buffalo Breeding Herds

Year	Northern Woodlands	Whole Park	Census Area
1958	—	27,000	Mara Park
1961	—	29,500	Serengeti and Mara
1965	—	41,000	Serengeti
1966	—	45,346	Serengeti
1967	—	47,889	Serengeti
1968a	32,887	52,463	Serengeti
1968b	—	47,507	Serengeti
1969	33,686	56,045	Serengeti (North)
1970	37,037	61,620	Serengeti and Mara
1971	36,774	61,182	Serengeti (North)
1972	36,494	60,716	Serengeti (North)
1973	38,759	64,484	Serengeti (North)

TABLE 25

Censuses of Serengeti Migratory Wildebeest (with 95% confidence limits)

Year	Total	Source
1961	263,362	Talbot and Talbot 1963
1963	356,124	Watson 1967
1965	439,124	Watson 1967
1967	483,292	R. H. V. Bell (pers. comm.)
1971	692,777 $\pm$ 57,650	This study
1972	773,014 $\pm$ 153,389	Norton-Griffiths 1973

TABLE 26

Survival of Yearling Buffalo per 100 Adult Females in the Serengeti

Year	Yearlings (North)	S.E.	% of Population	Yearlings (South)	S.E.
1965	32	—	11.97	33	—
1966	36	—	13.70	38	—
1967	34.0	1.0	12.62	31.2	2.1
1968	34.5	0.8	12.79	36.0	0.7
1969	43.0	0.7	16.00	39.8	0.8
1970	39.0	—	14.34	—	—
1971	34.5	1.5	12.79	—	—
1972	42.9	2.1	15.42	—	—
1973	42.4	2.0	16.00	—	—

TABLE 27

Mortality of Adult and Yearling Serengeti Buffalo

Year	Population Size Before Mortality	No. Adults Dying	No. Juveniles Dying	Mortality as a Percentage of the Live Population	
				Adult	Juvenile
1965–66	47,011	1,699	5,747	3.61	12.22
1966–67	51,783	3,186	8,205	6.15	15.84
1967–68	56,330	1,943	8,589	3.45	15.25
1968–69	59,119	4,893	8,110	8.28	13.72
1969–70	63,028	3,345	7,385	5.31	11.72
1970–71	69,722	8,585	15,762	12.31	22.61
1971–72	68,020	7,587	13,193	11.15	19.40
1972–73	68,228	4,994	8,903	7.32	13.05

TABLE 28

Life Table for the Serengeti Buffalo

Year	May Census	Adults + Yearlings	Adults, May	Potential Population, June	Actual Population, June
	(1)	(2)	(3)	(4)	(5)
1965	41,000	37,310	32,843	51,268	47,011
1966	45,346	41,264	35,611	56,398	51,783
1967	47,889	43,578	38,078	59,762	56,330
1968	52,463	47,741	41,635	65,436	59,119
1969	56,045	51,009	42,848	69,219	63,028
1970	61,620	55,643	47,664	75,900	69,722
1971	61,180	53,960	47,058	73,959	68,020
1972	60,716	54,827	46,373	74,536	68,228
1973	64,484	59,325	49,833	80,504	—

NOTES: Column (2) is derived from (1) by subtracting calves of the year already born. Column (4) is derived from (3) by adding calves born to all potentially fertile females, who make up 42.5% of the population. Column (5) is derived from (3) by the addition of calves calculated from the known proportion of pregnant females. For 1965, 1966, and 1970, the mean pregnancy rate (69.5% of females) of the other five years was used for the calculations but not for the k-value analysis.

TABLE 29
Parameters for the Model Populations of Serengeti Buffalo

Mean reduction in fertility $(\overline{kf})$	$= 0.0371$
Mean juvenile mortality $(\overline{kj})$	$= 0.0734$
Mean juvenile mortality during rinderpest $(\overline{kj'})$	$= 0.1398$
Regression slope for adult mortality (ka) (b_1)	$= 0.2357$
Regression slope for $(ka + kj)$ (b_2)	$= 0.3932$
Intercept for ka regression (a_1)	$= -1.0844$
Intercept for $(ka + kj)$ regression (a_2)	$= -1.7635$
Log production of newborn $(\log P)$	$= 0.1956$

TABLE 30
Life Table for Female Serengeti Buffalo

Age (x yr) (1)	N (2)	kdx' (3)	$kdx'er_x$ (4)	kdx (5)	klx (6)	kqx (7)	mx (8)
0	—	485	465	330	1,000	330	0
1	—	129	139	94	670	140	0
2	9	14	16	11	576	19	0
3	9	14	18	12	565	21	0.06
4	15	23	31	21	553	38	0.14
5	10	16	24	16	532	30	0.41
6	17	27	43	29	516	56	0.41
7	11	17	29	20	487	41	0.41
8	18	28	52	35	467	75	0.41
9	24	38	76	52	432	120	0.41
10	19	30	65	44	380	116	0.41
11	29	46	107	73	336	217	0.33
12	25	39	98	67	263	255	0.33
13	19	30	82	56	196	286	0.33
14	16	25	73	49	140	350	0.33
15	13	20	63	43	91	473	0.33
16	7	11	38	26	48	542	0.33
17	4	6	22	15	22	682	0.33
18	1	2	10	7	7	1,000	0.33
	246	1,000	1,471	1,000			

TABLE 31

Female Buffalo Life Tables for Different Rates of Increase

Age (x yr)	klx' (if r = 0)	klx (r = 0.077)	kqx'	kqx	Difference (4) & (5)	Difference as percentage of (4)
(1)	(2)	(3)	(4)	(5)	(6)	(7)
0	1,000	1,000	485	330	155	32
1	515	670	250	140	110	44
2	386	576	36	19	17	47
3	372	565	38	21	17	45
4	358	553	64	38	26	41
5	335	532	48	30	18	38
6	319	516	85	56	29	34
7	292	487	58	41	17	29
8	275	467	102	75	27	26
9	247	432	154	120	34	22
10	209	380	144	116	28	19
11	179	336	257	217	40	16
12	133	263	293	255	38	13
13	94	196	319	286	33	10
14	64	140	391	350	41	10
15	39	91	513	473	40	8
16	19	48	579	542	37	6
17	8	22	750	682	68	9
18	2	7	1,000	1,000	—	—

TABLE 32

Life Table for Northern Serengeti Male Buffalo

Age (x yr)	N	kdx'	kdx'erx	kdx	klx	kqx
0	—	485	485	319	1,000	319
1	—	129	139	91	681	134
2	2	5	6	4	590	7
3	5	13	16	10	586	17
4	6	15	20	13	576	23
5	4	10	15	10	563	18
6	7	17	27	18	553	33
7	9	22	38	25	535	47
8	16	40	74	49	510	96
9	13	32	64	42	461	91
10	14	35	76	50	419	119
11	11	27	63	41	369	111
12	19	47	118	78	328	237
13	13	32	87	57	250	228
14	14	35	103	68	193	352
15	12	30	95	63	125	504
16	7	17	58	38	62	612
17	1	3	11	7	24	292
18	1	3	12	8	17	471
19	1	3	13	9	9	1,000
	155	1,000	1,520	1,000		

TABLE 33

Life Table for Southern Serengeti Male Buffalo

Age (x yr)	N	kdx'	kdx'er$x$	kdx	klx	kqx
0	—	485	485	330	1,000	330
1	—	129	139	95	670	142
2	2	4	5	3	575	5
3	5	10	13	9	572	16
4	5	10	14	10	563	18
5	6	13	19	13	553	24
6	18	38	60	41	540	76
7	17	36	62	42	499	84
8	20	42	78	53	457	116
9	17	36	72	49	404	121
10	15	32	69	47	355	132
11	16	34	79	54	308	175
12	18	38	96	65	254	256
13	15	32	87	59	189	312
14	14	30	88	60	130	462
15	8	17	54	36	70	514
16	5	10	34	23	34	676
17	1	2	7	5	11	454
18	0	0	0	0	6	0
19	1	2	9	6	6	1,000
	183	1,000	1,470	1,000		

TABLE 34

Percentage Crude Protein in the Diet Made up by the Three Components of Grass Leaf, Sheath, and Stem

Month	Leaf	Sheath	Stem	Total in Diet
November	3.24	1.36	0.46	5.06
December	5.14	2.05	0.52	7.71
January	3.06	2.09	0.47	5.62
February	5.39	1.26	0.28	6.93
March	7.15	2.15	0.57	9.87
......[a]	...	...	...	...
May	2.80	2.12	0.34	5.26
June	3.10	2.26	0.24	5.60
July	2.67	2.01	0.54	5.22
August	1.64	2.00	0.47	4.11
September	0.78	1.44	0.65	2.87
October	0.51	1.01	0.66	2.18

[a]No data were available for April.

TABLE 35

The Quality of Diet in Different Classes of the Buffalo Population at the End of the Dry Season

Class	Number of Animals	Mean % Crude Protein (*CP*) in Diet	Range
Pregnant females	20	2.30	2.05–2.51
Bachelor males	6	2.32	2.29–2.64
Adult herd males	14	2.40	2.21–2.59
Juveniles < 2 yr old	10	2.12	1.97–2.52
Immature, 2–4 yr old	12	2.11	1.97–2.25

TABLE 36
Helminths, Pentastomids, and Ticks of African Buffalo

Species	No. of Herbivore Hosts	Incidence	Locality
Trematodes			
Cotylophoron cotylophoron	23		Chad, Zaire, East and South Africa
Paramphistomum microbothrium	11		Chad, Zaire, East and South Africa
Fasciola gigantica	10	58%	Sudan, East Africa
Stephanopharynx compactus	7		Chad
Schistosoma mattheei	6		South Africa
Dicrocoelium hospes	4		Chad
Fasciola hepatica	3		Zaire
Cotylophoron fulleborni	3		Cameroon, Zaire, East Africa
Carmyrius mancupatus	3		East Africa
Stephanopharynx secundus	2		East Africa
Carmyrius exoporus	2		Zaire
Carmyrius gregarius	2		Chad, Zaire, Sudan
Paramphistomum phillerouxi	2		East Africa
Carmyrius endopapillatus	1		Chad, Zaire
Schistosoma haematobium	1		South Africa
Paramphistomum sukari	1		East Africa
Paramphistomum sukumum	1		East Africa
Cotylophoron indicum	1		East Africa
Calicophoron raja	1		East Africa
Chabertina ovina	1		East Africa
Schistosoma sp.	—	62%	South Africa
Cestodes			
Avitellina centripunctata	21		South Africa, Zaire
Stilesia hepatica	13		Botswana
Echinococcus granulosus	8	17%, 6%	Ethiopia, Zaire East and South Africa
Cysticercus bovis	9		Angola
Cysticercus hyaenae	4		East Africa
Cysticercus gonyamae	?	5%	East Africa
Cysticercus sp.	—	29%	South Africa
Spargana sp.	—	0.7%	East Africa
Sarcocystis sp.	—		East Africa
Nematodes			
Haemonchus contortus	36	68%, 16%	East and South Africa
Haemonchus bedfordi	20		East and South Africa
Setaria labiatopapillosa	16		Chad, Zaire, Sudan East Africa
Trichuris globulosa	10		South Africa
Cooperia fulleborni	7		East and South Africa

Species	No. of Herbivore Hosts	Incidence	Locality
Cooperia pectinata	6		South Africa
Cooperia punctata	5		South Africa
Cordophilus sagittus	5		South Africa
Gaigeria pachyscelis	4		Chad, Zaire
Parabronema skrjabini	4	12%	East and South Africa
Trichostrongylus axei	4		South Africa
Longistrongylus meyeri	3		East Africa
Agriostomum gorgonis	3		South Africa
Thelazia rhodesii	3	12%, 5%	East Africa
Thelazia lacrymalis	2		South Africa
Setaria nelsoni	2		East Africa
Oesophagostomum radiatum	2		South Africa
Tricharis barbertonensis	1		East Africa
Ashworthius lerouxi	1	73%, 0%	Chad, Zaire, East Africa, Zambia
Elaeophora poeli	1	16%	Zaire, East Africa
Neoascaris vitalorum	1		Zaire
Onchocerca armillata	1		Zaire
Onchocerca gibsoni	1		Zaire
Onchocerca synceri	1	16%	Zaire, South Africa
Toxocara manzadiensis	1		Zaire
Mammomonogamus sp.	—		East Africa
Bunostomum sp.	—		East Africa
Ostertagia sp.	—	44%, 29%	East Africa

Pentastomids
Linguatula serrata	4	1%	East and South Africa
Linguatula multiannulata	10	79%	East and South Africa
Neolinguatula nuttalli	7	20%	East and South Africa

Ticks
Amblyoma cohaerens
Amblyoma gemma
Amblyoma variegatum
Amblyoma spargum
Amblyoma tholloni
Rhipicephalus simus
Rhipicephalus evertsi
Rhipicephaus appendiculatus
Rhipicephalus parvus
Rhipicephalus compositus
Rhipicephalus pulchellus
Rhipicephalus longus
Rhipicephalus tricuspis
Rhipicephalus dux
Hyalomma albiparmatum
Hyalomma rufipes
Boophilus decoloratus

TABLE 37
List of Helminths, Pentastomids, Ticks, and Oestrid Flies of Wildebeest

Trematodes
   Calicophoron calicophorum
B *Fasciola gigantica*
B *Schistosoma mattheei*
B *Cotylophoron cotylophoron*

Cestodes
B *Echinococcus granulosus*
   Monezia benedeni
   Monezia expansa
B *Stilezia hepatica*
   Thysaniezia connochaeti
B *Cysticercus gonyamae*
B *Cysticercus hyaenae*
   Cysticercus tenuicollis
   Spirometra sp.

Nematodes
B *Agriostomum gorgonis*
   Dictyocaulus viviparus
B *Haemonchus bedfordi*
B *Haemonchus contortus*
   Oesophagostomum columbianum
   Protostrongylus etoshai

   Strongyloides sp.
   Trichostrongylus colubriformis
   Trichostrongylus rugatus
   Pneumostrongylus calcaratus
   Protostrongylus africana
   Setaria pultoni
B *Cooperia fulleborni*

Pentastomids
B *Linguatula serrata*
B *Linguatula multiannulata*
B *Neolinguatula nuttalli*

Ticks
B *Rhipicephalus pulcellus*
B *Rhipicephalus appendiculatus*
B *Rhipicephalus evertsi*
   Rhipicephalus sanguineus
B *Boophilus decoloratus*

Oestrid flies
   Oestrus aureoargenteus
   Gedoelstia cristata
   Gedoelstia hassleri

NOTE: B = present in buffalo also.

TABLE 38

Potentially Important Diseases of Serengeti Buffalo

Diseases	Number of Animals Tested	% Affected	% Immune	Age Group Affected
Theileriasis	40	—	74–90	Calf
Allerton-type herpes virus	46	—	96	Calf
Infectious bovine rhinotracheitis	52	—	76	?
Babesiasis	27	—	78	Calf, Adult
Anaplasmosis	27	—	78	?
Foot-and-mouth	20	—	60	Calf
Brucellosis	98	5	16	Fetus
Trypanosomiasis	40	17	—	Calf
Corynebacterium pyogenes	24	50–70	—	Calf
Virus diarrhea	17	—	30	Calf, Adult
Bovine pleuropneumonia	98	0	0	—
Malignant catarrh	25	0	0	—
Tuberculosis	98	0	—	—

TABLE 39

Results of Tests for Serum Antibodies against Rinderpest in Serengeti Buffalo

Birth Year	Number Positive	Total	% Positive
Before 1955	2	2	100
1955–57	8	8	100
1958–59	8	10	80
1960–62	8	13	62
1963	4	7	57
1964	0	4	0
1965	0	5	0
1966	0	6	0
1967	0	2	0
1969	0	1	0

References

Abrams, J. T. 1968. Fundamental approach to the nutrition of the captive wild herbivore. In *Comparative nutrition of wild animals*, ed. M. A. Crawford. *Symp. Zool. Soc. Lond.*, no. 21, pp. 41–42.

Agricultural Research Council. 1965. *The nutrient requirements of farm livestock. 2. Ruminants.* London: Agricultural Research Council.

Anderson, A. E.; Medin, D. E.; and Ochs, D. P. 1969. Relationships of carcass fat indices in 18 wintering mule deer. *Proc. Western Assoc. State Game and Fish. Comm.* 49:329–40.

Andrewartha, H. G. 1961. *Introduction to the study of animal populations.* London: Methuen.

Andrewartha, H. G., and Birch, L. C. 1954. *The distribution and abundance of animals.* Chicago: University of Chicago Press.

Ansell, W. F. H. 1972. *Identification manual for African mammals*, ed. J. Meester and H. W. Setzer. Washington, D.C.: Smithsonian Institution.

Ardrey, R. 1970. *The social contract.* London: Collins.

Armstrong, D. G.; Blaxter, K. L.; and Waite, R. 1964. The evaluation of artificially dried grass as a source of energy for sheep. *J. Agric. Sci.* (Cambridge) 62:417–24.

Arnold, G. W. 1964. Factors within plant associations affecting the behaviour and performance of grazing animals. In *Grazing in terrestrial and marine environments*, ed. D. J. Crisp. *Symp. Brit. Ecol. Soc.*, no. 4, pp. 133–54.

Aschkenasy, A. 1974. Effect of a protein-free diet on meiotic activity of transplanted splenic lymphocytes. *Nature* (London) 250:325–27.

Asdell, S. A. 1965. *Patterns of mammalian reproduction.* 2d ed. London: Constable.

Atang, P. G., and Plowright, W. 1969. Extension of the JP-15 rinderpest control campaign to Eastern Africa: The epizootiological background. *Bull. Epizoot. Dis. Afr.* 17:161–70.

Azavedo, J. C. S., and Agnew A. D. Q. 1968. Rift valley impala food preferences. *E. Afr. Wildl. J.* 6:145–46.

Baker, A. A. 1969. Post partum anoestrus in cattle. *Aust. Vet. J.* 45:180–83.

Baker, J. R.; Sachs, R.; and Laufer, I. 1967. Trypanosomes of wild mammals in an area of the Serengeti National Park, Tanzania. *Z. Tropenmed. Parasit.* 18:280–84.

Balch, C. C. 1955. Sleep in ruminants. *Nature* (London) 175: 940–41.

Basson, P. A.; McCully, R. M.; Kruger, S. P.; van Niekerk, J. W.; Young, E.; and de Vos., V. 1970. Parasitic and other diseases of the African buffalo in the Kruger National Park. *Onderstepoort J. Vet. Res.* 37:11–28.

Bate, D. M. A. 1951. The mammals of Singa and Abu Hugar. In *Fossil mammals of Africa*, no. 2, pp. 1–29. London: British Museum of Natural History.

Beilharz, R. G., and Mylrea, P. J. 1963. Social position and movement orders of dairy heifers. *Anim. Behav.* 11:529–33.

Bell, R. H. V. 1969. The use of the herb layer by grazing ungulates in the Serengeti National Park, Tanzania. Ph.D. thesis, Manchester University.

———. 1970. The use of the herb layer by grazing ungulates in the Serengeti. In *Animal populations in relation to their food resources*, ed. A. Watson, pp. 111–23. Oxford: Blackwell.

———. 1971. A grazing ecosystem in the Serengeti. *Sci. Am.* 224(1): 86–93.

Beverton, R. J. H., and Holt, S. J. 1957. *On the dynamics of exploited fish populations.* Fishery Invest. Ser. II, vol. 19. London: Her Majesty's Stationery Office.

Bhattacharya, P. 1974. Reproduction. In *The husbandry and health of the domestic buffalo*, ed. W. R. Cockrill, pp. 105–58. Rome: F.A.O.

Bindernagel, J. A. 1971. *Elaeophora poeli* (Nematoda: Filaroidea) in African buffalo in Uganda, East Africa. *J. Wildl. Dis.* 7: 296–98.

———. 1972*a*. Liver fluke *Fasciola gigantica* in African buffalo and antelopes in Uganda, East Africa. *J. Wildl. Dis.* 8:315–17.

———. 1972*b*. *Thelazia rhodesi* (Nematoda: Spiraroidea) in African buffalo in Uganda, East Africa. *J. Parasitol.* 58:594.

Bindernagel, J. A., and Todd, A. C. 1972. The population dynamics of *Ashworthius lerouxi* (Nematoda: Trichostrongylidae) in African buffalo in Uganda. *Brit. Vet. J.* 128:452–55.

Blaxter, K. L. 1962. *The energy metabolism of ruminants.* London: Hutchinson.

———. 1964. Utilization of the metabolizable energy of grass. *J. Brit. Grassld. Soc.* 19:90–98.

———. 1970. The comparative biology of lactation. In *Lactation*, ed. I. R. Falconer, pp. 51–69. London: Butterworths.

Bligh, J., and Harthoorn, A. M. 1965. Continuous radiotelemetric records of the deep body temperature of some unrestrained African mammals under near-natural conditions. *J. Physiol.* 176:145–62.

Borowski, S., and Kossak, S. 1972. The natural food preferences of the European bison in seasons free of snow cover. *Acta Theriol.* 17:151–69.

Bourliere, F. 1965. Densities and biomass of some ungulate populations in eastern Congo and Ruanda, with notes on population structure and lion/ungulate ratios. *Zool. Afr.* 1:199–207.

Bourliere, F., and Verschuren, J. 1960. *Introduction à l'écologie des ongules du Parc National Albert.* Brussels: Institut des Parcs Nationaux du Congo Belge.

Braden, A. W. H., and Baker. A. A. 1973. Reproduction in sheep and cattle. In *The pastoral industries of Australia*, ed. G. Alexander and O. B. Williams, pp. 269–302. Sydney: Sydney University Press.

Branagan, D., and Hammond, J. A. 1965. Rinderpest in Tanganyika: A review. *Bull. Epizoot. Dis. Afr.* 13:225–46.

Brantas, G. C. 1968. On the dominance order in Friesian-Dutch dairy cows. *Z. Tierzucht. Zuchtbiol.* 84:127–51.

Braun, H. M. H. 1973. Primary production in the Serengeti; Purpose, methods and some results of research. *Ann. Univ. Abidjan*, (E) 6:171–88.

Bredon, R. M.; Harker, K. W., and Marshall, B. 1963. The nutritive value of grasses grown in Uganda when fed to Zebu cattle. *J. Agric. Sci.* (Cambridge) 61:101–04.

Bredon, R. M., and Wilson, J. 1963. The chemical composition and nutritive value of grasses from semi-arid areas of Karamoja, as related to ecology and types of soil. *E. Afr. Agric. For. J.* 29:134–42.

Brocklesby, D. W. 1965. A new theilerial parasite of the African buffalo (*Syncerus caffer*). *Bull. Epizoot. Dis. Afr.* 13:325–30.

Brocklesby, D. W., and Barnett, S. F. 1966. The isolation of *Theileria lawrencei* (Kenya) from a wild buffalo (*Syncerus caffer*) and its serial passage through captive buffaloes. *Brit. Vet. J.* 122:387–95.

Brocklesby, D. W., and Vidler, B. O. 1961. Haematozoa of the blue wildebeest. *Bull. Epizoot. Dis. Afr.* 9:245–49.

———. 1966. Haematozoa found in wild members of the order Artiodactyla in East Africa. *Bull. Epizoot. Dis. Afr.* 14:285–99.

Bwangamoi. O. 1968. Helminth parasites of domestic and wild animals in Uganda. *Bull. Epizoot. Dis. Afr.* 16:429–54.

———. 1970. A checklist of helminth parasites of animals in Tanzania. *Bull. Epizoot. Dis. Afr.* 18:229–42.

Cain, A. J. 1954. *Animal species and their evolution.* London: Hutchinson.

Campling, R. C.; Freer, M.; and Balch, C. C. 1961. Factors affecting the voluntary intake of food by cows. *Brit. J. Nutr.* 15:531–40.

Caughley, G. 1966. Mortality patterns in mammals. *Ecology* 47:906–18.

———. 1976. Wildlife management and the dynamics of ungulate populations. *Adv. Appl. Biol. A.P.*, in press

Caughley, G. and Birch, L. C. 1971. Rate of increase. *J. Wildl. Management* 35:658–63.

Chalmers, M. I. 1961. Protein synthesis in the rumen. In *Digestive physiology and nutrition in the ruminant*, ed. D. Lewis, pp. 205–22. London: Butterworth.

Chitty, D. 1960. Population processes in the vole and their relevance to general theory. *Can. J. Zool.* 38:99–113.

———. 1967. The natural selection of self-regulating behaviour in animal populations. *Proc. Ecol. Soc. Aust.* 2:51–78.

Christian, J. J. 1961. Phenomena associated with population density. *Proc. Nat. Acad. Sci. U.S.A.* 47:428–49.

Christian, J. J., and Davis, D. E. 1964. Endocrines, behaviour, and population. *Science* 146:1550-60.

Christian, J. J.; Lloyd, J. A.; and Davis, D. E. 1965. The role of endocrines in the self-regulation of mammalian populations. *Recent Progr. Horm. Res.* 21:501-78.

Christy, C. 1929. The African buffaloes. *Proc. Zool. Soc. Lond.*, pp. 445-62.

Ciba Foundation. 1974. Parasites in the immunized host: Mechanisms of survival. Ciba foundation Symp. no. 25 (new series). Amsterdam: Associated Scientific Publishers.

Clark, L. R.; Geier, P. W.; Hughes, R. D.; and Morris, R. F. 1967. *The ecology of insect populations in theory and practice.* London: Methuen.

Cockrill. W. R. 1967. The water buffalo. *Sci. Am.* 217(6): 118-25.

Cole, L. C. 1949. The measurement of interspecific association. *Ecology* 30:411-24.

Condy, J. B.; Herniman, K. A. J.; and Hedger, R. S. 1969. Foot-and-mouth disease in wildlife in Rhodesia and other African territories. *J. comp. Path.* 79:27-31.

Cooke, H. B. S., and Coryndon, S. C. 1970. Pleistocene mammals from the Kaiso formation and other related deposits in Uganda. In *Fossil vertebrates of Africa*, ed. L. S. B. Leakey and R. J. G. Savage, 2:107-224. London: Academic Press.

Cooper, A. C. D., and Carmichael, I. H. 1974. The incidence of brucellosis in game in Botswana. *Bull. Epizoot. Dis. Afr.* 22:119-24.

Corbin, K. W., and Uzzell, T. 1970. Natural selection and mutation rates in mammals. *Am. Nat.* 104:37-54.

Cornevin, C., and Lesbre, X. 1894. Traité de l'âge des animaux domestiques d'après les dents et les productions épidermiques. Paris: Baillière et Fils.

Council on Environmental Quality. 1974. *Environmental quality.* 5th Annual Report. Washington, D.C.

Crofton, H. D. 1958. Nematode parasite populations in sheep on lowland pasture. VI. Sheep behaviour and nematode infections. *Parasitology* 48:251-60.

Croze, H. 1974a. The Seronera bull problem. I. The elephants. *E. Afr. Wildl. J.* 12:1-28.

———. 1974b. The Seronera bull problem. II. The trees. *E. Afr. Wildl. J.* 12:29-47.

Curry-Lindahl, K. 1974. The conservation story in Africa during the 1960s. *Biol. Conserv.* 6:170-78.

Dagg, A. I., and Taub, A. 1970. Flehmen. *Mammalia* 34:686-95.

Daniel, J. C., and Grubh, B. R. 1966. The Indian wild buffalo *Bubalus bubalis* (Linn.) in peninsula India: A preliminary survey. *Bombay Nat. Hist. Soc. J.* 63:32-53.

Darling, F. F. 1960. *An ecological reconnaisance of the Mara Plains in Kenya Colony.* Wildl. Monogr., no. 5. Chestertown: The Wildlife Society.

Dassman, R. F. 1972. Towards a system for classifying natural regions of the world and their representation by national parks and reserves. *Biol. Conserv.* 4:247–55.

Dassman, R. F., and Mossman, A. S. 1962. Reproduction in some ungulates in Southern Rhodesia. *J. Mammal.* 43:533–37.

Davidson, B. R. 1972. *The northern myth: Limits to agriculture and pastoral development in tropical Australia.* 3d ed. Melbourne: Melbourne University Press.

Davis, D. E., and Golley, F. B. 1963. *Principles in mammalogy.* New York: Rheinhold.

Delius, J. D. 1969. A stochastic analysis of the maintenance behaviour of skylarks. *Behaviour* 33:137–78.

Densham, W. D. 1974. A method of capture and translocation of wild herbivores using opaque plastic material and a helicopter. *Lammergeyer* 21:1–25.

De Ruiter, L. 1952. Some experiments on the camouflage of stick caterpillars. *Behaviour* 4:222–32.

Diamond, J. M. 1975. The island dilemma: Lessons of modern biogeographic studies for the design of natural reserves. *Biol. Conserv.* 7:129–46.

Dinnick, J. A.; Walker, J. B.; Barnett, S. F.; and Brocklesby, D. W. 1963. Some parasites obtained from game animals in western Uganda. *Bull. Epizoot. Dis. Afr.* 11:37–44.

Douglas-Hamilton, I. 1972. On the ecology and behaviour of the African elephant: The elephants of Lake Manyara. D.Phil. thesis, Oxford.

Eberhard, M. J. W. 1975. The evolution of social behaviour by kin selection. *Quart. Rev. Biol.* 50:1–33.

Ehrlich, P. R., and Birch, L. C. 1967. The "balance of nature" and "population control." *Am. Nat.* 101:97–107.

Ehrlich, P. R.; Breedlove, D. E.; Brussard, P. F.; and Sharp, M. A. 1972. Weather and the "regulation" of subalpine populations. *Ecology* 53:243–47.

Ellerman, J. R., and Morrison-Scott, T. C. S. 1951. *Checklist of Palaearctic and Indian mammals, 1758–1946.* London: British Museum.

Eltringham, S. K. 1974. Changes in the large mammal community of Mweya Peninsula, Rwensori National Park, Uganda, following removal of hippopotamus. *J. Appl. Ecol.* 11:855–66.

Eltringham, S. K., and Woodford, M. H. 1973. The numbers and distribution of buffalo in the Ruwenzori National Park, Uganda. *E. Afr. Wildl. J.* 11:151–64.

Epstein, H. 1971. *The origin of the domestic animals of Africa.* Vol. 1. New York: Africana Publishing Corp.

Erkert, H. G. 1974. Der Einfluss des Mondlichtes auf die Aktivitatsperiodik nachtaktiver Säugetiere. *Oecologia* (Berlin) 14:269–87.

Estes, R. D. 1966. Behaviour and life history of the wildebeest (*Connochaetes taurinus* Burchell) *Nature* (London) 212:999–1000.

———. 1969. Territorial behaviour of the wildebeest (*Connochaetes taurinus* Burchell, 1823) *Z. Tierpsychol.* 26:284–370.

———. 1972. The role of the vomeronasal organ in mammalian reproduction. *Mammalia* 36:315–51.

———. 1974. Social organization of the African Bovidae. In *The behaviour of ungulates and its relation to management,* ed. V. Geist and F. Walther, pp. 166–205. Morges, Switzerland: I.U.C.N. Publications, new series no. 24.

———. 1976. The significance of breeding synchrony in the wildebeest. *E. Afr. Wildl. J.* 14:135–52.

Everitt, G. C. 1968. Prenatal development of uniparous animals with particular reference to the influence of maternal nutrition in sheep. In *Growth and development of mammals,* ed. G. A. Lodge and G. E. Lamming, pp. 131–57. London: Butterworth.

Fairall, N. 1968. The reproductive seasons of some mammals in the Kruger National Park. *Zool. Afr.* 3:189–210.

Field, C. R. 1968a. The food habits of some wild ungulates in Uganda. Ph.D. thesis, Cambridge University.

———. 1968b. Methods of studying the food habits of some wild ungulates in Uganda. *Proc. Nutr. Soc.* 27:172–77.

———. 1968c. A comparative study of the food habits of some wild ungulates in the Queen Elizabeth Park, Uganda: Preliminary report. In *Comparative nutrition of wild large mammals,* ed. M. A. Crawford, pp. 135–51. Symp. Zool. Soc. Lond. no. 21. London: Academic Press.

———. 1970. Observations on the food habits of tame warthog and antelope in Uganda. *E. Afr. Wildl. J.* 8: 1–18.

Field, C. R., and Laws, R. M. 1970. The distribution of the larger herbivores in the Queen Elizabeth National Park, Uganda. *J. Appl. Ecol.* 7:273–94.

Flatt, W. P., and Moe, P. W. 1974. Nutritional requirements for lactation. In *Lactation: A comprehensive treatise.* Vol. 3. *Nutrition and biochemistry of milk/maintenance,* ed. B. L. Larson and V. R. Smith, pp. 311–47. New York: Academic Press.

Follett, B. K. 1973. Circadian rhythms and photoperiodic time measurement in birds. *J. Reprod. Fert.,* suppl. 19:5–18.

Ford, J. 1971. *The role of the trypanosomiases in African ecology.* Oxford: Clarendon Press.

Frazer, A. F. 1968. *Reproductive behaviour in ungulates.* London: Academic Press.

French, M. H. 1957. Nutritional value of tropical grasses and fodders. *Herbage Abstr.* 27:1–9.

French, M. H.; Glover, J.; and Duthie, D. W. 1957. The apparent digestibility of crude protein in the ruminant. II. The general equation and some of its implications. *J. Agric. Sci.* (Cambridge) 48:379–83.

Fuller, W. A. 1961. The ecology and management of the American bison. *Terre Vie* 108:286–304.

Gebczynska, Z., and Krasinska, M. 1972. Food preferences and requirements of the European bison. *Acta Theriol.* 17:105–17.

Geist, V. 1971. The relation of social evolution and dispersal in ungulates during the pleistocene with emphasis on the old world deer and the genus *Bison. Quat. Res.* 1:285–315.

———. 1974a. On the evolution of reproductive potential in moose. *Nat. Can.* 101:527–37.

———. 1974b. On the relationship of social evolution and ecology in ungulates. *Amer. Zool.* 14:205–20.

Gentry, A. W. 1967. *Pelorovis oldowayensis* Reck, an extinct bovid from East Africa. *Bull. Brit. Mus. (Nat. Hist.), Geol.* 14:245–99.

Glover, J., and Duthie, D. W. 1958. The apparent digestibility of crude protein by non-ruminants and ruminants. *J. Agric. Sci.* 51:289–93.

Graaf, G. de; Schulz, K. C. A.; and Walt, P. T. van der. 1973. Notes on rumen contents of cape buffalo *Syncerus caffer* in the Addo Elephant National Park. *Koedoe* 16:45–58.

Graber, M. 1969. Helminthes parasites de certains animaux domestiques et sauvages du Tchad. *Bull. Epizoot. Dis. Afr.* 17:403–28.

Greenway, P. J., and Vesey-Fitzgerald, D. F. 1969. The vegetation of Lake Manyara National Park. *J. Ecol.* 57:127–49.

Griffiths, R. B. 1974. Parasites and parasitic diseases. In *The husbandry and health of the domestic buffalo,* ed. W. R. Cockrill, pp. 236–75. Rome: F.A.O.

Grimsdell, J. J. R. 1969. The ecology of the buffalo, *Syncerus caffer,* in western Uganda. Ph.D. thesis, Cambridge University.

———. 1973a. Age determination of the African buffalo, *Syncerus caffer* Sparrman. *E. Afr. Wildl. J.* 11:31–54.

———. 1973b. Reproduction in the African buffalo, *Syncerus caffer,* in western Uganda. *J. Reprod. Fert.,* suppl. 19:301–16.

———. 1975. *Annual report, 1973–74.* Serengeti Research Institute, p. 21. Arusha: Tanzania National Parks.

Grubb, P. 1972. Variation and incipient speciation in the African buffalo. *Z. Säugetierk.* 37:121–44.

Grzimek, B. 1970. *Among animals of Africa.* Trans. J. Maxwell Brownjohn. London: Collins.

Guilbride, P. D. L.; Rollinson, D. H. L.; McAnulty, E. G.; Alley, J. G.; and Wells, E. A. 1963. Tuberculosis in the free-living African (Cape) buffalo *(Syncerus caffer caffer* Sparrman) *J. Comp. Path.* 73:337–48.

Guthrie, R. D. 1970. Bison evolution and zoogeography in North America during the Pleistocene. *Quart. Rev. Biol.* 45:1–15.

Gwynne, M. D., and Bell, R. H. V. 1968. Selection of grazing components by grazing ungulates in the Serengeti National Park. *Nature* (London) 220:390–93.

Hafez, E. S. E.; Schein, M. W.; and Ewbank, W. 1969. The behaviour of cattle. In *The behaviour of domestic animals.* 2d ed., ed. E. S. E. Hafez, pp. 235–96. Baltimore: Williams and Wilkins.

Hairston, N. G.; Smith, F. E.; and Slobodkin, L. B. 1960. Community structure, population control, and competition. *Am. Nat.* 94:421–25.

Hamilton, W. D. 1971. Geometry for the selfish herd. *J. Theor. Biol.* 31:295–311.

Hammond, J. A., and Branagan, D. 1965. Contagious bovine pleuro-pneumonia in Tanganyika. *Bull. Epizoot. Dis. Afr.* 13:121–47.

Hancock, J. 1954. Studies on grazing behaviour in relation to grassland management. *J. Agric. Sci.* 44:420–33.

Hanks, J. 1972. Growth of the African elephant (*Loxodonta africana*). *E. Afr. Wildl. J.* 10:251–72.

Harker, K. W.; Taylor, J. I.; and Rollinson, D. H. L. 1954. Studies on the habits of zebu cattle. I. Preliminary observations on grazing habits. *J. Agric. Sci.* 44:193–98.

Harris, L. D. 1972. *An ecological description of a semi-arid East African ecosystem.* Range. Sci. Dept., ser. no. 11. Fort Collins: Colorado State University.

Hedger, R. S. 1972. Foot-and-mouth disease and the African buffalo (*Syncerus caffer*) *J. Comp. Path.* 82:19–28.

Hedger, R. S.; Forman, A. J.; and Woodford, M. H. 1973. Le virus de la fièvre aphteuse chez le buffle est-africain. *Bull. Epizoot. Dis. Afr.* 21:101–3.

Hendrichs, H. 1970. Schatzungen der Huftierbiomasse in der Dornbusch-savanne nordlich und westlich der Serengetisteppe in Ostafrika nach einem neuen Vefahren und Bemerkungen zur Biomasse der anderen pflanzenfressenden Tierarten. *Säugetierk. Mitt.* 18:237–55.

Herlocker, D. 1975. *Woody vegetation of the Serengeti National Park.* College Station: Caesar Kleberg Research Program, Texas A & M University.

Herrig, D. M., and Haugen, A. O. 1969. Bull bison behaviour traits. *Proc. Iowa Acad. Sci.* 76:245–62.

Hinde, S. L., and Hinde, H. 1901. *The last of the Masai.* London: Heine-mann.

Hornocker, M. G. 1970. *An analysis of mountain lion predation upon mule deer and elk in the Idaho Primitive Area.* Wildl. Monogr., no. 21. Chestertown: The Wildlife Society.

Houston, D. B. 1971. Ecosystems of national parks. *Science* 172:648–51.

Hugget, A. St. G., and Widdas, W. F. 1951. The relationship between mammalian foetal weight and conception age. *J. Physiol.* 114:306–17.

Ito, Y. 1972. On the methods for determining density-dependence by means of regression. *Oecologia* (Berlin) 10:347–72.

Jaczewski, Z. 1958. Reproduction of the European bison *Bison bonasus* (L) in reserves. *Acta Theriol.* 1:333–76.

Jarman, M. V., and Jarman, P. J. 1973. Daily activity of impala. *E. Afr. Wildl. J.* 11:75–92.

Jarman, P. J. 1968. The effect of the creation of Lake Kariba upon the terrestrial ecology of the Middle Zambesi Valley, with particular reference to the large mammals. Ph.D. thesis, Manchester University.

———. 1971. Diets of large mammals in the woodlands around Lake Kariba, Rhodesia. *Oecologia* (Berlin) 8:157–78.

———. 1974. The social organization of antelope in relation to their ecology. *Behaviour* 48:215–66.

Jenkins, R. E., and Bedford, W. B. 1973. The use of natural areas to establish environmental baselines. *Biol. Conserv.* 5:168–74.

Jenness, R. 1974. The composition of milk. In *Lactation: A comprehensive treatise.* Vol. 3. *Nutrition and biochemistry of milk/maintenance,* ed. B. L. Larson and V. R. Smith, pp. 1–107. New York: Academic Press.

Jewell, P. A. 1966. The concept of home range in mammals. In *Play, exploration and territory in mammals,* ed. P. A. Jewell and C. Loizos, pp. 85–109. *Symp. Zool. Soc. Lond.,* no. 18.

Joblin, A. D. H. 1960. The influence of night grazing on the growth rates of zebu cattle in East Africa. *J. Brit. Grassld. Soc.* 15:212–15.

Joubert, D. M. 1963. Puberty in female farm animals. *Anim. Breed. Abstr.* 31:295–306.

Kaliner, G., and Staak, C. 1973. A case of orchitis caused by *Brucella abortus* in the African Buffalo. *J. Wildl. Dis.* 9:251–53.

Kay, H. D. 1974. Milk and milk production. In *The husbandry and health of the domestic buffalo,* ed. W. R. Cockrill, pp. 329–76. Rome: F.A.O.

Klapp, E. 1960. The influence of pasture, hay, silage, and type of animal on forage utilization. *Proc. VIII Int. Grassld. Congr.,* pp. 570–73.

Kleiber, M. 1961. *The fire of life: An introduction to animal energetics.* New York: Wiley.

Klomp, H. 1961. The concepts "similar ecology" and "competition" in animal ecology. *Arch. Neerl. Zool.* 14:90–102.

———. 1962. The influence of climate and weather on the mean density level, the fluctuations and the regulation of populations. *Arch. Neerl. Zool.* 15:68–109.

Kowalski, K. 1967. The evolution and fossil remains of the European bison. *Acta Theriol.* 12:335–38.

Krasinski, Z. 1967. Free living European bisons. *Acta Theriol.* 12:391–405.

Krasinski, Z., and Raczynski, J. 1967. The reproduction biology of European bison living in reserves and in freedom. *Acta Theriol.* 12: 407–44.

Krebs, C. J. 1972. *Ecology: The experimental analysis of distribution and abundance.* New York: Harper and Row.

Krebs, C. J.; Gaenes, M. S.; Keller, B. L.; Myers, J. H.; and Tamarin, R. H. 1973. Population cycles in small rodents. *Science* 179:35–41.

Krebs, C. J., and Myers, J. H. 1974. Population cycles in small mammals. *Adv. Ecol. Res.* 8:267–399.

Kreulen, D. 1975. Wildebeest habitat selection on the Serengeti plains, Tanzania, in relation to calcium and lactation: A preliminary report. *E. Afr. Wildl. J.* 13:297–304.

Kruuk, H. 1972. *The spotted hyena.* Chicago: University of Chicago Press.

Krysiak, K. 1967. The history of the European bison in the Bialowieza Forest and the results of its protection. *Acta Theriol.* 12:323–31.

Kukla, G. J., and Kukla, H. J. 1974. Increased surface albedo in the northern hemisphere. *Science* 183:709–14.

Kuno, E. 1973. Statistical characteristics of the density-independent population fluctuations and the evaluation of density-dependence and regulation in animal populations. *Res. Popul. Ecol., Kyoto* 15:99–120.

Kuttler, K. 1965. Serological survey of anaplasmosis incidence in East Africa, using the compliment-fixation test. *Bull. Epizoot. Dis. Afr.* 13: 257–62.

Lack, D. 1966. *Population studies of birds.* Oxford: Oxford University Press.

Lamond, D. R. 1970. The influence of undernutrition on reproduction in the cow. *Anim. Breed. Abstr.* 38:359–72.

Lamprey, H. F. 1963*a*. Ecological separation of the large mammal species in the Tarangire Game Reserve, Tanganyika. *E. Afr. Wildl. J.* 1:63–92.

———. 1963*b*. The Tarangire Game Reserve. *Tanganyika Notes Rec.* 60: 10–22.

———. 1964. Estimation of the large mammal densities, biomass and energy exchange in the Tarangire Game Reserve and the Masai Steppe in Tanganyika. *E. Afr. Wildl. J.* 2:1–46.

Lamprey, H. F.; Glasgow, J. P.; Lee-Jones, F.; and Weitz, B. 1962. A simultaneous census of the potential and actual food sources of the tsetse fly *Glossina swynnertoni* Austen. *J. Anim. Ecol.* 31:151–56.

Lamprey, H. F.; Glover, P. E.; Turner, M.; and Bell, R. H. V. 1967. Invasion of the Serengeti National Park by elephants. *E. Afr. Wildl. J.* 5:151–66.

Laws, R. M. 1969. Aspects of reproduction in the African elephant, *Loxodonta africana. J. Reprod. Fert.*, suppl. 6: 193–217.

Laws, R. M.; Parker, I. S. C.; and Johnstone, R. C. B. 1975. *Elephants and the habitats.* Oxford: Oxford University Press.

Leuthold, W. 1972. Home range, movements and food of a buffalo herd in Tsavo National Park. *E. Afr. Wildl. J.* 10:237–43.

Leuthold, W., and Leuthold, B. M. 1976. Density and biomass of ungulates in Tsavo National Park, Kenya. *E. Afr. Wildl. J.* 14:49–58.

Levin, D. A. 1971. Plant phenolics. *Am. Nat.* 105:157–81.

Littlejohn, K. G. 1938. Field notes on bushcow. *Niger. Fld.* 7:17–20.

Lott, D. F. 1974. Sexual and aggressive behaviour of American bison *Bison bison.* In *The behaviour of ungulates and its relation to manage-*

ment, ed. V. Geist and F. Walther, pp. 382–94. Morges, Switzerland: I.U.C.N. Publications, new series no. 24.

Lydekker, R. 1908. *The game animals of Africa*. London: Rowland Ward.

MacArthur, R. H., and Wilson, E. O. 1963. An equilibrium theory of island biogeography. *Evolution* 17:373–87.

McConnell, E. E.; Tustin, R. C.; and Vos, V. de. 1972. Anthrax in an African buffalo (*Syncerus caffer*) in the Kruger National Park. *J. S. Afr. Vet. Med. Ass.* 43:181–87.

McCulloch, B.; Suda, B'Q. J.; Tungaraza, R.; and Kalaye, W. J. 1968. A study of East Coast fever, drought and social obligations in relation to the need for the economic development of the livestock industry in Sukumaland, Tanzania. *Bull. Epizoot. Dis. Afr.* 16:303–26.

McEwan, E. H. 1963. Seasonal annuli in the cementum of the teeth of barren ground cariboo. *Can. J. Zool.* 41:111–13.

McHugh, T. 1958. Social behaviour of the American buffalo. Zoologica 43:1–40.

McKay, G. M., and Eisenberg, J. F. 1974. Movement patterns and habitat utilization of ungulates in Ceylon. In *The behaviour of ungulates and its relation to management*, ed. V. Geist and F. Walther, pp. 708–21. Morges, Switzerland: I.U.C.N. Publications, new services no. 24.

McNaughton, S. J. 1976. Serengeti migratory wildebeest: Facilitation of energy flow by grazing. *Science* 191:92–94.

Mason, I. L. 1974. Environmental physiology. In *The husbandry and health of the domestic buffalo*, ed. W. R. Cockrill, pp. 88–104. Rome: F.A.O.

Maynard-Smith, J. 1964. Group selection and kin selection. *Nature* (London) 201:1145–47.

Meagher, M. M. 1973. *The bison of Yellowstone National Park*. Nat. Park Serv. Sci. Monogr., ser. no. 1.

Milford, R., and Minson, D. J. 1966. The feeding values of tropical pastures. In *Tropical pastures*, ed. W. Davies and C. L. Skidmore, pp. 106–14. London: Faber and Faber.

Mitchell, B. L.; Skenton, J. B.; and Uys, J. C. M. 1965. Predation on large mammals in Kafue National Park, Zambia. *Zool. Afr.* 1:297–318.

Moore, A. 1938. *Serengeti*. London: Country Life.

Moran, J. 1973. Heat tolerance of brahman cross, buffalo, banting, and shorthorn steers during exposure to sun as a result of exercise. *Aust. J. Agric. Res.* 24:775–82.

Moreau, R. E. 1966. *The bird faunas of Africa and its islands*. London: Academic Press.

Morris, D. 1958. The function and causation of courtship ceremonies. In *L'instinct dans le comportement des animaux et de l'homme*. Paris: Foundation Singer Polignac.

Moss, R.; Watson, A.; and Parr, R. 1975. Maternal nutrition and breeding success in red grouse (*Lagopus lagopus scoticus*). *J. Anim. Ecol.* 44:233–44.

Mross, G. A., and Doolittle, R. F. 1967. Amino-acid sequence studies on Artiodactyl fibrinopeptides. *Arch. Biochem. Biophys.* 122: 674–84.

Murdoch, W. W. 1970. Population regulation and population inertia. *Ecology* 51:497–502.

Murphy, D. A., and Coates, J. A. 1966. Effects of dietary protein on deer. *Trans. N. Am. Wildl. and Nat. Res. Conf.* 31: 124–39.

Murton, R. K. 1971. Why do some bird species feed in flocks? *Ibis* 113: 534–36.

Myers, N. 1973. Tsavo National Park, Kenya, and its elephants: An interim appraisal. *Biol. Conserv.* 5:123–32.

———. 1976. An expanded approach to the problem of disappearing species. *Science* 193:198–202.

National Research Council. 1970. *Nutrient requirements of domestic animals.* No. 4. *Nutrient requirements of beef cattle.* 4th ed. Washington, D.C.: National Academy of Sciences.

Nicholson, A. J. 1933. The balance of animal populations. *J. Anim. Ecol.* 2:132–78.

Norton-Griffiths, M. 1973. Counting the Serengeti migratory wildebeest using two-stage sampling. *E. Afr. Wildl. J.* 11: 135–49.

———. 1975. The numbers and distribution of large mammals in Ruaha National Park, Tanzania. *E. Afr. Wildl. J.* 13:121–40.

Norton-Griffiths, M.; Herlocker, D.; and Pennycuick, L. 1975. The patterns of rainfall in the Serengeti ecosystem, Tanzania. *E. Afr. Wildl. J.* 13:347–74.

Oh, H. K.; Jones, M. B.; and Longhurst, W. M. 1968. A comparison of rumen microbial inhibition resulting from various essential oils isolated from relatively unpalatable species. *Appl. Microbiol.* 16:39–44.

Owen, J. S. 1972. Some thoughts on management of national parks. *Biol. Conserv.* 4:241–46.

Patterson, I. J. 1965. Timing and spacing of broods in the black-headed gull. *Ibis* 107:433–59.

Payne, P. R., and Wheeler, E. F. 1968. Comparative nutrition in pregnancy and lactation. *Proc. Nutr. Soc.* 27:129–38.

Pennycuick, L. 1975. Movements of the migratory wildebeest population in the Serengeti area between 1960 and 1973. *E. Afr. Wildl. J.* 13:65–87.

Percival, A. B. 1924. *A game ranger's note book.* London: Nisbet and Co.

———. 1928. *A game ranger on safari.* London: Nisbet and Co.

Pereira, H. C. 1961. Conference on land management problems in areas containing game: Lake Manyara, Tanganyika. *E. Afr. Agric. For. J.* 27:40–46.

Pester, F. R. N., and Laurence, B. R. 1974. The parasite load of some African game animals. *J. Zool.* (London) 174: 397–406.

Pfeffer, P. 1969. Considerations sur l'écologie des forêts claires du Cambodge oriental. *Terre Vie* 7:3–24.

Phillipson, J. 1975. Rainfall, primary production and "carrying capacity" of Tsavo National Park (East), Kenya. *E. Afr. Wildl. J.* 13:171–202.

Pianka, E. R. 1974. *Evolutionary ecology.* New York: Harper and Row.

Pienaar, U. de V. 1969. Observations on the developmental biology, growth and some aspects of the population ecology of African buffalo in the Kruger National Park. *Koedoe* 12:29–52.

Pilgrim, G. E. 1947. The evolution of the buffaloes, oxen, sheep, and goats. *J. Linn. Soc., Zool.* 41:272–86.

Pitman, C. R. S. 1943. *A game warden among his charges.* Harmondsworth, England: Penguin.

Plowes, D. C. H. 1957. The seasonal variation of crude protein in twenty common veld grasses at Matopos, Southern Rhodesia, and related observations. *Rhod. Agric. J.* 54:33–55.

Plowright, W. 1963. The role of game animals in the epizootiology of rinderpest and malignant catarrhal fever in East Africa. *Bull. Epizoot. Dis. Afr.* 11:149–62.

————. 1965. Malignant catarrhal fever in East Africa. 1. Behaviour of the virus in free-living populations of blue wildebeest (*Gorgon taurinus taurinus* Burchell). *Res. Vet. Sci.* 6:56–68.

Plowright, W. and Jessett, D. M. 1971. Investigations of Allerton-type herpes virus infection in East African game animals and cattle. *J. Hyg.* (Cambridge) 69:209–22.

Plowright, W., and McCulloch, B. 1967. Investigations on the incidence of rinderpest virus infection in game animals of N. Tanganyika and S. Kenya 1960/63. *J. Hyg.* (Cambridge) 65:343–58.

Podoler, H., and Rogers, D. 1975. A new method for the identification of Key Factors from life-table data. *J. Anim. Ecol.* 44:85–114.

Quick, H. F. 1963. Animal population analysis. In *Wildlife investigational techniques* 2d ed., ed. H. S. Mosby. pp. 190–228, Blacksburg: The Wildlife Society.

Ransom, A. B. 1965. Kidney and marrow fat as indicators of white-tailed deer condition. *J. Wildl. Management* 29:397–98.

————. 1966. Determining age of white-tailed deer from layers in cementum molars. *J. Wildl. Management* 30:197–99.

Reddingius, J. 1971. Gambling for existence. *Acta Biotheoretica,* suppl. 1, 20:1–208.

Reimers, E., and Nordby, O. 1968. Relationships between age and tooth cementum layers in Norwegian reindeer. *J. Wildl. Management.* 32:957–61.

Reveron, A. E., and Topps, J. H. 1970. Nutrition and gastrointestinal parasitism in ruminants. *Outlook Agric.* 6:131–36.

Reveron, A. E.; Topps, J. H.; MacDonald, D. C.; and Pratt, G. 1974. The intake, digestion, and utilization of food and growth rate of lambs affected by *Trichostrongylus colubriformis. Rev. Vet. Sci.* 16:299–399.

Richards, O. W., and Waloff, N. 1954. Studies on the biology and population dynamics of British grasshoppers. *Antilocust Bull.* no. 17.

Robertshaw, D., and Taylor, C. R. 1969. A comparison of sweat gland activity in eight species of East African bovids. *J. Physiol.* 203:135–43.

Rogerson, A. 1968. Energy utilization by the eland and wildebeest. In *Comparative nutrition of wild animals*, ed. M. A. Crawford, pp. 153–61. *Symp. Zool. Soc. Lond.*, no. 21.

Rollinson, D. H. L. 1962. Brucella agglutinins in East African game animals. *Vet. Rec.* 74:904.

———. 1974. Calculating age from teeth and horns. In *The husbandry and health of the domestic buffalo*, ed. W. R. Cockrill, pp. 296–301. Rome: F.A.O.

Roosevelt, T. 1910. *African game trails*. London: John Murray.

Rose, G. A. 1975. Buffalo increase and seasonal use of Ngorongoro Crater. *E. Afr. Wildl. J.* 13:385–87.

Roseby, F. B. 1973. Effects of *Trichostrongylus colubriformis* (Nematoda) on the nutrition and metabolism of sheep. 1. Feed intake, digestion and utilization. *Aust. J. Agric. Res.* 24:947–53.

Roth, H. H. 1967. A survey of brucellosis in game animals in Rhodesia. *Bull Epizoot. Dis. Afr.* 15:133–42.

Round, M. C. 1968. *Checklist of the Helminth parasites of African mammals*. Tech. Com. Commonwealth Bur. Helminth. no. 38. Farnham Royal, England: Commonwealth Agric. Bureaux.

Russell, E. W. 1968. *Management policy in the national parks*. Arusha: Tanzania National Parks.

Rweyemamu, M. M. 1970. Observations on foot-and-mouth disease type SAT 2 in Tanzania. *Bull. Epizoot. Dis. Afr.* 18:87–100.

———. 1974. The incidence of infectious bovine rhinotracheitis antibody in Tanzanian game animals and cattle. *Bull. Epizoot. Dis. Afr.* 22:19–22.

Sachs, R. 1967. Liveweights and body measurements of Serengeti game animals. *E. Afr. Wildl. J.* 5:24–36.

Sachs, R.; Frank, H.; and Bindernagel, J. A. 1969. New host records for *Mammomonogamus* in African game animals through application of a simple method of collection. *Vet. Rec.* 84:562–63.

Sachs R.; Rack, G.; and Woodford, M. H. 1973. Observations on pentastomid infestation of East African game animals. *Bull. Epizoot. Dis. Afr.* 21:401–10.

Sachs, R., and Sachs, C. 1968. A survey of parasitic infestation of wild herbivores in the Serengeti region in northern Tanzania and the Lake Rukwa region in southern Tanzania. *Bull. Epizoot. Dis. Afr.* 16:455–72.

Sachs, R.; Staak, C.; and Groocock, C. M. 1968. Serological investigation of brucellosis in game animals in Tanzania. *Bull. Epizoot. Dis. Afr.* 16:93–100.

Sadlier, R. M. F. S. 1969. *The ecology of reproduction in wild and domestic mammals*. London: Methuen.

Schaller, G. B. 1967. *The deer and the tiger*. Chicago: University of Chicago Press.

———. 1972. *The Serengeti lion*. Chicago: University of Chicago Press.

———. 1976. Agressive behaviour of domestic yak. *J. Bombay Nat. Hist. Soc.*, in press.

Schindler, R.; Sachs, R.; Hilton, P. J.; and Watson, R. M. 1969. Some veterinary aspects of the utilization of African game animals. *Bull. Epizoot. Dis. Afr.* 17:215–21.

Schloeth, R. 1958. Cycle annuel et comportement social du taurau de Camargue. *Mammalia* 22:121–39.

———. 1961. Das Sozialleben des Camargue-Rindes: Qualitative und quantitative Untersuchungen über die sozialen Beziehungen-insbesondere die soziale Rangornungdes halbwilden franzosisohen Kampfrindes. *Z. Tierpsychol.* 18:574–627.

Scrimshaw, N. S.; Taylor, C. E.; and Gordon, J. E. 1968. *Interactions of nutrition and infection.* Geneva: W.H.O. no. 57.

Shifrine, M., and Domermuth, C. H. 1967. Contagious bovine pleuropneumonia in wildlife. *Bull. Epizoot. Dis. Afr.* 15:319–22.

Shifrine, M.; Stone, S. S.; and Staak, C. 1970. Contagious bovine pleuropneumonia in African buffalo (*Syncerus caffer*). *Bull. Epizoot. Dis. Afr.* 18:201–5.

Short, H. L.; Newson, J. D.; MçCoy, G. L.; and Fowler, J. F. 1969. Effects of nutrition and climate on southern deer. *Trans. N. Am. Wildl. and Nat. Res. Conf.* 34:137–46.

Sidney, J. 1965. The past and present distribution of some African ungulates. *Trans. Zool. Soc. Lond.* 30:1–396.

Siegel, S. 1956. *Nonparametric statistics.* New York: McGraw-Hill.

Simpson, G. G. 1945. The principles of classification and a classification of mammals. *Bull. Am. Mus. Nat. Hist.* 85:1–350.

Sinclair, A. R. E. 1970. Studies of the ecology of the East African buffalo. D.Phil. thesis, Oxford University.

———. 1972. Long term monitoring of mammal populations in the Serengeti: Census of non-migratory ungulates, 1971. *E. Afr. Wildl. J.* 10:287–97.

———. 1973a. Population increases of buffalo and wildebeest in the Serengeti. *E. Afr. Wildl. J.* 11:93–107.

———. 1973b. Regulation, and population models for a tropical ruminant. *E. Afr. Wildl. J.* 11:307–16.

———. 1974a. The natural regulation of buffalo populations in East Africa. I. Introduction and resource requirements. *E. Afr. Wildl. J.* 12:135–54.

———. 1974b. The natural regulation of buffalo populations in East Africa. II. Reproduction, recruitment and growth. *E. Afr. Wildl. J.* 12:169–83.

———. 1974c. The natural regulation of buffalo populations in East Africa. III. Population trends and mortality. *E. Afr. Wildl. J.* 12:185–200.

———. 1974d. The natural regulation of buffalo populations in East Africa. IV. The food supply as a regulating factor, and competition. *E. Afr. Wildl. J.* 12:291–311.

———. 1974e. The social organization of the East African Buffalo (*Syncerus caffer* Sparrman). In *The behaviour of ungulates and its relation to management*, ed. V. Geist and F. Walther, pp. 676–89. Morges, Switzerland: I.U.C.N. Publications, new series no. 24.

————. 1975. The resource limitation of trophic levels in tropical grassland ecosystems. *J. Anim. Ecol.* 44:497–520.

Sinclair, A. R. E., and Duncan, P. 1972. Indices of condition in tropical ruminants. *E. Afr. Wildl. J.* 10:143–49.

Sinclair, A. R. E., and Gwynne, M. D. 1972. Food selection and competition in the East African buffalo (*Syncerus caffer* Sparrman). *E. Afr. Wildl. J.* 10:77–89.

Skinner, J. D.; Van Zyl, J. H. M.; and Van Heerden, J. A. H. 1973. The effect of season on reproduction in the black wildebeest and red hartebeest in South Africa. *J. Reprod. Fert.,* suppl. 19:101–10.

Slobodkin, L. B.; Smith, F. E.; and Hairston, N. G. 1967. Regulation in terrestrial ecosystems and the implied balance of nature. *Am. Nat.* 101:109–24.

Smith, C. A. 1959. Studies on the Northern Rhodesia *Hyparrhenia* veld. 1. The grazing behaviour of indigenous cattle grazed at light and heavy stocking rates. *J. Agric. Sci.* (Cambridge) 53:369–75.

Smith, N. S. 1970. Appraisal of condition estimation methods for East African ungulates. *E. Afr. Wildl. J.* 8:123–29.

Solomon, M. E. 1964. Analysis of processes involved in the natural control of insects. *Adv. Ecol. Res.* 2:1–58.

Spinage, C. 1967. Aging the Uganda defassa waterbuck, *Kobus defassa ugandae,* Neuman. *E. Afr. Wildl. J.* 5: 1–15.

————. 1968. A quantitative study of the daily activity of the Uganda defassa waterbuck. *E. Afr. Wildl. J.* 6:89–93.

————. 1969. Reproduction in the Uganda defassa waterbuck, *Kobus defassa ugandae,* Neuman. *J. Reprod. Fert.* 18:445–57.

Staak, C.; Sachs, R.; and Groocock, C. M. 1968. Bruzellose beim afrikanischen Buffel (*Syncerus caffer*) in Tanzania. *Vet. Med. Nachr.* 68:245–49.

Stewart, D. R. M. 1964. Rinderpest among wild animals in Kenya, 1960–2. *Bull. Epizoot. Dis. Afr.* 12:39–42.

Stewart, D. R. M., and Stewart, J. 1963. The distribution of some large mammals in Kenya. *J. E. Afr. Nat. Hist. Soc.* 24:107.

Stewart, D. R. M., and Talbot, L. M. 1962. Census of wildlife on the Serengeti, Mara and Loita Plains. *E. Afr. Agric. For. J.* 28:58–60.

Stobbs, T. H. 1973. The effect of plant structure on the intake of tropical pastures. 1. Variation in the bite size of grazing cattle. *Aust. J. Agric. Res.* 24:809–19.

Symons, L. E. A. 1969. Pathology of gastrointestinal helminthiases. *Int. Rev. Trop. Med.* 3:49–100.

Talbot, L. M. 1966. *Wild animals as a source of food.* Special Scientific Report, Wildlife no. 98. Washington, D.C.: Bureau of Sport, Fisheries and Wildlife.

Talbot, L.M., and Talbot, M. H. 1962. Food preferences of some East African wild ungulates. *E. Afr. Agric. For. J.* 27:131–38.

————. 1963. *The wildebeest in western Masailand.* Wildl. Monogr., no. 12. Chestertown: The Wildlife Society.

———. 1966. The tamarau (*Bubalus mindorensis* Heude): Observations and recommendations. *Mammalia* 30:1–12.

Tassell, R. 1967. The effects of diet on reproduction in pigs, sheep, and cattle. 5. Plane of nutrition in cattle. *Brit. Vet. J.* 123:459–63.

Taylor, C. R. 1968. The minimum water requirements of some East African bovids. In *Comparative nutrition of wild animals*, ed. M. A. Crawford, pp. 195–206. London: Symp. Zool. Soc. Lond.

———. 1970a. Strategies of temperature regulation: Effect on evaporation in East African ungulates. *Am. J. Physiol.* 219:1131–35.

———. 1970b. Dehydration and heat: Effects on temperature regulation of East African ungulates. *Am. J. Physiol.* 219:1136–39.

———. 1973. Energy cost of animal locomotion. In *Comparative physiology*, ed. L. Bolis, K. Schmidt-Nielsen, and S. H. P. Maddrell, pp. 23–42. Amsterdam: North-Holland.

Taylor, W. P., and Watson, R. M. 1967. Studies on the epizootiology of rinderpest in blue wildebeest and other game species of northern Tanzania and southern Kenya, 1965–7. *J. Hyg.* (Cambridge) 65:537–45.

Terborgh, J. 1974. Preservation of natural diversity: The problem of extinction prone species. *BioScience* 24: 715–22.

Thenius, E. 1969. Phylogenie der Mammalia: Stammesgeschichte der Säugetiere (einschliesslich der Hominiden). In *Handbuch der Zoologie*, vol. 8, no. 48 (2):369–722. Berlin: Walter de Gruyter.

Thresher, P. 1972. African National Parks and tourism: An interlinked future. *Biol. Conserv.* 4:279–84.

Tinbergen, N. 1964. The evolution of signaling devices. In *Social behavior and organization among vertebrates*, ed. W. Etkin, pp. 206–30. Chicago: University of Chicago Press.

———. 1965. Behaviour and natural selection. In *Ideas in modern biology*, ed. J. A. Moore, pp. 521–42. Proc. XVI Int. Zool. Congr., vol. 6.

Tulloch, D. G. 1967. The distribution, density and social behaviour of the water buffalo (*Bubalus bubalis* Lydekker, 1913) in the Northern Territory. M.Sc. thesis, University of Queensland.

———. 1969. Home range in feral water buffalo *Bubalus bubalis* Lydekker. *Aust. J. Zool.* 17:143–52.

———. 1970. Seasonal movements and distribution of the sexes in the water buffalo, *Bubalus bubalis*, in the Northern Territory. *Aust. J. Zool.* 18:399–414.

Ullrich, W. 1968. Festotellungen über das Verhalten des Gaur (*Bos gaurus gaurus*) in den Reservaten von Bandipur und Mudumalai in Sudindien. *Zool. Gart., Frankf.* 36: 80–89.

Varley, G. C., and Gradwell, G. R. 1960. Key factors in population studies. *J. Anim. Ecol.* 29:399–401.

———. 1968. Population models for the winter moth. In *Insect abundance.*, ed. T. R. E. Southwood, pp. 132–42. London: Oxford University Press.

———. 1970. Recent advances in insect population dynamics. *Ann. Rev. Ent.* 15:1–24.

Varley, G. C.; Gradwell, G. R.; and Hassell, M. P. 1973. *Insect population ecology: An analytical approach.* Oxford: Blackwell Scientific Publications.

Vercoe, J. E., and Springell, P. H. 1969. Effect of subclinical helminthosis on nitrogen metabolism in beef cattle. *J. Agric. Sci.* (Cambridge) 73: 203–9.

Verme, L. J. 1963. Effect of nutrition on white-tailed deer fawns. *Trans. N. Am. Wildl. and Nat. Res. Conf.* 28:431–42.

Vesey-Fitzgerald, D. F. 1960. Grazing succession amongst East African game animals. *J. Mammal.* 41:161–70.

———. 1969. Utilization of the habitat by buffalo in the Lake Manyara National Park. *E. Afr. Wildl. J.* 7:131–45.

———. 1974. Utilization of the grazing resources by buffaloes in the Arusha National Park. *E. Afr. Wildl. J.* 12:107–34.

Vidler, B. O.; Harthoorn, A. M.; Brocklesby, D. W.; and Robertshaw, D. 1963. The gestation and parturition of the African buffalo. *E. Afr. Wildl. J.* 1:122.

Vos, A. de. 1975. *Africa, the devastated continent?* The Hague: Dr. W. Junk.

Vos, V. de, and Niekerk, C. A. W. J. van. 1969. Brucellosis in the Kruger National Park. *J. S. Afr. Vet. Med. Ass.* 40:331–34.

Wagner, F. H. 1969. Ecosystem concepts in fish and game management. In *The ecosystem concept in natural resource management*, ed. G. M. Van Dyne, pp. 259–307. New York: Academic Press.

Walther, F. R. 1973. Round-the-clock activity of Thomson's gazelle (*Gazella thomsoni* Gunther 1884) in the Serengeti National Park. *Z. Tierpsychol.* 32:75–105.

Watson, R. M. 1967. The population ecology of the Serengeti wildebeest. Ph.D. thesis, Cambridge University.

Watson, R. M., and Bell, R. H. V. 1969. The distribution, abundance and status of elephant in the Serengeti region of Northern Tanzania. *J. Appl. Ecol.* 6:115–32.

Watson, R. M., and Turner, M. I. M. 1965. A count of the large mammals of the Lake Manyara National Park: Results and discussion. *E. Afr. Wildl. J.* 3:95–98.

Weir, J., and Davison, E. 1965. Daily occurrence of African game animals at their water holes during dry weather. *Zool. Afr.* 1:353–68.

Weston, R. H., and Hogan, J. P. 1973. Nutrition of herbage-fed ruminants. In *The pastoral industries of Australia*, ed. G. Alexander and O. B. Williams, pp. 233–68. Sydney: Sydney University Press.

Wharton, C. H. 1957. *An ecological study of the Kouprey*, Novibos sauveli (*Urbain*). Manila: Monogr. Inst. Sci. and Tech. Manila no. 5.

———. 1968. *Man, fire and wild cattle in southeast Asia.* Proc. 8th. Ann. Tall Timbers Fire Ecology Conf., pp. 107–67. Tallahassee, Fla.: Tall Timbers Res. Stn.

White, S. E. 1915. The rediscovered country. New York: Doubleday, Page.

Wiens, J. A. 1966. On group selection and Wynne-Edwards' hypothesis. *Am. Sci.* 54:273–87.

Wilson, E. O. 1975. *Sociobiology.* Cambridge, Mass.: Belknap Press.

Wilson, P. N. 1961. The grazing behaviour of free-water intake of East African shorthorned zebu heifers at Serere, Uganda. *J. Agric. Sci.* (Cambridge) 56:351–64.

Wiltbank, J. N.; Rowden W. W.; Ingalls, J. E.; Gregory, K. E.; and Koch, R. M. 1962. Effect of energy level of reproductive phenomena of mature Hereford cows. *J. Anim. Sci.* 21:219–25.

Woodford, M. H., and Sachs, R. 1973. The incidence of cysticercosis, hydatidosis, and sparganosis in wild herbivores of the Queen Elizabeth National Park, Uganda. *Bull. Epizoot. Dis. Afr.* 21:265–72.

Wright, B. 1960. Predation on big game in East Africa. *J. Wildl. Management* 24:1–15.

Wynne-Edwards, V. C. 1962. *Animal dispersion in relation to social behaviour.* Edinburgh: Oliver and Boyd.

———. 1963. Intergroup selection in the evolution of social systems. *Nature* (London) 200:623–26.

———. 1965. Social organization as a population regulator. In *Social organization of animal communities,* ed. P. E. Ellis, pp. 173–78. Symp. Zool. Soc. Lond., no. 14.

Young, A. S.; Branagan, D.; Brown, C. G. D.; Burridge, M. J.; Cunningham, M. P.; and Purnell, R. E. 1973. Preliminary observations on a theilerial species pathogenic to cattle isolated from buffalo (*Syncerus caffer*) in Tanzania. *Brit. Vet. J.* 129:382–89.

Zeuner, F. E. 1963. *A history of domesticated animals.* London: Hutchinson.

Index

Acacia woodland, 300
Activity cycle, 82–88; total daily, 88–90
Addo National Park, 10; food types in, 70
Aerial photography, 170, 204; and horn shape, 163, 164; and male horns, 158
Age-determination methods, 158–65; for fetuses, 158; by tooth eruption, 158, 159; by cementum lines and tooth wear, 159–63; by horn shape, 163, 164; for males in field, 164, 165
Agonistic behavior: of buffalo, 108–13; of other Bovini, 113–17; of bachelor males, 124
Albert National Park, 69
Allerton-type herpes virus, 243–45
Altruisim, 101; and genes, 101; and antipredator behavior, 132
Amino-acid sequence fibrinopeptides, 22, 23
Anaplasma, 247
Anestrus, 168, 169; in cattle, 169; and lactation, 191
Anthrax, 248
Antipredator behavior, 126–32; of wildebeest, 129, 130; and calf distress call, 130; and group defense, 130; against hyena, 131, 132; evolution of, 149, 150
Appeasement behavior, 111, 112
Arusha National Park, 25, 31, 47–50
Asian buffalo. *See* Water buffalo
Association coefficient, 54–66; methods, 297–98
Aurochs, 21
Australia, water buffalo breeding in, 179–81

Autocorrelation: and grazing, 83–86; and ruminating, 86, 87

Babesia, 247
Baboon, 37, 46, 51
Bachelor males, 122–25; habitat selection of, 60–62; energy use by, 99; seasonal numbers of, 122; group size of, 122; reproductive activity of, 124; home range of, 124, 125; and human settlement, 125; longevity of, 125; seasonal splitting away of, 142; censuses of, 203, 205
Banagi: rainfall at, 32; bachelor males at, 122, 124, 125; as home range, 134, 136, 139
Banteng, 14, 15; food, 15; agonistic behavior, 113–15
Bat-eared fox, 47
Bellowing: submissive, 111; of other Bovini, 114
Birth, 103–8; and mother attachment, 106; attacks by mother after, 117; weight at, 167, 193; season of, 183, 192; and rainfall, 177; of wildebeest, 177; of water buffalo, 180
Bison, 12, 14, 15, 21–23
Bison: food of, 15, 16; phylogeny of, 21–24
Bison, American, 16; agonistic behavior in, 113–16; dominance hierarchy among, 119; herd leader among, 122; gestation in, 166; twins in, 166; pregnancy rate in, 168; sex ratio of, 170
Bison, European. *See* Wisent
Black-headed heron, 47
Black-shouldered kite, 47

Note: Entries refer to the African buffalo unless otherwise indicated.